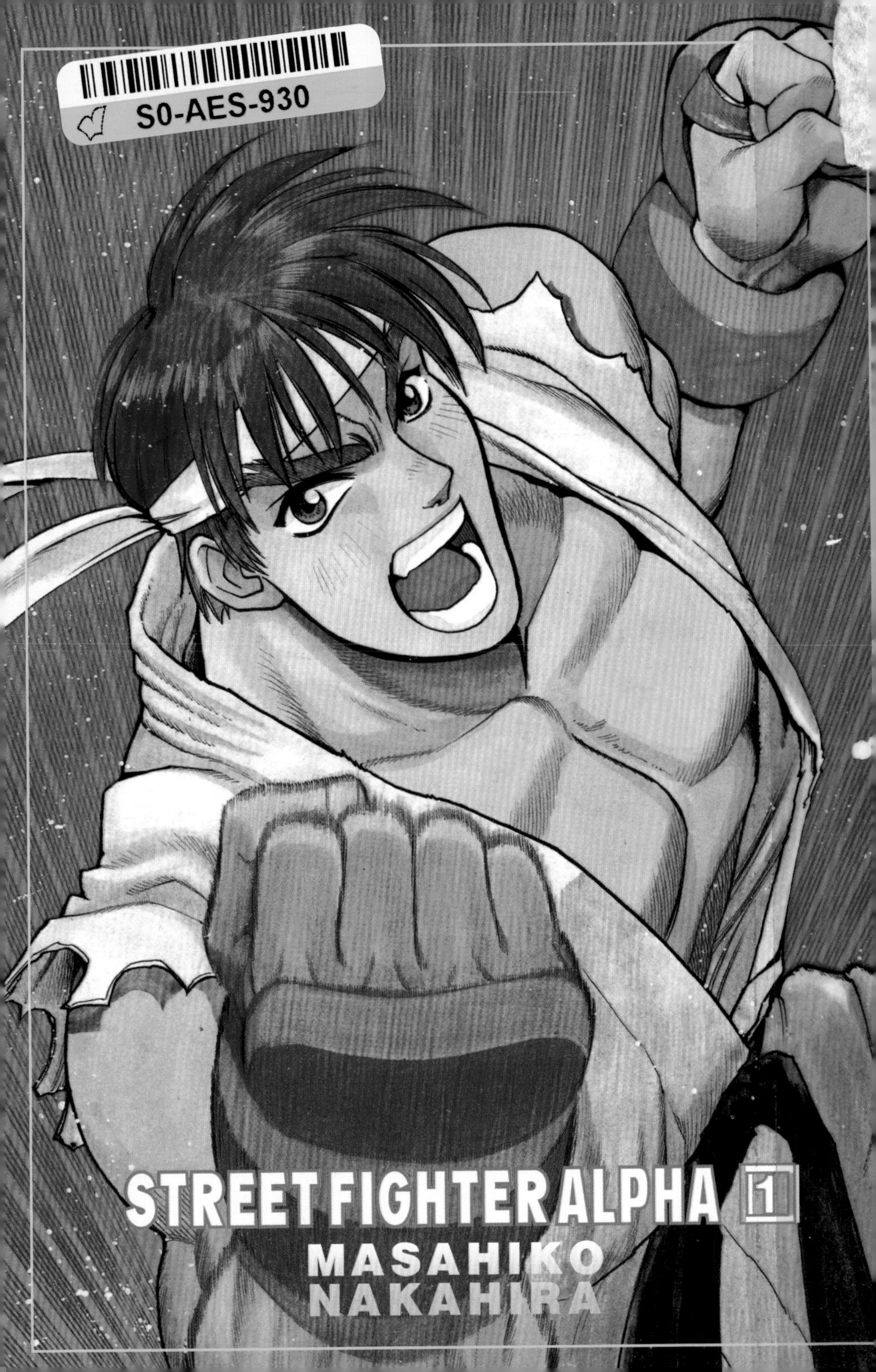

STREET FIGHTER ALPHA 1

MASAHIKO NAKAHIRA

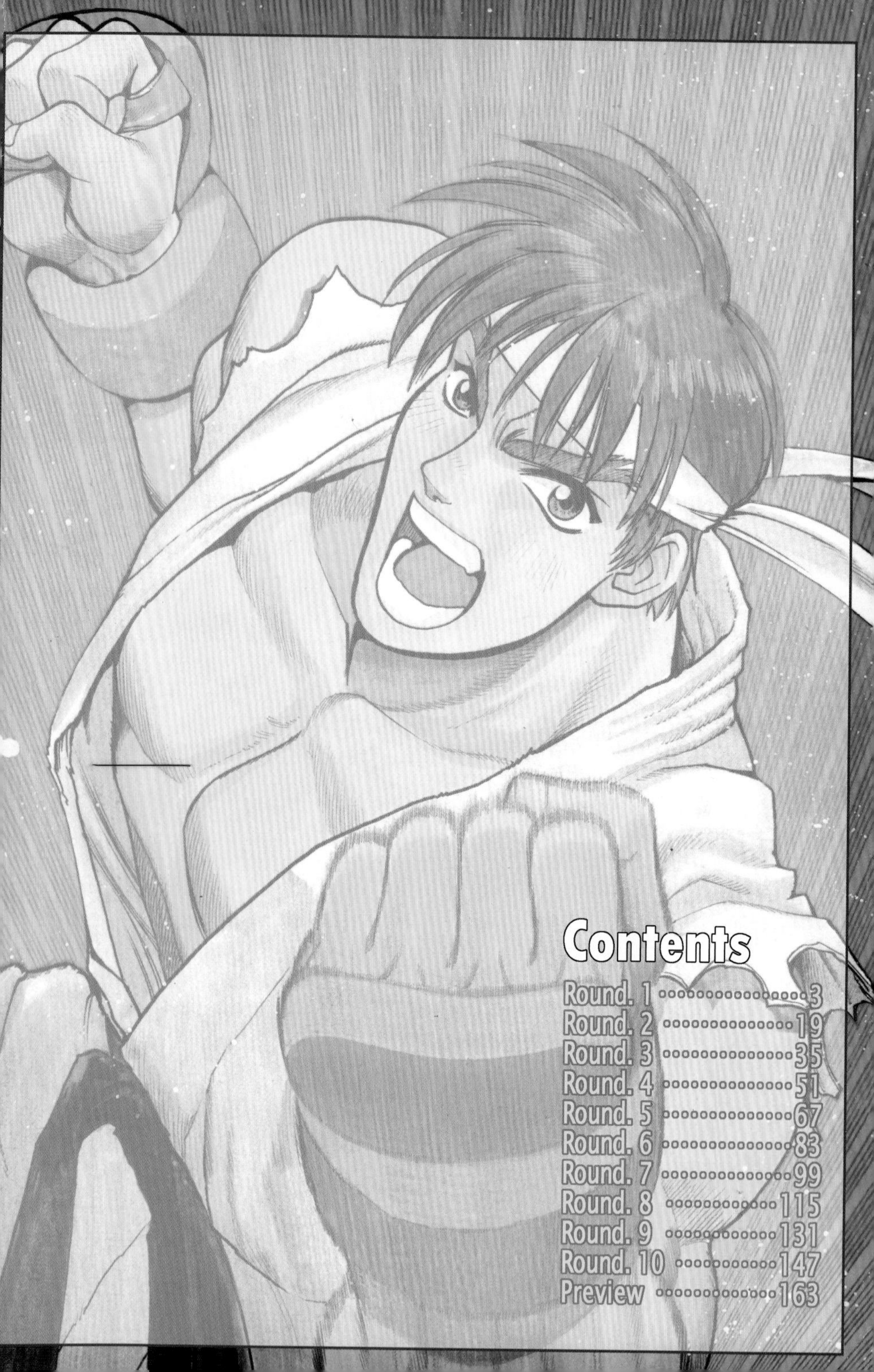

Contents

Round. 1

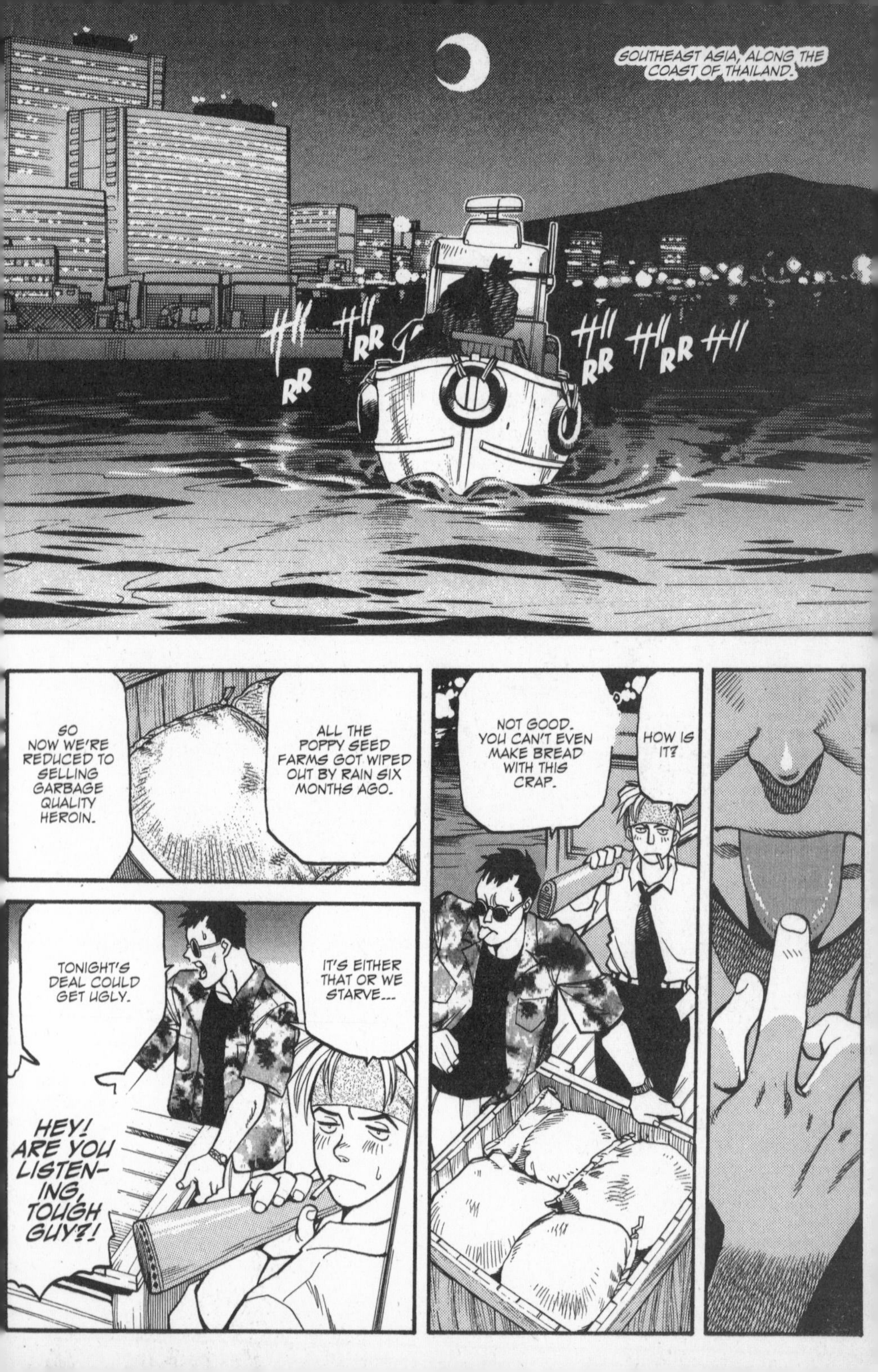
SOUTHEAST ASIA, ALONG THE COAST OF THAILAND.
HOW IS IT?
NOT GOOD. YOU CAN'T EVEN MAKE BREAD WITH THIS CRAP.
ALL THE POPPY SEED FARMS GOT WIPED OUT BY RAIN SIX MONTHS AGO.
SO NOW WE'RE REDUCED TO SELLING GARBAGE QUALITY HEROIN.
IT'S EITHER THAT OR WE STARVE...
TONIGHT'S DEAL COULD GET UGLY.
HEY! ARE YOU LISTENING, TOUGH GUY?!

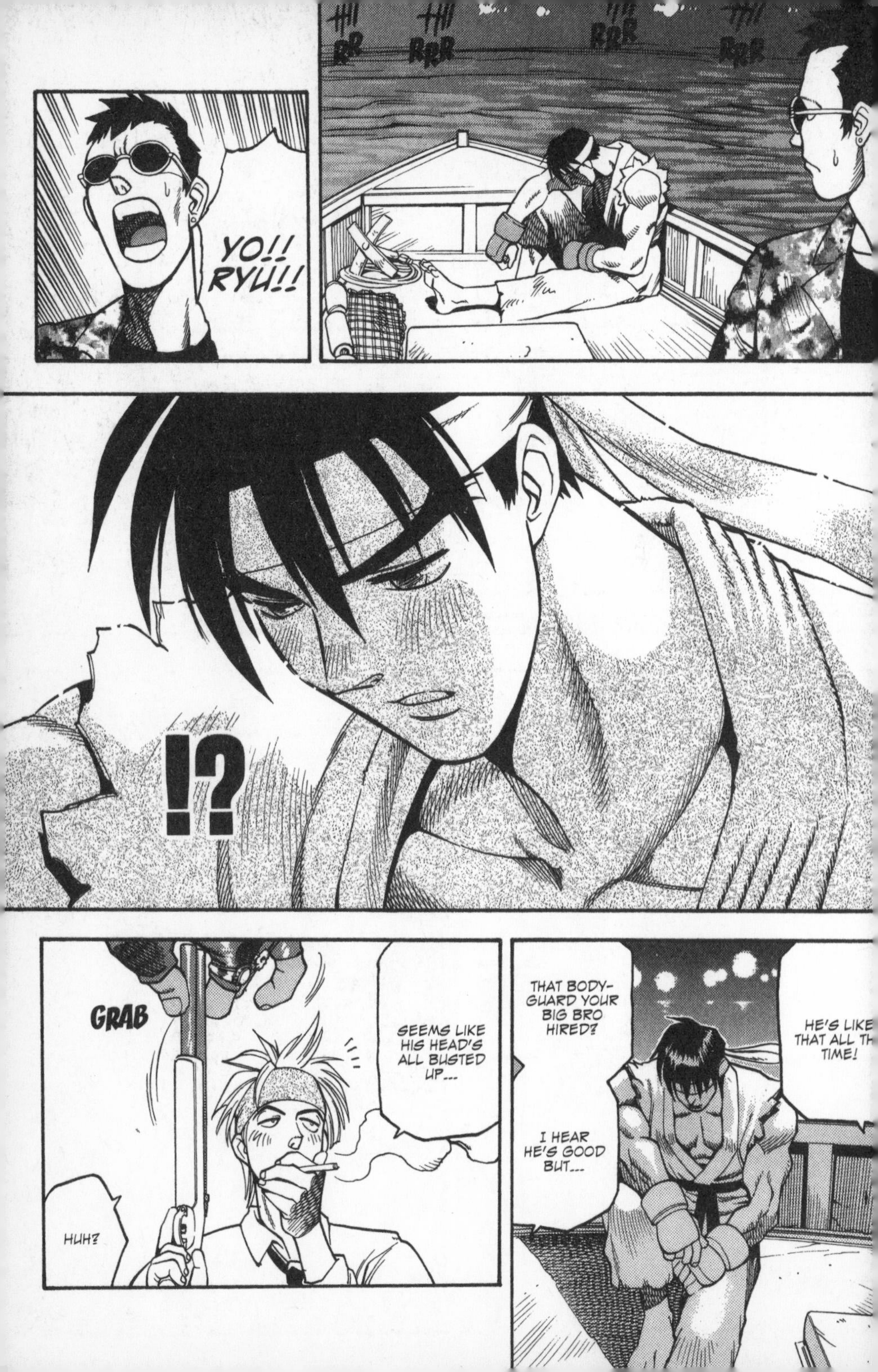

RRR
RRR
RRR
RRR
YO!! RYU!!
!?
HE'S LIKE THAT ALL TH TIME!
THAT BODY-GUARD YOUR BIG BRO HIRED?
I HEAR HE'S GOOD BUT...
SEEMS LIKE HIS HEAD'S ALL BUSTED UP...
GRAB
HUH?

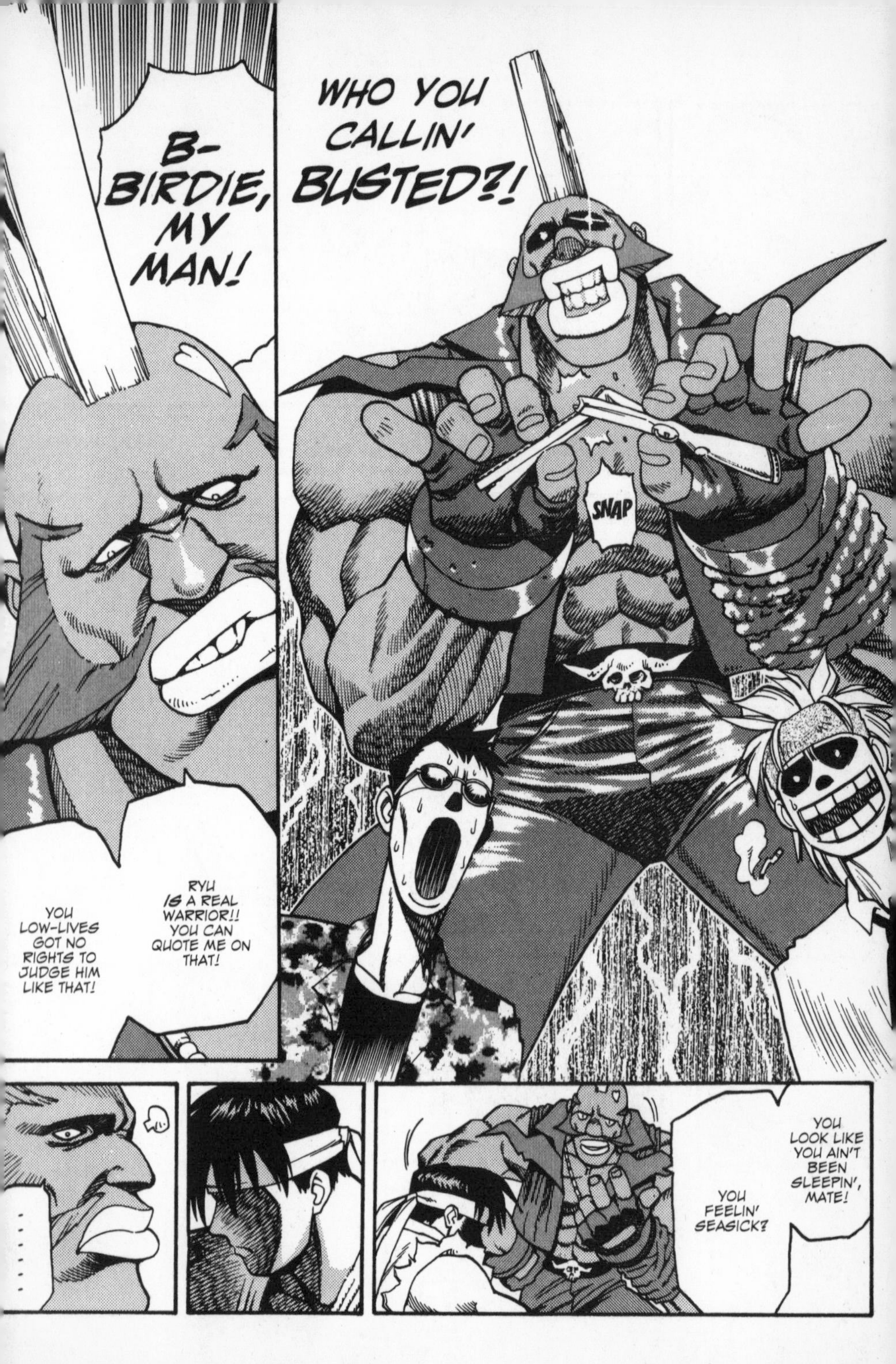
WHO YOU CALLIN' BUSTED?!
SNAP
B-BIRDIE, MY MAN!
RYU IS A REAL WARRIOR!! YOU CAN QUOTE ME ON THAT!
YOU LOW-LIVES GOT NO RIGHTS TO JUDGE HIM LIKE THAT!
YOU LOOK LIKE YOU AIN'T BEEN SLEEPIN', MATE!
YOU FEELIN' SEASICK?

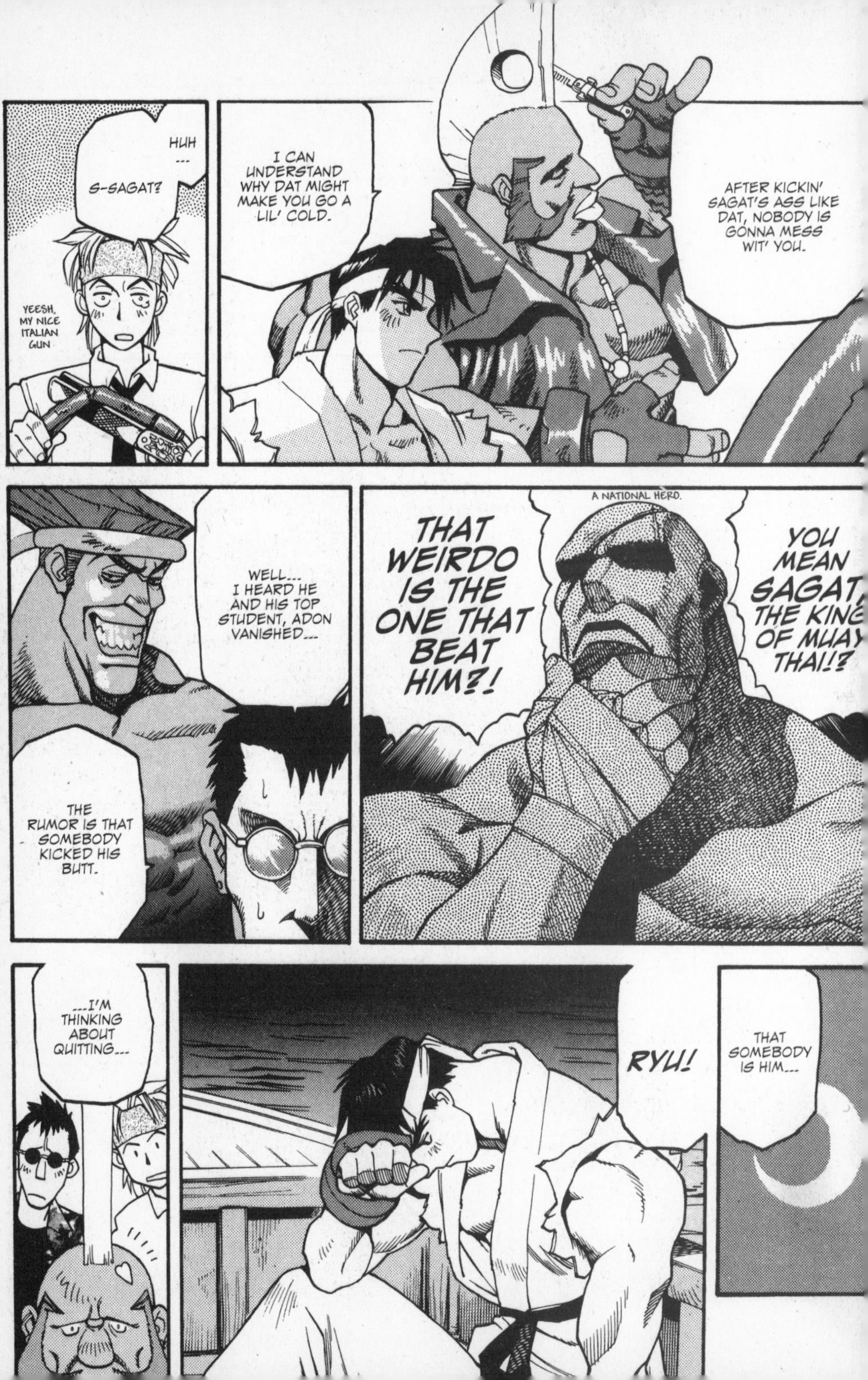
AFTER KICKIN' SAGAT'S ASS LIKE DAT, NOBODY IS GONNA MESS WIT' YOU.
I CAN UNDERSTAND WHY DAT MIGHT MAKE YOU GO A LIL' COLD.
HUH --- S-SAGAT?
YEESH, MY NICE ITALIAN GUN.
YOU MEAN SAGAT, THE KING OF MUAY THAI!?
A NATIONAL HERO.
THAT WEIRDO IS THE ONE THAT BEAT HIM?!
WELL... I HEARD HE AND HIS TOP STUDENT, ADON VANISHED...
THE RUMOR IS THAT SOMEBODY KICKED HIS BUTT.
THAT SOMEBODY IS HIM...
RYU!
...I'M THINKING ABOUT QUITTING...

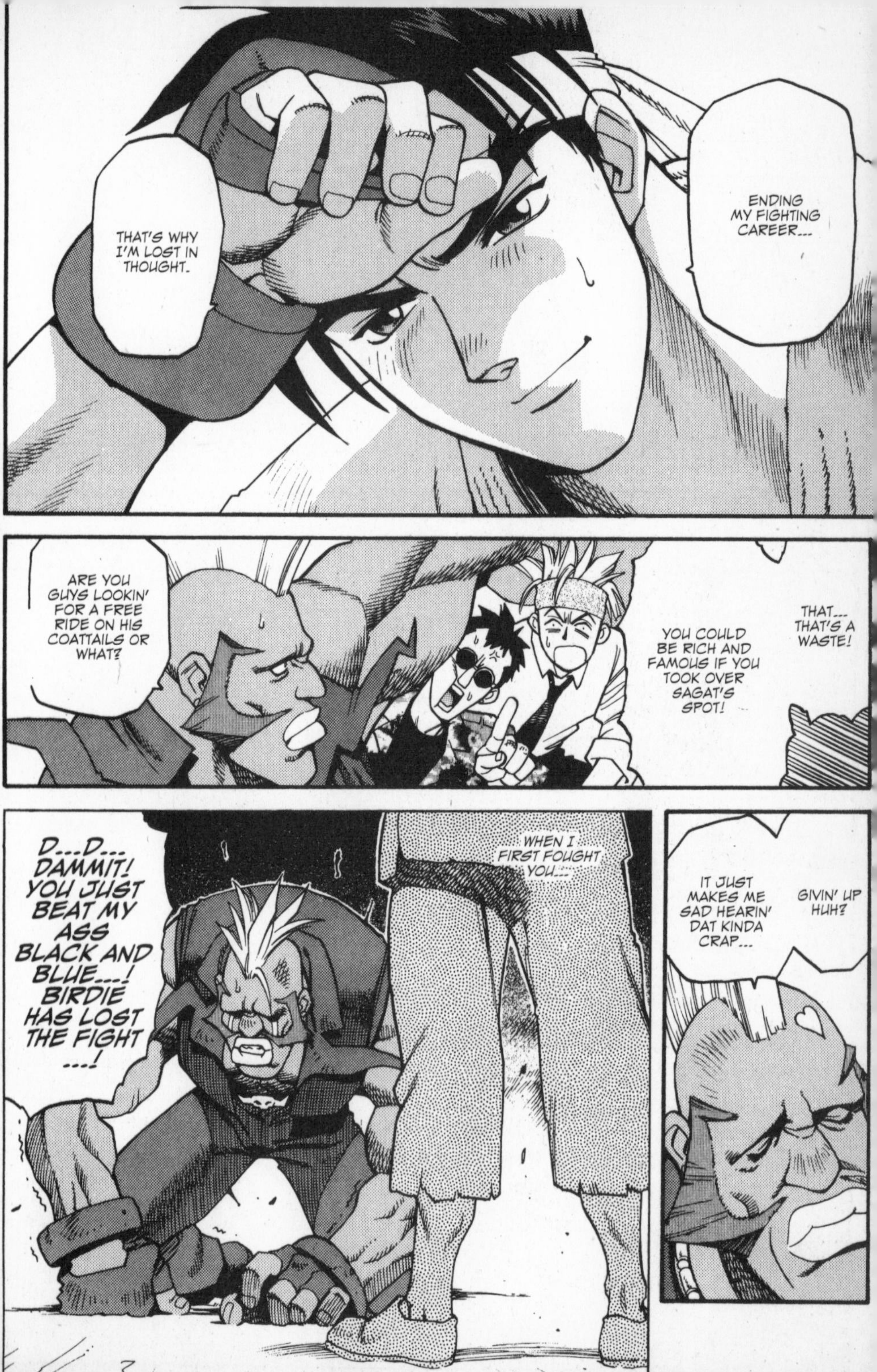
ENDING MY FIGHTING CAREER...
THAT'S WHY I'M LOST IN THOUGHT.
THAT... THAT'S A WASTE!
YOU COULD BE RICH AND FAMOUS IF YOU TOOK OVER SAGAT'S SPOT!
ARE YOU GUYS LOOKIN' FOR A FREE RIDE ON HIS COATTAILS OR WHAT?
GIVIN' UP HUH?
IT JUST MAKES ME SAD HEARIN' DAT KINDA CRAP...
WHEN I FIRST FOUGHT YOU...
D...D... DAMMIT! YOU JUST BEAT MY ASS BLACK AND BLUE...! BIRDIE HAS LOST THE FIGHT...!

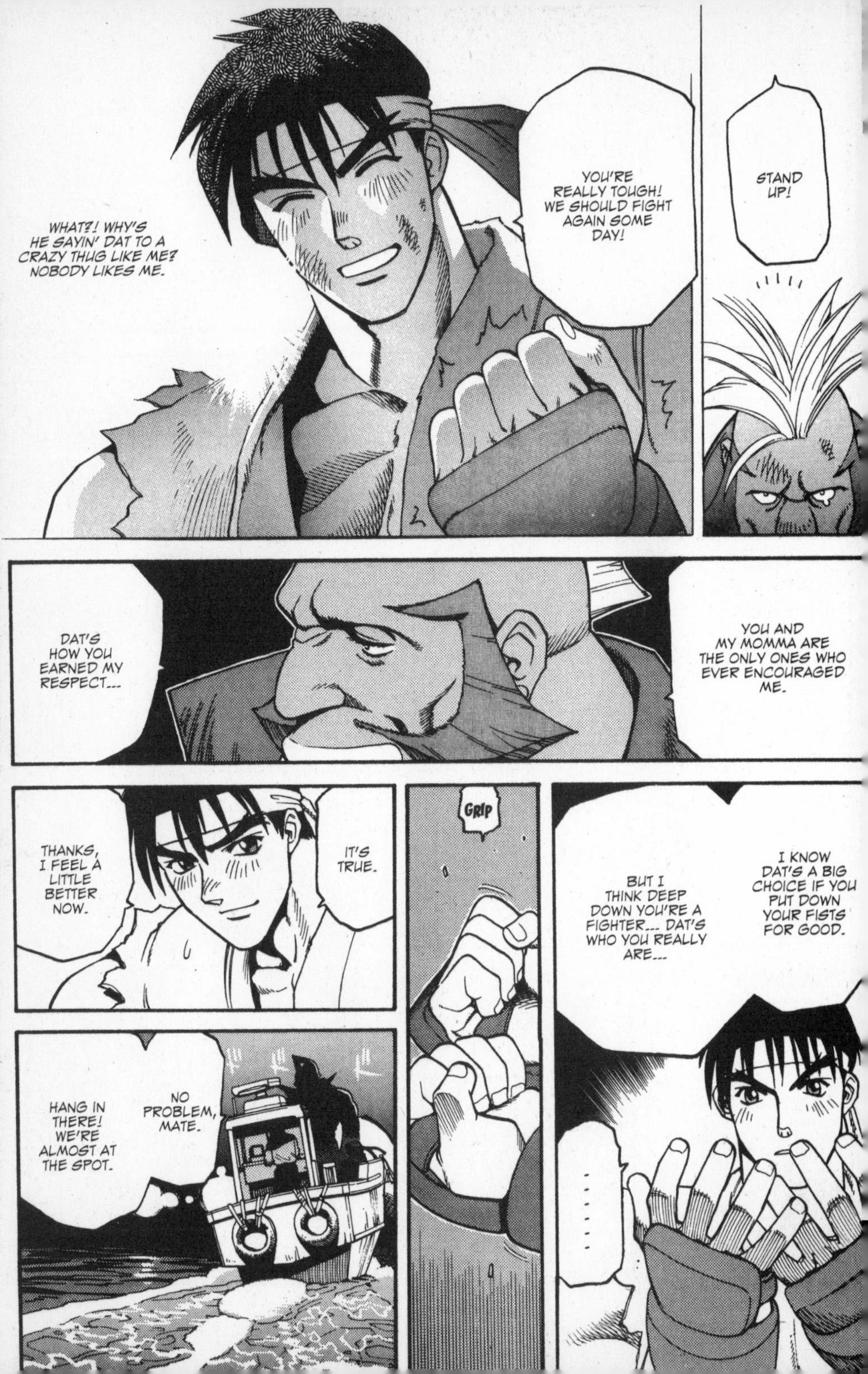
STAND UP!
YOU'RE REALLY TOUGH! WE SHOULD FIGHT AGAIN SOME DAY!
WHAT?! WHY'S HE SAYIN' DAT TO A CRAZY THUG LIKE ME? NOBODY LIKES ME.
YOU AND MY MOMMA ARE THE ONLY ONES WHO EVER ENCOURAGED ME.
DAT'S HOW YOU EARNED MY RESPECT...
I KNOW DAT'S A BIG CHOICE IF YOU PUT DOWN YOUR FISTS FOR GOOD.
BUT I THINK DEEP DOWN YOU'RE A FIGHTER... DAT'S WHO YOU REALLY ARE...
......
GRIP
IT'S TRUE.
THANKS, I FEEL A LITTLE BETTER NOW.
NO PROBLEM, MATE.
HANG IN THERE! WE'RE ALMOST AT THE SPOT.

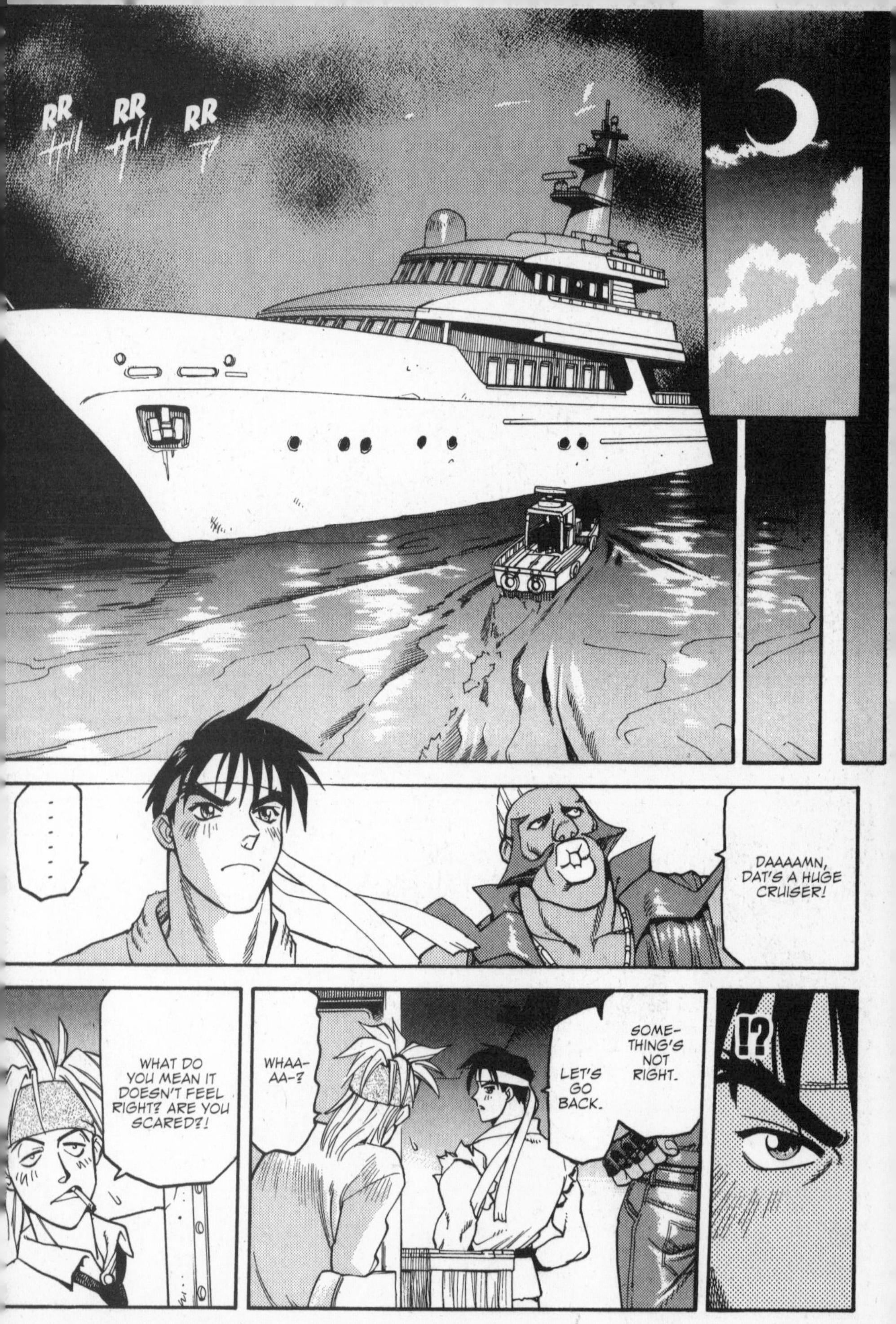
RR
RR
RR
DAAAAMN, DAT'S A HUGE CRUISER!
......
!?
SOME-THING'S NOT RIGHT.
LET'S GO BACK.
WHAAA-AA-?
WHAT DO YOU MEAN IT DOESN'T FEEL RIGHT? ARE YOU SCARED?!

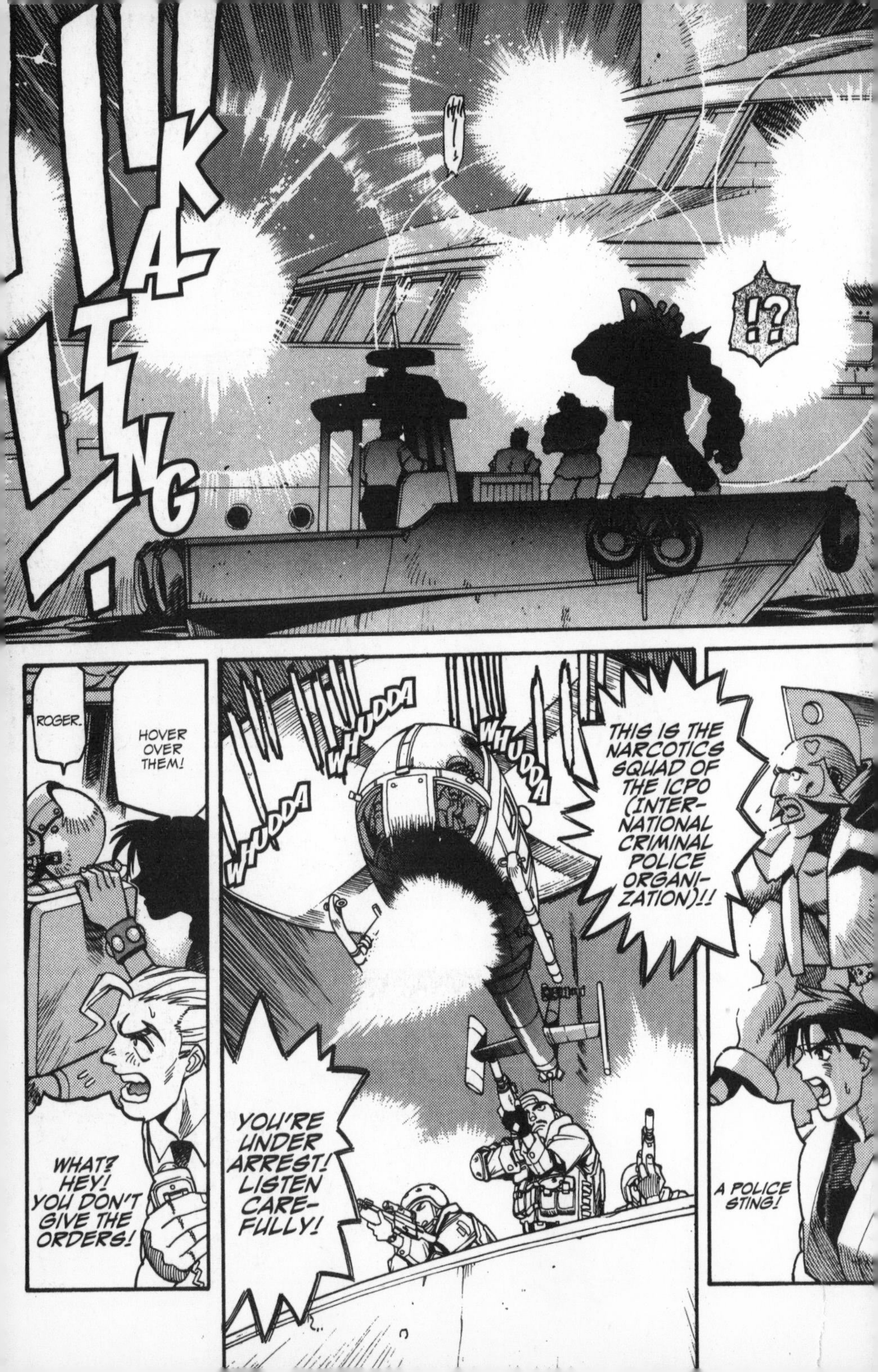
KA-TING!
!?
A POLICE STING!
THIS IS THE NARCOTICS SQUAD OF THE ICPO (INTER-NATIONAL CRIMINAL POLICE ORGANI-ZATION)!!
WHUDDA
WHUDDA
WHUDDA
WHUDDA
YOU'RE UNDER ARREST! LISTEN CARE-FULLY!
HOVER OVER THEM!
ROGER.
WHAT? HEY! YOU DON'T GIVE THE ORDERS!

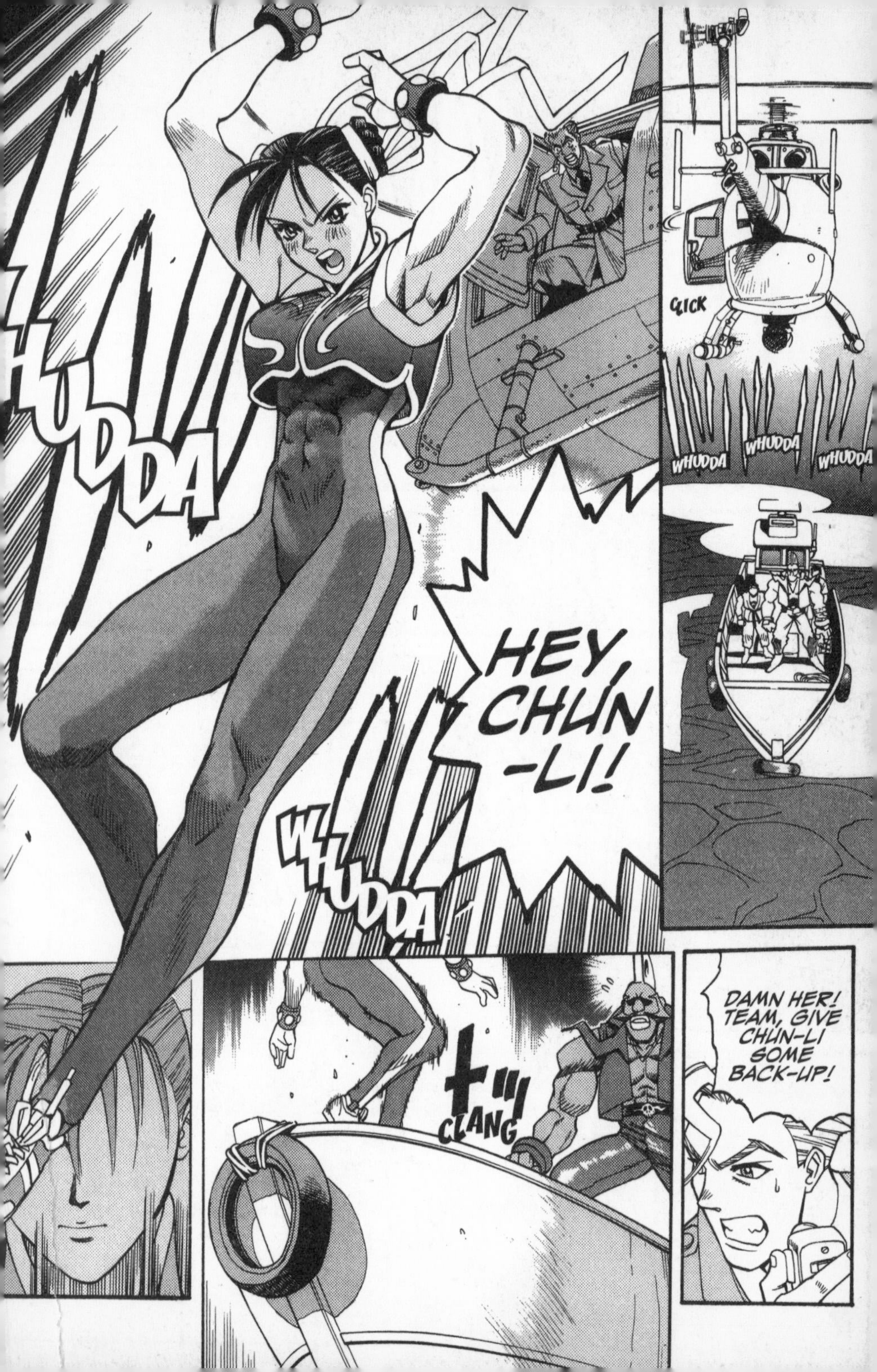
CLICK
WHUDDA
WHUDDA
WHUDDA
WHUDDA
HEY CHUN-LI!
WHUDDA
DAMN HER! TEAM, GIVE CHUN-LI SOME BACK-UP!
CLANG

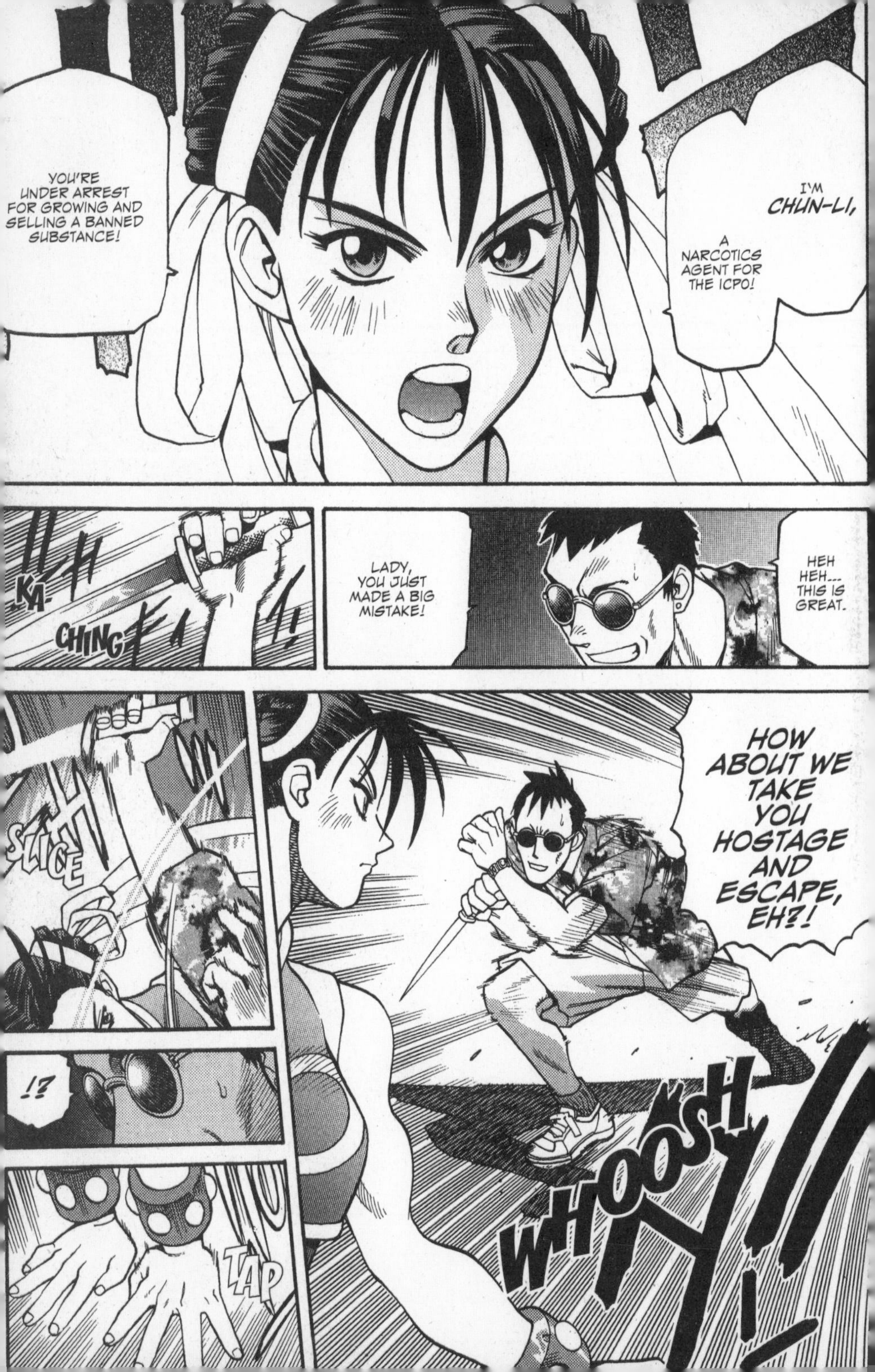
I'M CHUN-LI,
A NARCOTICS AGENT FOR THE ICPO!
YOU'RE UNDER ARREST FOR GROWING AND SELLING A BANNED SUBSTANCE!
HEH HEH... THIS IS GREAT.
LADY, YOU JUST MADE A BIG MISTAKE!
KA-CHING
HOW ABOUT WE TAKE YOU HOSTAGE AND ESCAPE, EH?!
WHOOSH
SLICE
!?
TAP

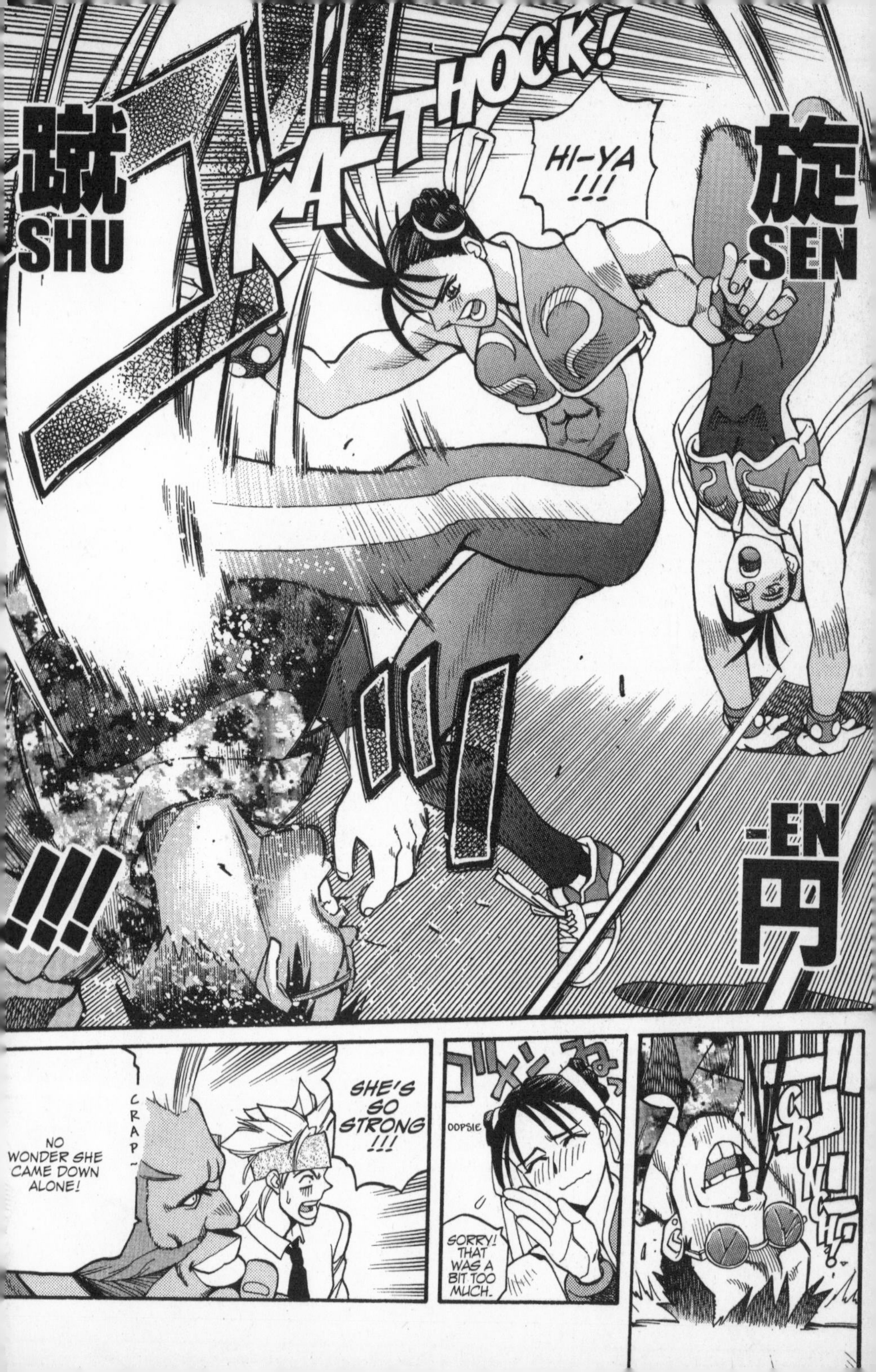
旋
SEN
HI-YA
!!!
KA-THOCK!
蹴
SHU
-EN
円
!!!
CRUNCH!
ゴメンねっ
OOPSIE
SORRY! THAT WAS A BIT TOO MUCH.
SHE'S SO STRONG !!!
CRAP~
NO WONDER SHE CAME DOWN ALONE!

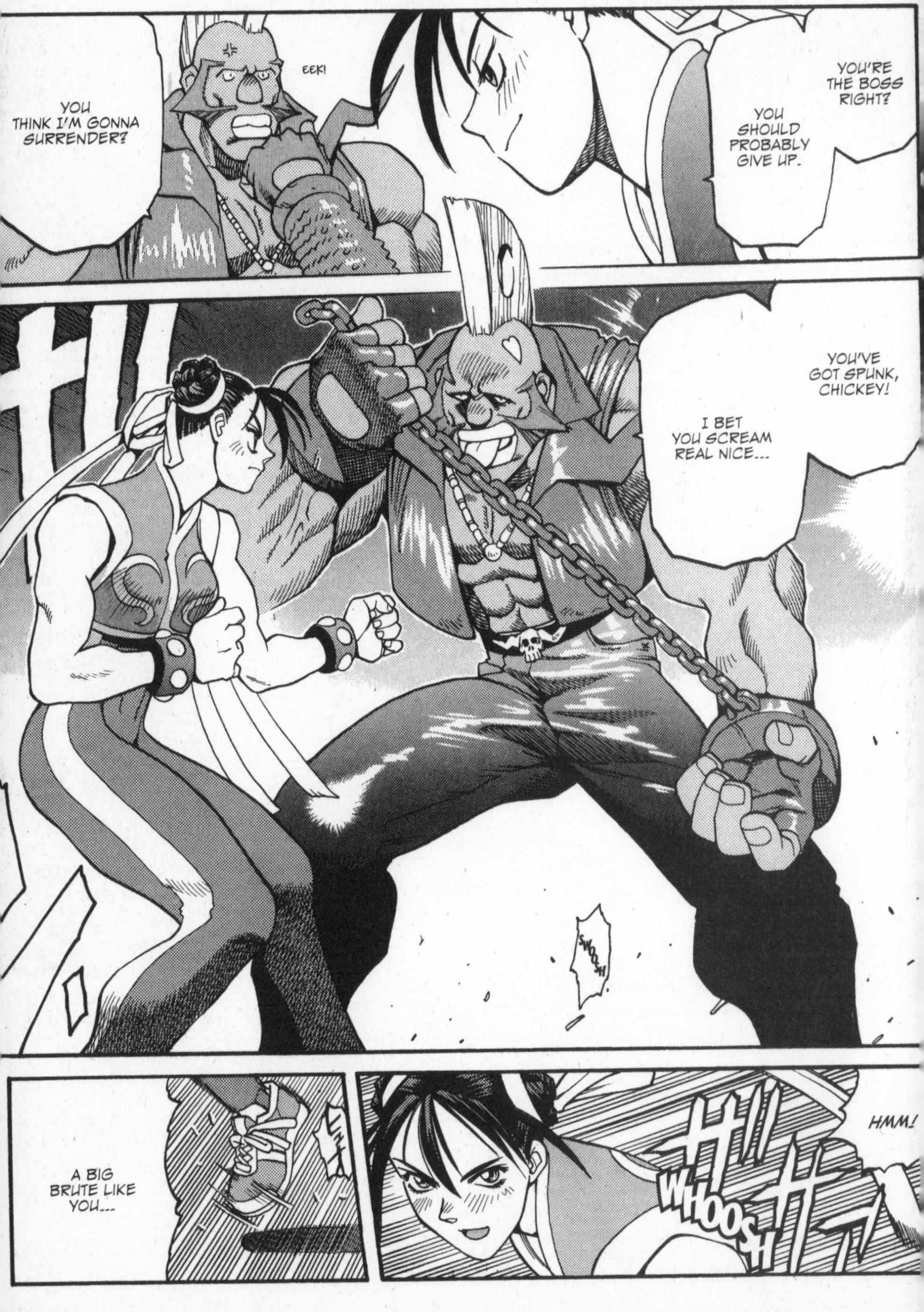
YOU'RE THE BOSS RIGHT?
YOU SHOULD PROBABLY GIVE UP.
EEK!
YOU THINK I'M GONNA SURRENDER?
YOU'VE GOT SPUNK, CHICKEY!
I BET YOU SCREAM REAL NICE...
SWOOSH
HMM!
WHOOSH
A BIG BRUTE LIKE YOU...

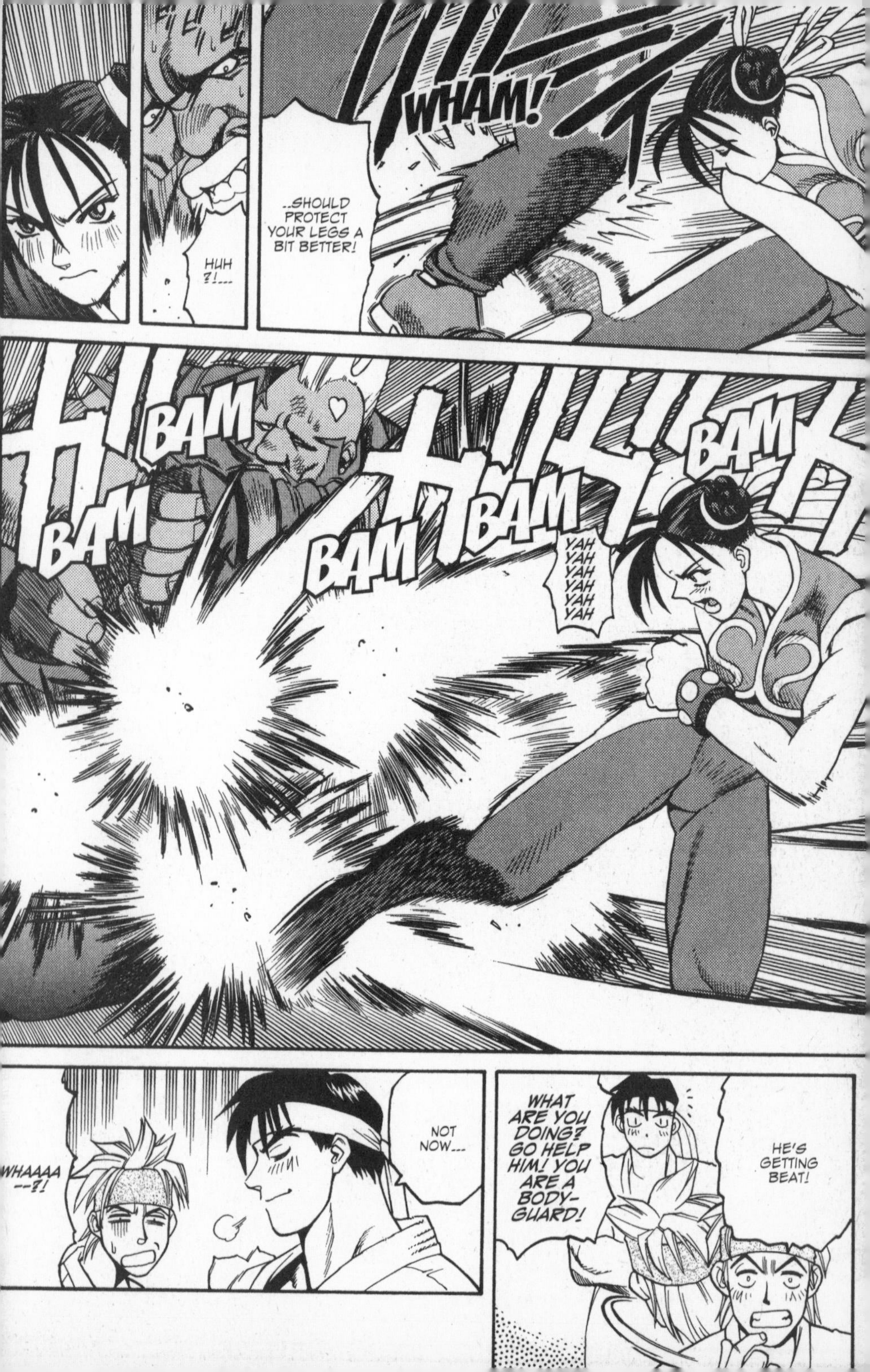
WHAM!
..SHOULD PROTECT YOUR LEGS A BIT BETTER!
HUH ?!...
BAM
YAH YAH YAH YAH YAH YAH
BAM
BAM
BAM
BAM
BAM
HE'S GETTING BEAT!
WHAT ARE YOU DOING? GO HELP HIM! YOU ARE A BODY-GUARD!
NOT NOW...
WHAAAA --?!

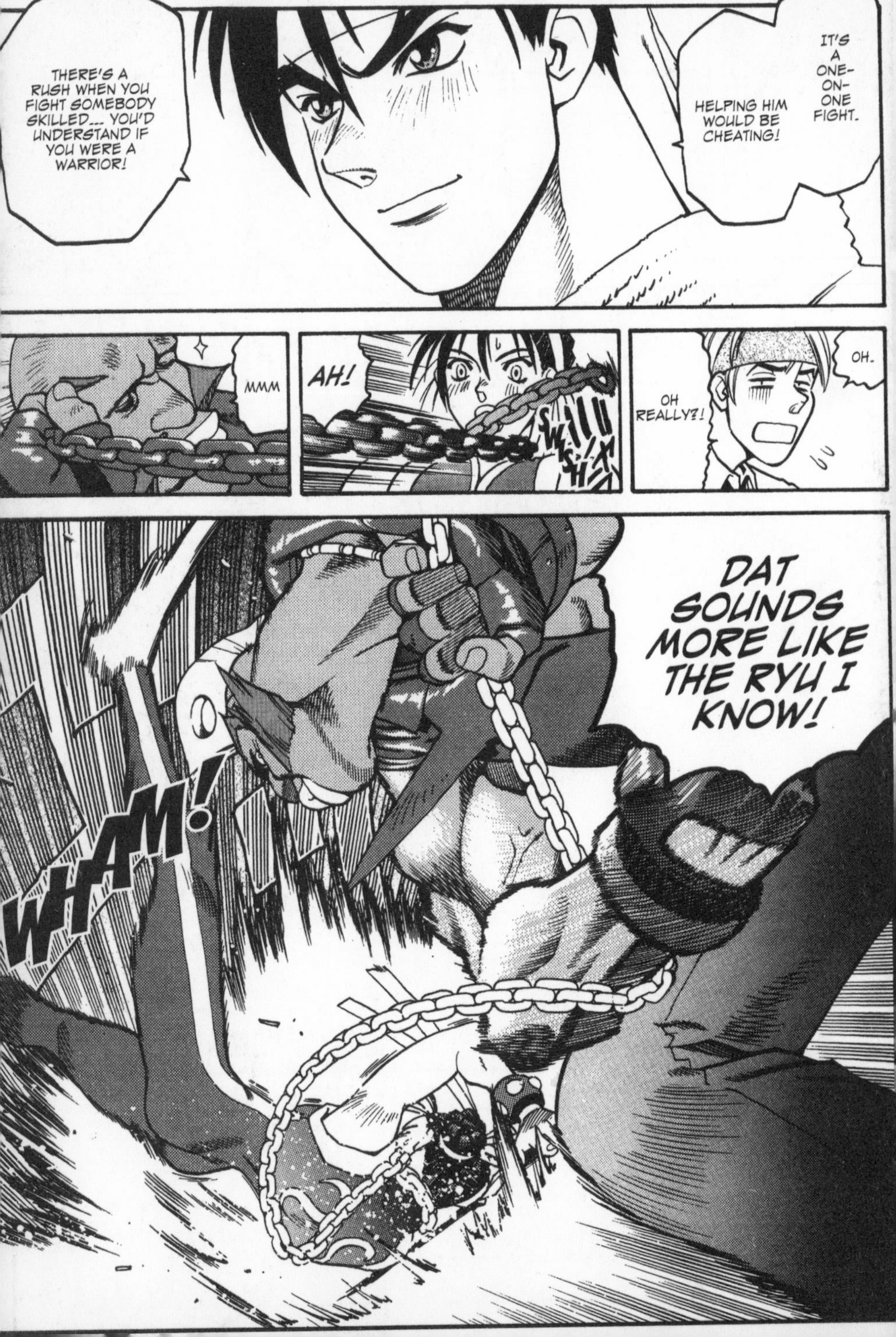
IT'S A ONE-ON-ONE FIGHT.
HELPING HIM WOULD BE CHEATING!
THERE'S A RUSH WHEN YOU FIGHT SOMEBODY SKILLED... YOU'D UNDERSTAND IF YOU WERE A WARRIOR!
OH.
OH REALLY?!
AH!
SWISH
MMM
DAT SOUNDS MORE LIKE THE RYU I KNOW!
WHAM!

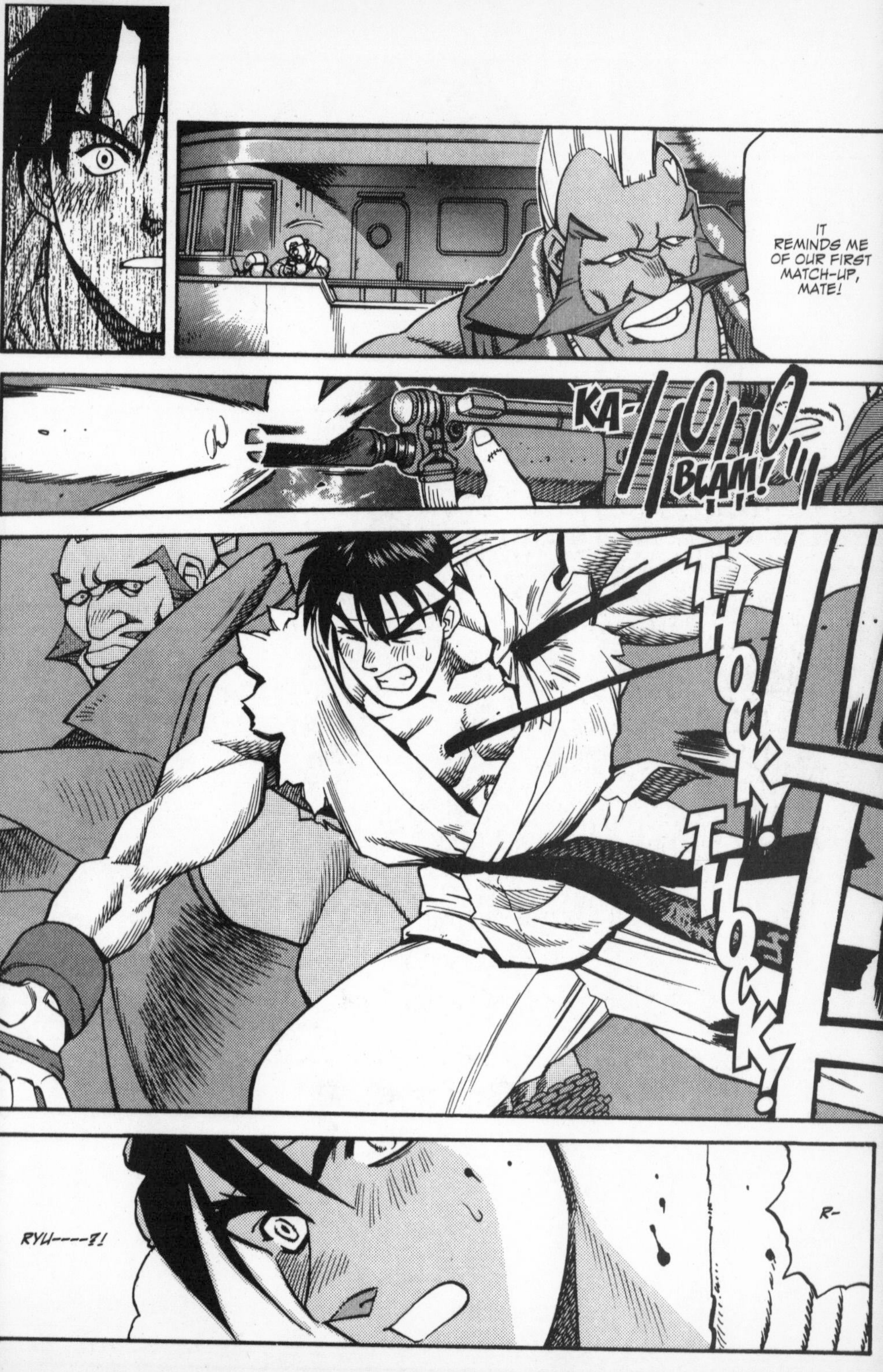
IT REMINDS ME OF OUR FIRST MATCH-UP, MATE!
KA-BLAM!
THOCK! THOCK!
R-
RYU----?!

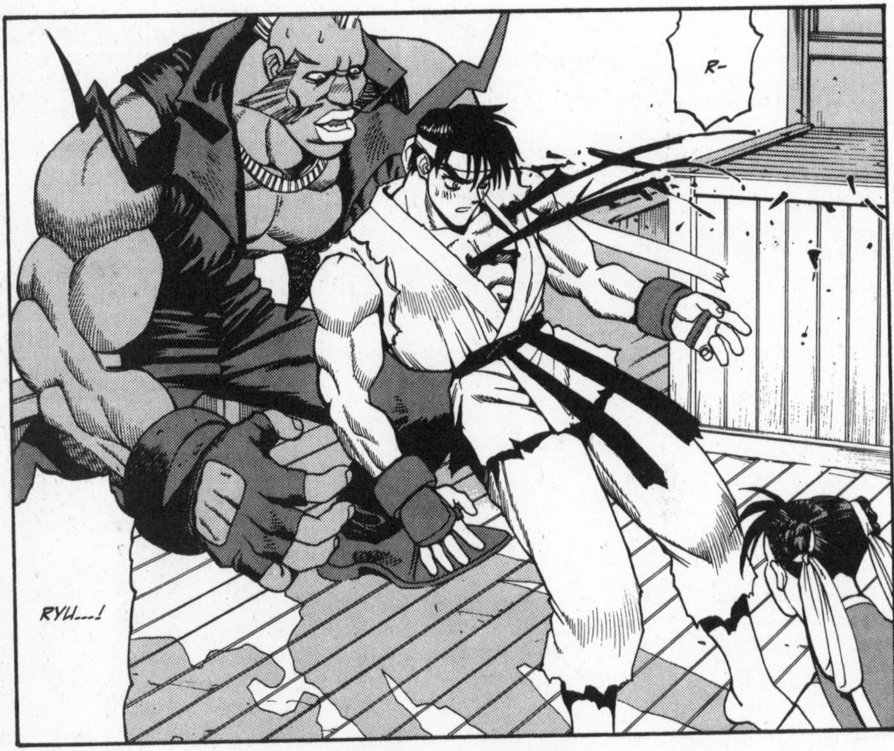
R-
RYU...!

Round. 2

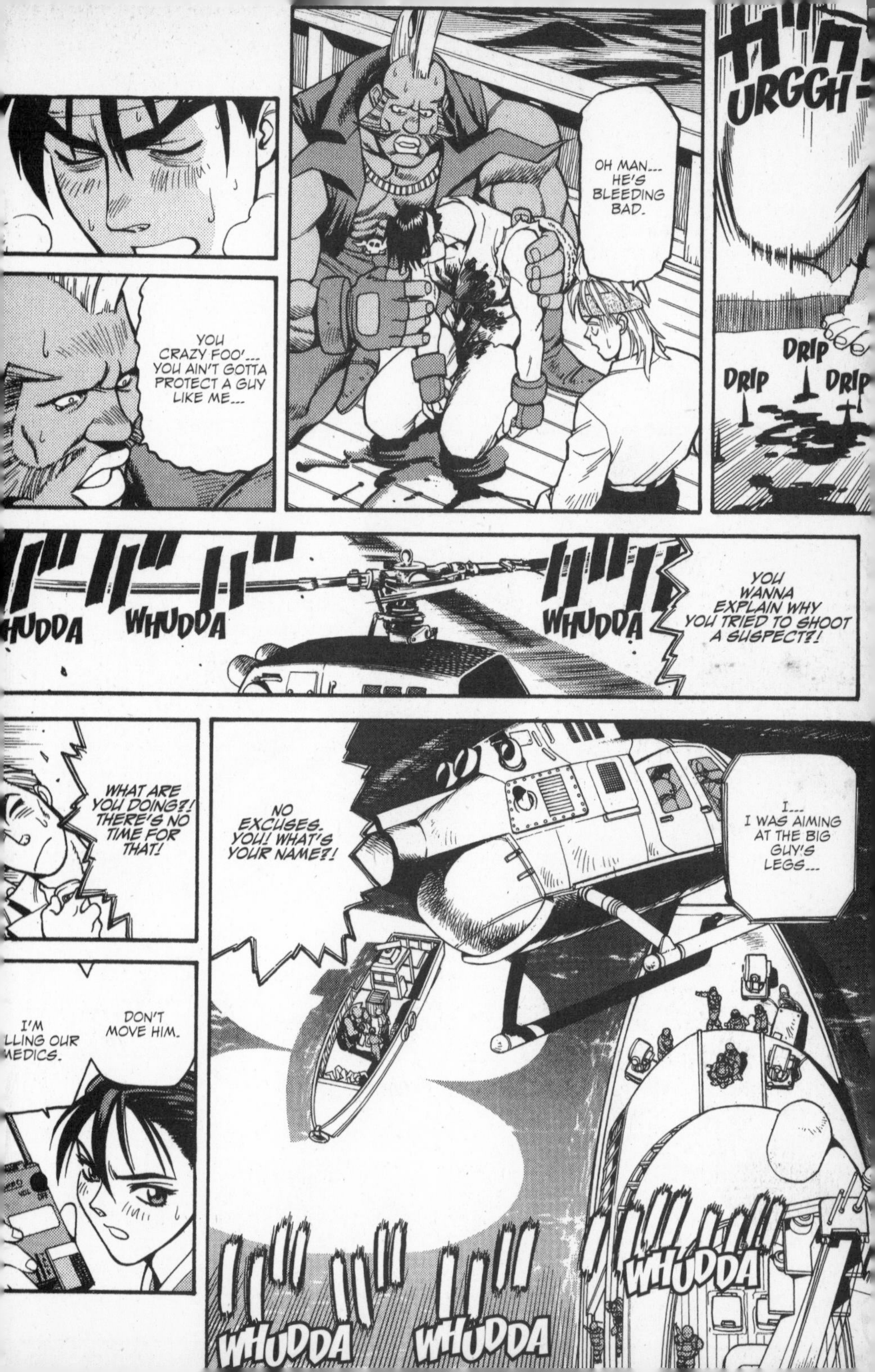
URGGH
DRIP
DRIP
DRIP
OH MAN... HE'S BLEEDING BAD.
YOU CRAZY FOO'... YOU AIN'T GOTTA PROTECT A GUY LIKE ME...
YOU WANNA EXPLAIN WHY YOU TRIED TO SHOOT A SUSPECT?!
WHUDDA
WHUDDA
HUDDA
I... I WAS AIMING AT THE BIG GUY'S LEGS...
NO EXCUSES. YOU! WHAT'S YOUR NAME?!
WHUDDA
WHUDDA
WHUDDA
WHAT ARE YOU DOING?! THERE'S NO TIME FOR THAT!
DON'T MOVE HIM.
I'M LLING OUR MEDICS.

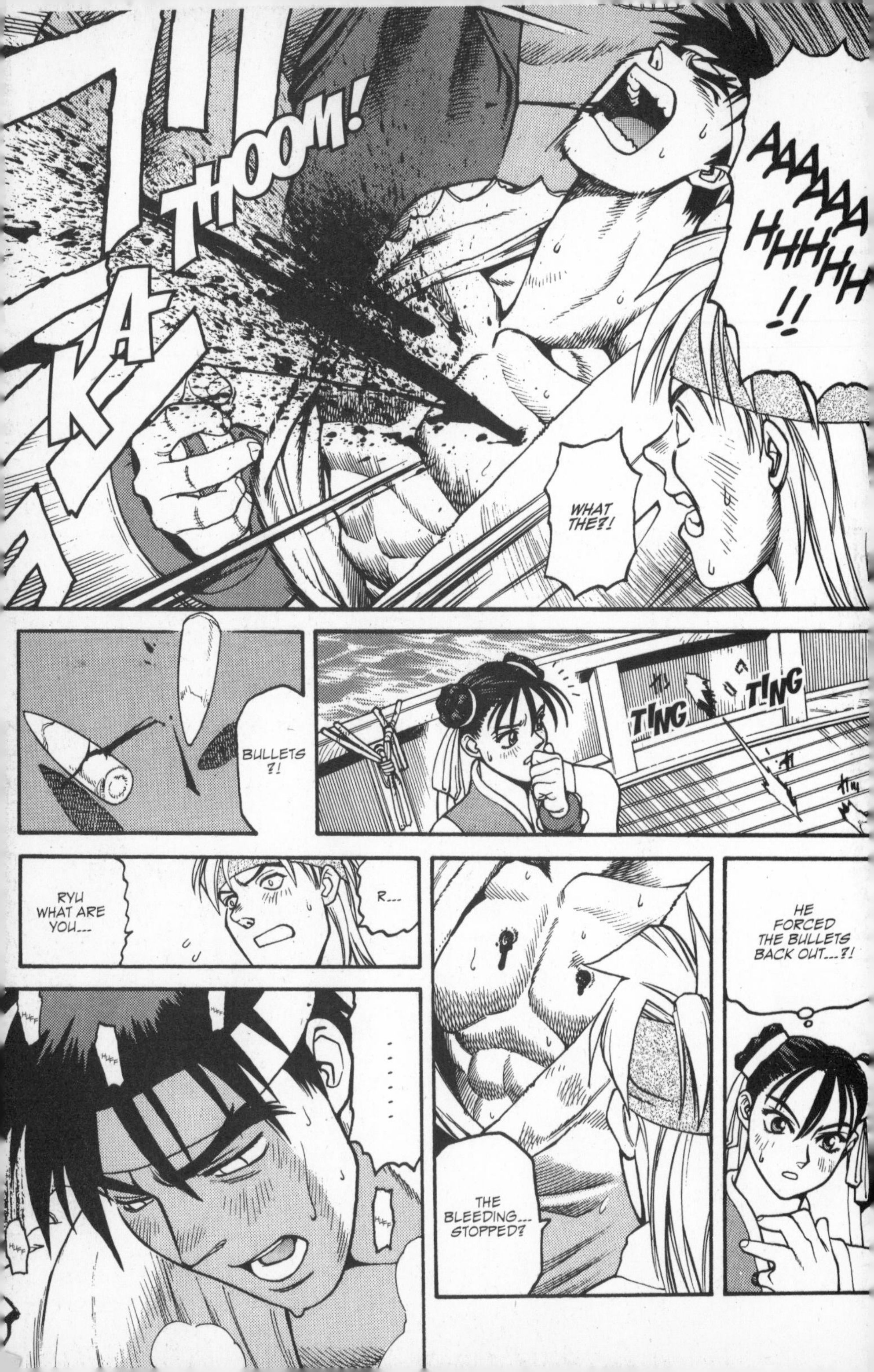
AAAAAAHHHHHH!!
KA-THOOM!
WHAT THE?!
TING
TING
BULLETS?!
HE FORCED THE BULLETS BACK OUT...?!
THE BLEEDING... STOPPED?
R...
RYU WHAT ARE YOU...
......

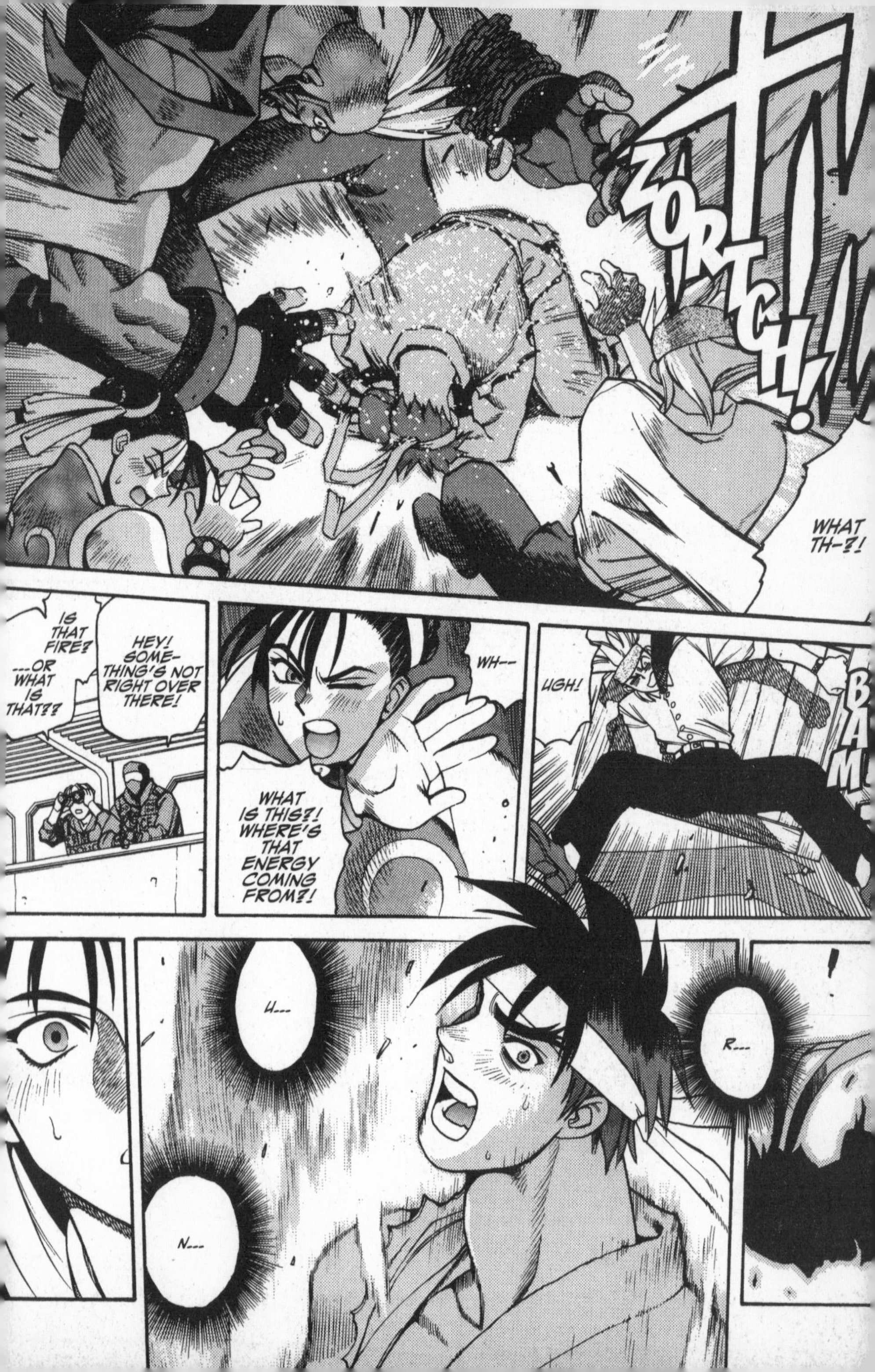
ZORTCH!
WHAT TH-?!
BAM
UGH!
WH--
WHAT IS THIS?! WHERE'S THAT ENERGY COMING FROM?!
HEY! SOME-THING'S NOT RIGHT OVER THERE!
IS THAT FIRE? ---OR WHAT IS THAT??
R---
U---
N---

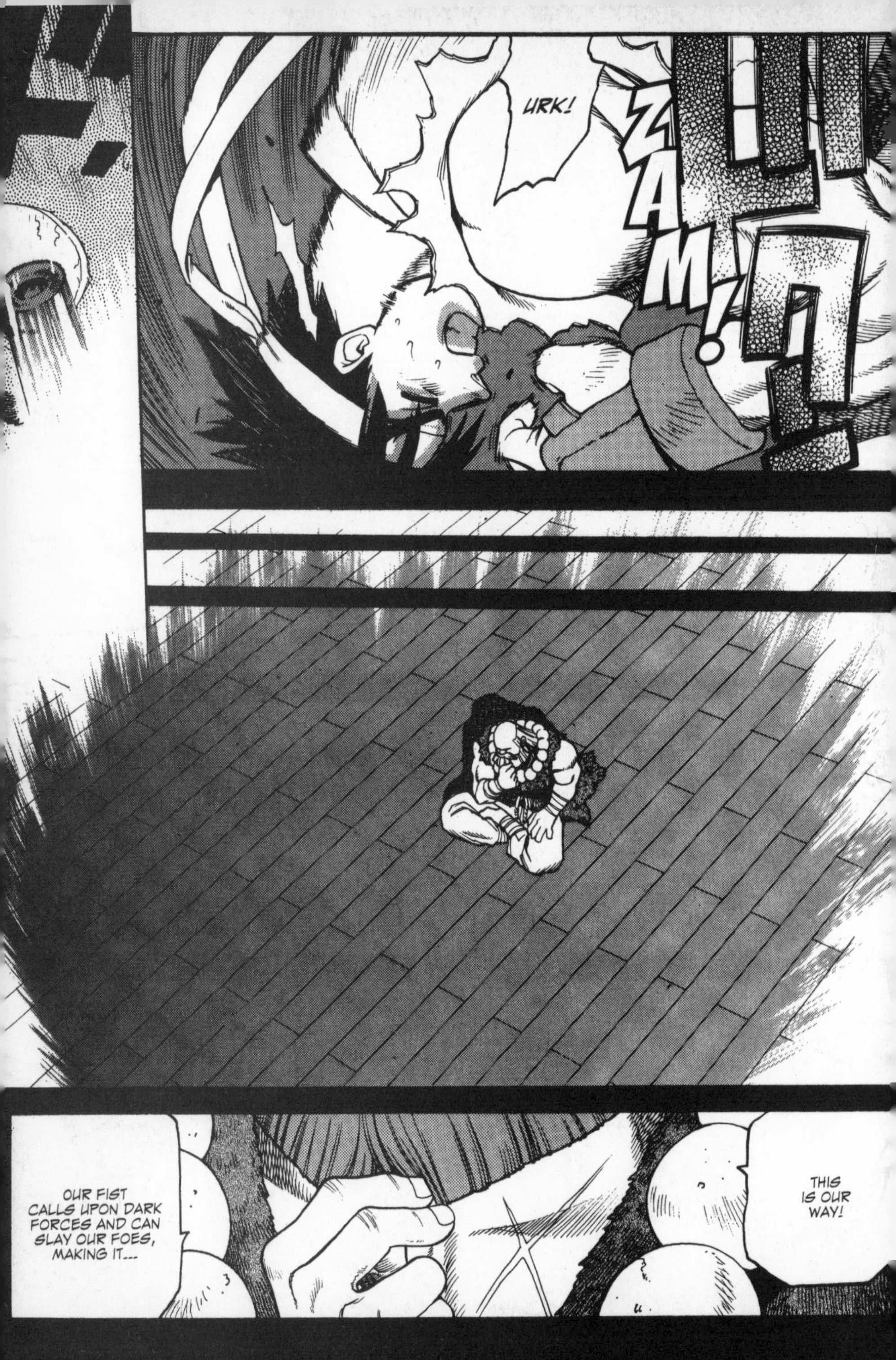
URK!
ZAM!!
OUR FIST CALLS UPON DARK FORCES AND CAN SLAY OUR FOES, MAKING IT...
THIS IS OUR WAY!

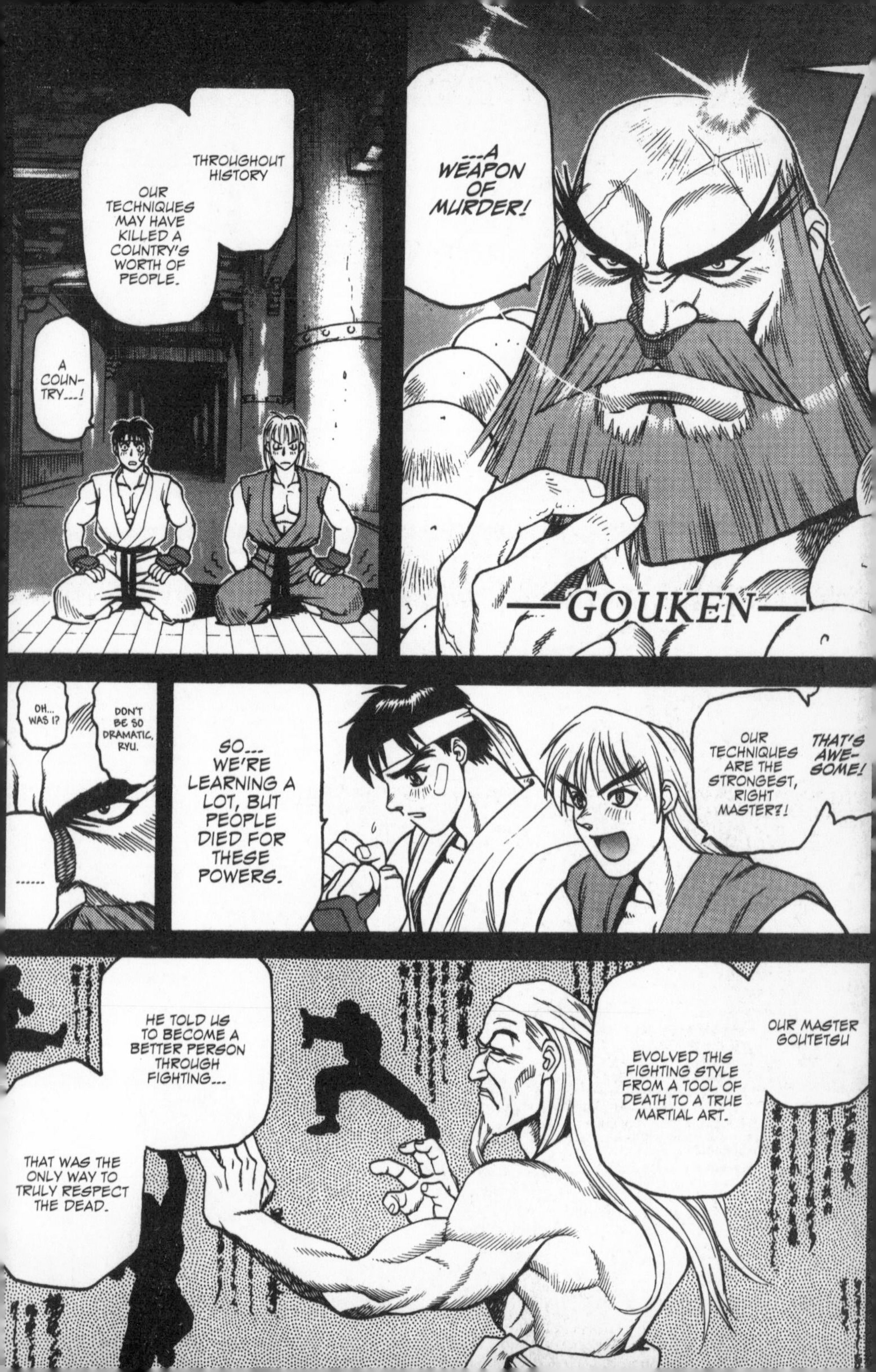
...A WEAPON OF MURDER!
—GOUKEN—
THROUGHOUT HISTORY
OUR TECHNIQUES MAY HAVE KILLED A COUNTRY'S WORTH OF PEOPLE.
A COUN-TRY...!
THAT'S AWE-SOME!
OUR TECHNIQUES ARE THE STRONGEST, RIGHT MASTER?!
SO... WE'RE LEARNING A LOT, BUT PEOPLE DIED FOR THESE POWERS.
DON'T BE SO DRAMATIC, RYU.
OH... WAS I?
......
OUR MASTER GOUTETSU
EVOLVED THIS FIGHTING STYLE FROM A TOOL OF DEATH TO A TRUE MARTIAL ART.
HE TOLD US TO BECOME A BETTER PERSON THROUGH FIGHTING...
THAT WAS THE ONLY WAY TO TRULY RESPECT THE DEAD.

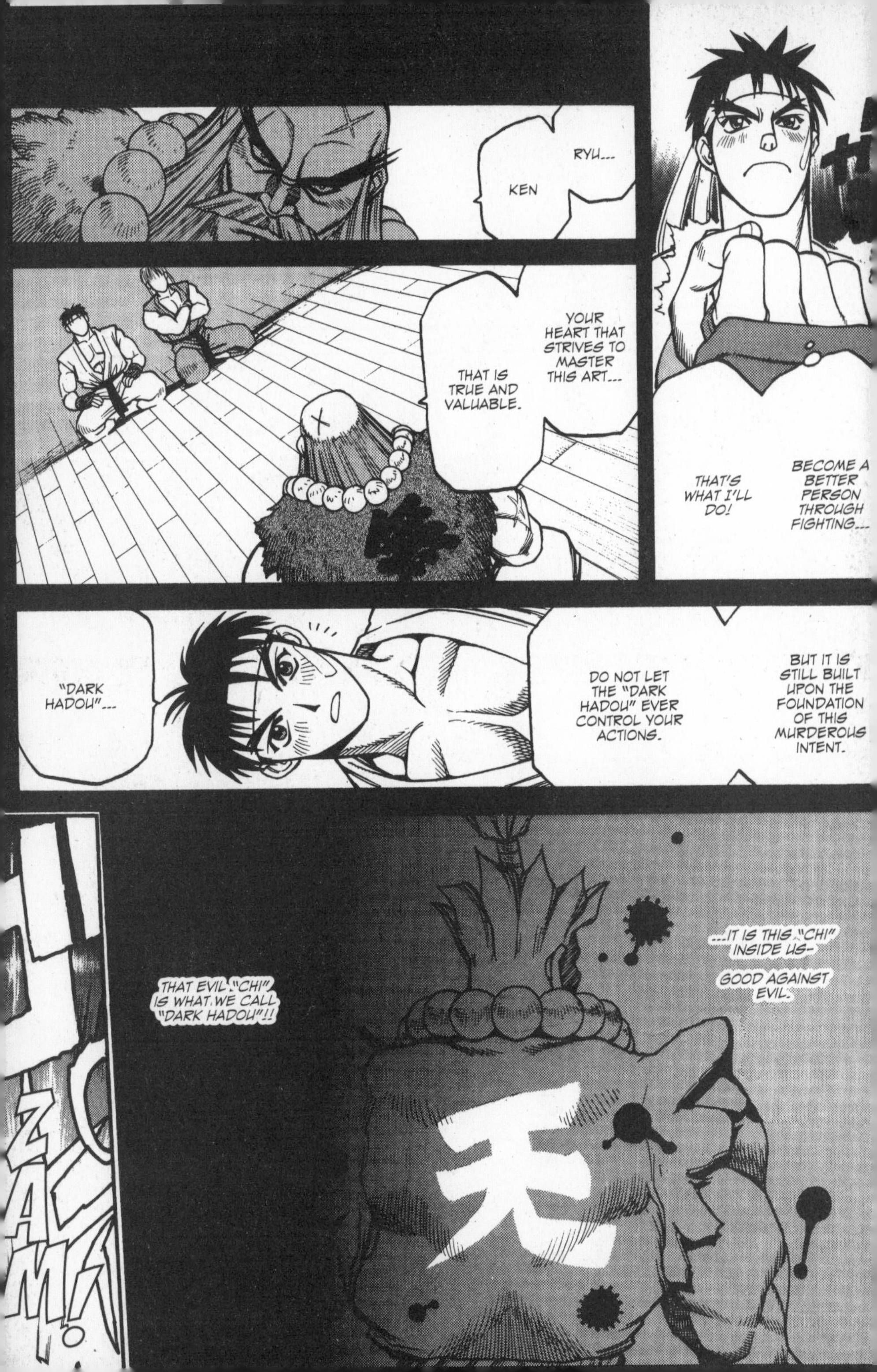
BECOME A BETTER PERSON THROUGH FIGHTING...
THAT'S WHAT I'LL DO!
RYU...
KEN
YOUR HEART THAT STRIVES TO MASTER THIS ART...
THAT IS TRUE AND VALUABLE.
BUT IT IS STILL BUILT UPON THE FOUNDATION OF THIS MURDEROUS INTENT.
DO NOT LET THE "DARK HADOU" EVER CONTROL YOUR ACTIONS.
"DARK HADOU"...
...IT IS THIS "CHI" INSIDE US-
GOOD AGAINST EVIL.
THAT EVIL "CHI" IS WHAT WE CALL "DARK HADOU"!!
ZAM!
天

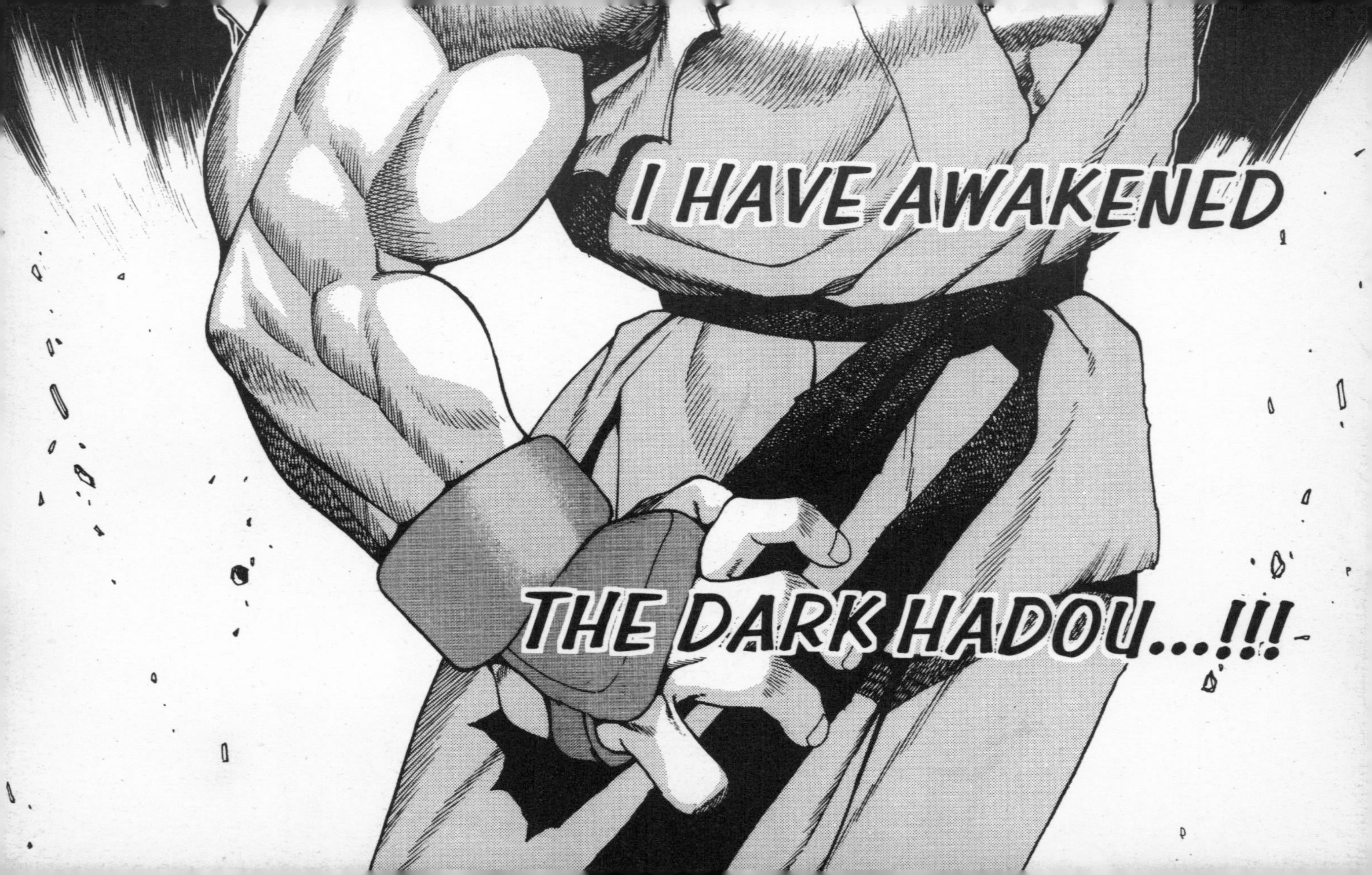
I HAVE AWAKENED
THE DARK HADOU...!!!

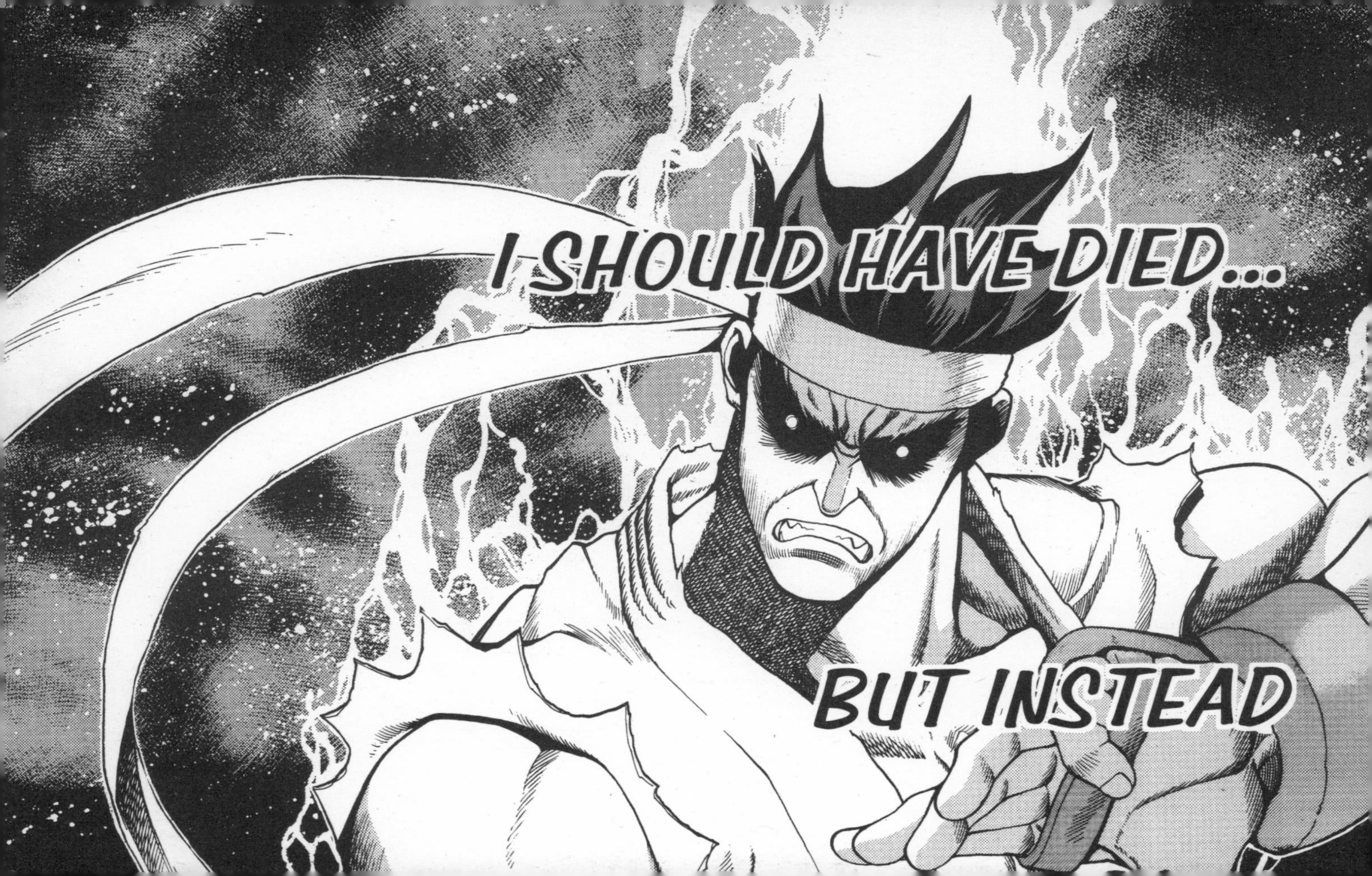
I SHOULD HAVE DIED...
BUT INSTEAD

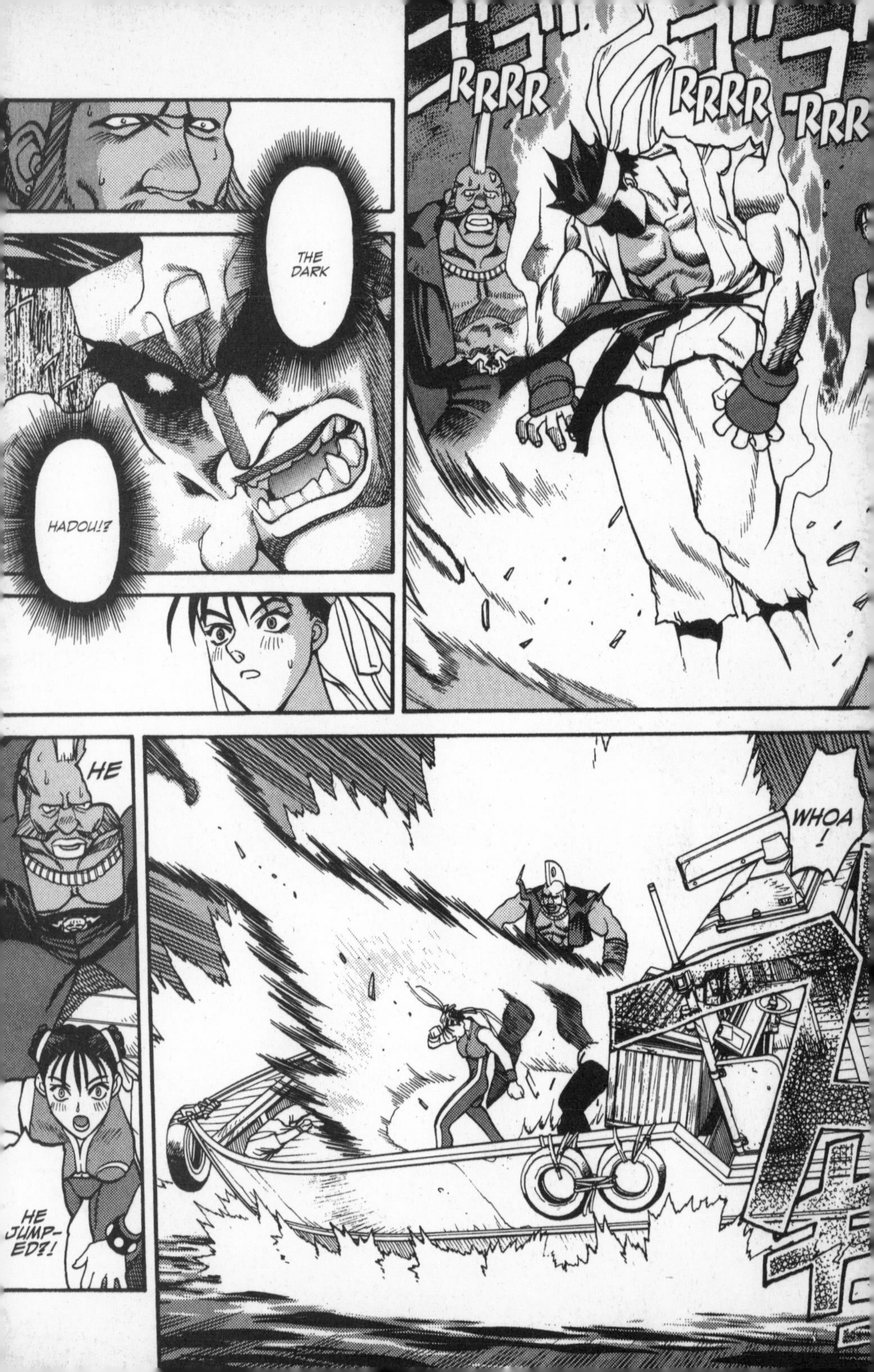
RRR
RRRR
RRRR
THE DARK
HADOU!?
WHOA!
HE
HE JUMPED?!

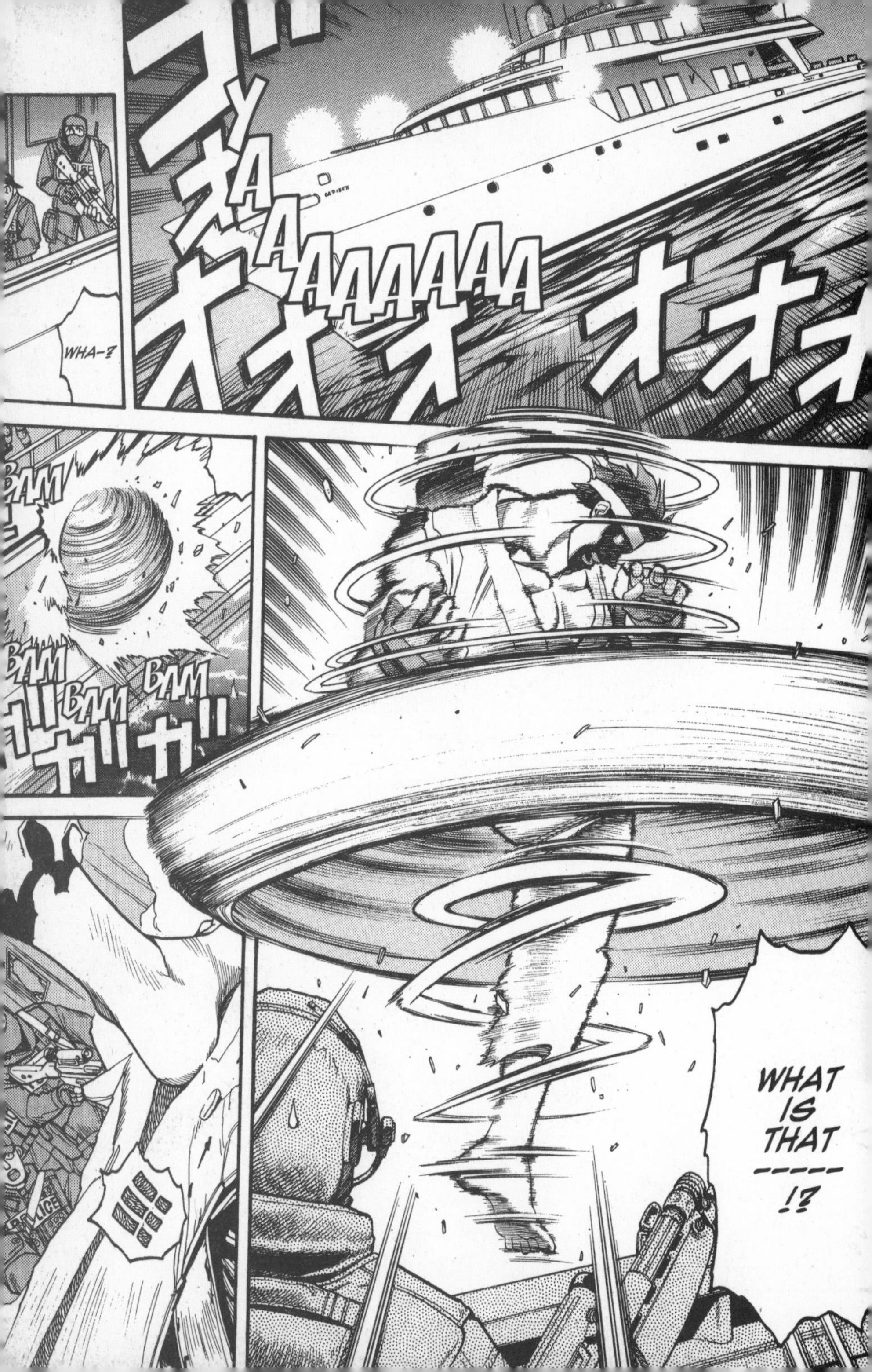
YAAAAAAAA
WHA-!?
BAM
BAM
BAM
BAM
WHAT IS THAT -----!?

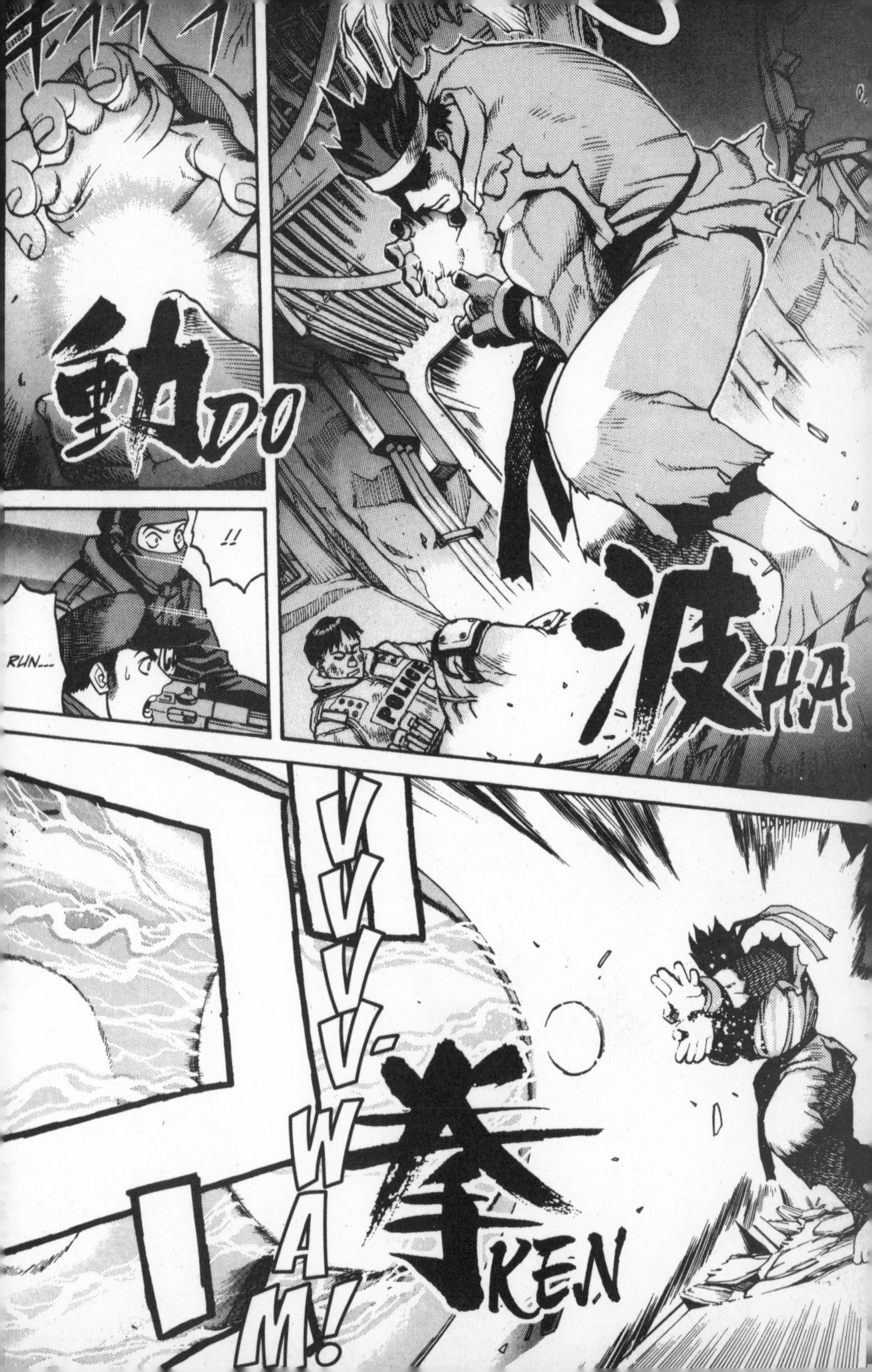

波 HA
動 DO
!!
RUN...
拳 KEN
VVVVV-WAM!

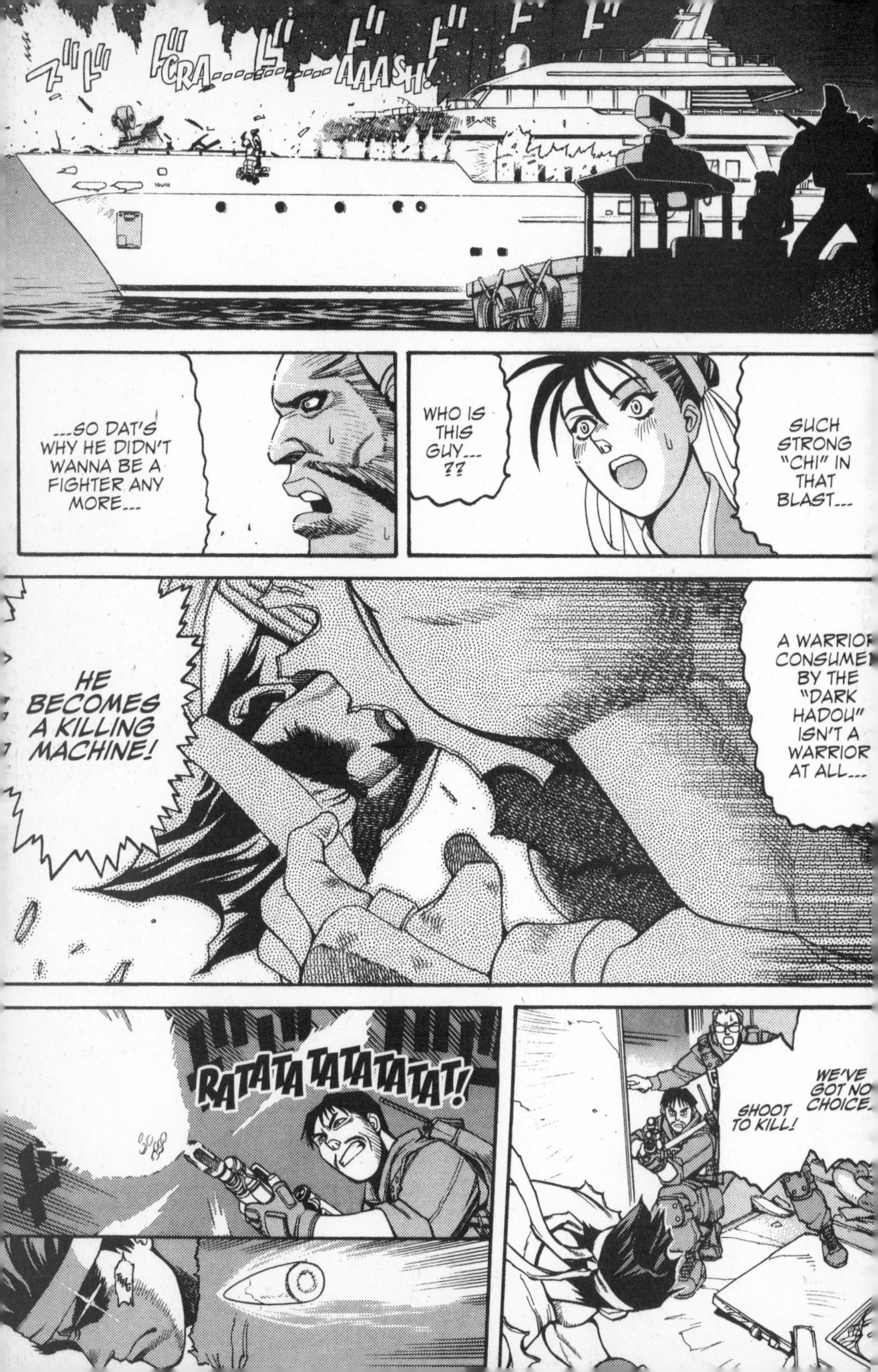
CRA.........AAASH!
SUCH STRONG "CHI" IN THAT BLAST...
WHO IS THIS GUY... ??
...SO DAT'S WHY HE DIDN'T WANNA BE A FIGHTER ANY MORE...
A WARRIOR CONSUMED BY THE "DARK HADOU" ISN'T A WARRIOR AT ALL...
HE BECOMES A KILLING MACHINE!
WE'VE GOT NO CHOICE.
SHOOT TO KILL!
RATATA TATATATAT!

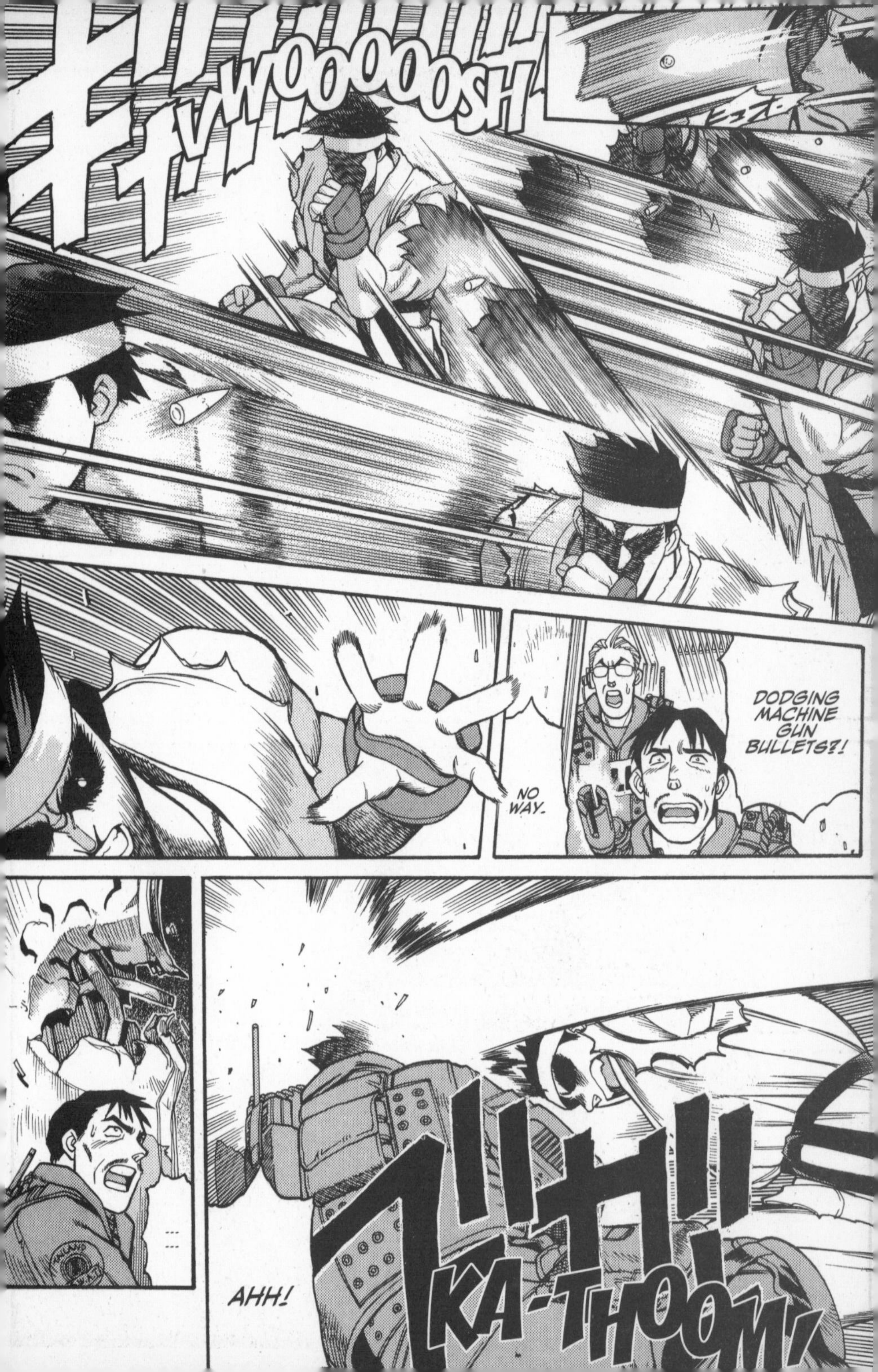
VWOOOOOSH
DODGING MACHINE GUN BULLETS?!
NO WAY...
AHH!
KA-THOOM!

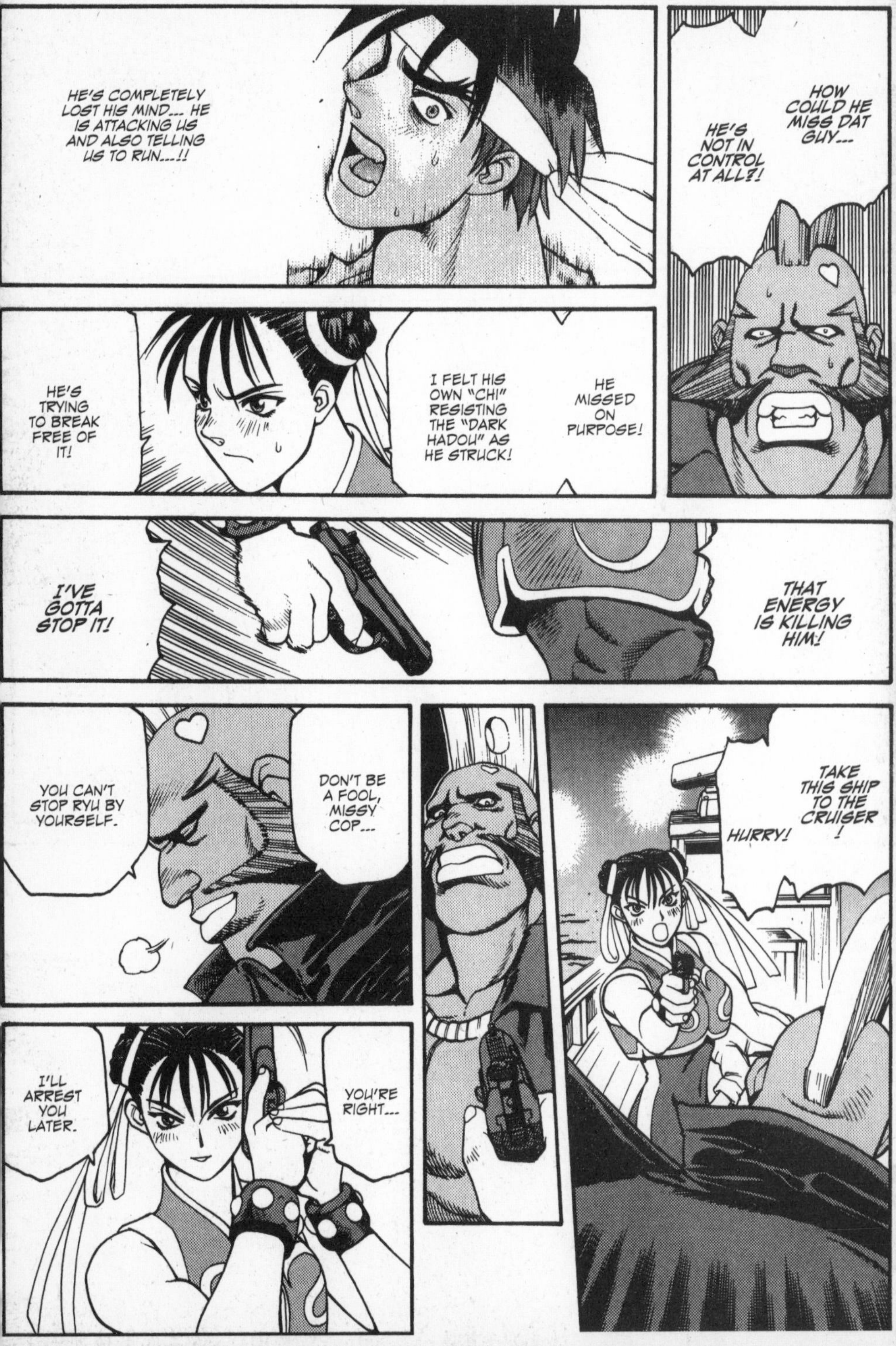
HOW COULD HE MISS DAT GUY---
HE'S NOT IN CONTROL AT ALL?!
HE'S COMPLETELY LOST HIS MIND--- HE IS ATTACKING US AND ALSO TELLING US TO RUN---!!
HE MISSED ON PURPOSE!
I FELT HIS OWN "CHI" RESISTING THE "DARK HADOU" AS HE STRUCK!
HE'S TRYING TO BREAK FREE OF IT!
THAT ENERGY IS KILLING HIM!
I'VE GOTTA STOP IT!
TAKE THIS SHIP TO THE CRUISER!
HURRY!
DON'T BE A FOOL, MISSY COP---
YOU CAN'T STOP RYU BY YOURSELF.
YOU'RE RIGHT---
I'LL ARREST YOU LATER.

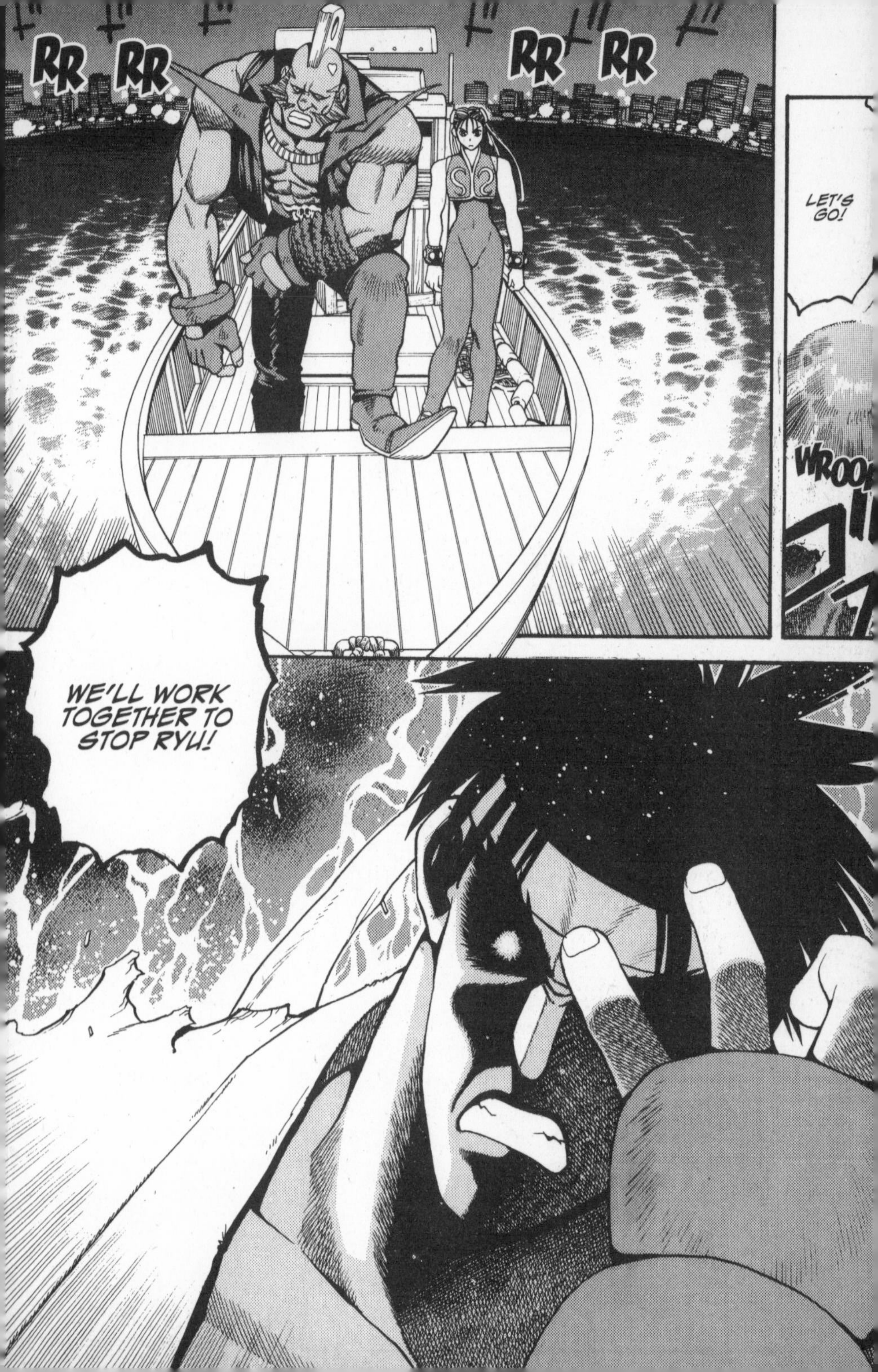
LET'S GO!
RR RR
RR RR
WE'LL WORK TOGETHER TO STOP RYU!

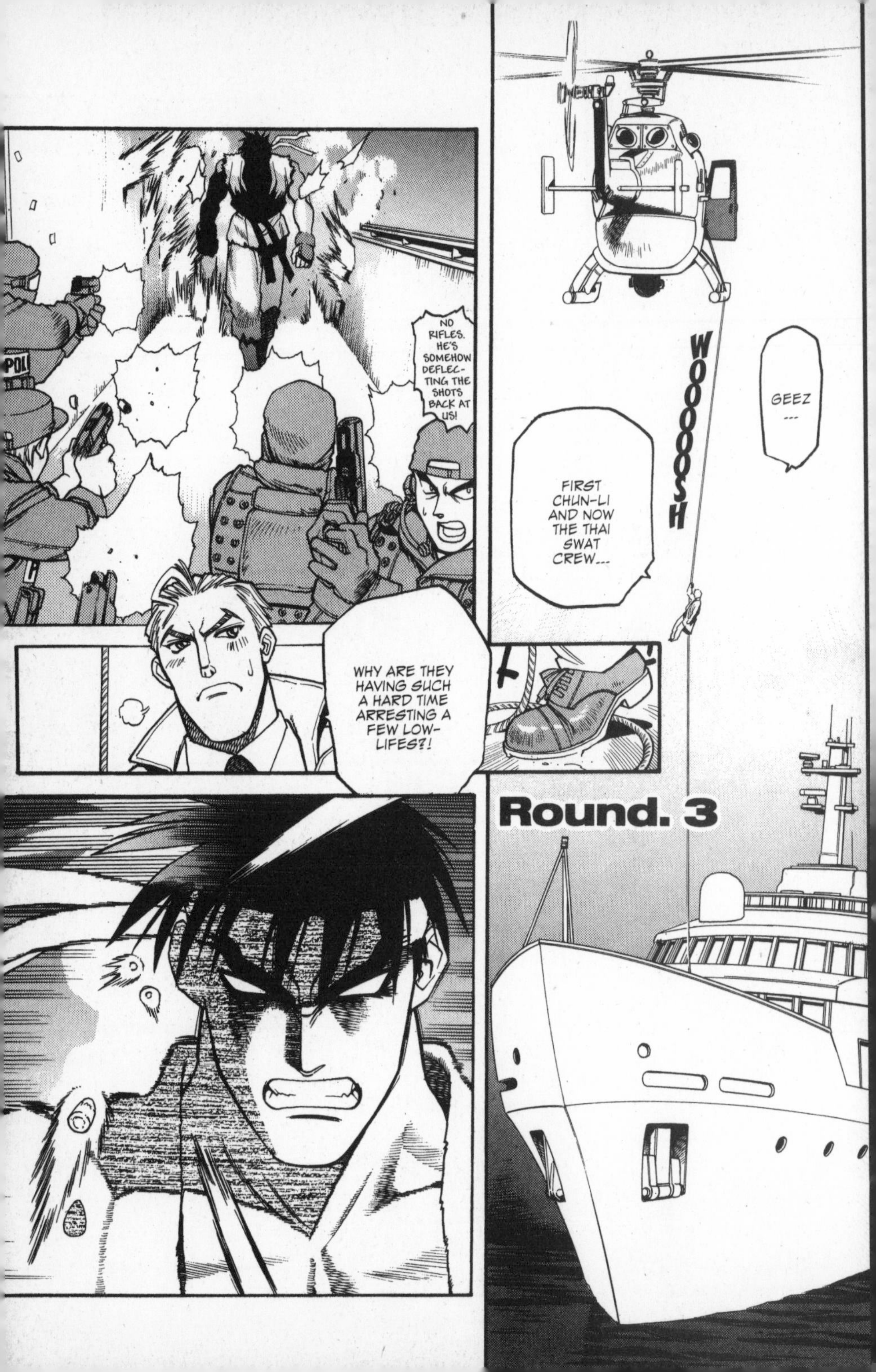
GEEZ ---
WOOOOOOSH
FIRST CHUN-LI AND NOW THE THAI SWAT CREW...
Round. 3
NO RIFLES. HE'S SOMEHOW DEFLECTING THE SHOTS BACK AT US!
POL
WHY ARE THEY HAVING SUCH A HARD TIME ARRESTING A FEW LOW-LIFES?!

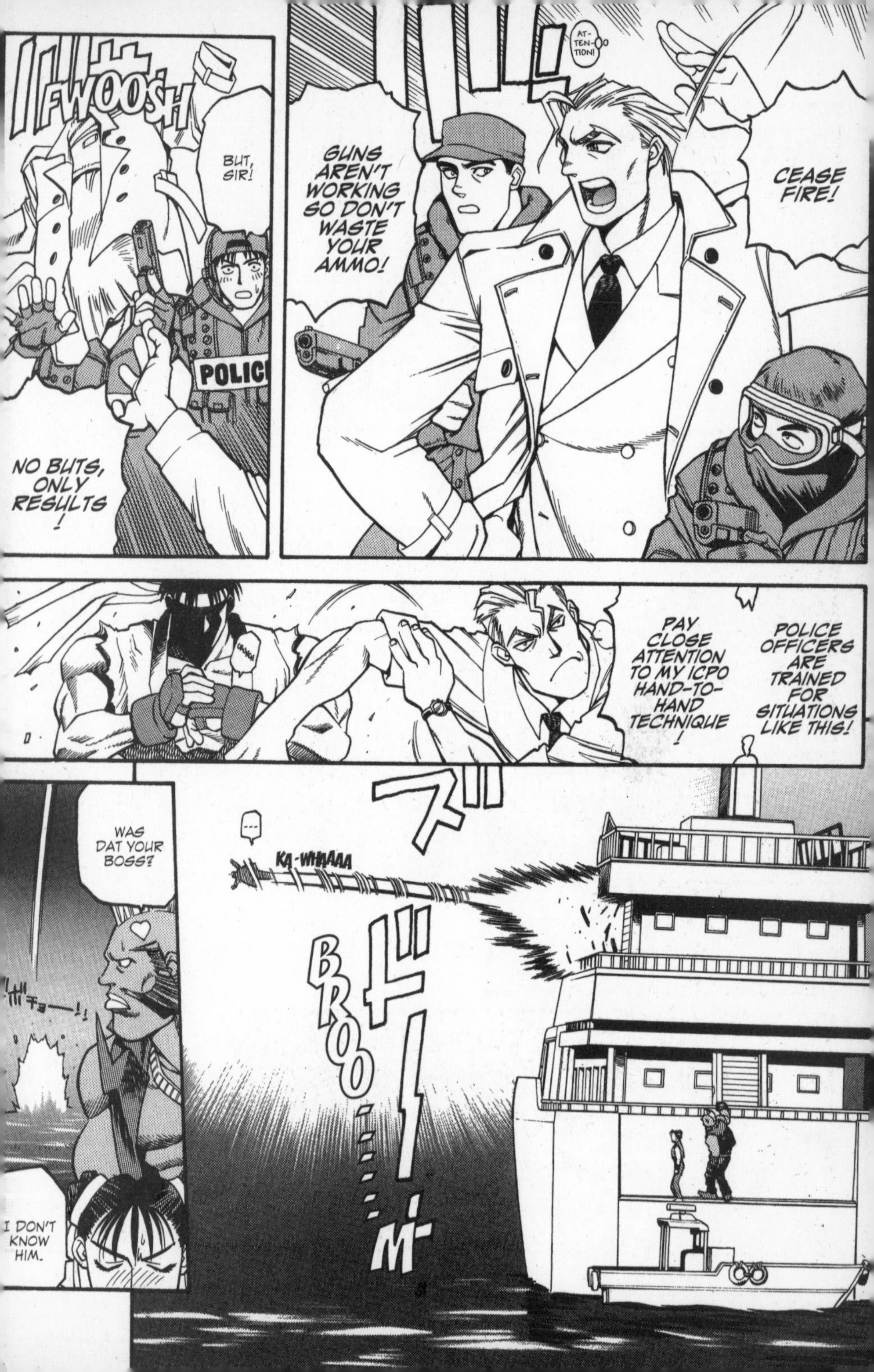
AT-TEN-TION!
CEASE FIRE!
GUNS AREN'T WORKING SO DON'T WASTE YOUR AMMO!
FWOOSH
BUT, SIR!
NO BUTS, ONLY RESULTS!
POLICE
POLICE OFFICERS ARE TRAINED FOR SITUATIONS LIKE THIS!
PAY CLOSE ATTENTION TO MY ICPO HAND-TO-HAND TECHNIQUE!
...
KA-WHAAAA
BROOM
WAS DAT YOUR BOSS?
I DON'T KNOW HIM.

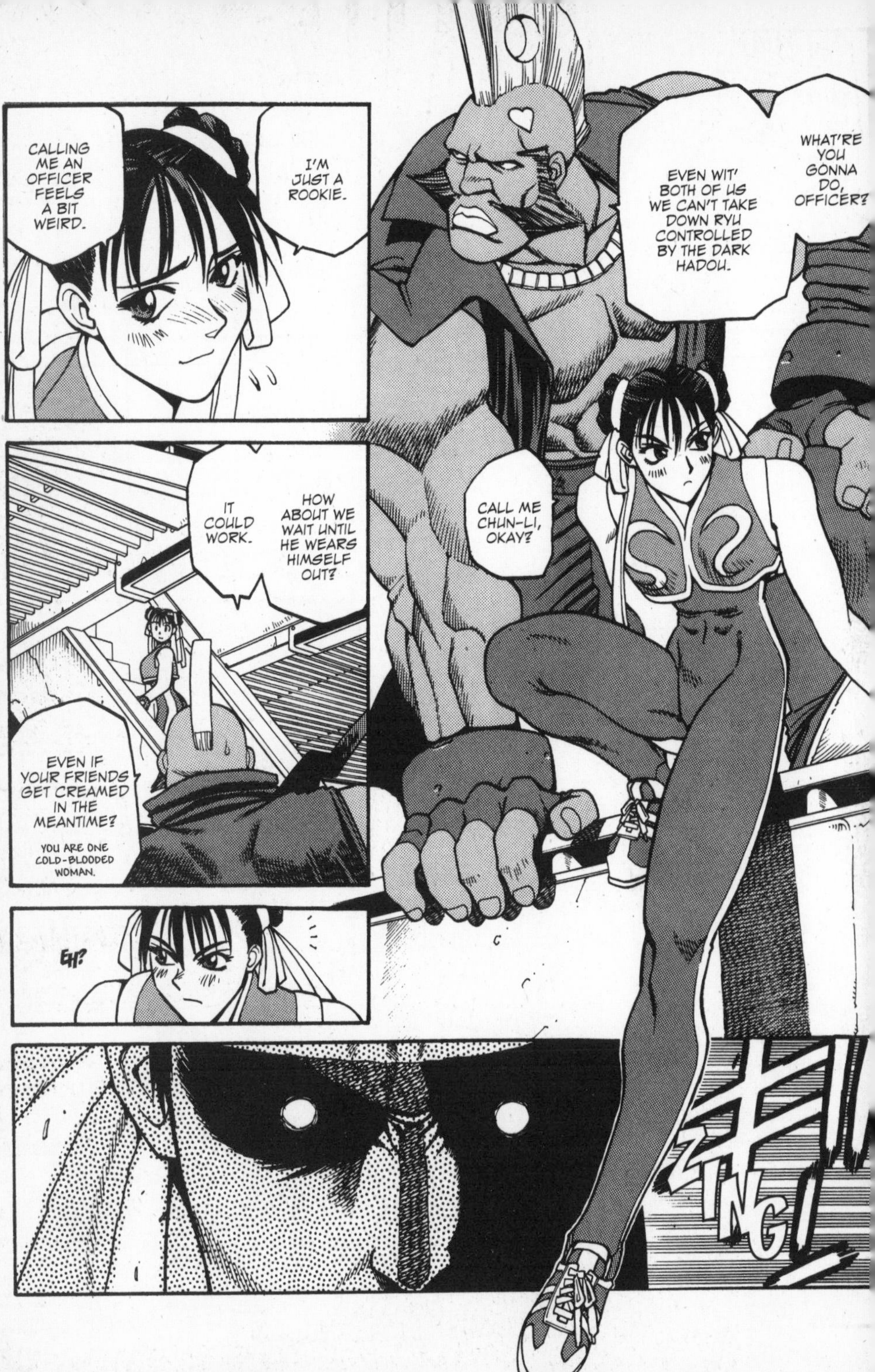
WHAT'RE YOU GONNA DO, OFFICER?
EVEN WIT' BOTH OF US WE CAN'T TAKE DOWN RYU CONTROLLED BY THE DARK HADOU.
CALL ME CHUN-LI, OKAY?
I'M JUST A ROOKIE.
CALLING ME AN OFFICER FEELS A BIT WEIRD.
HOW ABOUT WE WAIT UNTIL HE WEARS HIMSELF OUT?
IT COULD WORK.
EVEN IF YOUR FRIENDS GET CREAMED IN THE MEANTIME?
YOU ARE ONE COLD-BLOODED WOMAN.
EH?
ZING!

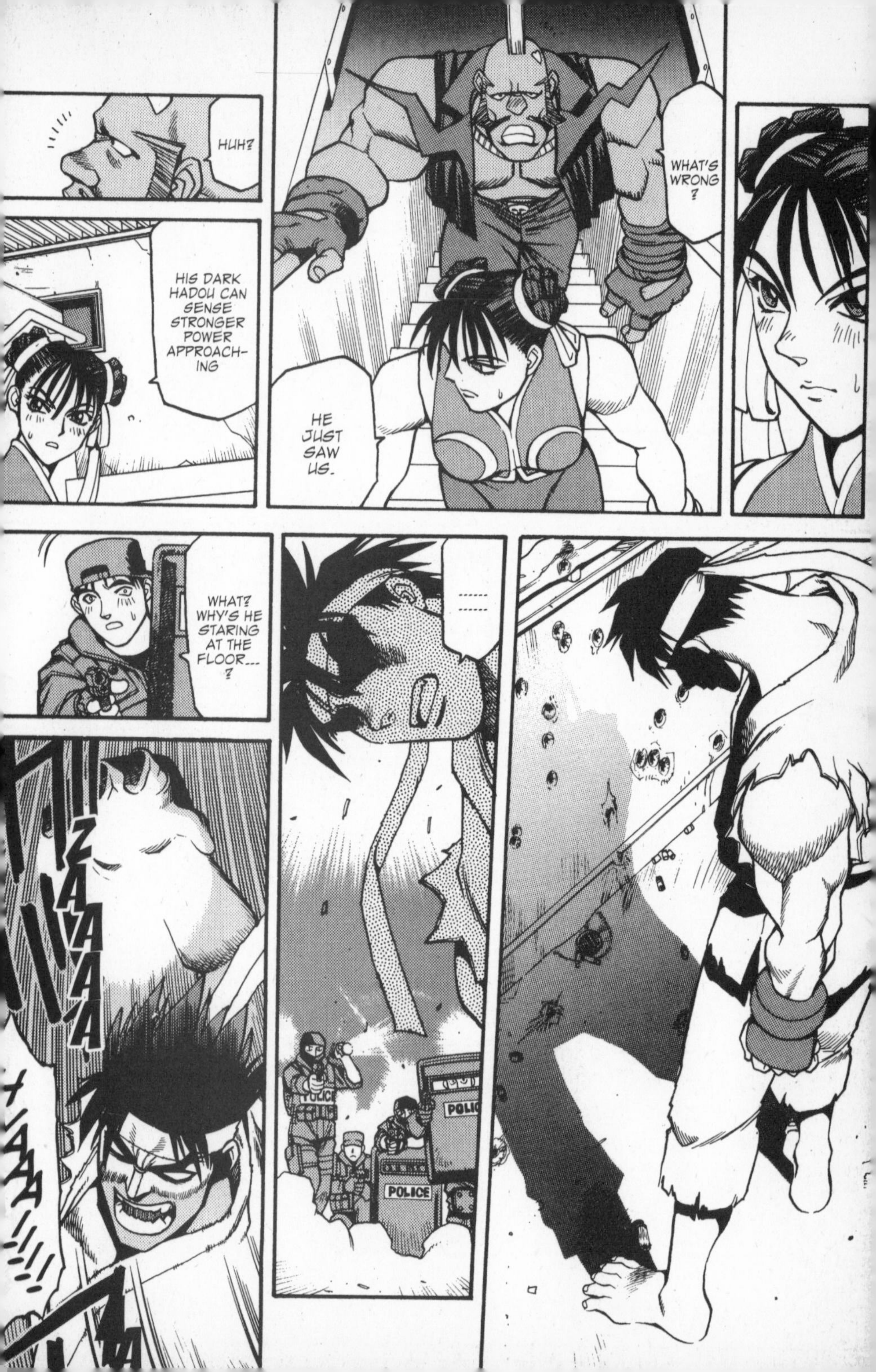
WHAT'S WRONG ?
HE JUST SAW US.
HUH?
HIS DARK HADOU CAN SENSE STRONGER POWER APPROACHING
......
POLICE
POLICE
POLICE
WHAT? WHY'S HE STARING AT THE FLOOR...?
ZAAAAA
AAAAA!!!!

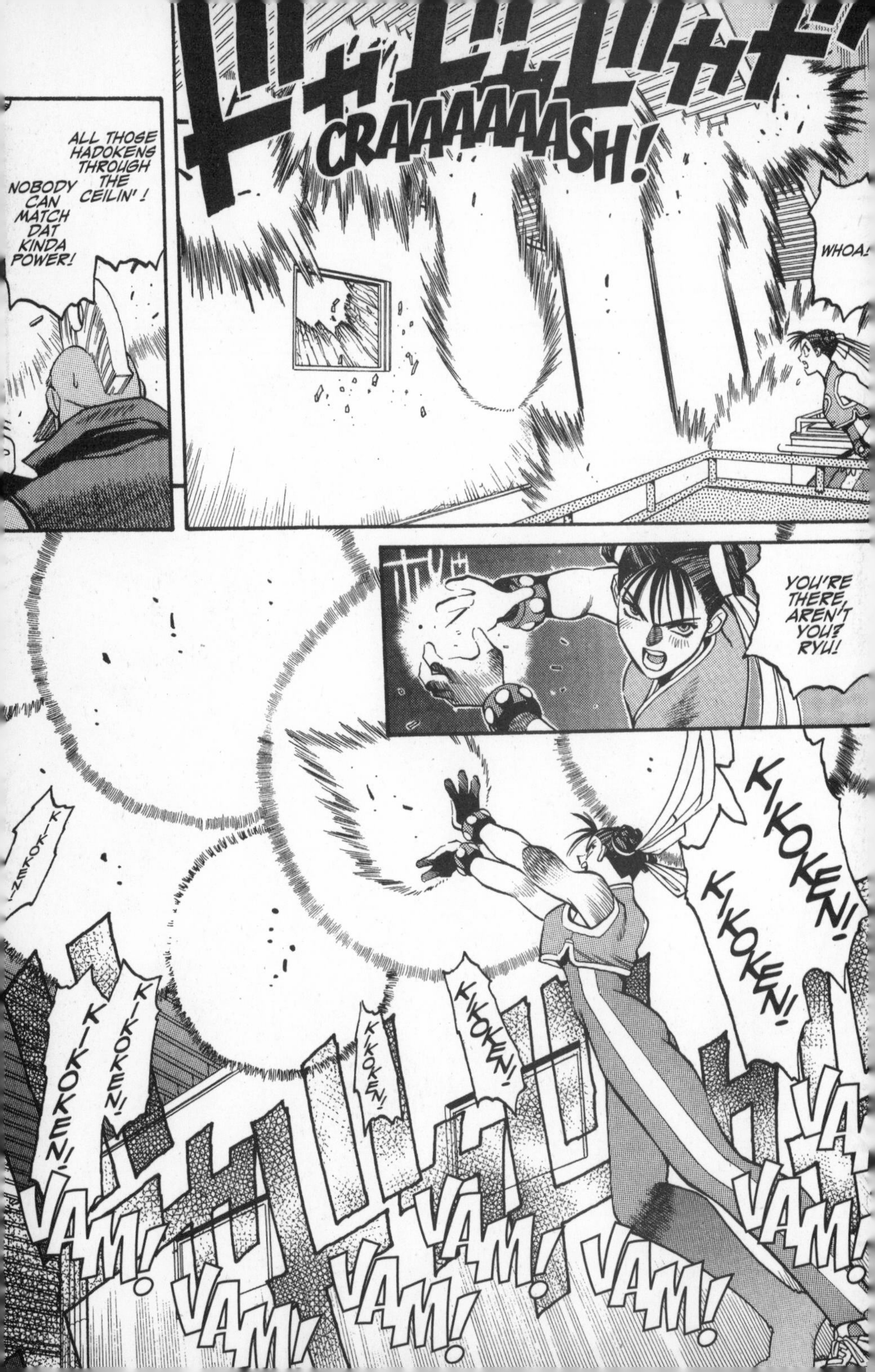
CRAAAAAAASH!
WHOA!
ALL THOSE HADOKENS THROUGH THE CEILIN'!
NOBODY CAN MATCH DAT KINDA POWER!
YOU'RE THERE, AREN'T YOU? RYU!
KIKOKEN!
KIKOKEN!
KIKOKEN!
KIKOKEN!
KIKOKEN!
KIKOKEN!
KIKOKEN!
VAM!
VAM!
VAM!
VAM!
VAM!
VAM!
VAM!
VAM!

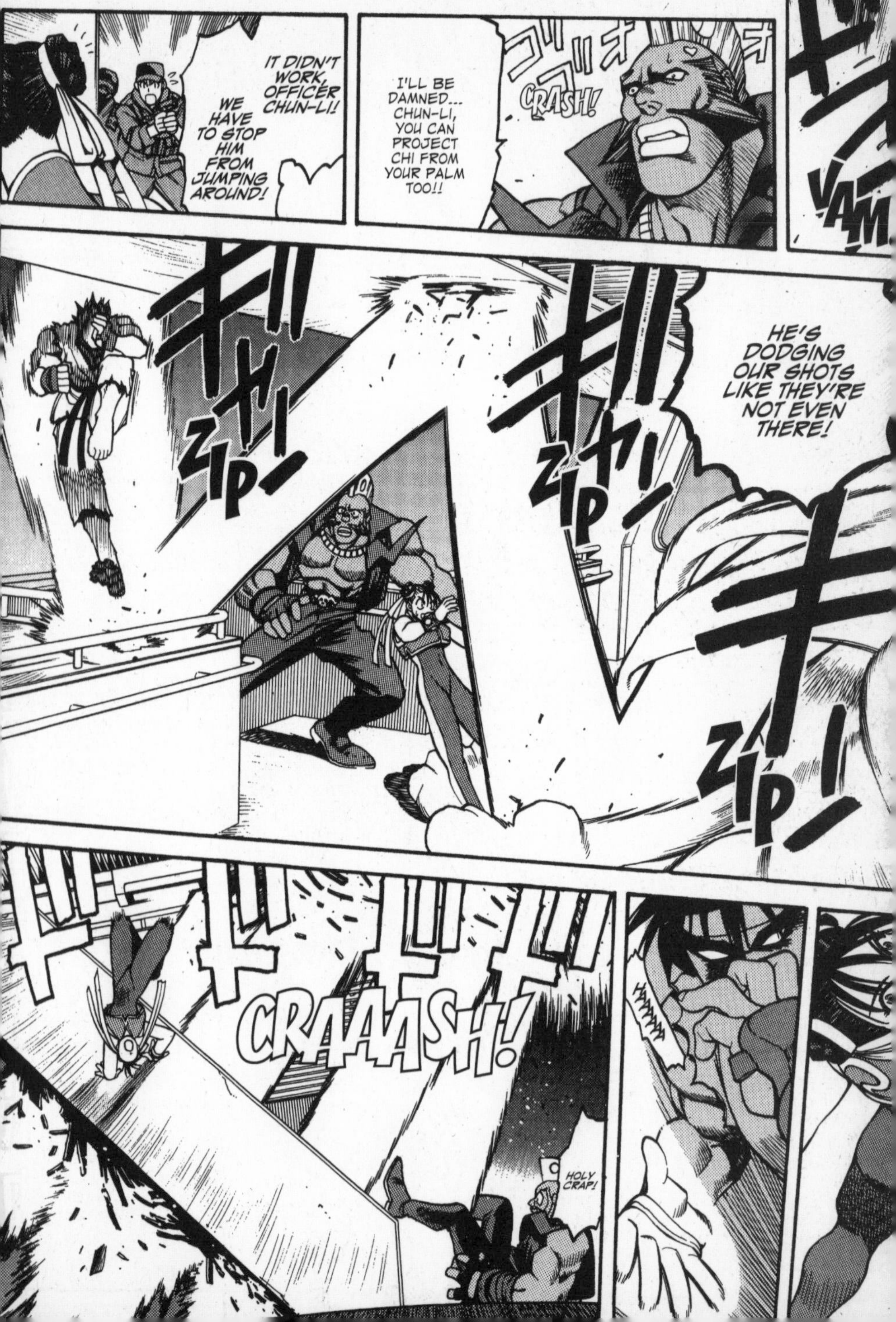
VAM
CRASH!
I'LL BE DAMNED... CHUN-LI, YOU CAN PROJECT CHI FROM YOUR PALM TOO!!
IT DIDN'T WORK, OFFICER CHUN-LI!
WE HAVE TO STOP HIM FROM JUMPING AROUND!
HE'S DODGING OUR SHOTS LIKE THEY'RE NOT EVEN THERE!
ZIP
ZIP
ZIP
CRAAASH!
HOLY CRAP!

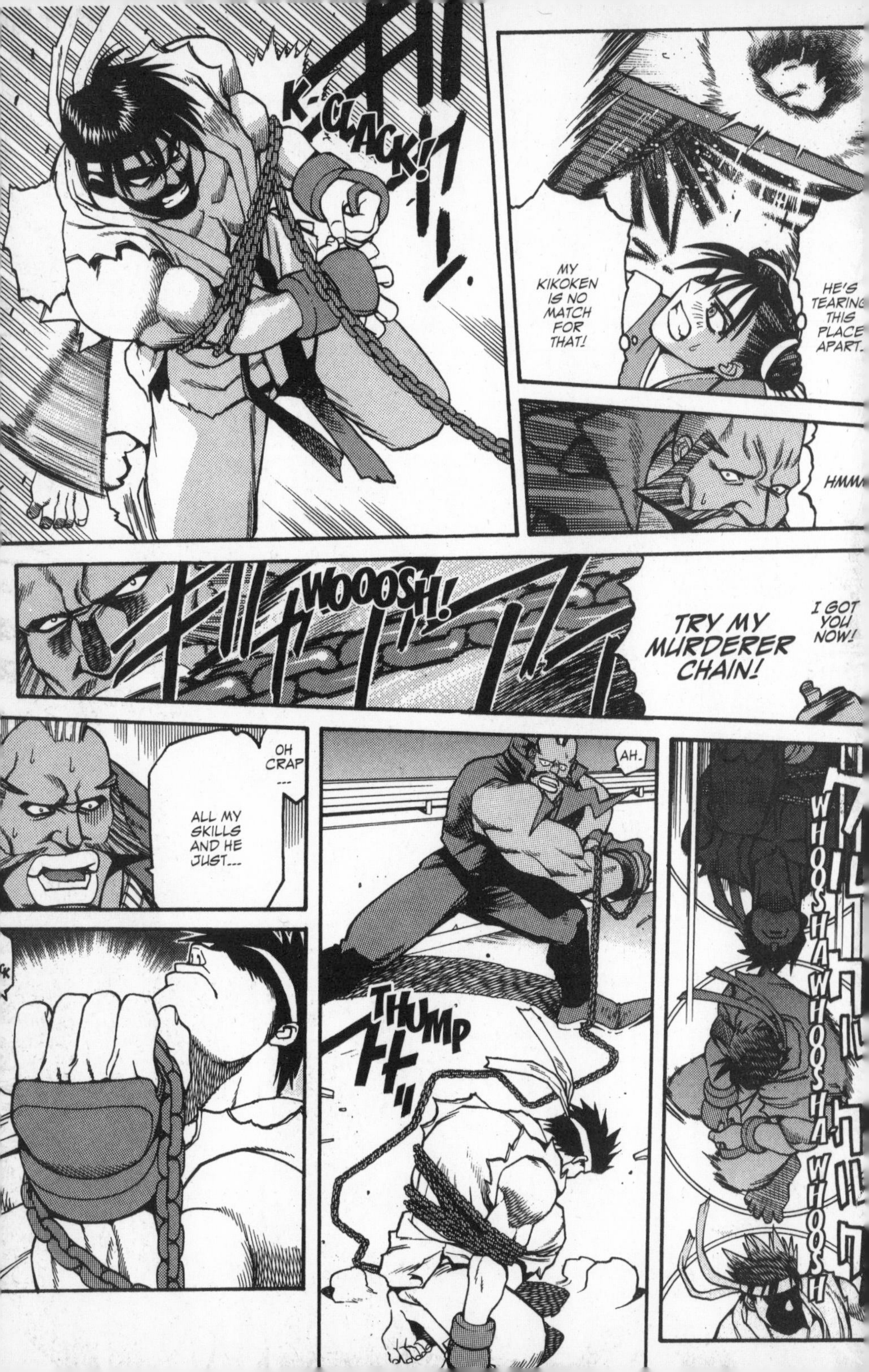
HE'S TEARING THIS PLACE APART...
MY KIKOKEN IS NO MATCH FOR THAT!
HMM
K-CLACK!!
I GOT YOU NOW!
TRY MY MURDERER CHAIN!
WOOOSH!
WHOOSHA
WHOOSHA
WHOOSH
AH...
THUMP
OH CRAP ---
ALL MY SKILLS AND HE JUST---

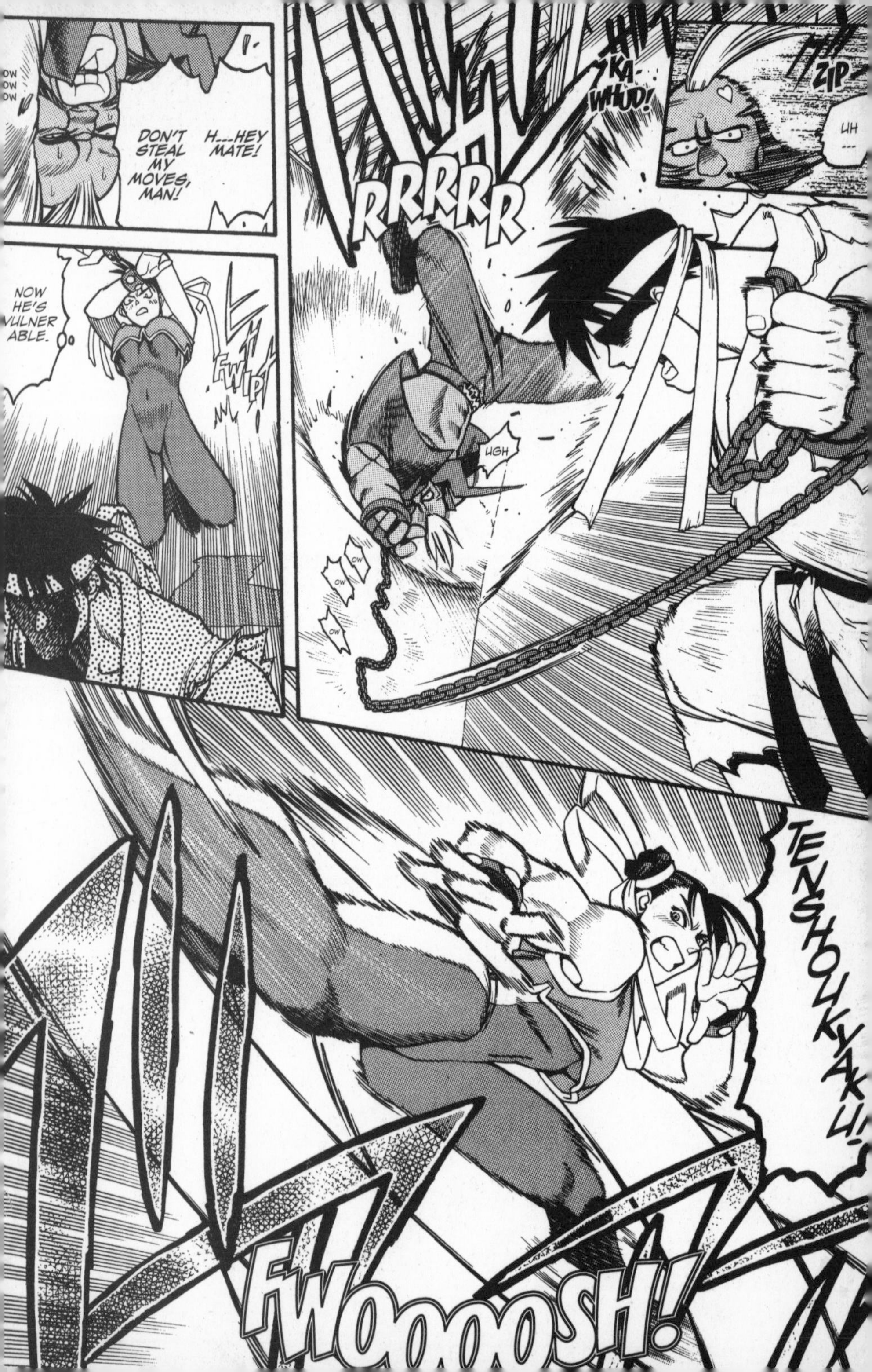
ZIP
UH...
KA-WHUD!
RRRRRR
UGH
OW
OW
OW
OW
OW
OW
H...HEY MATE!
DON'T STEAL MY MOVES, MAN!
NOW HE'S VULNERABLE..
FWIP
TENSHOUKYAKU!
FWOOOOOSH!

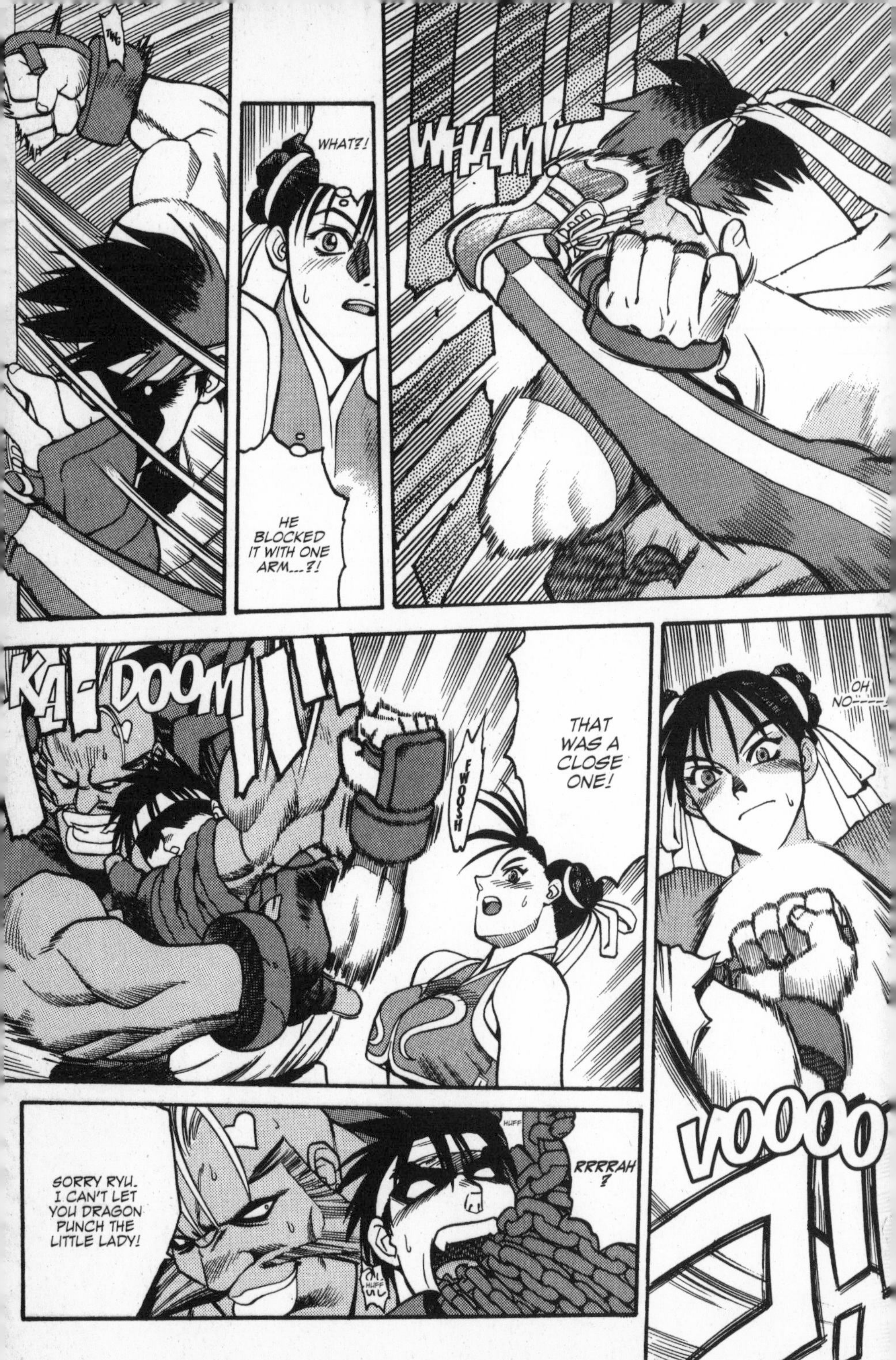
WHAM!!
WHAT?!
HE BLOCKED IT WITH ONE ARM...?!
TING
OH NO...!
THAT WAS A CLOSE ONE!
FWOOSH
KA-DOOM!!!
VOOOO
RRRRAH?
HUFF
SORRY RYU. I CAN'T LET YOU DRAGON PUNCH THE LITTLE LADY!
HUFF

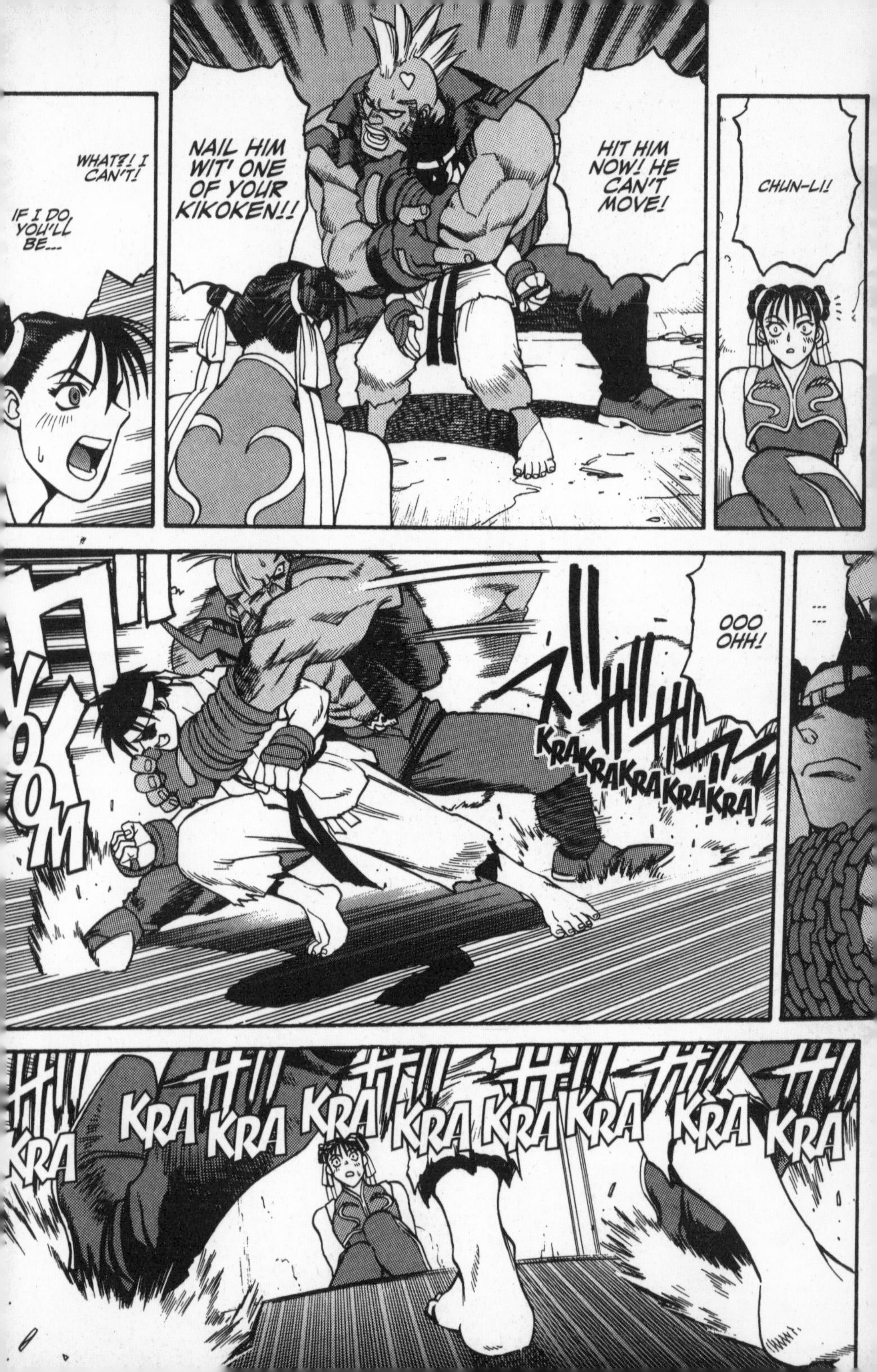
CHUN-LI!
HIT HIM NOW! HE CAN'T MOVE!
NAIL HIM WIT' ONE OF YOUR KIKOKEN!!
WHAT?! I CAN'T!
IF I DO, YOU'LL BE...
...
...
OOO OHH!
KRAKRAKRAKRAKRAKRA!
VOOOM
KRA KRA KRA KRA KRA KRA KRA KRA KRA

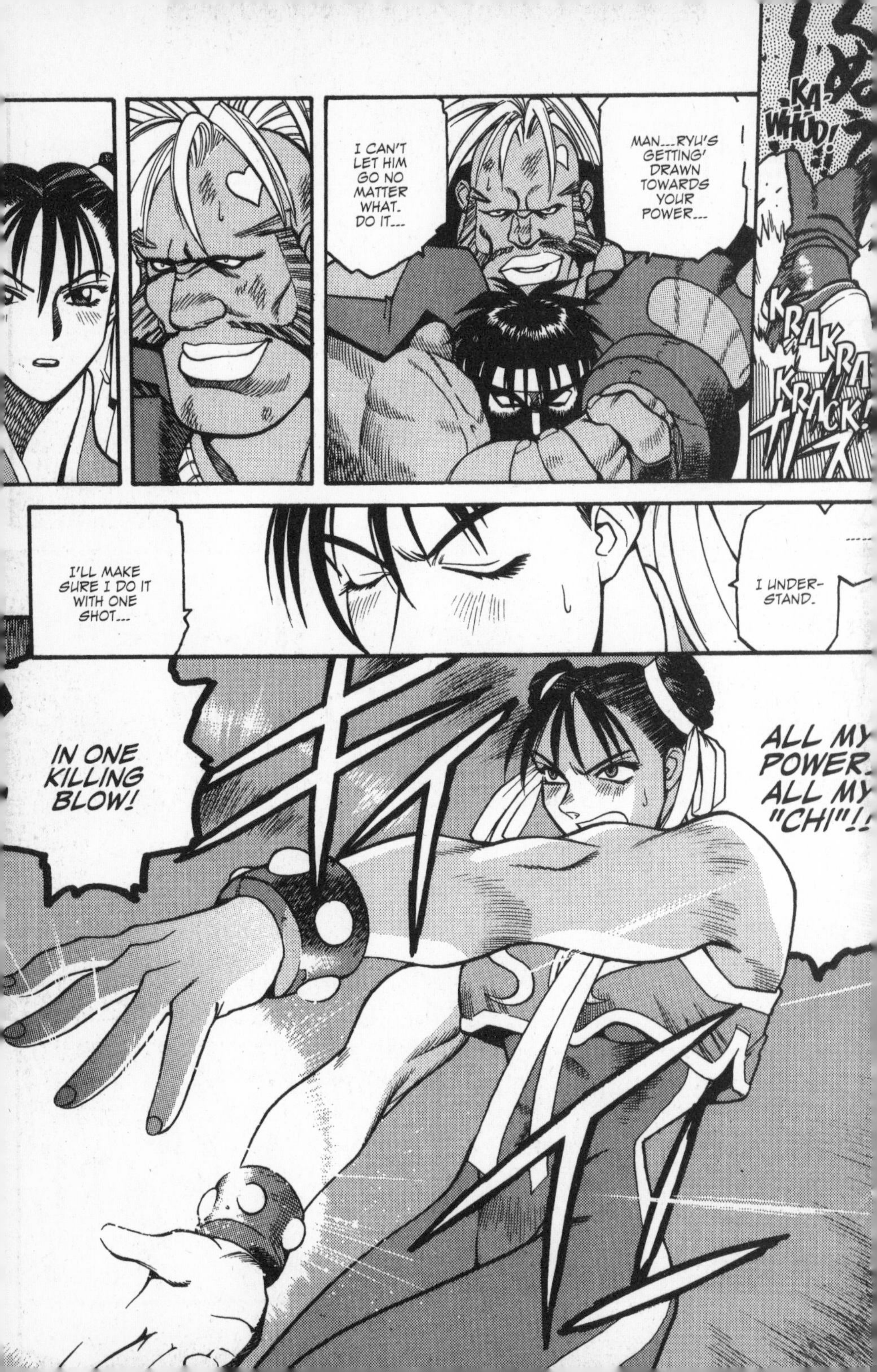
KA-WHUD!
KRAKRA KRACK!
MAN... RYU'S GETTING' DRAWN TOWARDS YOUR POWER...
I CAN'T LET HIM GO NO MATTER WHAT. DO IT...
......
I UNDER-STAND.
I'LL MAKE SURE I DO IT WITH ONE SHOT...
ALL MY POWER. ALL MY "CHI"!!
IN ONE KILLING BLOW!

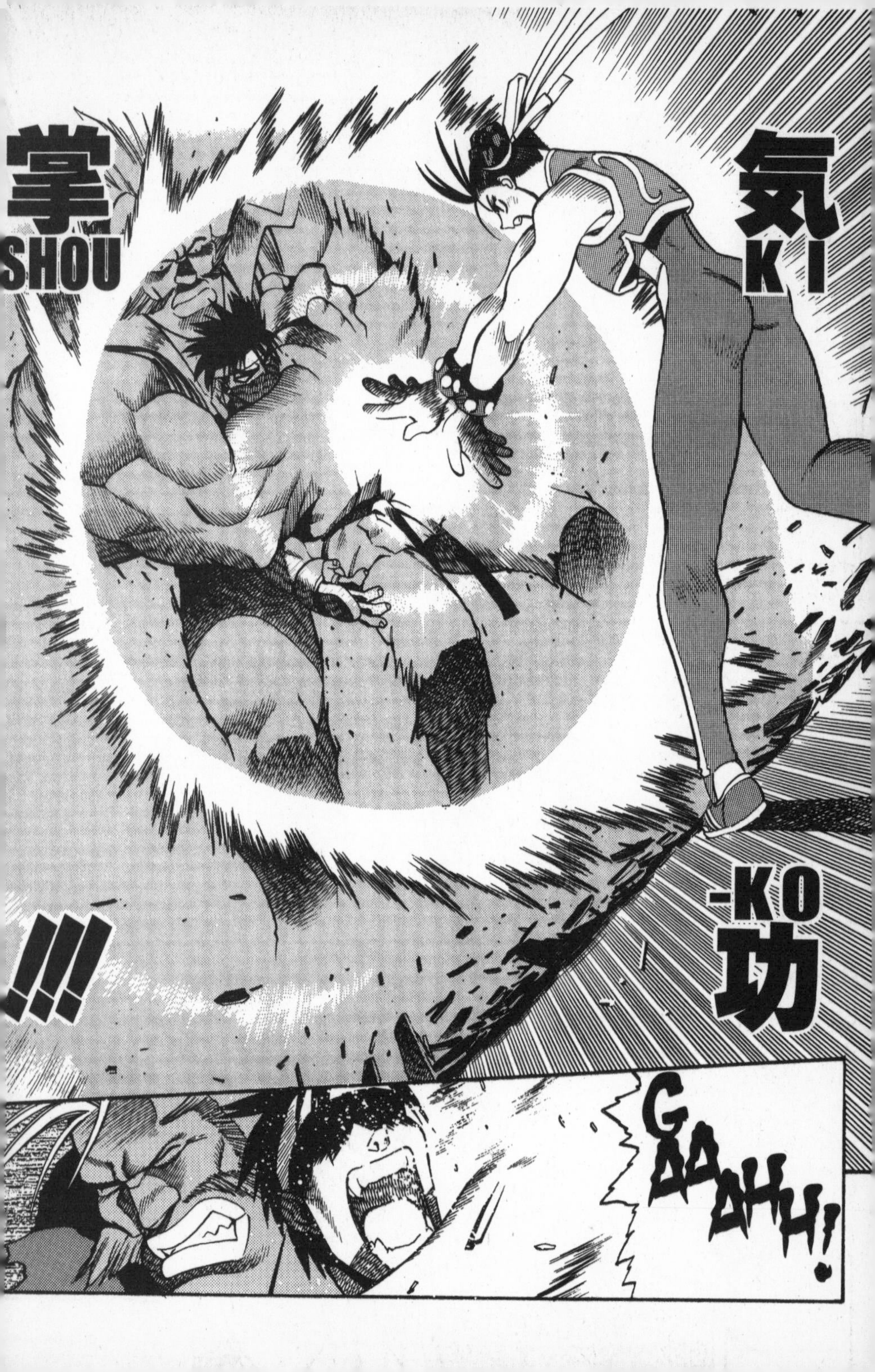

気
-KI
掌
SHOU
-KO
功
!!!
GAAHH!

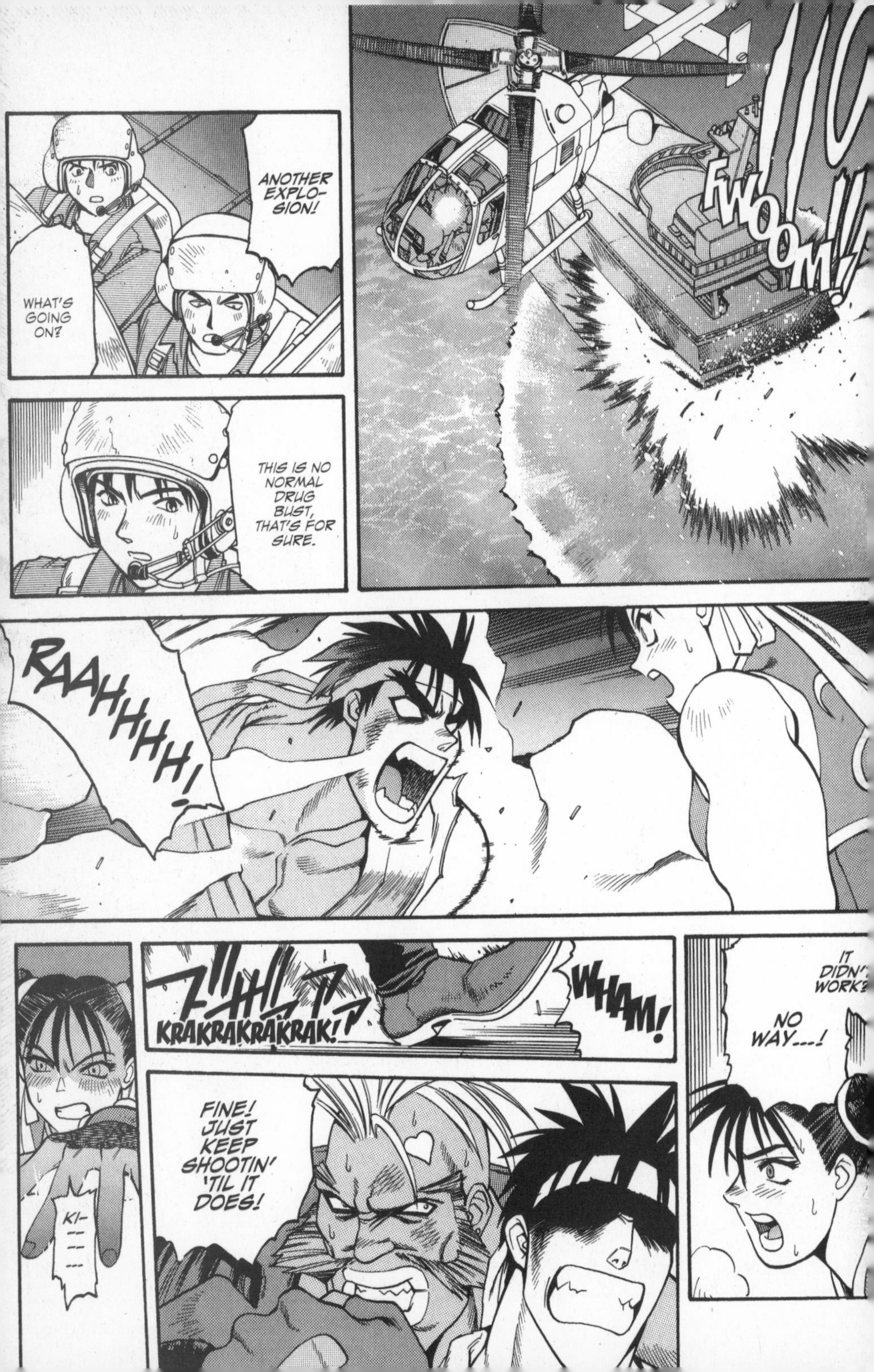
FWOOM!!
ANOTHER EXPLOSION!
WHAT'S GOING ON?
THIS IS NO NORMAL DRUG BUST, THAT'S FOR SURE.
RAAHHHHH!
IT DIDN'T WORK?
NO WAY...!
WHAM!
KRAKRAKRAKRAK!
FINE! JUST KEEP SHOOTIN' 'TIL IT DOES!
KI------

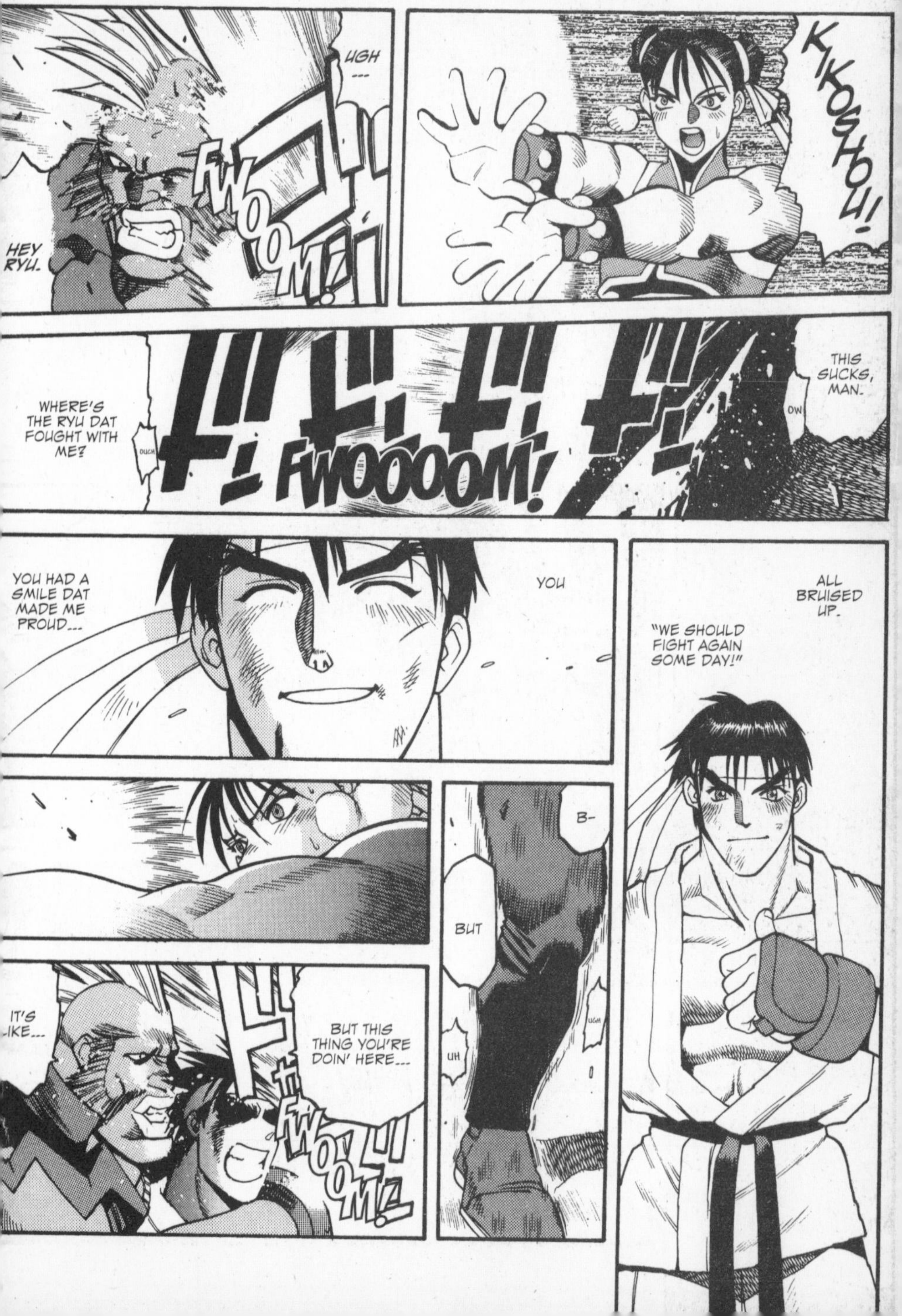
KIKOSHOU!
UGH ---
FWOOOM!
HEY RYU.
THIS SUCKS, MAN.
OW
FWOOOOM!
OUCH
WHERE'S THE RYU DAT FOUGHT WITH ME?
ALL BRUISED UP.
"WE SHOULD FIGHT AGAIN SOME DAY!"
YOU
YOU HAD A SMILE DAT MADE ME PROUD...
B-
BUT
UGH
UH
BUT THIS THING YOU'RE DOIN' HERE...
FWOOM!
IT'S LIKE...

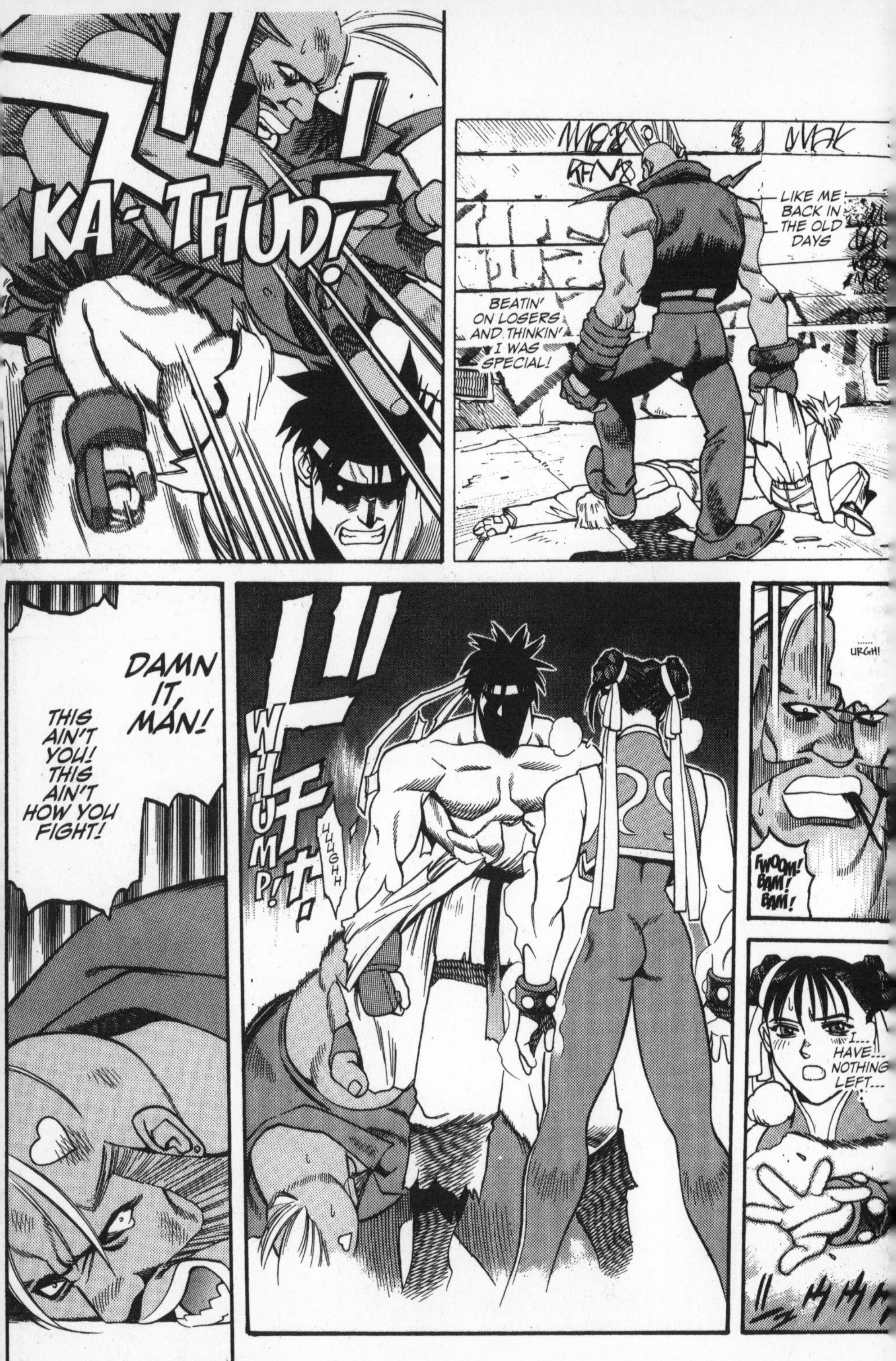
LIKE ME BACK IN THE OLD DAYS
BEATIN' ON LOSERS AND THINKIN' I WAS SPECIAL!
KA-THUD!
......URGH!
FWOOM! BAM! BAM!
I... HAVE... NOTHING LEFT...
WHUMP!
UUGHH
DAMN IT, MAN!
THIS AIN'T YOU! THIS AIN'T HOW YOU FIGHT!

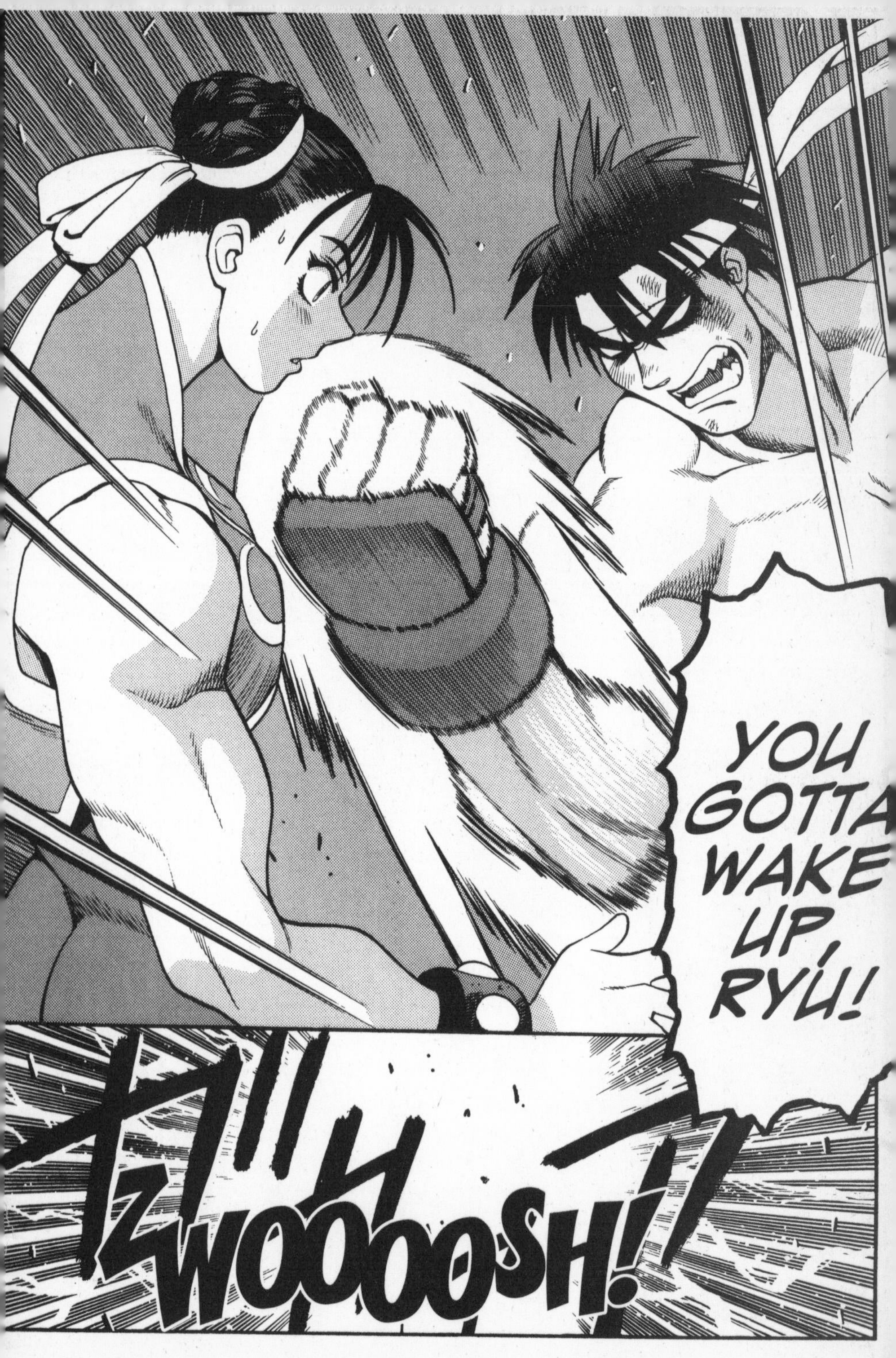
YOU GOTTA WAKE UP, RYU!
ZWOOOOSH!

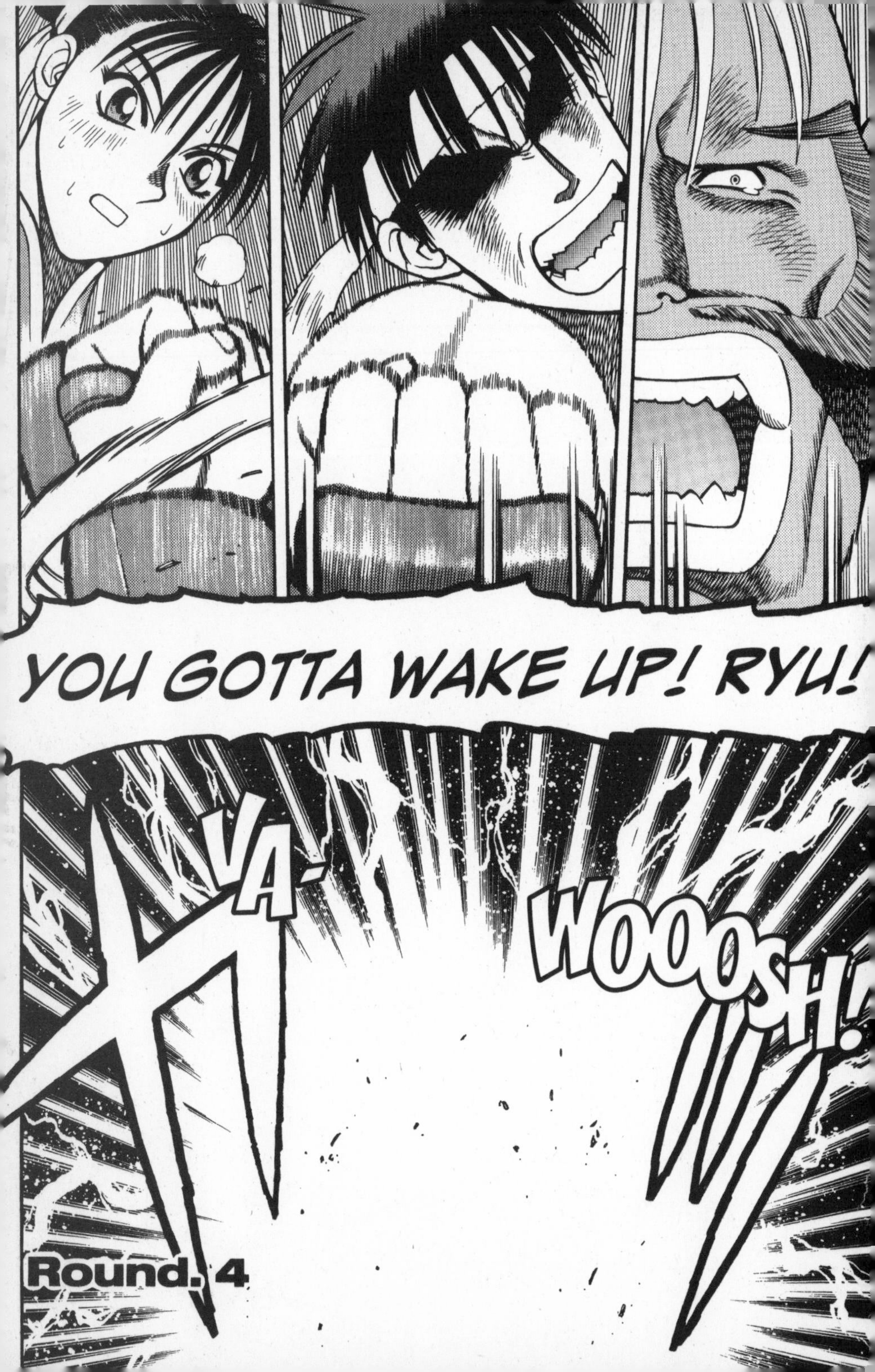
YOU GOTTA WAKE UP! RYU!
VA-
WOOOSH!
Round. 4

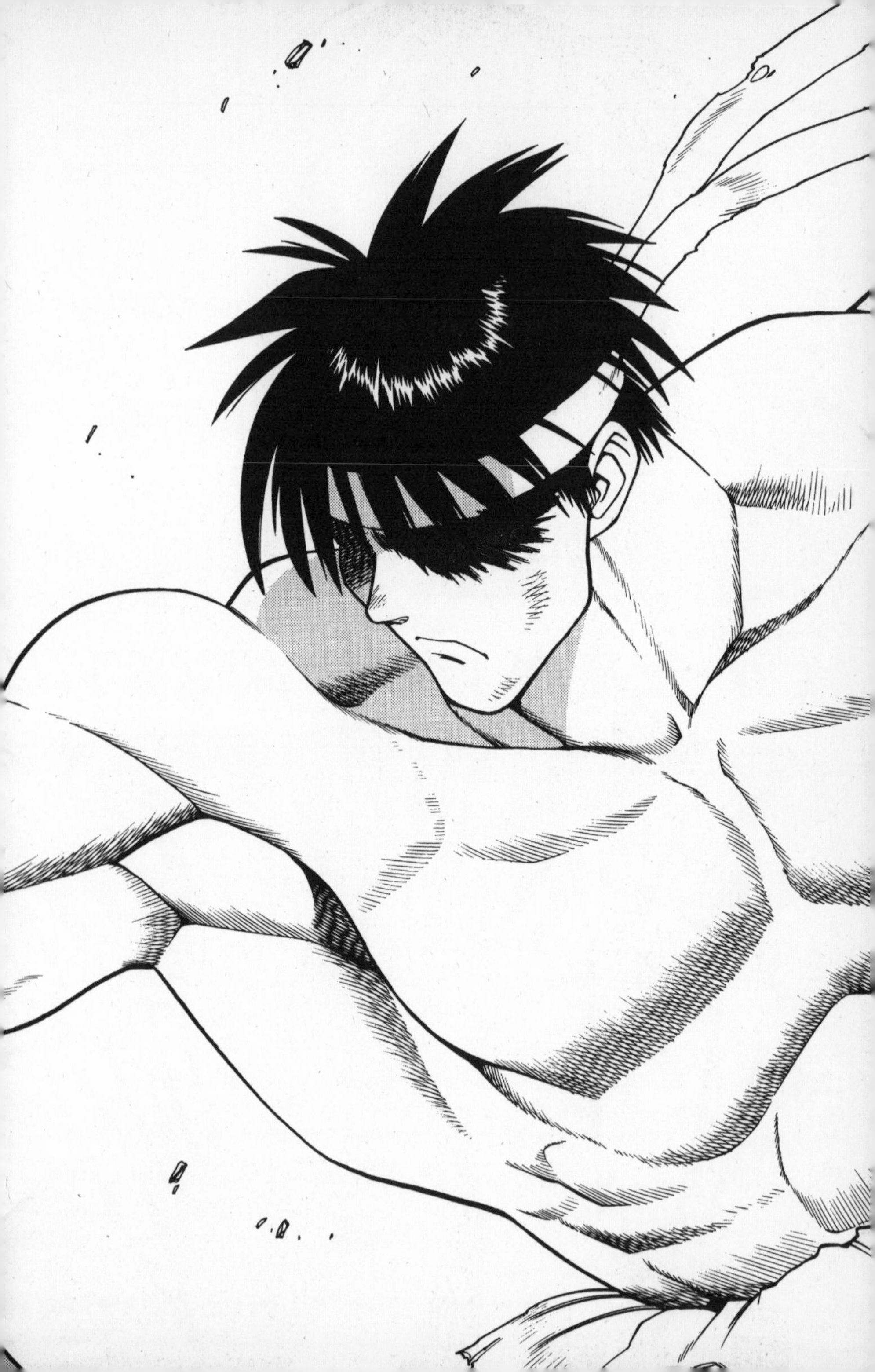

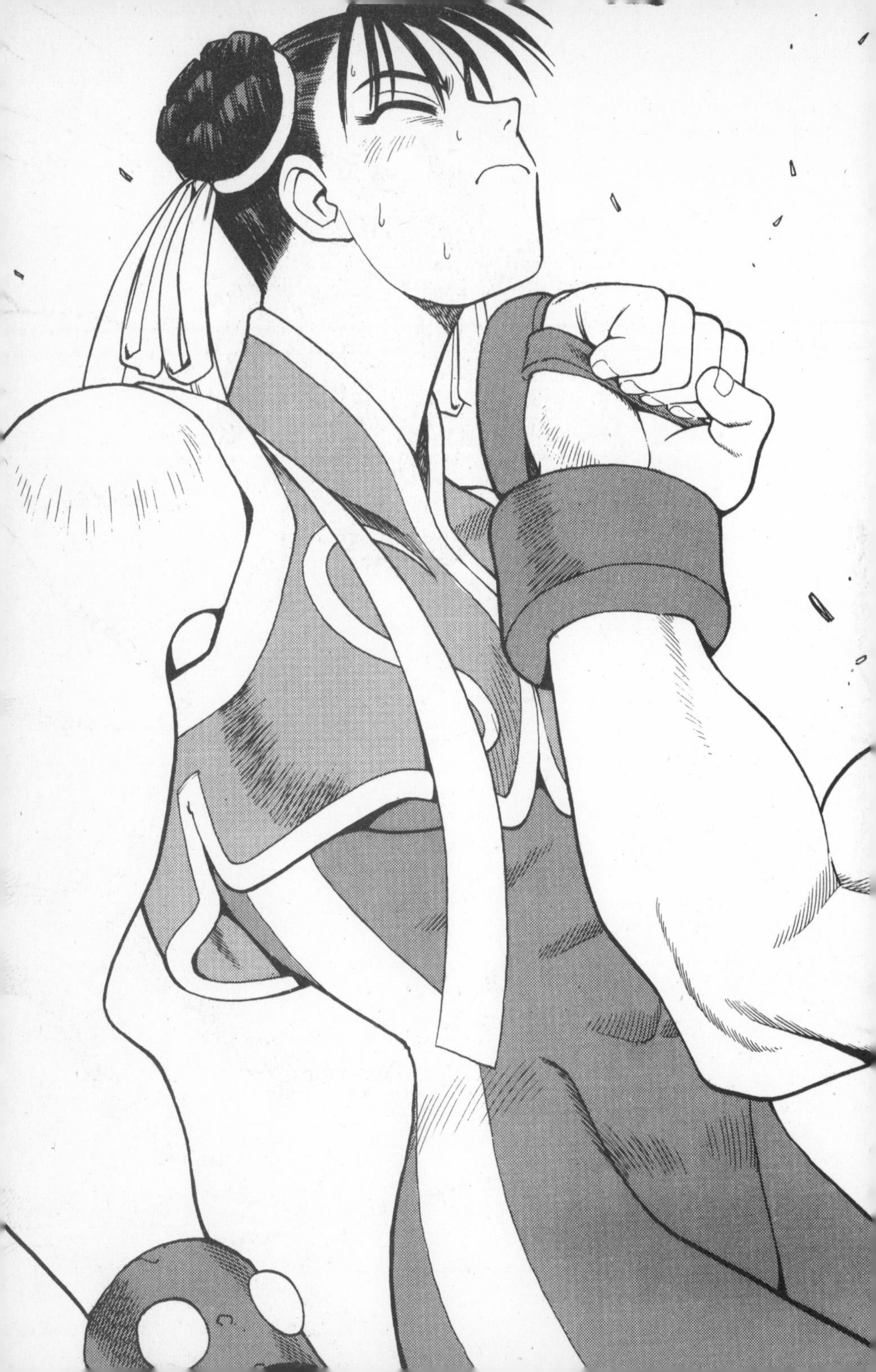

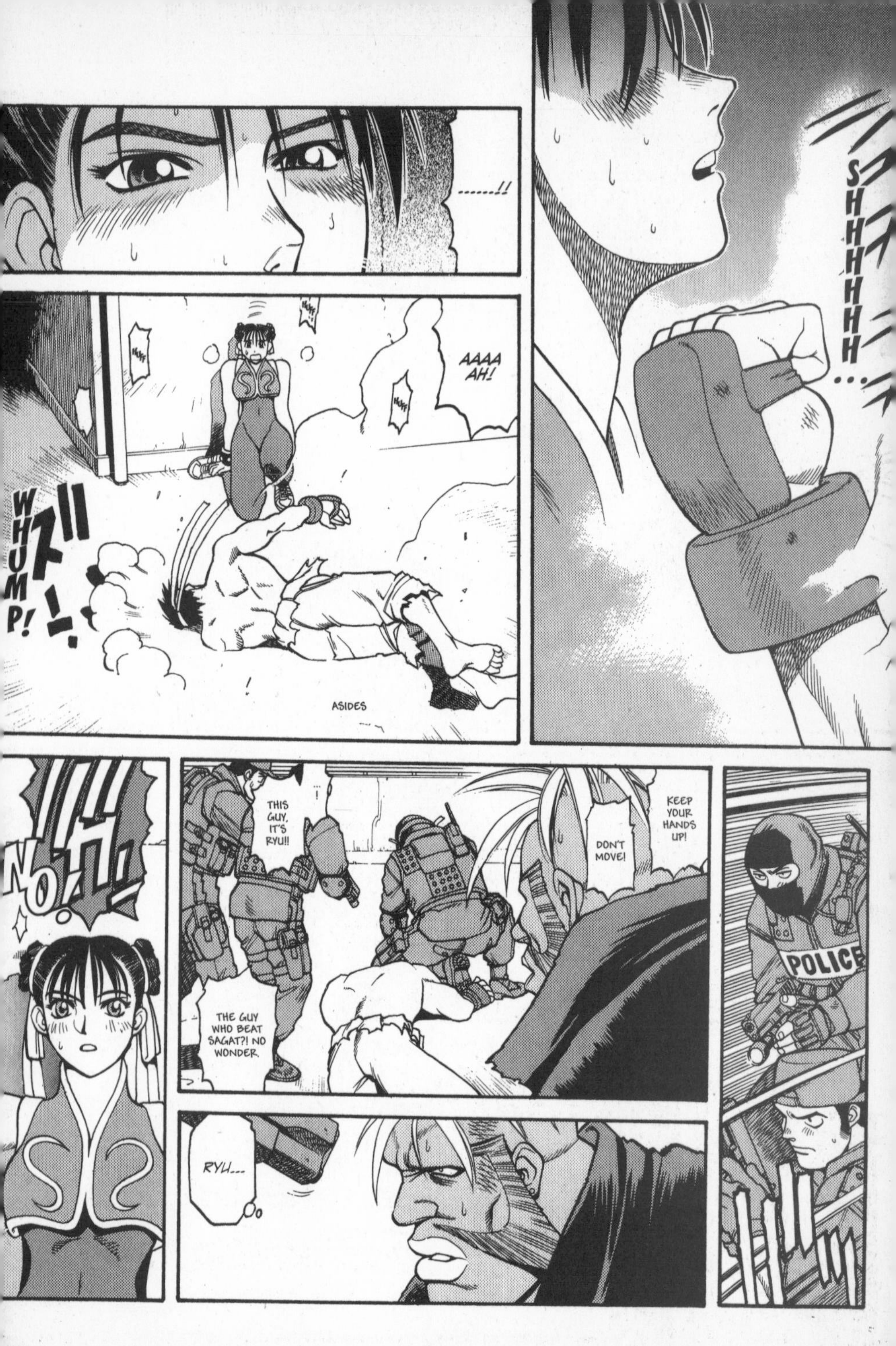
SHHHHHHH...
......!!
AAAA AH!
WHUMP!
ASIDES
KEEP YOUR HANDS UP!
DON'T MOVE!
THIS GUY, IT'S RYU!!
THE GUY WHO BEAT SAGAT?! NO WONDER
RYU...
NO!

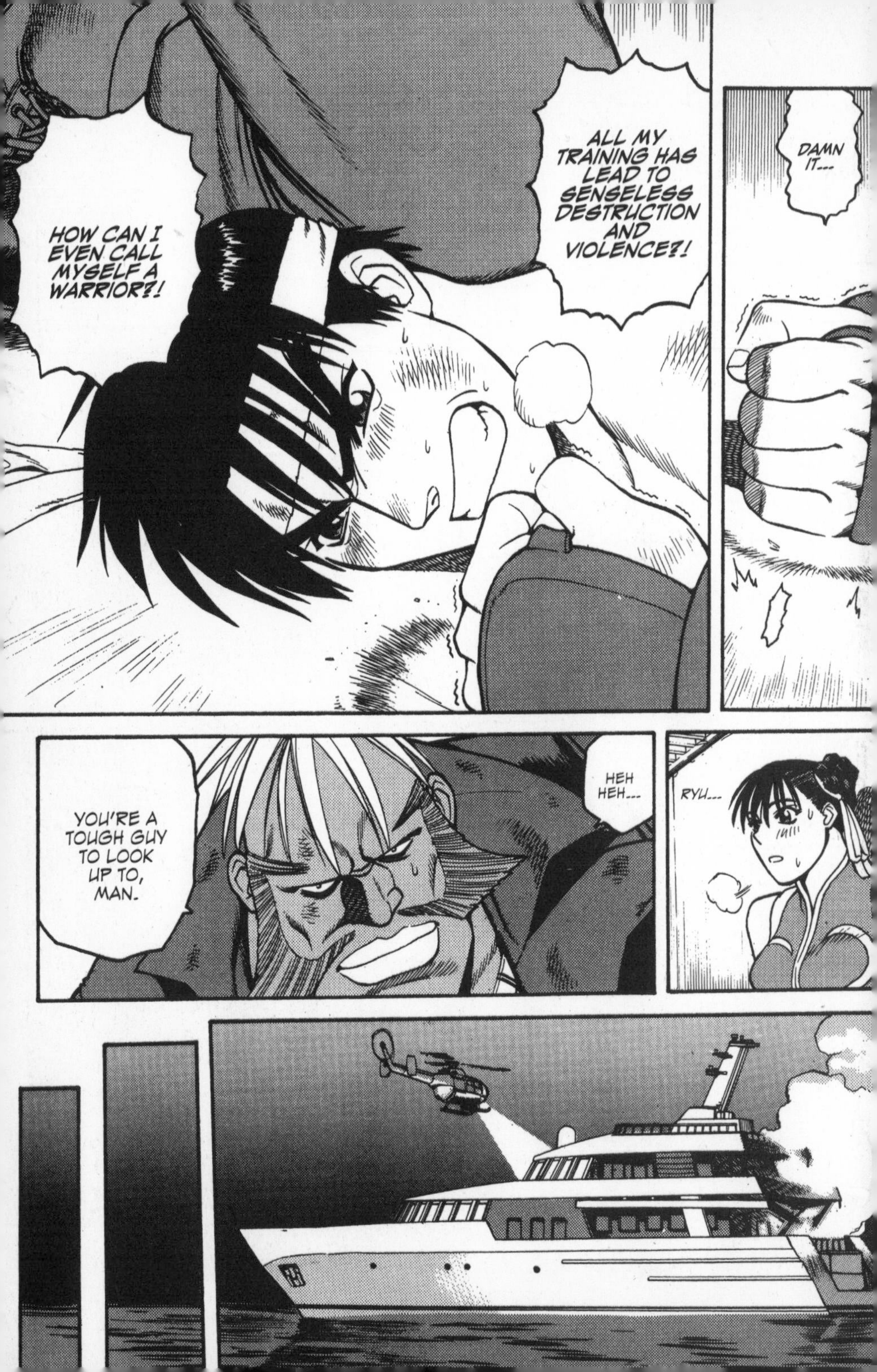
DAMN IT...
ALL MY TRAINING HAS LEAD TO SENSELESS DESTRUCTION AND VIOLENCE?!
HOW CAN I EVEN CALL MYSELF A WARRIOR?!
RYU...
HEH HEH...
YOU'RE A TOUGH GUY TO LOOK UP TO, MAN.

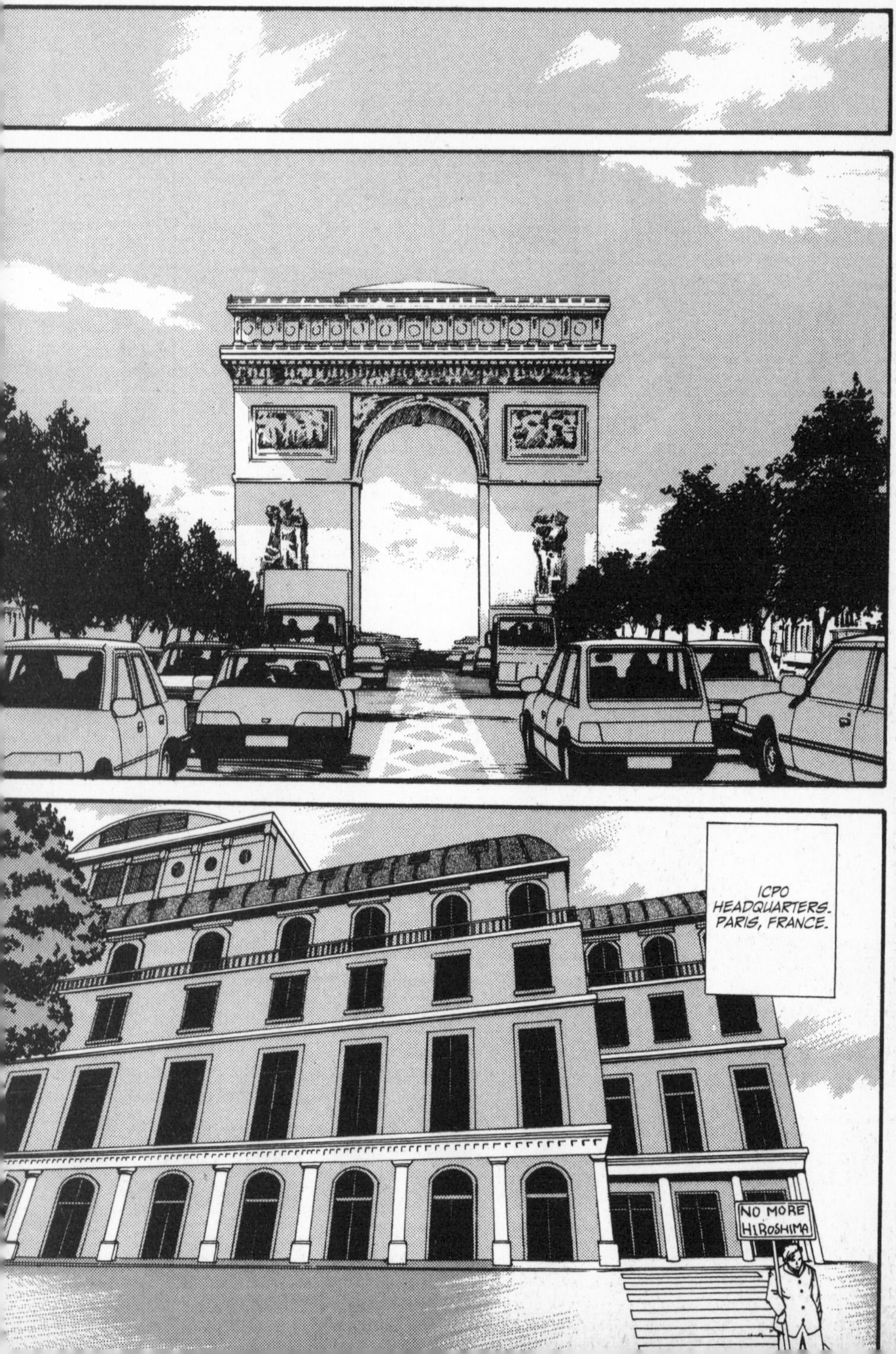
ICPO HEADQUARTERS. PARIS, FRANCE.
NO MORE HIROSHIMA

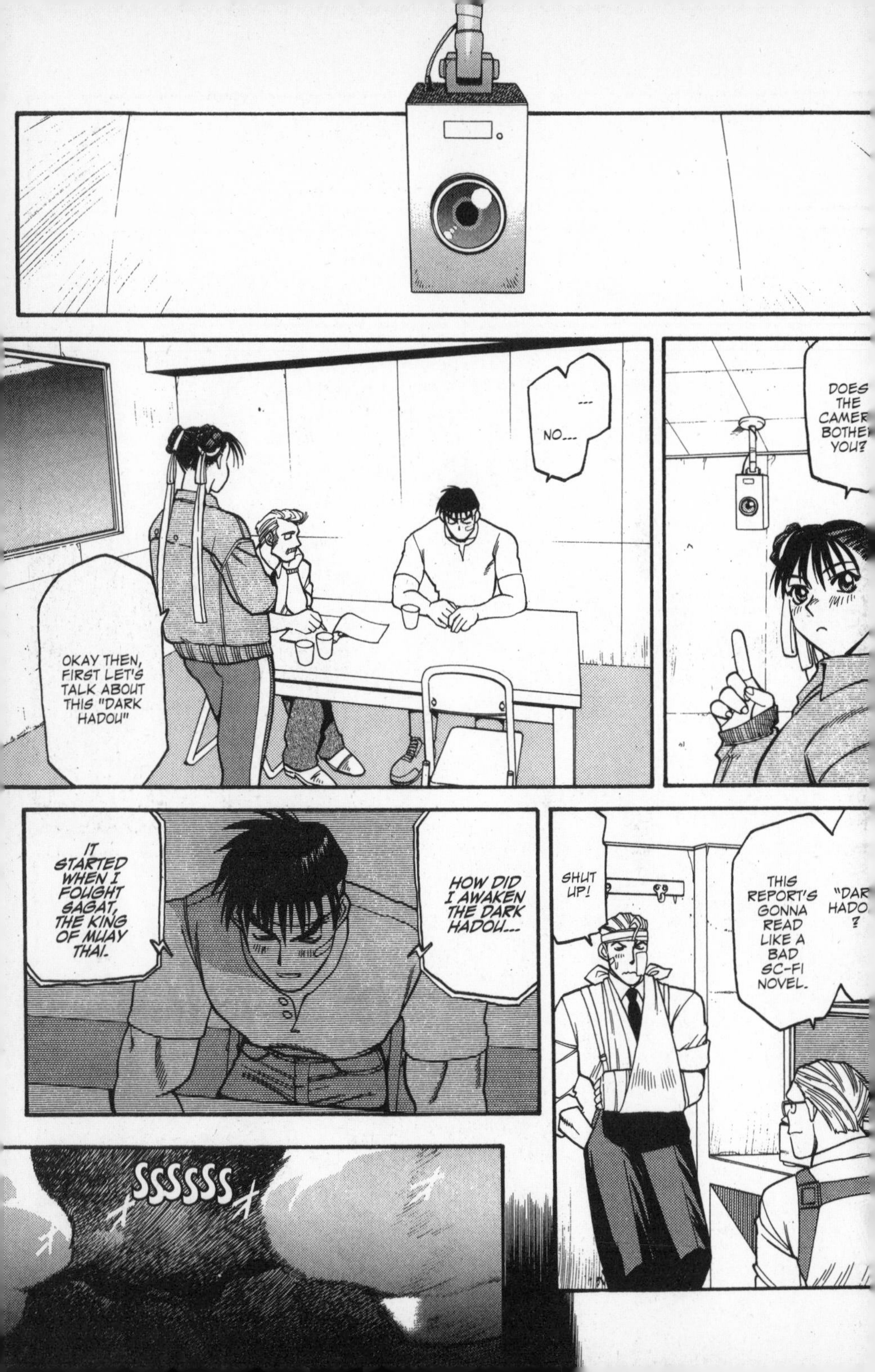
DOES THE CAMER BOTHEI YOU?
... NO...
OKAY THEN, FIRST LET'S TALK ABOUT THIS "DARK HADOU"
"DAR HADO ?
THIS REPORT'S GONNA READ LIKE A BAD SC-FI NOVEL.
SHUT UP!
HOW DID I AWAKEN THE DARK HADOU...
IT STARTED WHEN I FOUGHT SAGAT, THE KING OF MUAY THAI.
SSSSSS

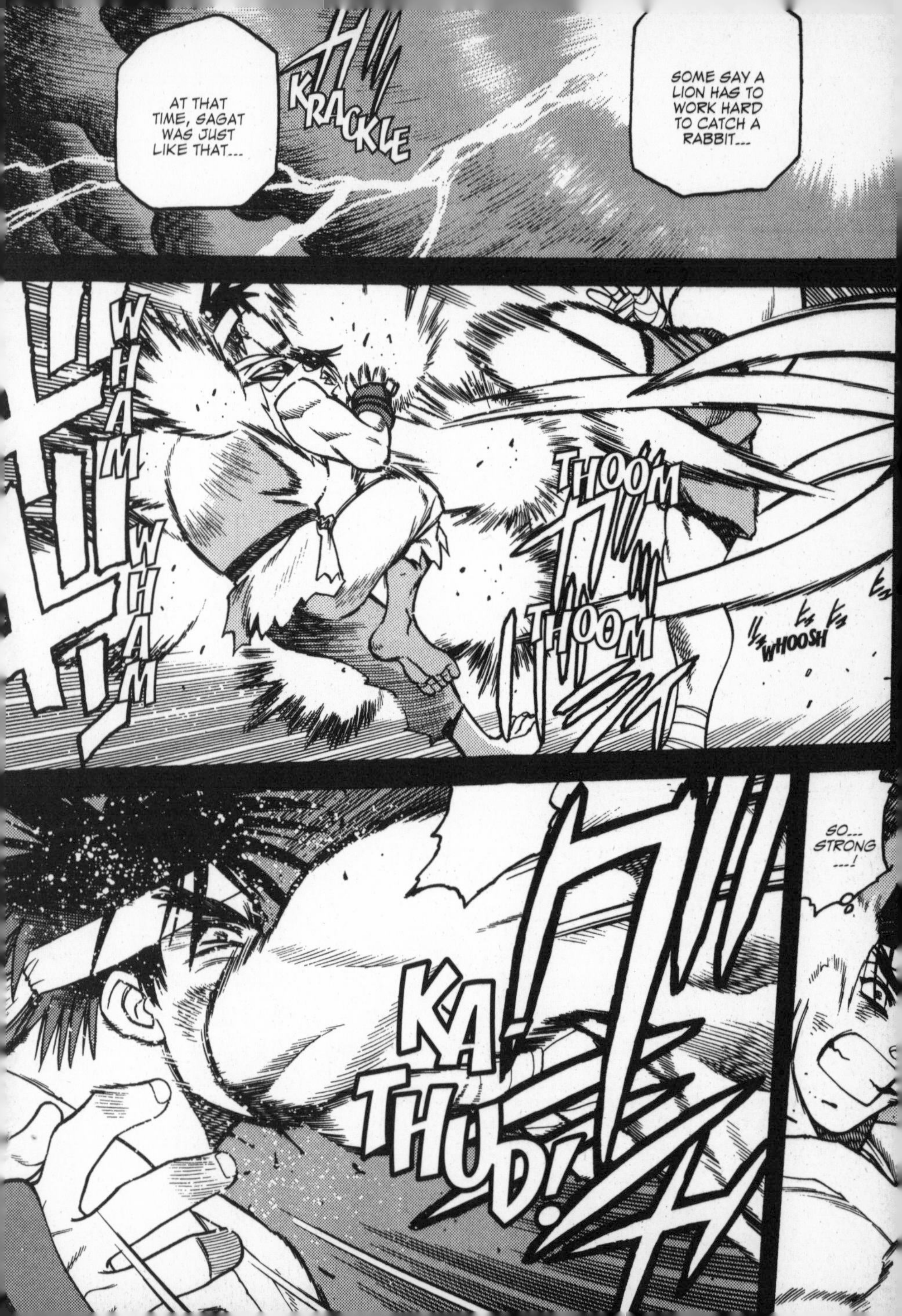
SOME SAY A LION HAS TO WORK HARD TO CATCH A RABBIT---
KRACKLE
AT THAT TIME, SAGAT WAS JUST LIKE THAT---
WHOOSH
THOOM
THOOM
WHAM
WHAM
SO--- STRONG ---!
KA-THUD!

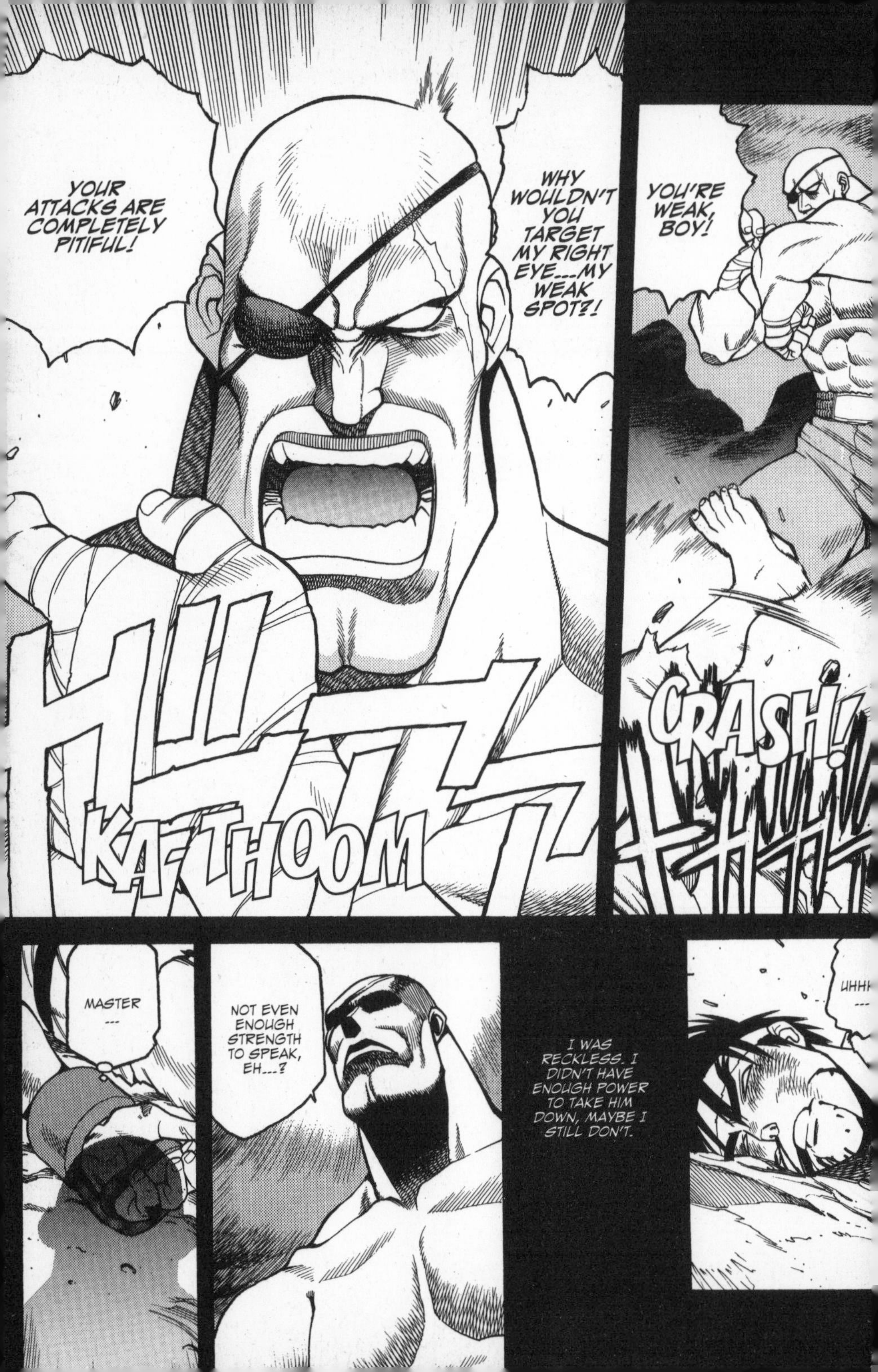
YOU'RE WEAK, BOY!
CRASH!
WHY WOULDN'T YOU TARGET MY RIGHT EYE...MY WEAK SPOT?!
YOUR ATTACKS ARE COMPLETELY PITIFUL!
KA-THOOM
UHHH
I WAS RECKLESS. I DIDN'T HAVE ENOUGH POWER TO TAKE HIM DOWN, MAYBE I STILL DON'T.
NOT EVEN ENOUGH STRENGTH TO SPEAK, EH...?
MASTER ...

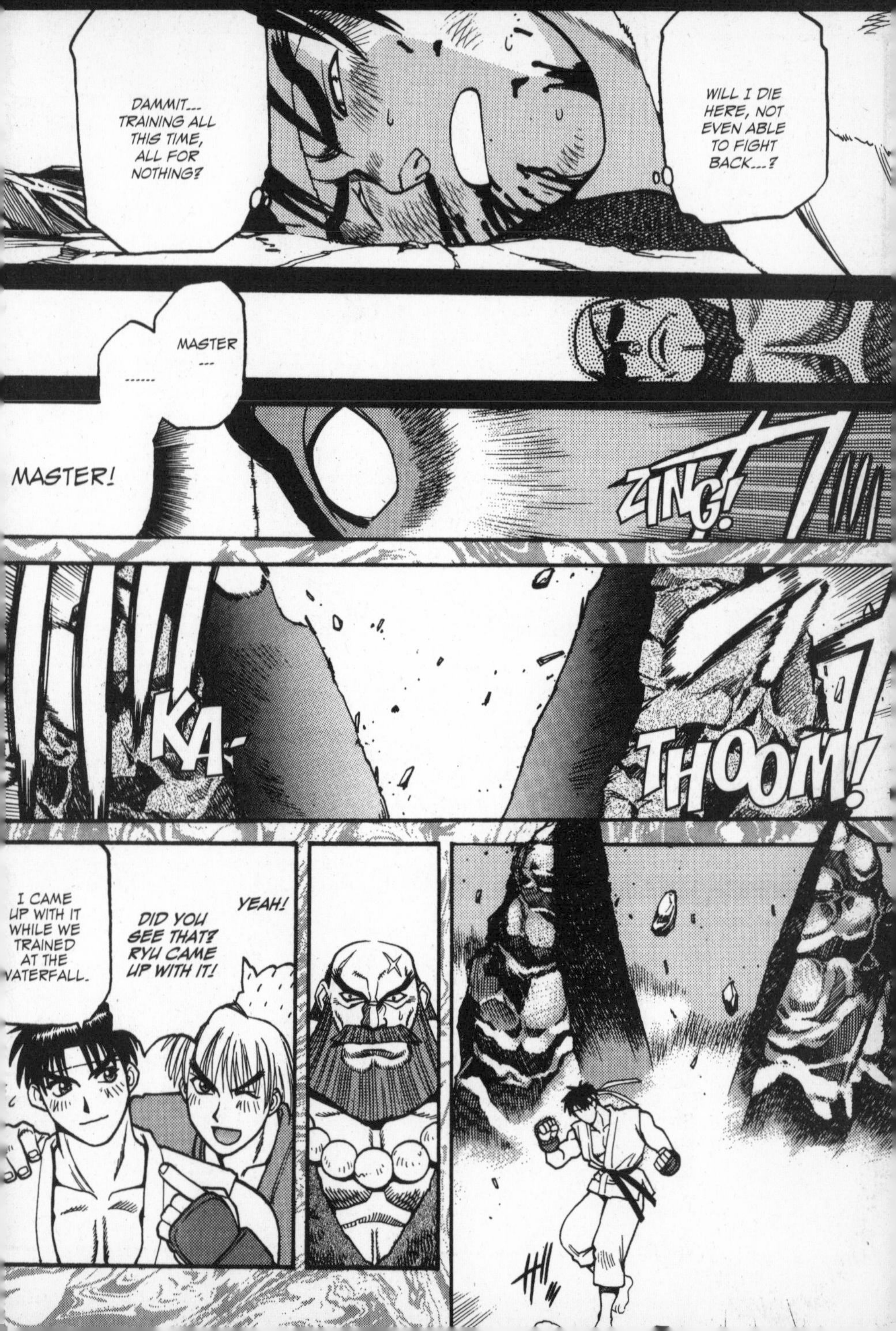
WILL I DIE HERE, NOT EVEN ABLE TO FIGHT BACK...?
DAMMIT... TRAINING ALL THIS TIME, ALL FOR NOTHING?
MASTER ...
......
ZING!
MASTER!
KA-
THOOM!
YEAH!
DID YOU SEE THAT? RYU CAME UP WITH IT!
I CAME UP WITH IT WHILE WE TRAINED AT THE WATERFALL.

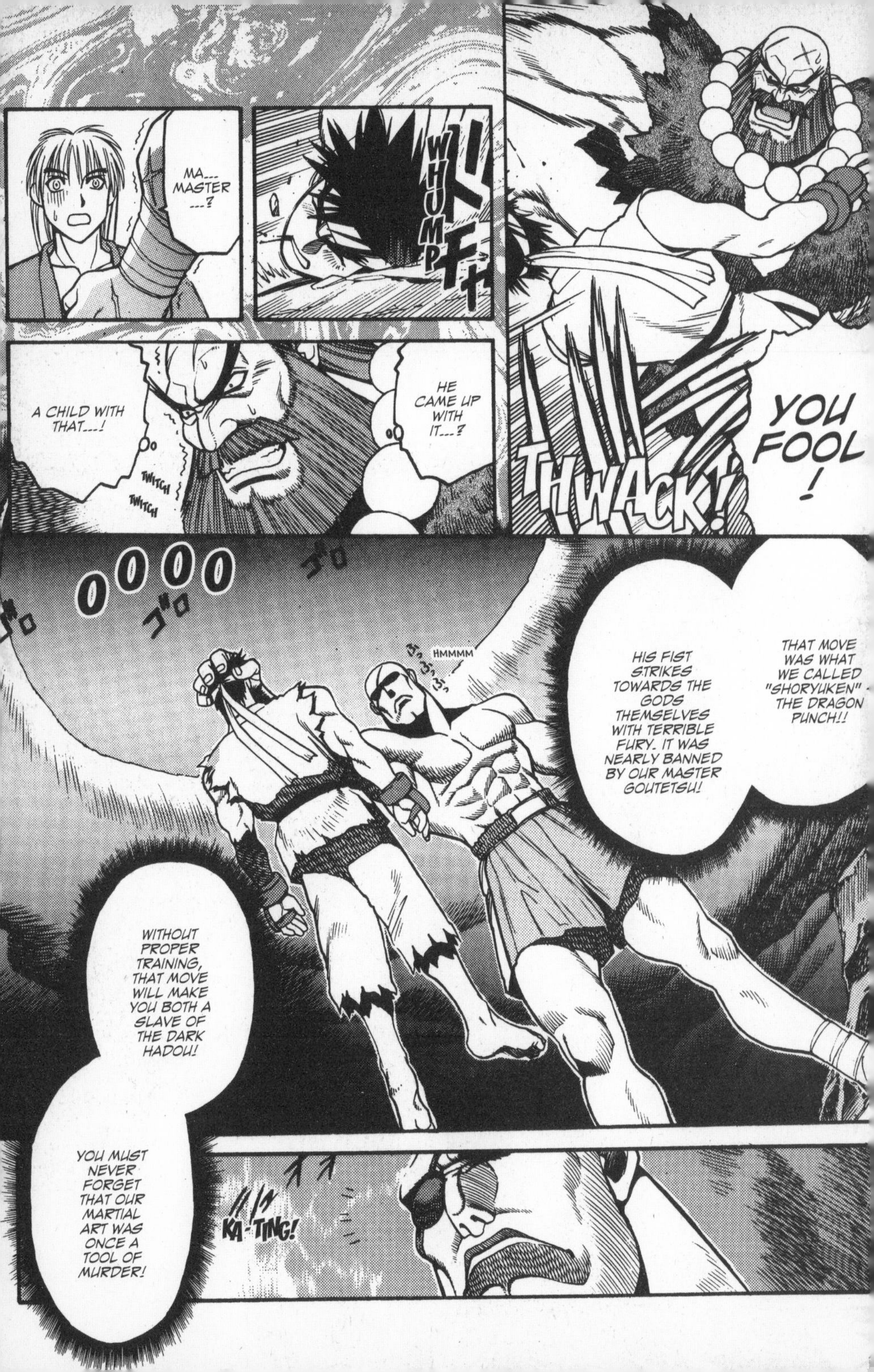
YOU FOOL!
THWACK!
WHUMP
MA... MASTER ...?
HE CAME UP WITH IT...?
A CHILD WITH THAT...!
TWITCH TWITCH
THAT MOVE WAS WHAT WE CALLED "SHORYUKEN" THE DRAGON PUNCH!!
HIS FIST STRIKES TOWARDS THE GODS THEMSELVES WITH TERRIBLE FURY. IT WAS NEARLY BANNED BY OUR MASTER GOUTETSU!
HMMMM
WITHOUT PROPER TRAINING, THAT MOVE WILL MAKE YOU BOTH A SLAVE OF THE DARK HADOU!
YOU MUST NEVER FORGET THAT OUR MARTIAL ART WAS ONCE A TOOL OF MURDER!
KA-TING!

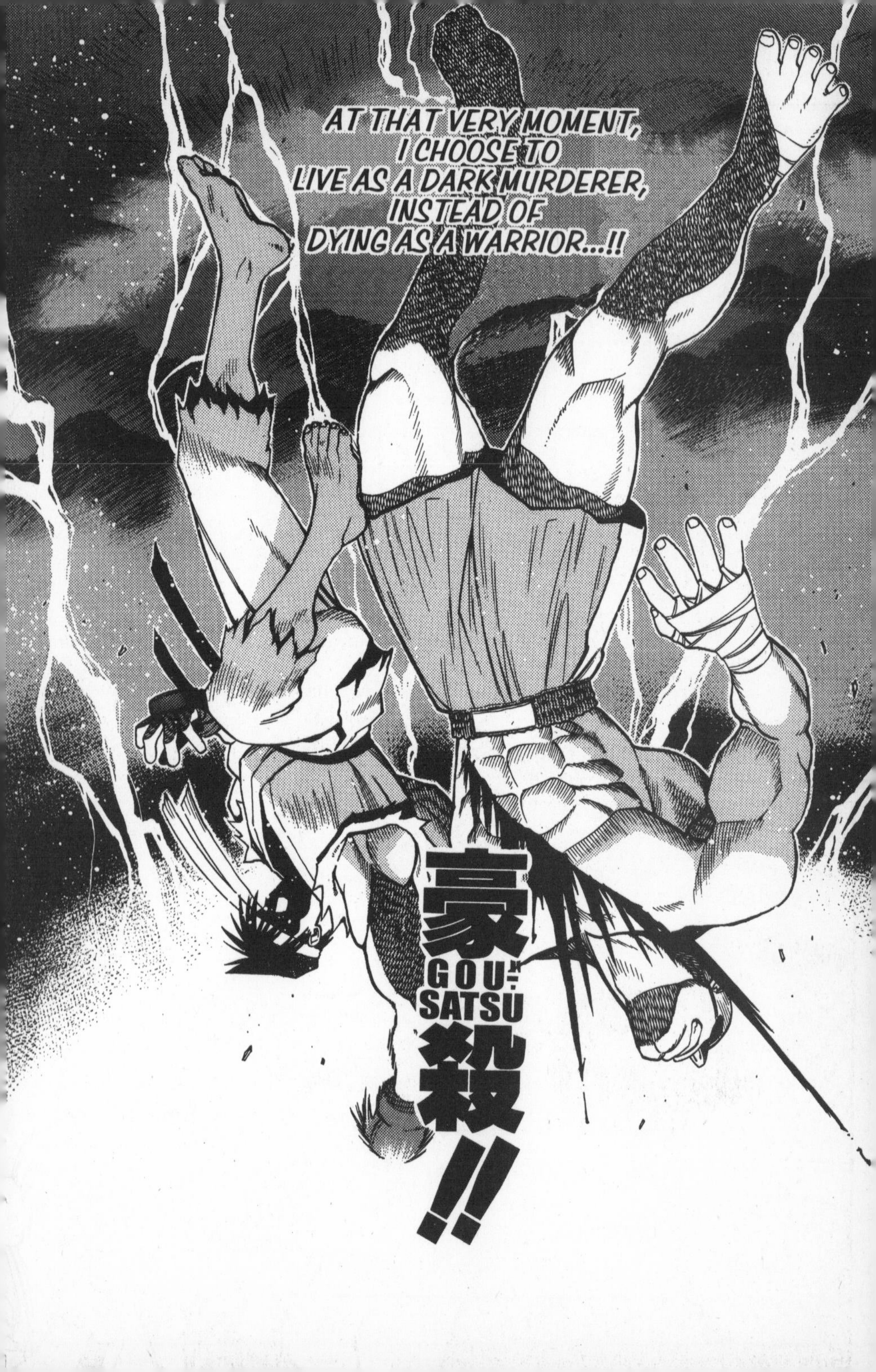
AT THAT VERY MOMENT,
I CHOOSE TO
LIVE AS A DARK MURDERER,
INSTEAD OF
DYING AS A WARRIOR...!!
豪GOU-SATSU殺!!

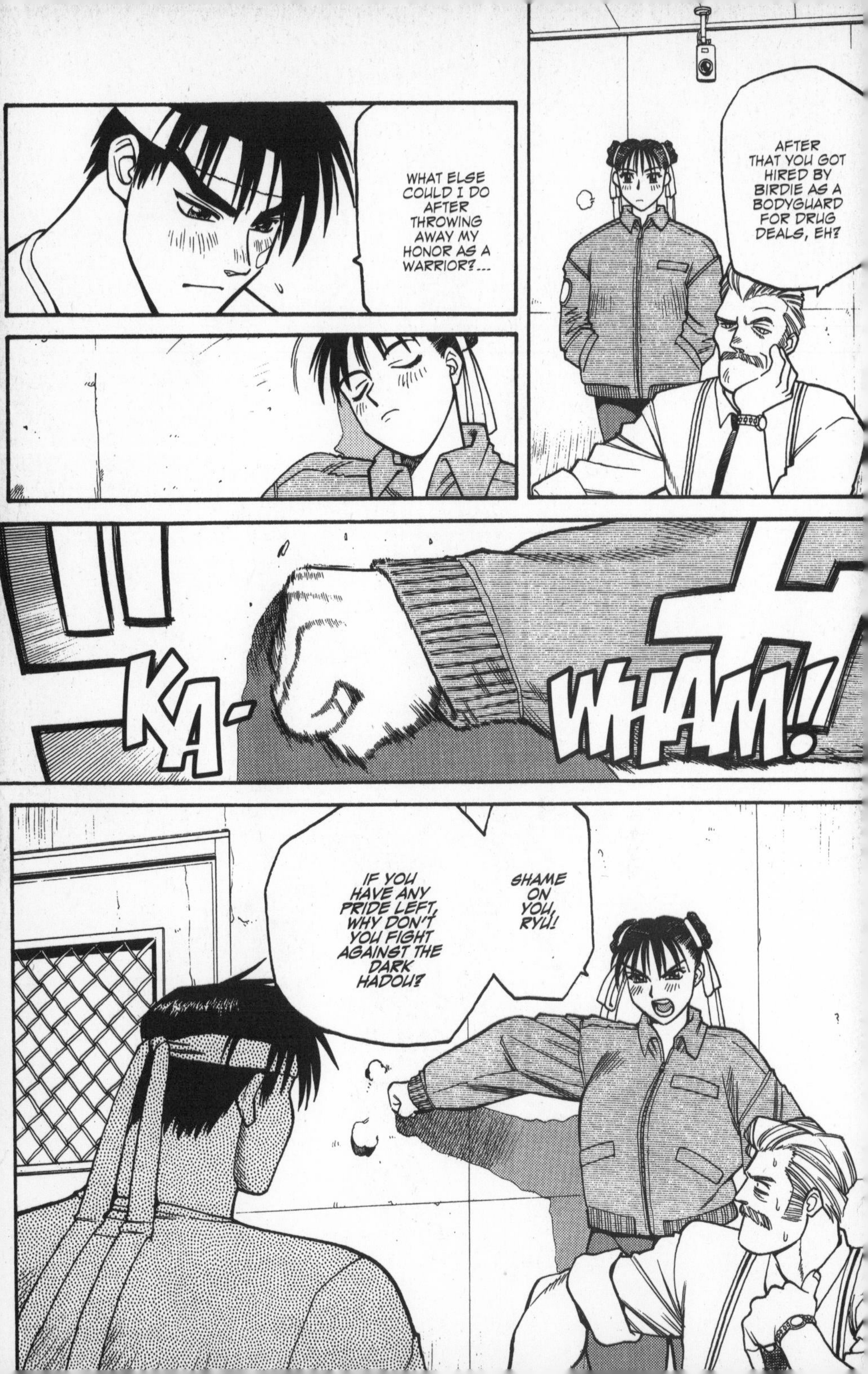
AFTER THAT YOU GOT HIRED BY BIRDIE AS A BODYGUARD FOR DRUG DEALS, EH?
WHAT ELSE COULD I DO AFTER THROWING AWAY MY HONOR AS A WARRIOR?...
KA-WHAM!!
SHAME ON YOU, RYU!
IF YOU HAVE ANY PRIDE LEFT, WHY DON'T YOU FIGHT AGAINST THE DARK HADOU?

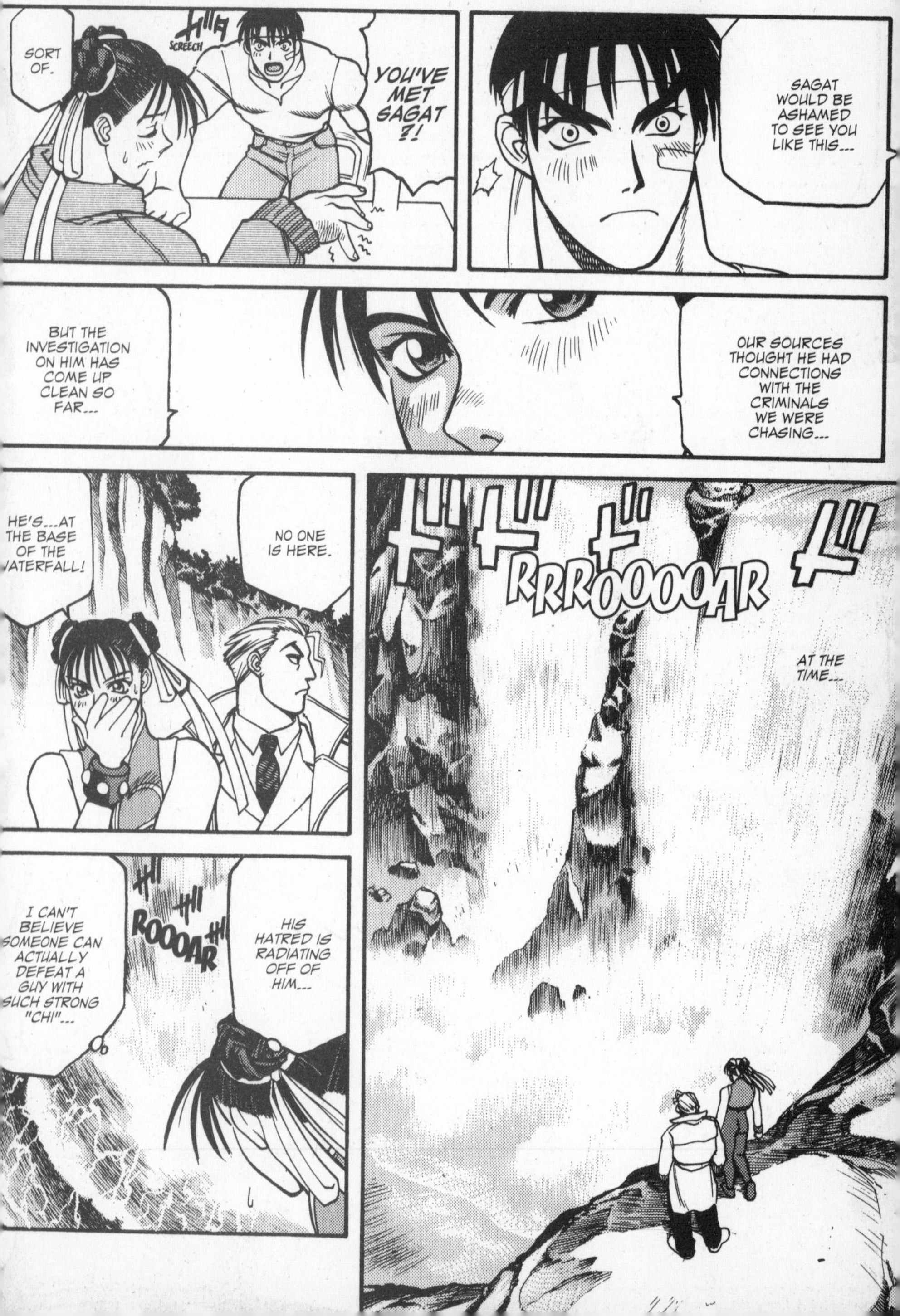
SAGAT WOULD BE ASHAMED TO SEE YOU LIKE THIS...
YOU'VE MET SAGAT ?!
SCREECH
SORT OF.
OUR SOURCES THOUGHT HE HAD CONNECTIONS WITH THE CRIMINALS WE WERE CHASING...
BUT THE INVESTIGATION ON HIM HAS COME UP CLEAN SO FAR...
RRROOOOAR
AT THE TIME...
NO ONE IS HERE.
HE'S...AT THE BASE OF THE WATERFALL!
HIS HATRED IS RADIATING OFF OF HIM...
ROOOAR
I CAN'T BELIEVE SOMEONE CAN ACTUALLY DEFEAT A GUY WITH SUCH STRONG "CHI"...

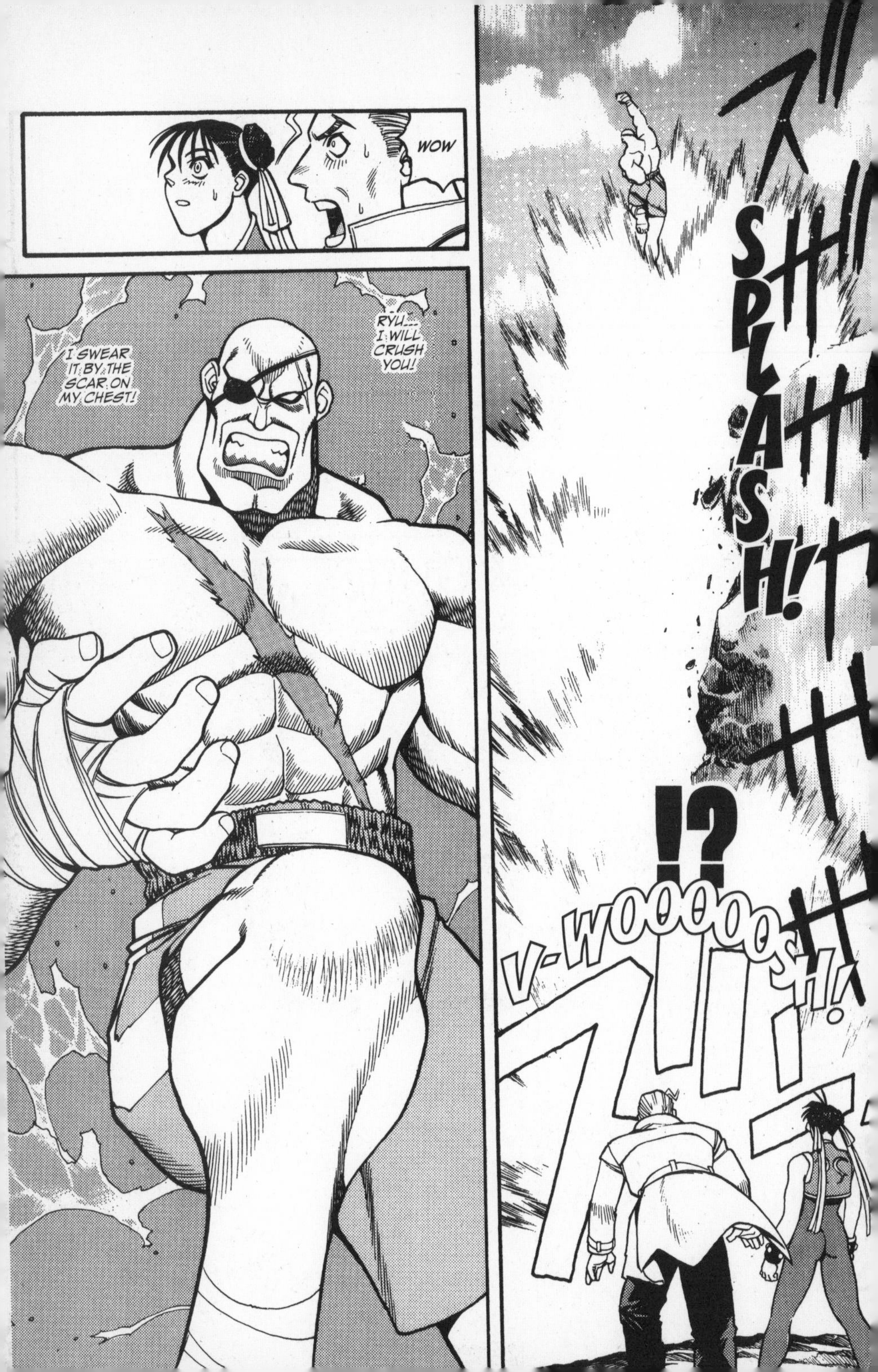
SPLASH!
!?
V-WOOOOOSH!
WOW
RYU... I WILL CRUSH YOU!
I SWEAR IT BY THE SCAR ON MY CHEST!

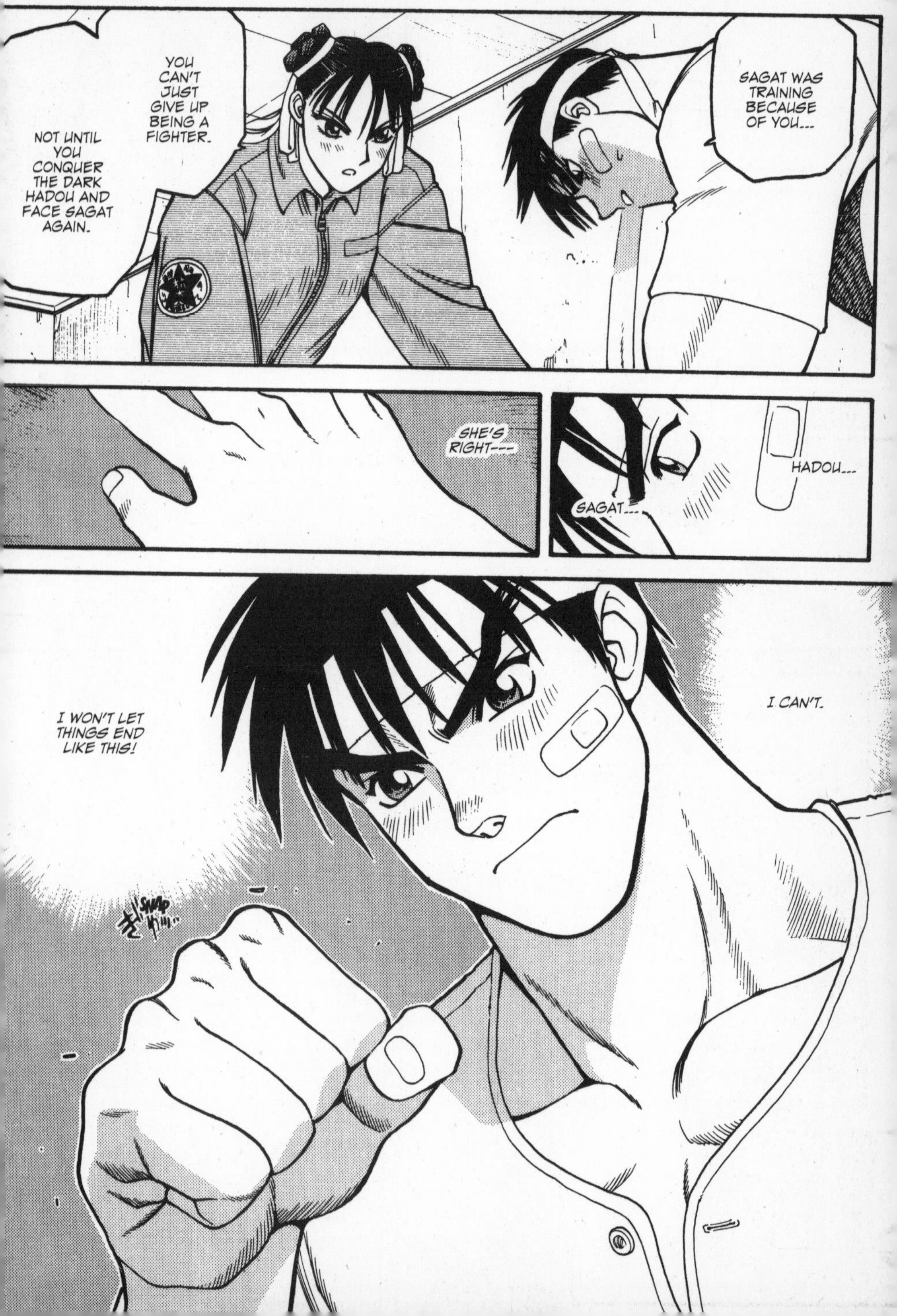
SAGAT WAS TRAINING BECAUSE OF YOU...
YOU CAN'T JUST GIVE UP BEING A FIGHTER.
NOT UNTIL YOU CONQUER THE DARK HADOU AND FACE SAGAT AGAIN.
HADOU...
SAGAT...
SHE'S RIGHT...
I CAN'T.
I WON'T LET THINGS END LIKE THIS!
SNAP

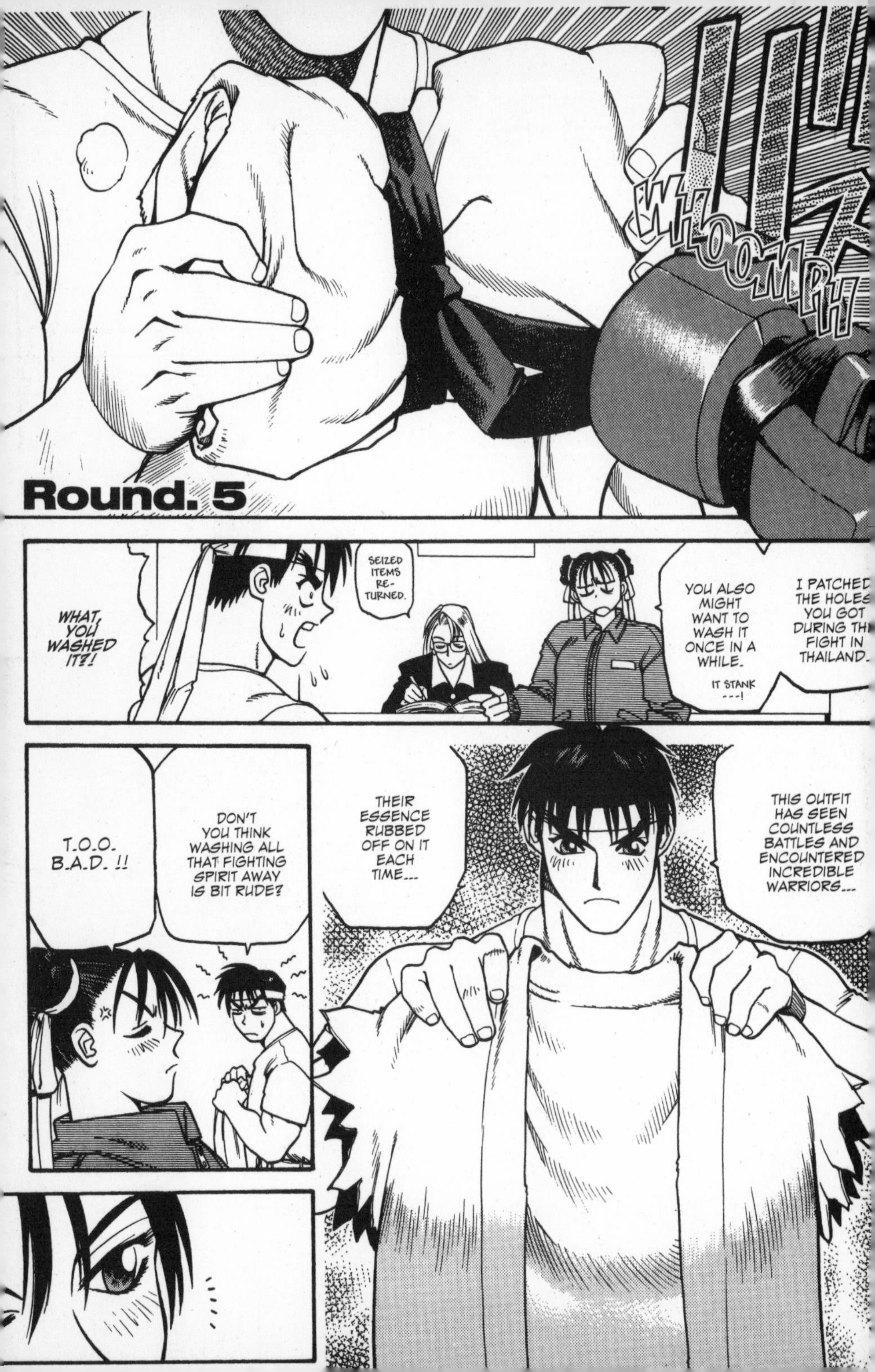
WHOOMPH
Round. 5
I PATCHED THE HOLES YOU GOT DURING THE FIGHT IN THAILAND...
YOU ALSO MIGHT WANT TO WASH IT ONCE IN A WHILE.
IT STANK---!
SEIZED ITEMS RE-TURNED.
WHAT, YOU WASHED IT?!
THIS OUTFIT HAS SEEN COUNTLESS BATTLES AND ENCOUNTERED INCREDIBLE WARRIORS...
THEIR ESSENCE RUBBED OFF ON IT EACH TIME...
DON'T YOU THINK WASHING ALL THAT FIGHTING SPIRIT AWAY IS BIT RUDE?
T.O.O. B.A.D. !!

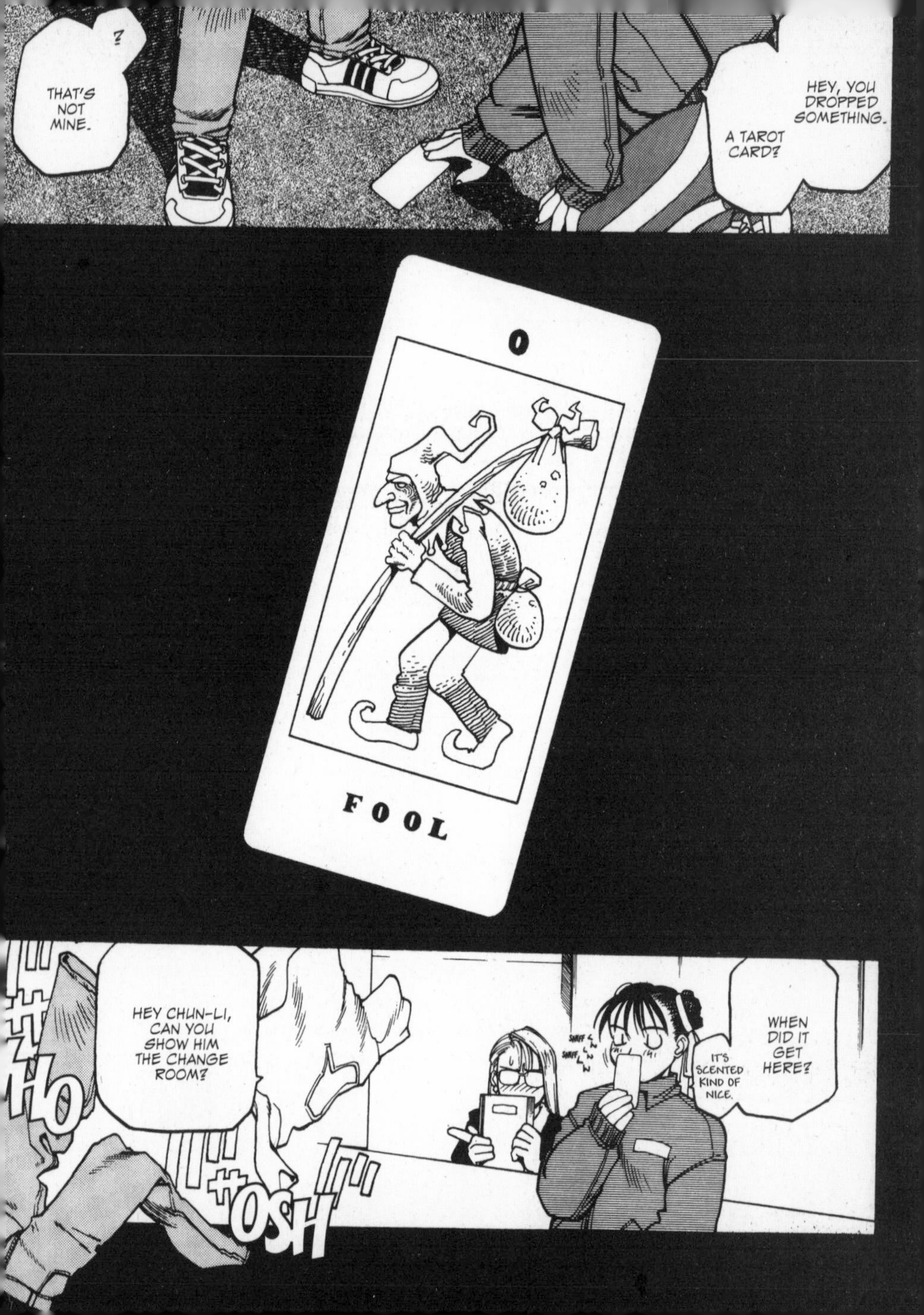
HEY, YOU DROPPED SOMETHING.
A TAROT CARD?
?
THAT'S NOT MINE.
0
FOOL
WHEN DID IT GET HERE?
IT'S SCENTED KIND OF NICE.
HEY CHUN-LI, CAN YOU SHOW HIM THE CHANGE ROOM?

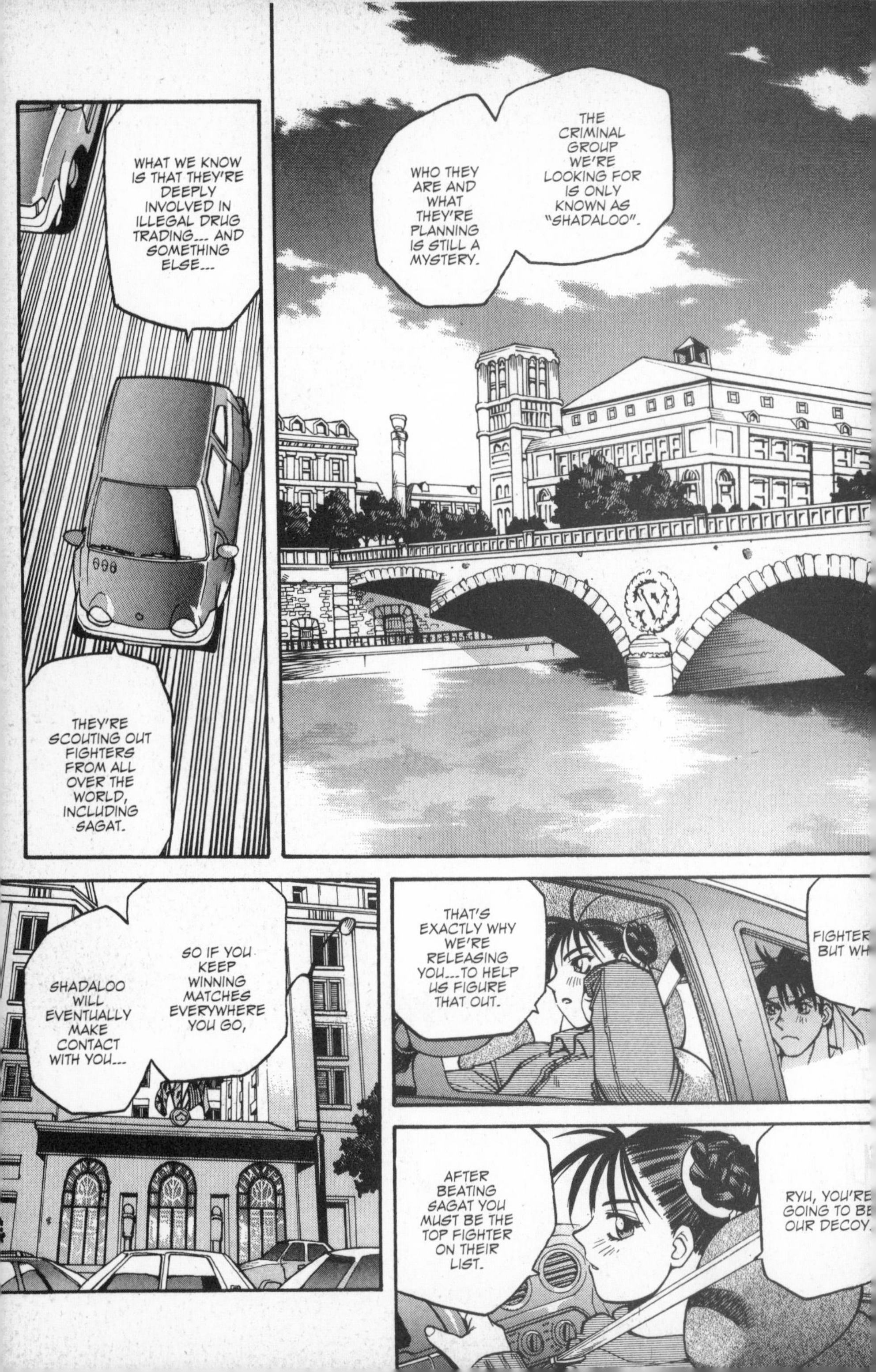
THE CRIMINAL GROUP WE'RE LOOKING FOR IS ONLY KNOWN AS "SHADALOO".
WHO THEY ARE AND WHAT THEY'RE PLANNING IS STILL A MYSTERY.
WHAT WE KNOW IS THAT THEY'RE DEEPLY INVOLVED IN ILLEGAL DRUG TRADING... AND SOMETHING ELSE...
THEY'RE SCOUTING OUT FIGHTERS FROM ALL OVER THE WORLD, INCLUDING SAGAT.
THAT'S EXACTLY WHY WE'RE RELEASING YOU...TO HELP US FIGURE THAT OUT.
RYU, YOU'RE GOING TO BE OUR DECOY.
AFTER BEATING SAGAT YOU MUST BE THE TOP FIGHTER ON THEIR LIST.
SO IF YOU KEEP WINNING MATCHES EVERYWHERE YOU GO,
SHADALOO WILL EVENTUALLY MAKE CONTACT WITH YOU...

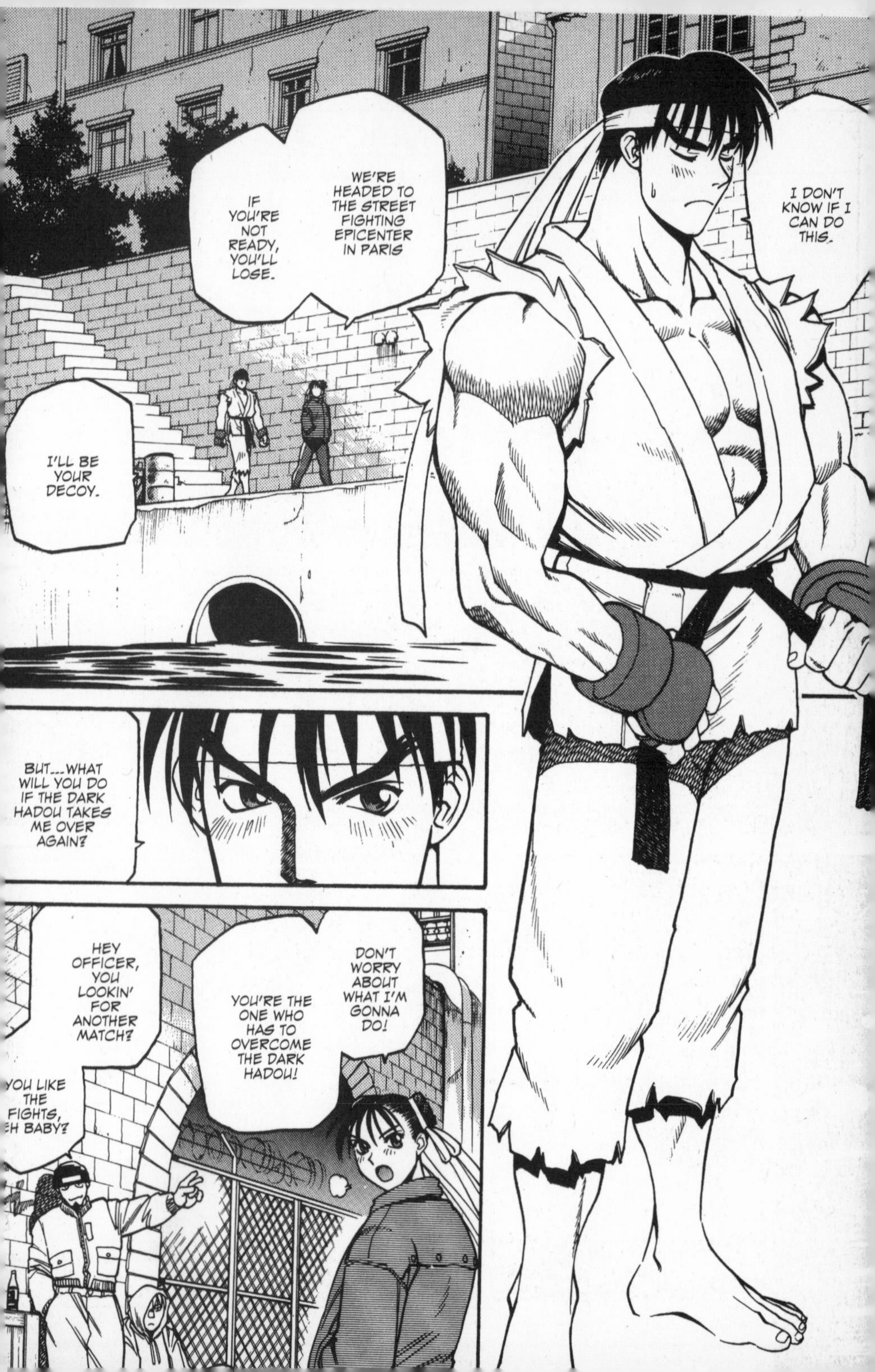
I DON'T KNOW IF I CAN DO THIS.
WE'RE HEADED TO THE STREET FIGHTING EPICENTER IN PARIS
IF YOU'RE NOT READY, YOU'LL LOSE.
I'LL BE YOUR DECOY.
BUT... WHAT WILL YOU DO IF THE DARK HADOU TAKES ME OVER AGAIN?
DON'T WORRY ABOUT WHAT I'M GONNA DO!
YOU'RE THE ONE WHO HAS TO OVERCOME THE DARK HADOU!
HEY OFFICER, YOU LOOKIN' FOR ANOTHER MATCH?
YOU LIKE THE FIGHTS, EH BABY?

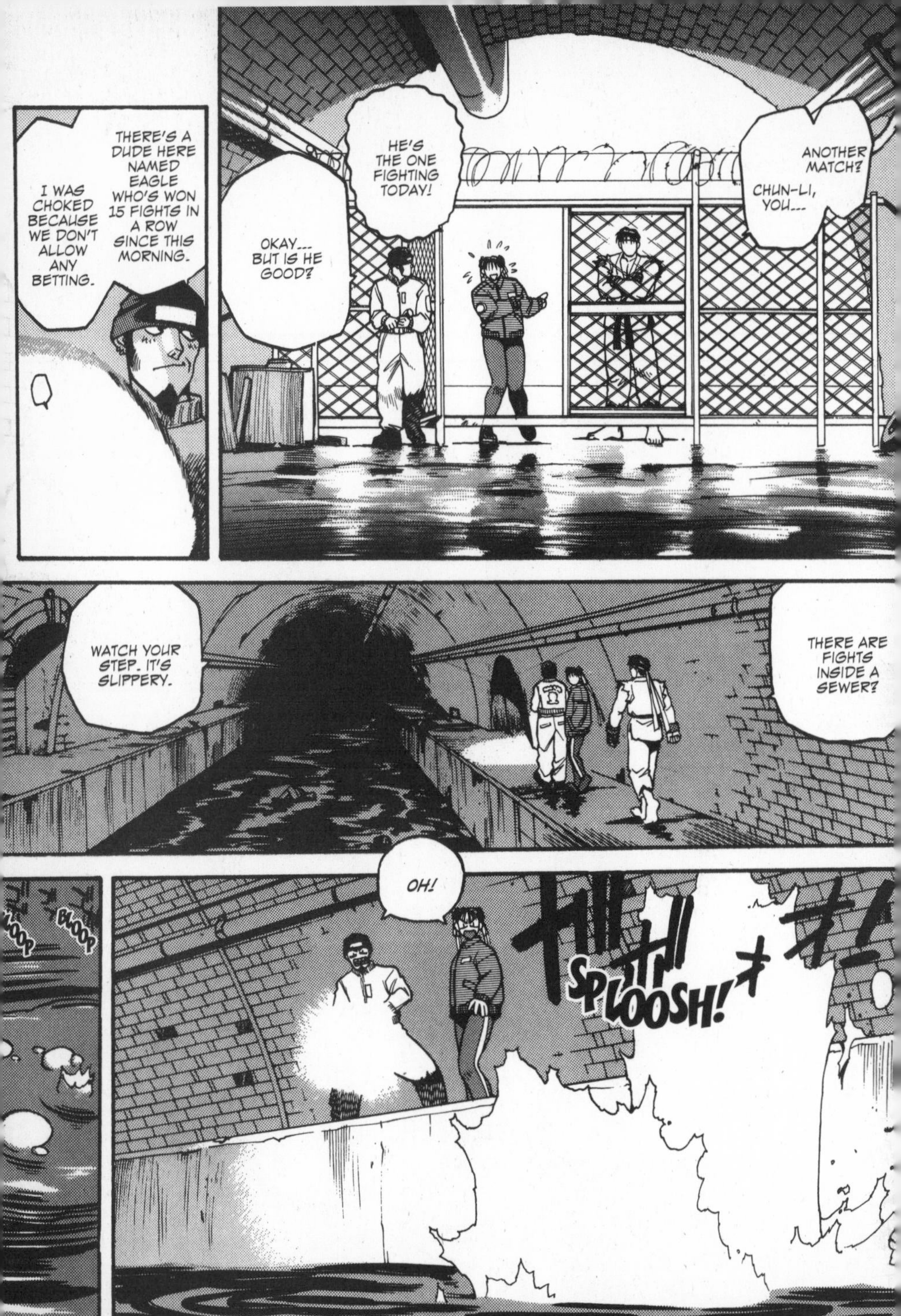
ANOTHER MATCH? CHUN-LI, YOU...
HE'S THE ONE FIGHTING TODAY!
OKAY... BUT IS HE GOOD?
THERE'S A DUDE HERE NAMED EAGLE WHO'S WON 15 FIGHTS IN A ROW SINCE THIS MORNING.
I WAS CHOKED BECAUSE WE DON'T ALLOW ANY BETTING.
THERE ARE FIGHTS INSIDE A SEWER?
WATCH YOUR STEP. IT'S SLIPPERY.
OH!
SPLOOSH!
BLOOP
BLOOP

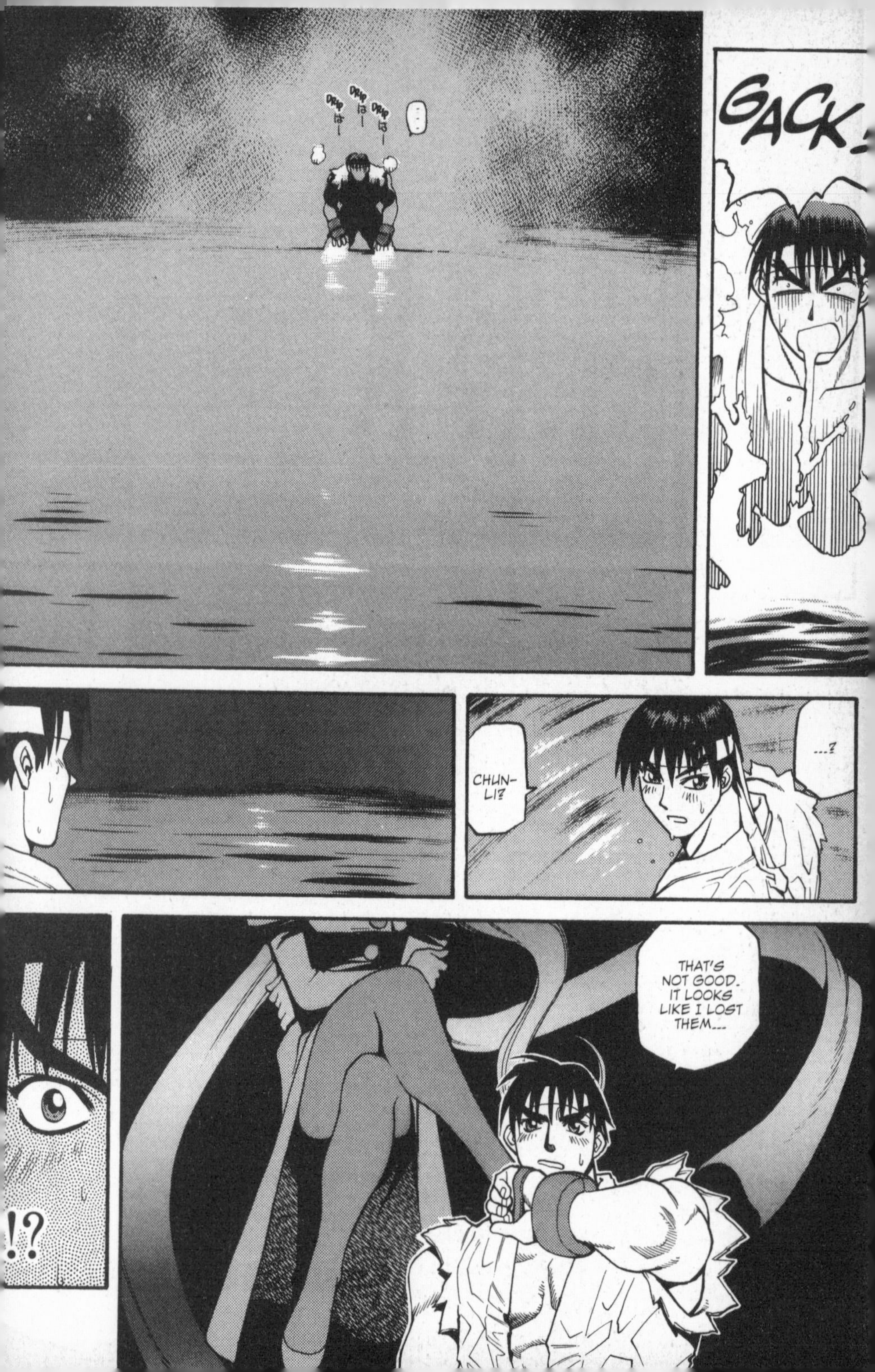
GACK
DRIP は
DRIP は
DRIP は
...
...?
CHUN-LI?
THAT'S NOT GOOD. IT LOOKS LIKE I LOST THEM...
!?

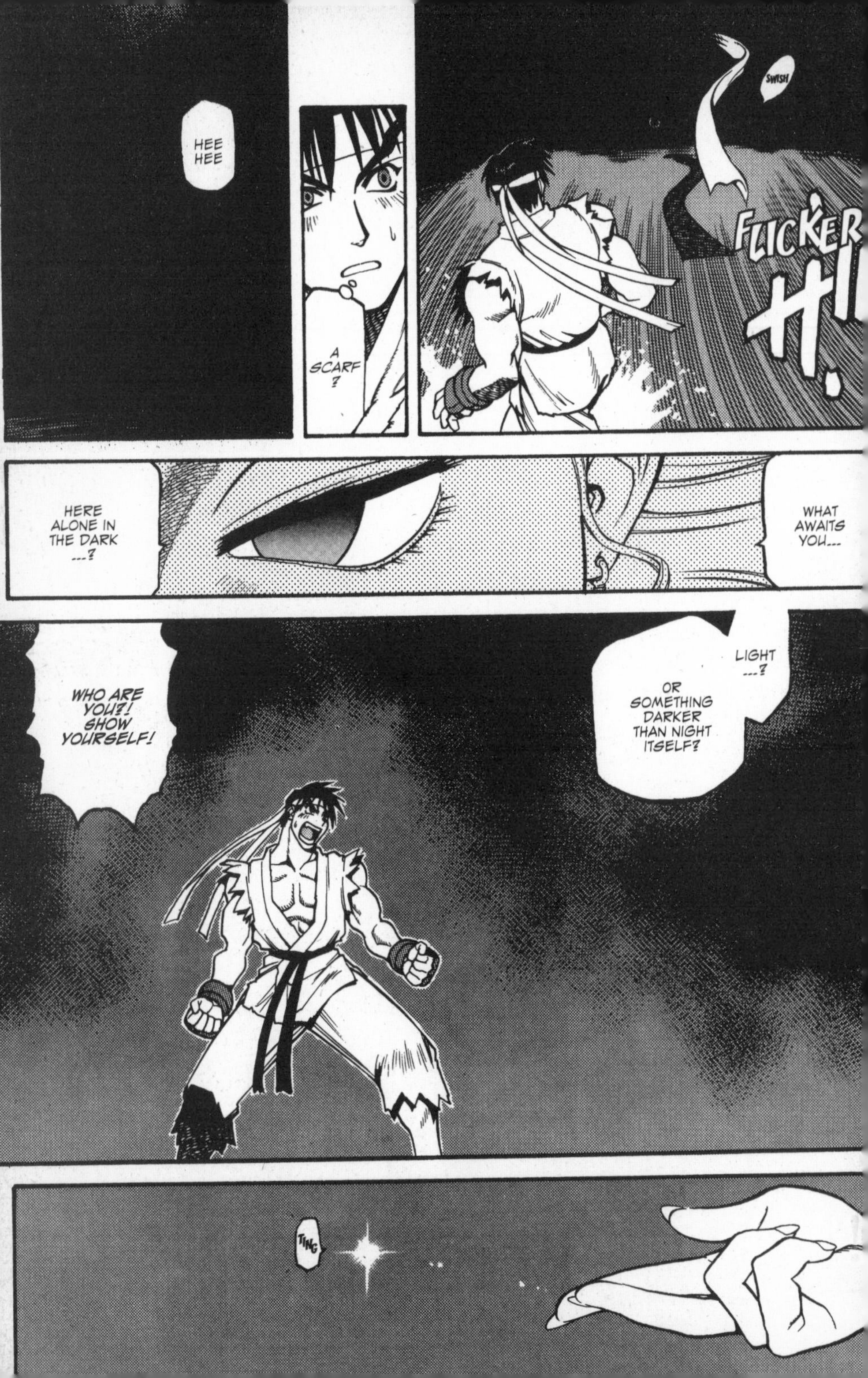
SWISH
FLICKER
A SCARF ?
HEE HEE
WHAT AWAITS YOU---
HERE ALONE IN THE DARK ---?
LIGHT ---?
OR SOMETHING DARKER THAN NIGHT ITSELF?
WHO ARE YOU?! SHOW YOURSELF!
TING

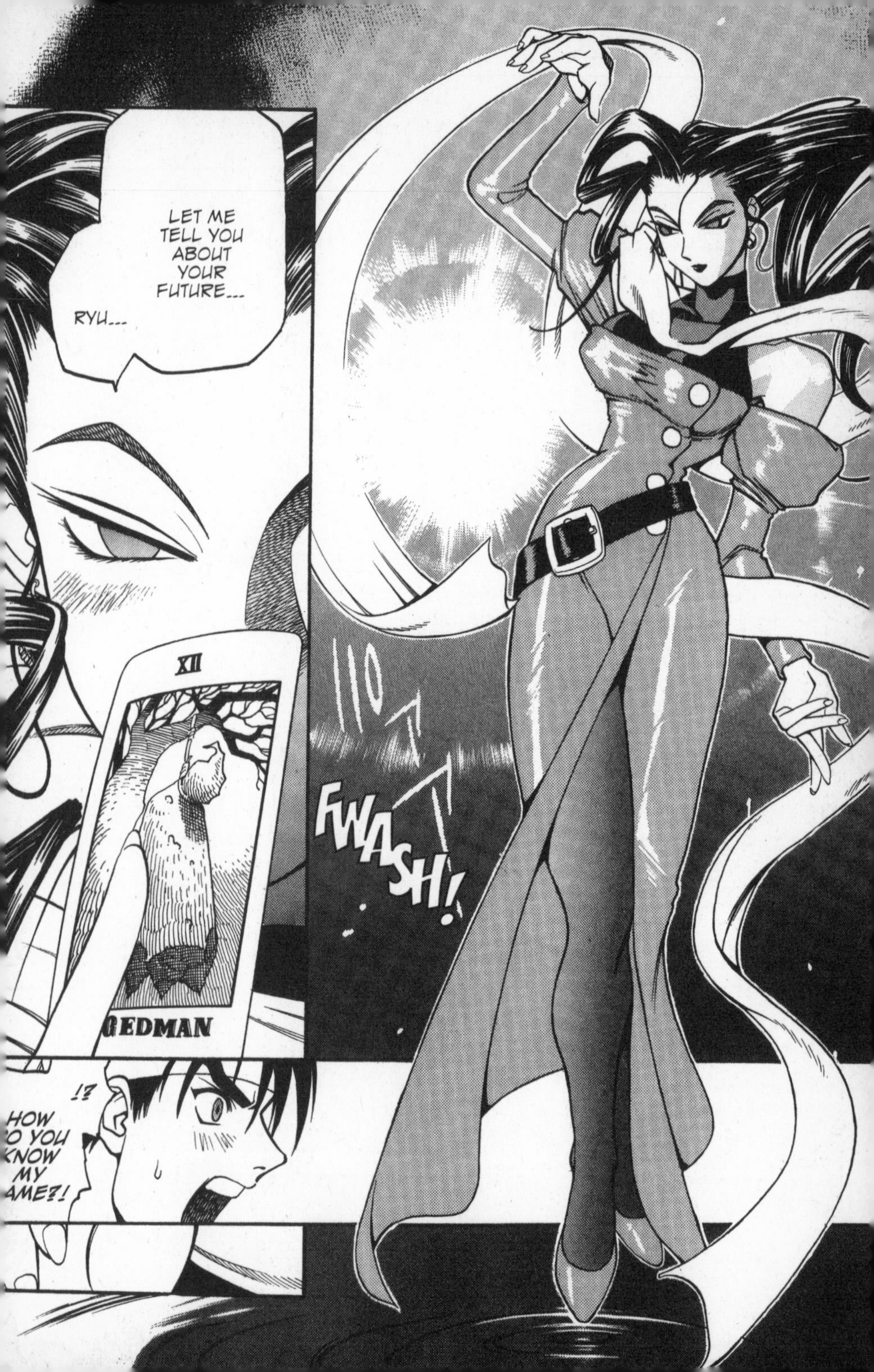
FWASH!
LET ME TELL YOU ABOUT YOUR FUTURE...
RYU...
XII
GEDMAN
!?
HOW O YOU NOW MY AME?!

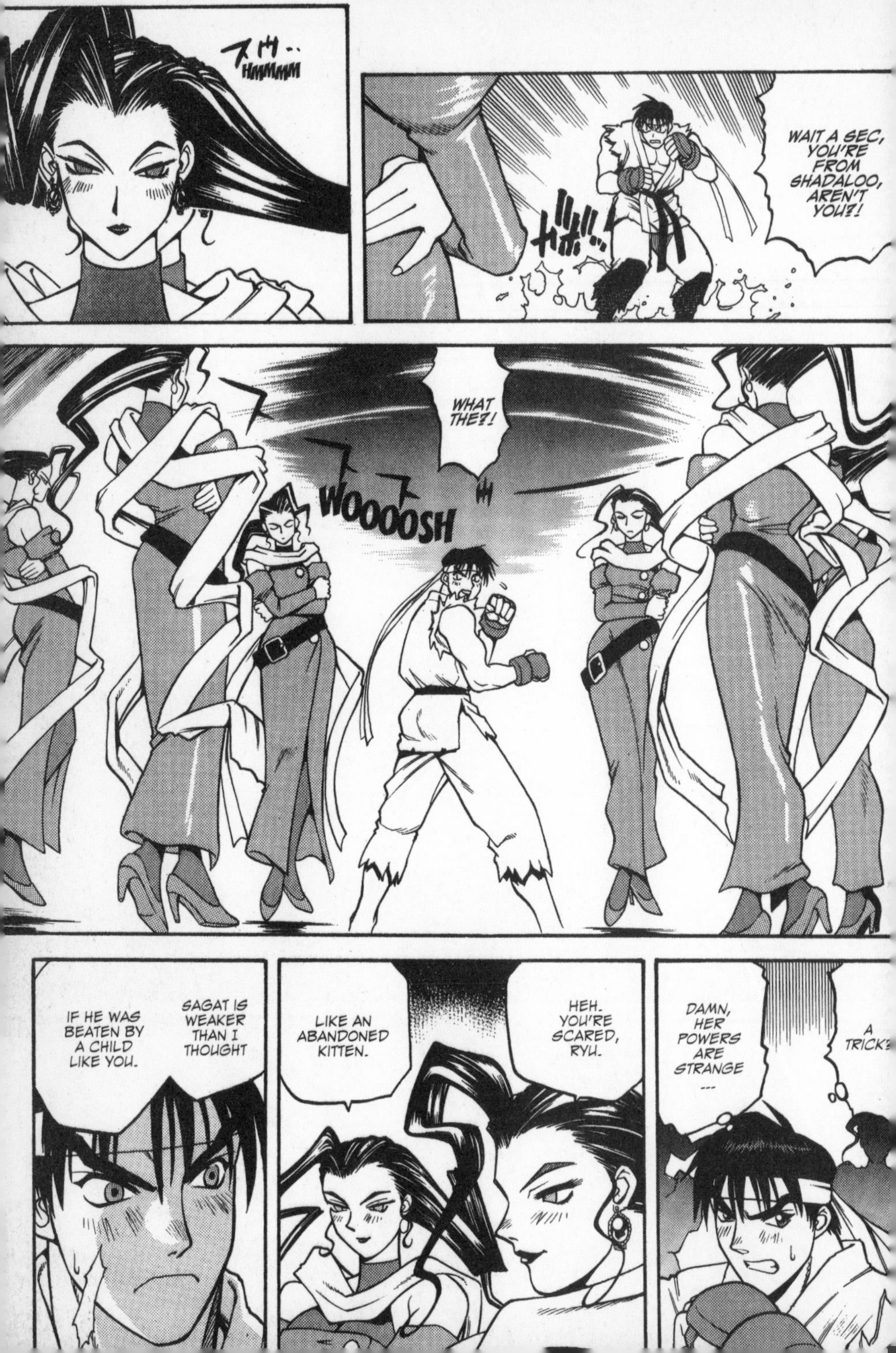
WAIT A SEC, YOU'RE FROM SHADALOO, AREN'T YOU?!
HMMMMM
WHAT THE?!
WOOOOSH
A TRICK?
DAMN, HER POWERS ARE STRANGE ---
HEH. YOU'RE SCARED, RYU.
LIKE AN ABANDONED KITTEN.
SAGAT IS WEAKER THAN I THOUGHT
IF HE WAS BEATEN BY A CHILD LIKE YOU.

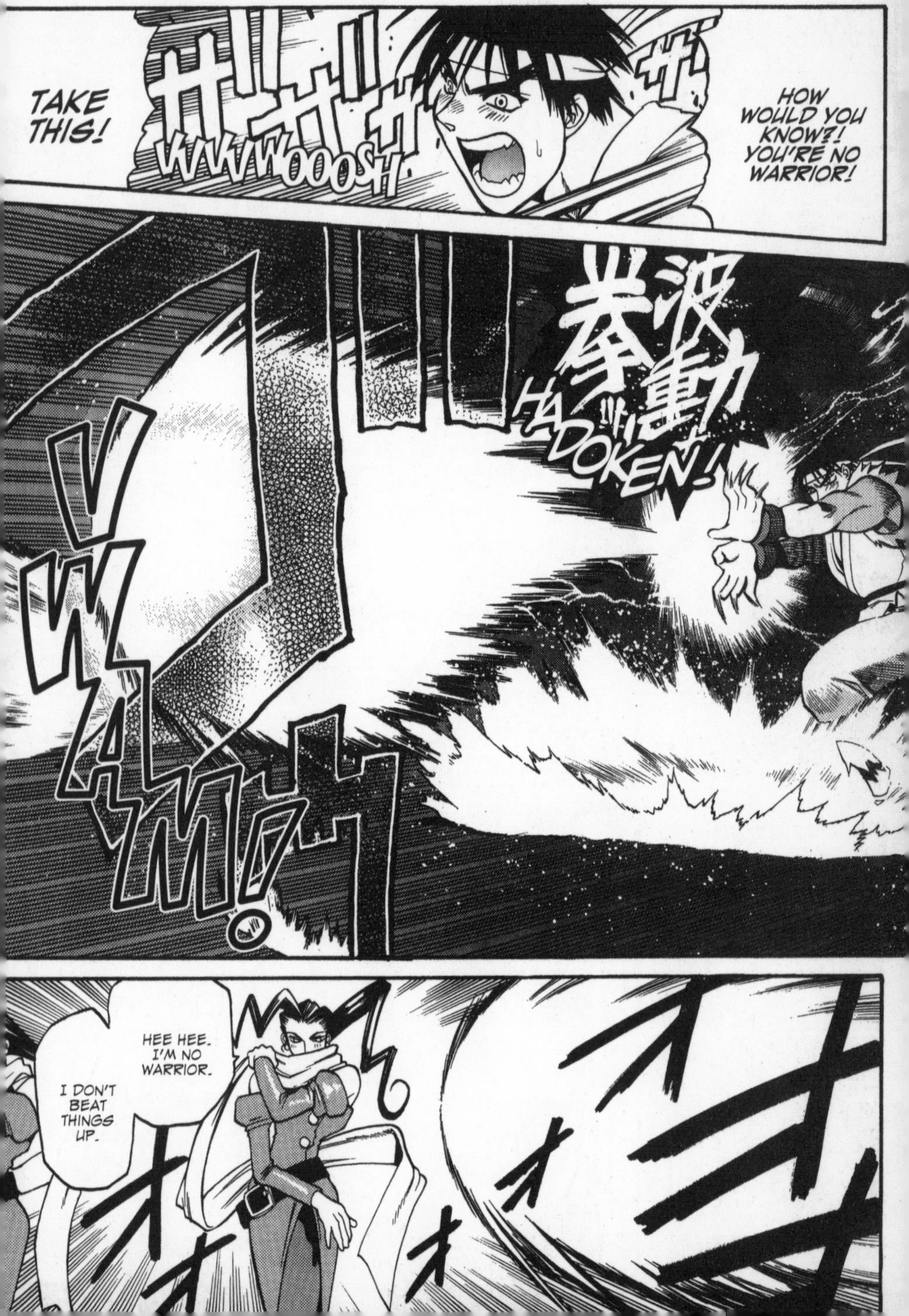
HOW WOULD YOU KNOW?! YOU'RE NO WARRIOR!
TAKE THIS!
WWWWOOOSH
波動拳
HADOKEN!
HEE HEE. I'M NO WARRIOR.
I DON'T BEAT THINGS UP.

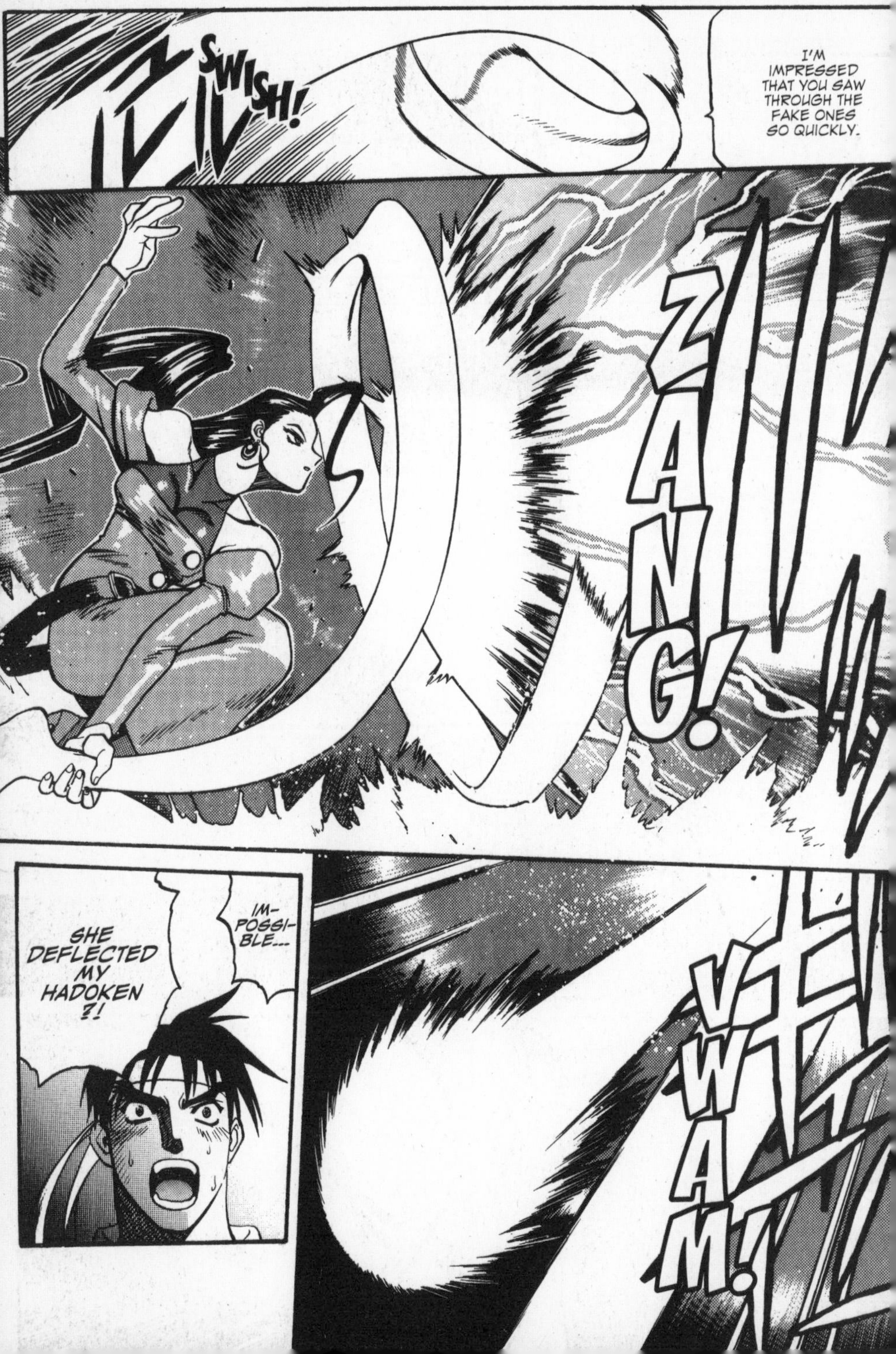
I'M IMPRESSED THAT YOU SAW THROUGH THE FAKE ONES SO QUICKLY.
SWISH!
ZANG!
VWAM!
IM-POSSI-BLE...
SHE DEFLECTED MY HADOKEN ?!

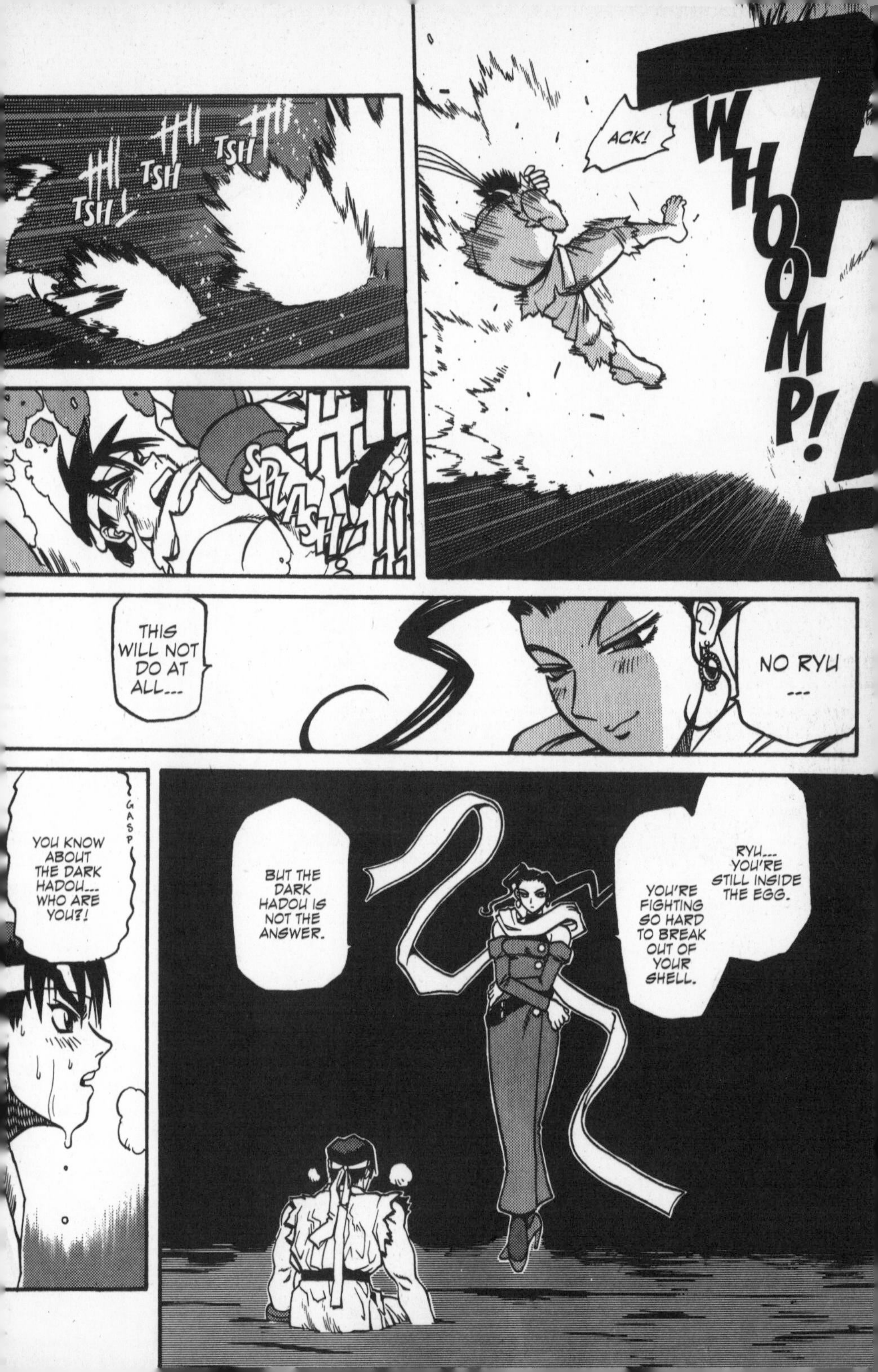
WHOOMP!
ACK!
TSH
TSH
TSH!
SPLASH!
NO RYU ---
THIS WILL NOT DO AT ALL...
RYU... YOU'RE STILL INSIDE THE EGG.
YOU'RE FIGHTING SO HARD TO BREAK OUT OF YOUR SHELL.
BUT THE DARK HADOU IS NOT THE ANSWER.
GASP
YOU KNOW ABOUT THE DARK HADOU... WHO ARE YOU?!

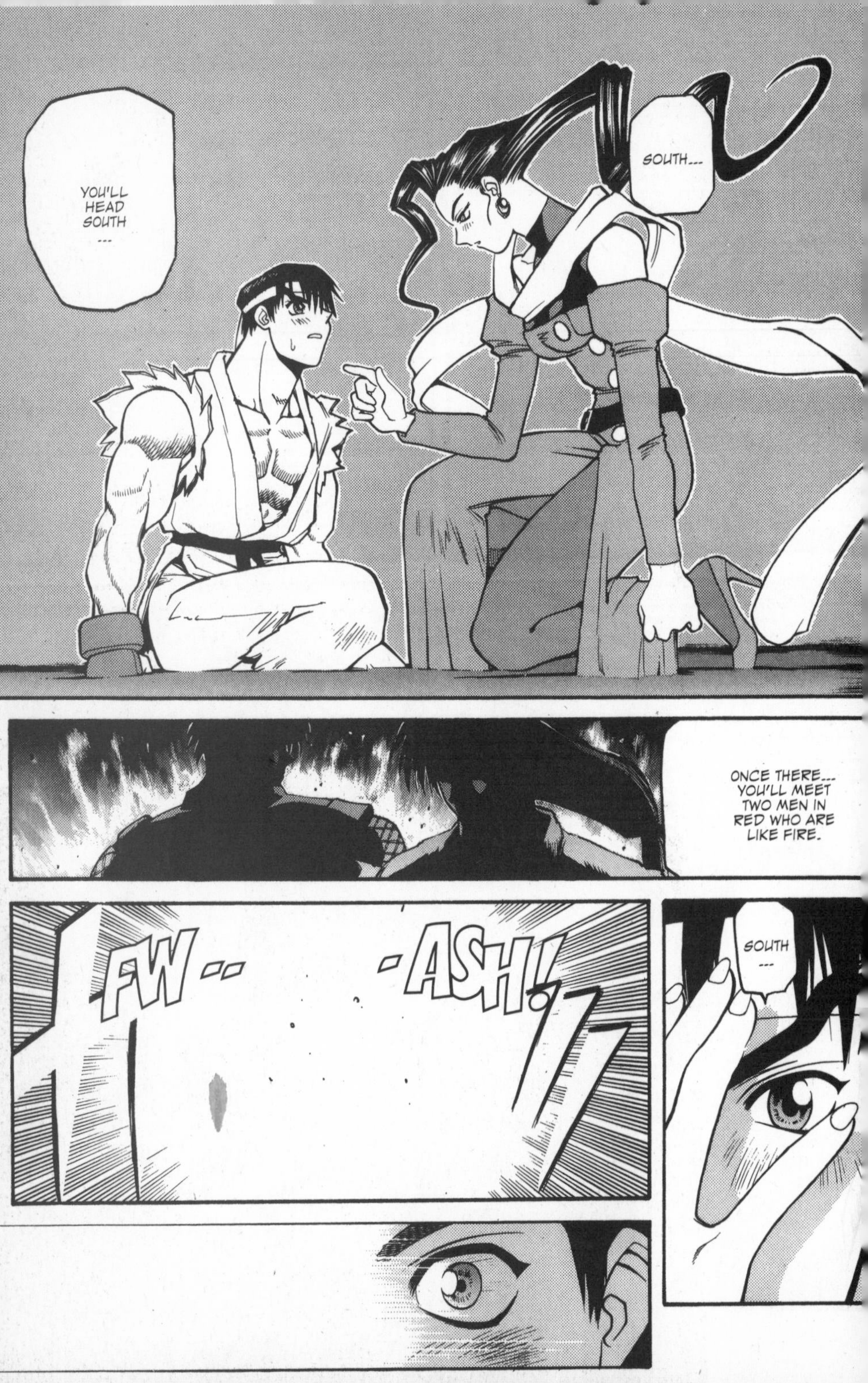
SOUTH...
YOU'LL HEAD SOUTH ...
ONCE THERE... YOU'LL MEET TWO MEN IN RED WHO ARE LIKE FIRE.
SOUTH ...
FW-- -ASH!

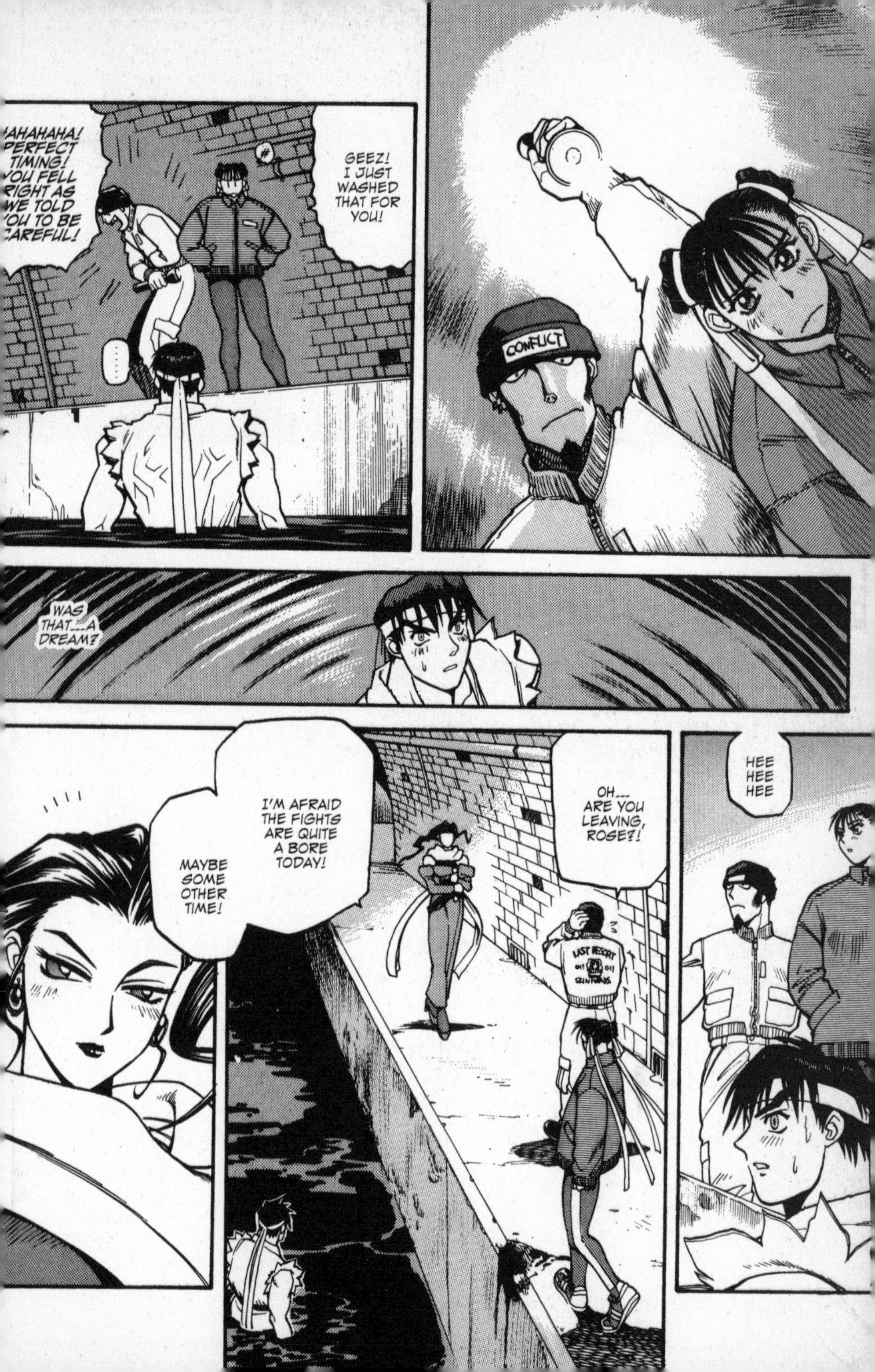
CONFLICT
GEEZ! I JUST WASHED THAT FOR YOU!
HAHAHAHA! PERFECT TIMING! YOU FELL RIGHT AS WE TOLD YOU TO BE CAREFUL!
......
WAS THAT...A DREAM?
HEE HEE HEE
OH... ARE YOU LEAVING, ROSE?!
LAST RESORT
I'M AFRAID THE FIGHTS ARE QUITE A BORE TODAY!
MAYBE SOME OTHER TIME!

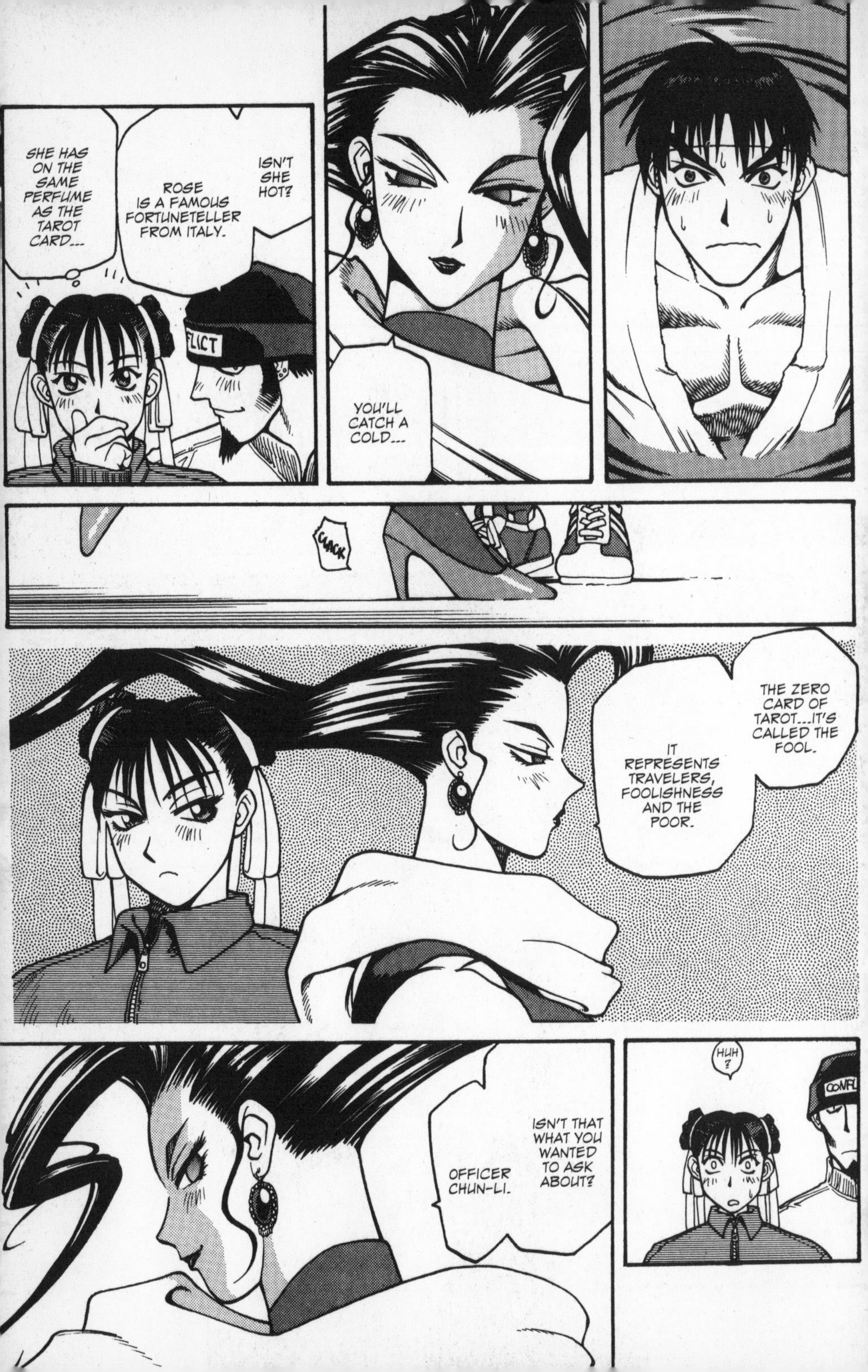
YOU'LL CATCH A COLD...
ISN'T SHE HOT?
ROSE IS A FAMOUS FORTUNETELLER FROM ITALY.
SHE HAS ON THE SAME PERFUME AS THE TAROT CARD...
CLACK
THE ZERO CARD OF TAROT...IT'S CALLED THE FOOL.
IT REPRESENTS TRAVELERS, FOOLISHNESS AND THE POOR.
HUH?
ISN'T THAT WHAT YOU WANTED TO ASK ABOUT?
OFFICER CHUN-LI.

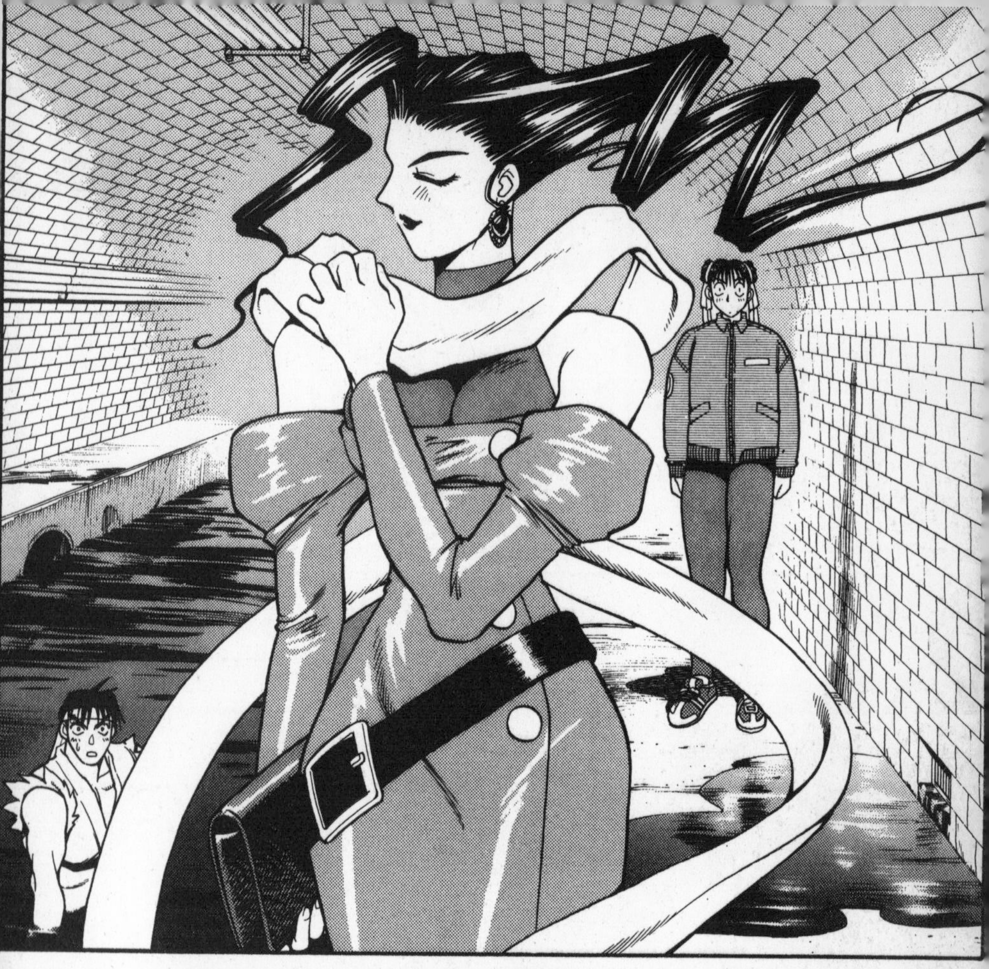

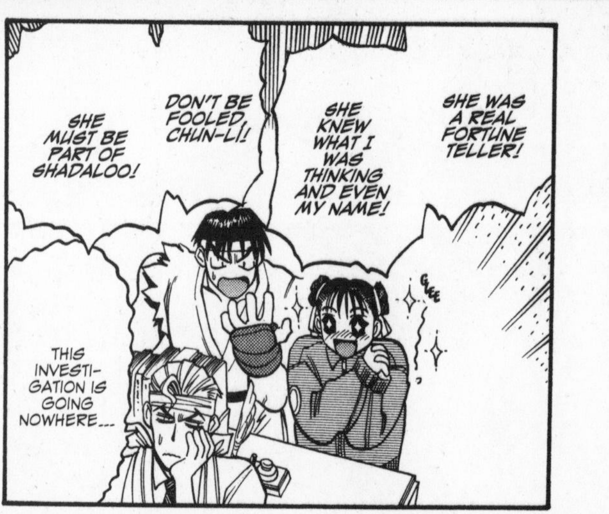
SHE WAS A REAL FORTUNE TELLER!
SHE KNEW WHAT I WAS THINKING AND EVEN MY NAME!
DON'T BE FOOLED, CHUN-LI!
SHE MUST BE PART OF SHADALOO!
THIS INVESTI-GATION IS GOING NOWHERE...

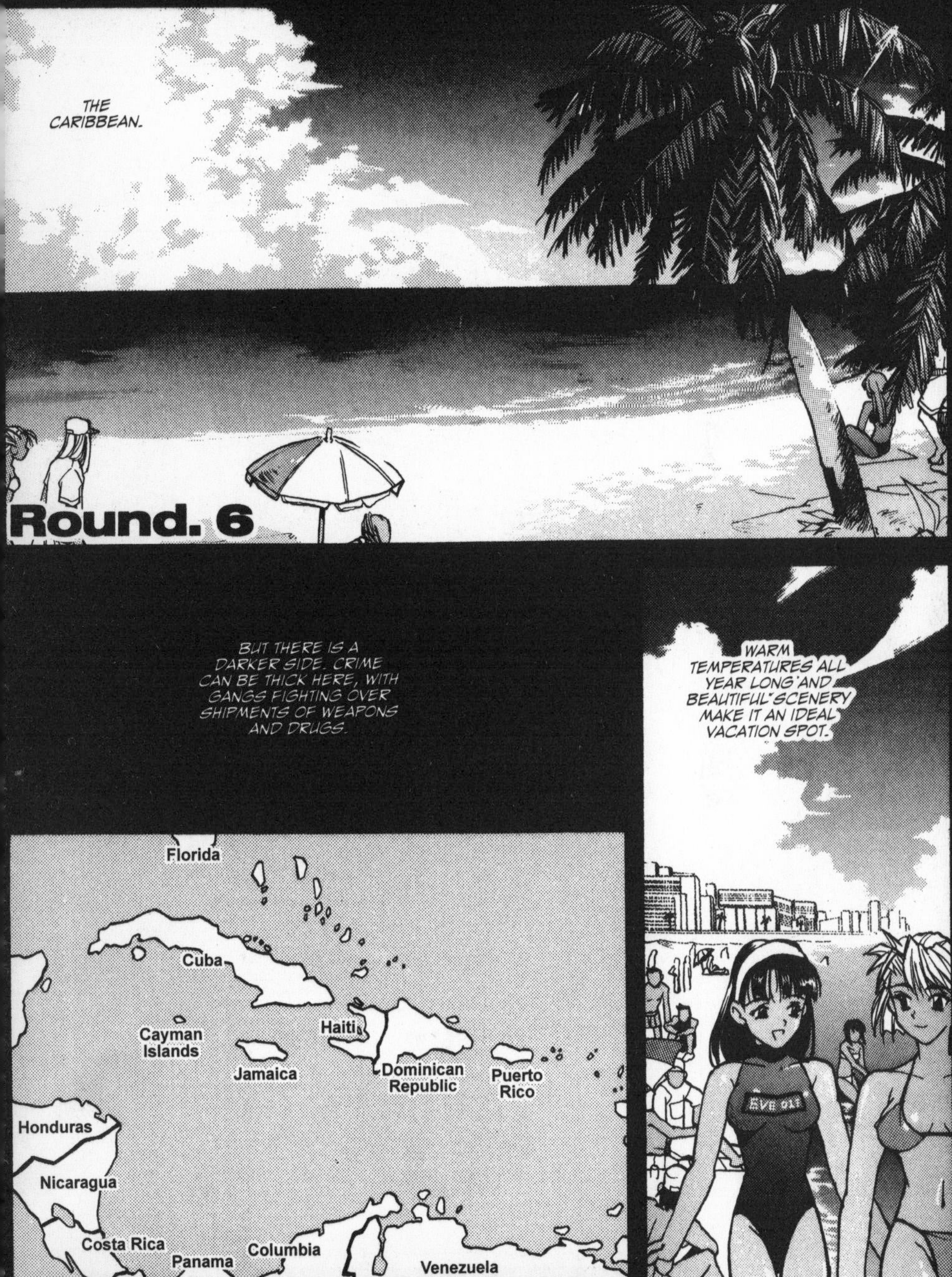
THE CARIBBEAN.
Round. 6
WARM TEMPERATURES ALL YEAR LONG AND BEAUTIFUL SCENERY MAKE IT AN IDEAL VACATION SPOT.
BUT THERE IS A DARKER SIDE. CRIME CAN BE THICK HERE, WITH GANGS FIGHTING OVER SHIPMENTS OF WEAPONS AND DRUGS.
Florida
Cuba
Cayman Islands
Jamaica
Haiti
Dominican Republic
Puerto Rico
Honduras
Nicaragua
Costa Rica
Panama
Columbia
Venezuela
EVE 011

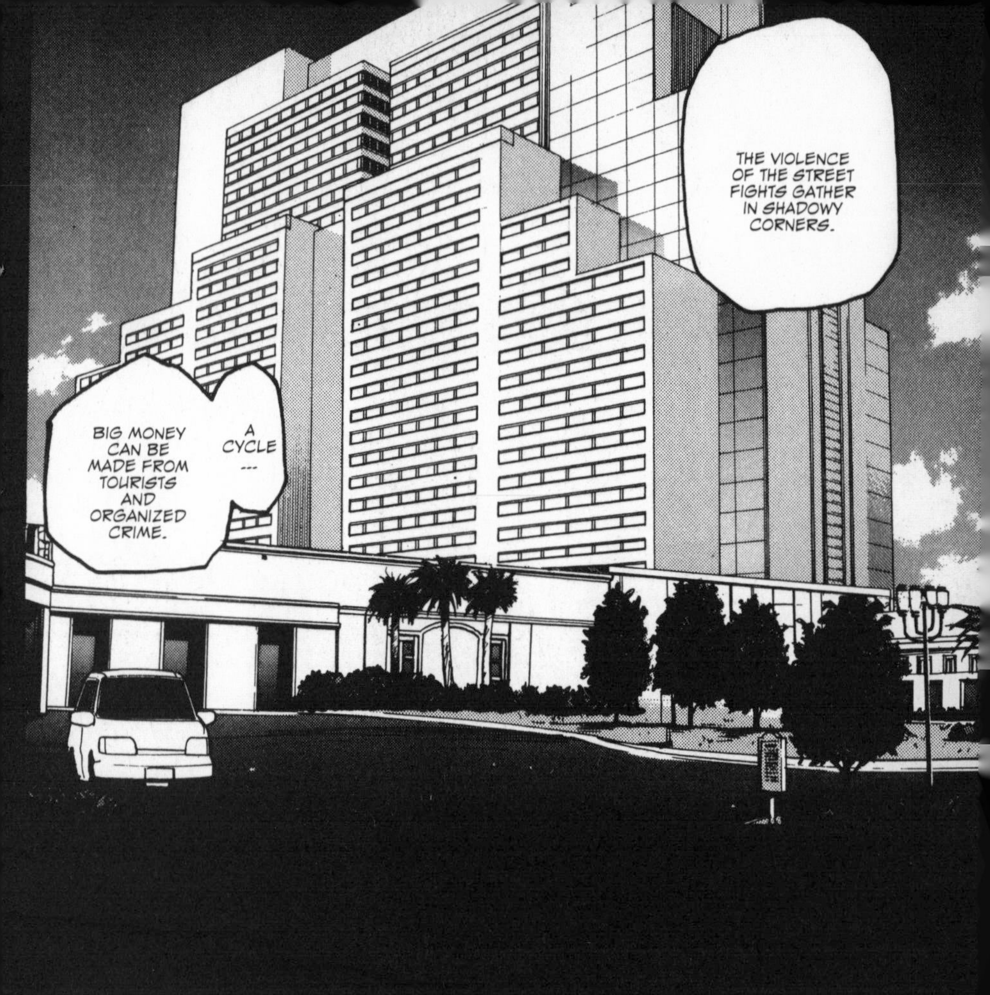
THE VIOLENCE OF THE STREET FIGHTS GATHER IN SHADOWY CORNERS.
A CYCLE ---
BIG MONEY CAN BE MADE FROM TOURISTS AND ORGANIZED CRIME.

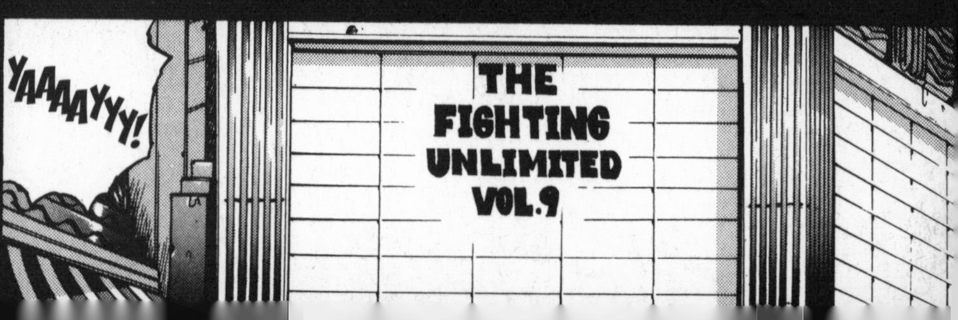
THE FIGHTING UNLIMITED VOL.9
YAAAAYYY!

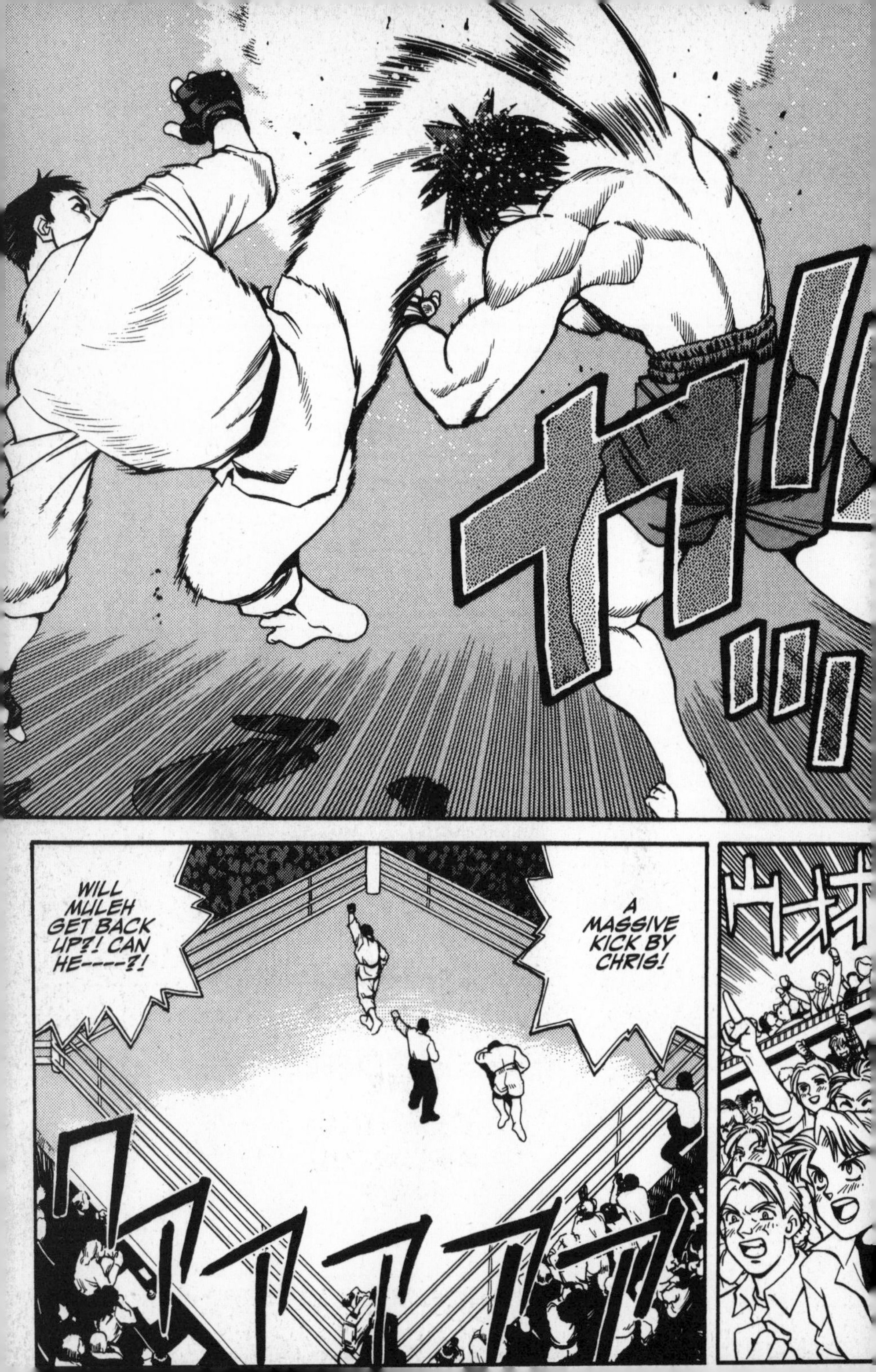
A MASSIVE KICK BY CHRIS!
WILL MULEH GET BACK UP?! CAN HE----?!

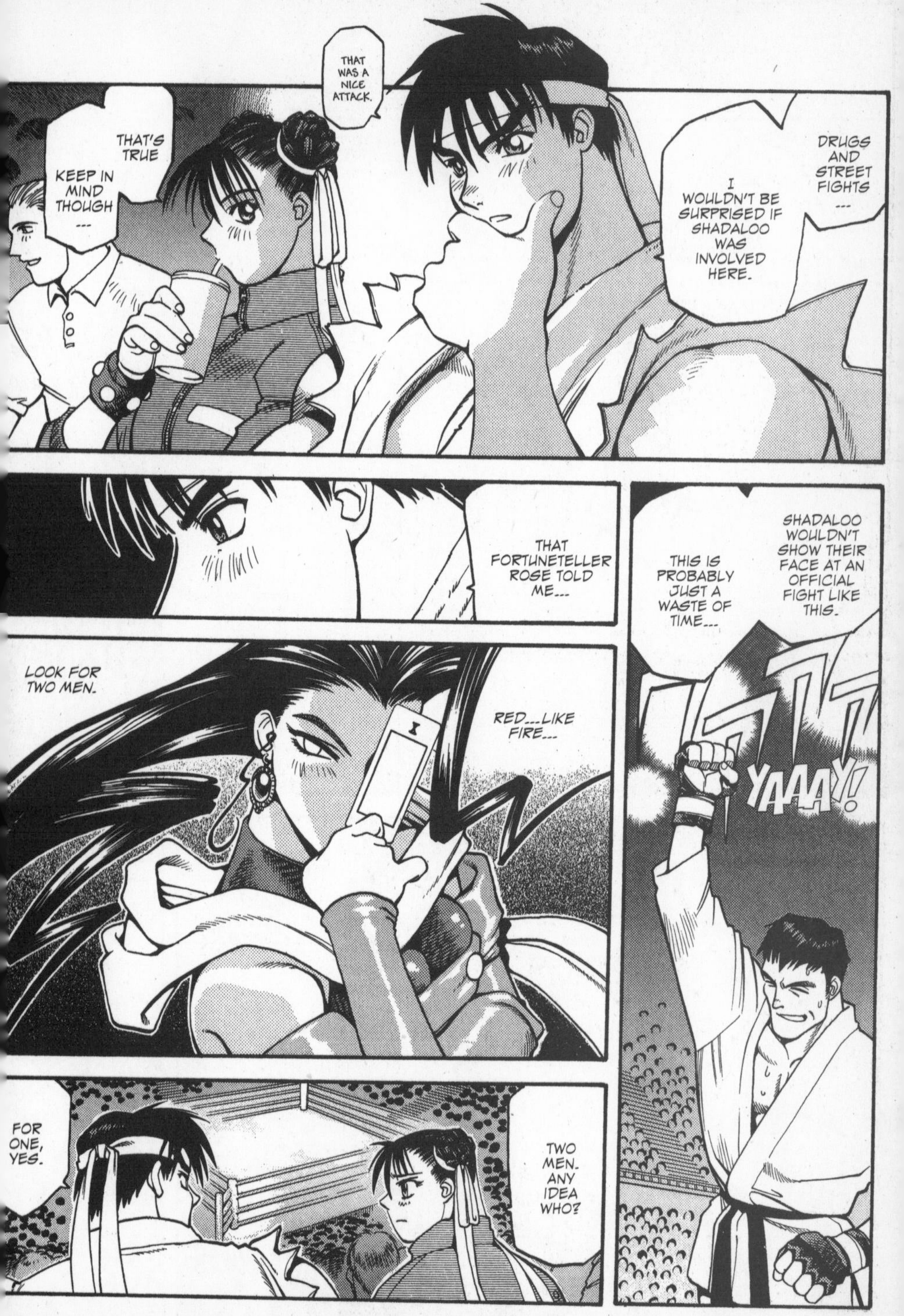
DRUGS AND STREET FIGHTS ---
I WOULDN'T BE SURPRISED IF SHADALOO WAS INVOLVED HERE.
THAT WAS A NICE ATTACK.
THAT'S TRUE
KEEP IN MIND THOUGH ---
SHADALOO WOULDN'T SHOW THEIR FACE AT AN OFFICIAL FIGHT LIKE THIS.
THIS IS PROBABLY JUST A WASTE OF TIME---
YAAAY!
THAT FORTUNETELLER ROSE TOLD ME---
LOOK FOR TWO MEN.
RED---LIKE FIRE---
TWO MEN. ANY IDEA WHO?
FOR ONE, YES.

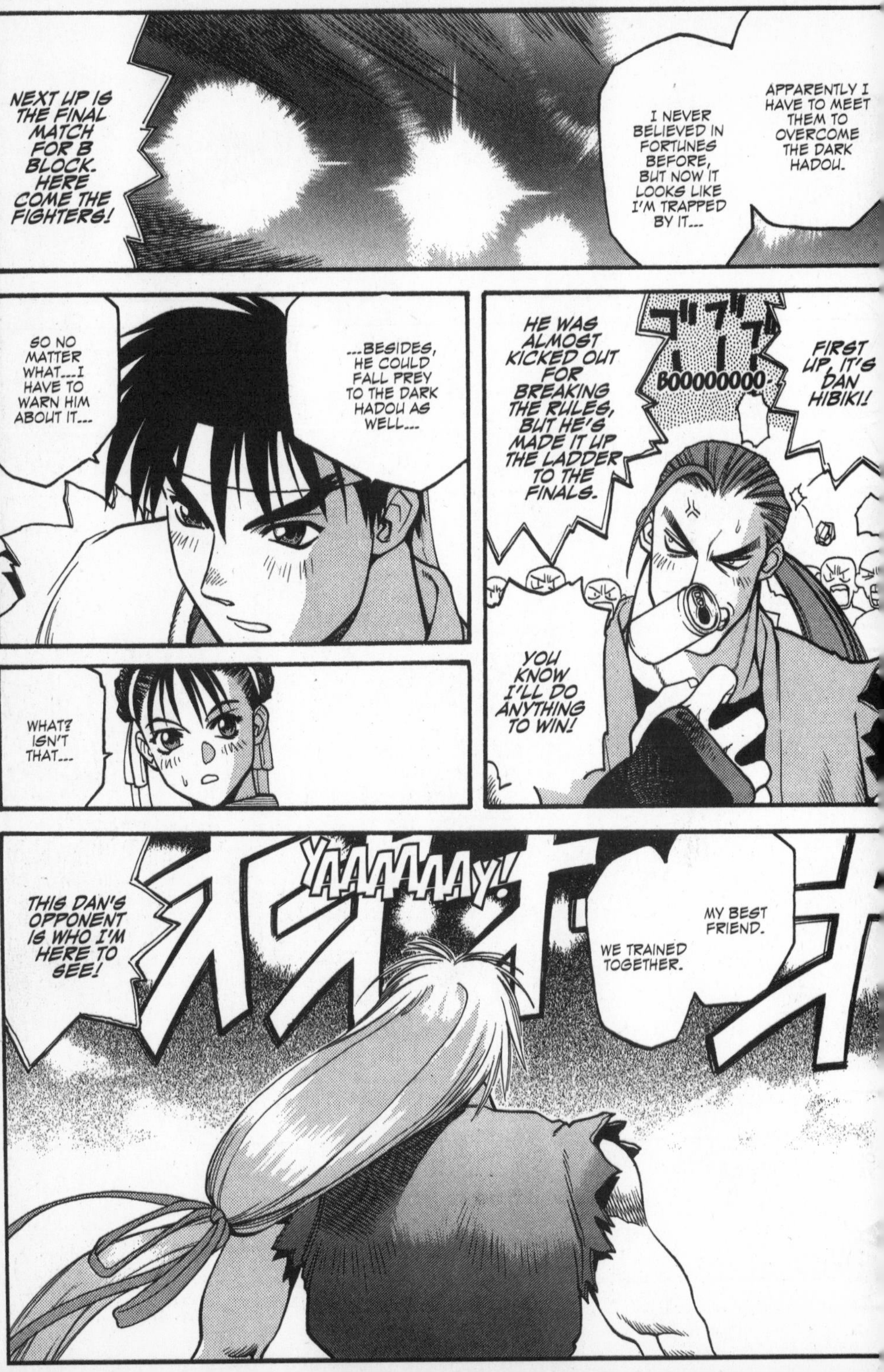
I NEVER BELIEVED IN FORTUNES BEFORE, BUT NOW IT LOOKS LIKE I'M TRAPPED BY IT...
APPARENTLY I HAVE TO MEET THEM TO OVERCOME THE DARK HADOU.
NEXT UP IS THE FINAL MATCH FOR B BLOCK. HERE COME THE FIGHTERS!
FIRST UP, IT'S DAN HIBIKI!
BOOOOOOOO
HE WAS ALMOST KICKED OUT FOR BREAKING THE RULES, BUT HE'S MADE IT UP THE LADDER TO THE FINALS.
YOU KNOW I'LL DO ANYTHING TO WIN!
...BESIDES, HE COULD FALL PREY TO THE DARK HADOU AS WELL...
SO NO MATTER WHAT...I HAVE TO WARN HIM ABOUT IT...
WHAT? ISN'T THAT...
MY BEST FRIEND.
WE TRAINED TOGETHER.
YAAAAAAAY!
THIS DAN'S OPPONENT IS WHO I'M HERE TO SEE!

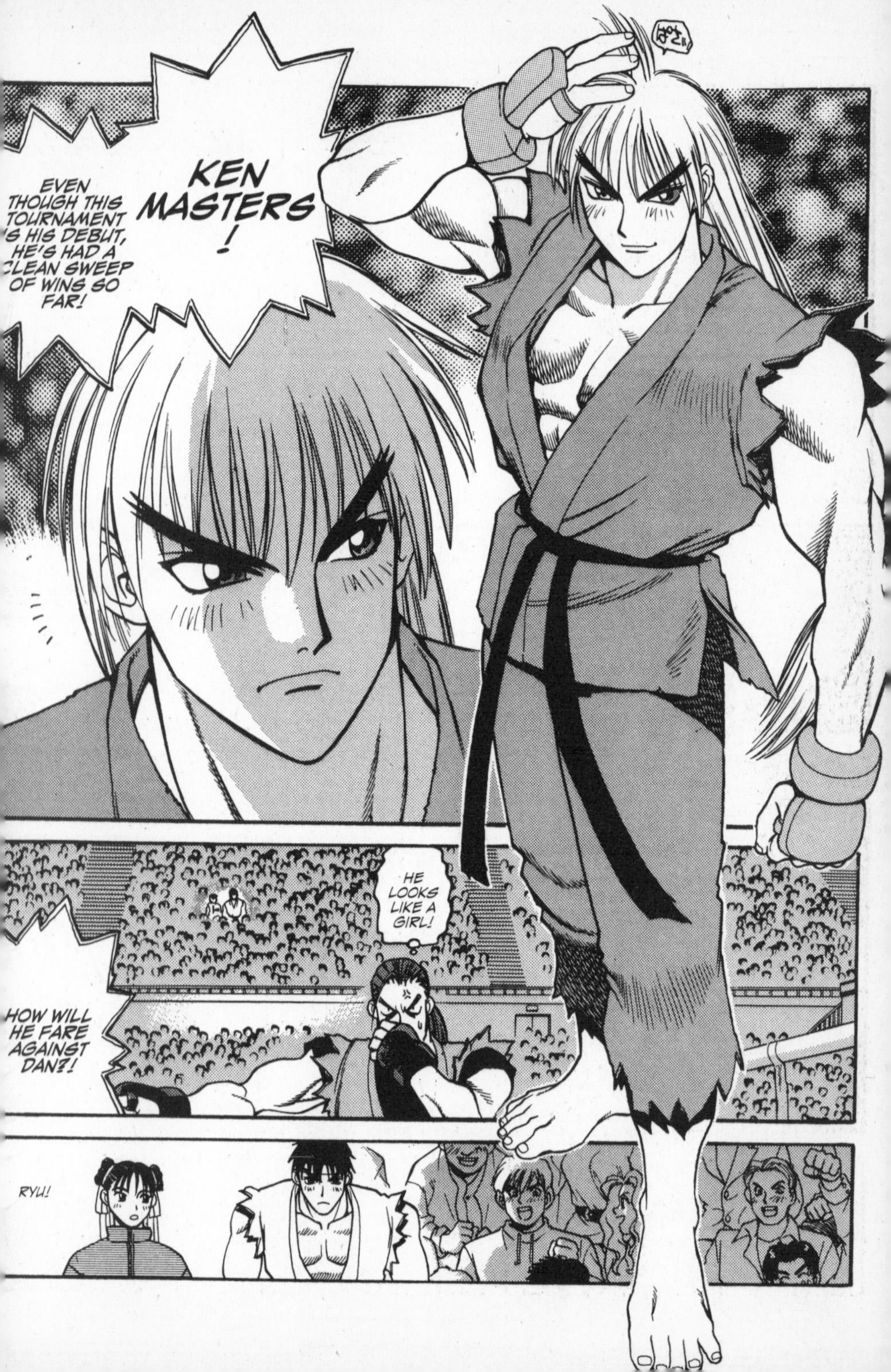
KEN MASTERS!
EVEN THOUGH THIS TOURNAMENT IS HIS DEBUT, HE'S HAD A CLEAN SWEEP OF WINS SO FAR!
HE LOOKS LIKE A GIRL!
HOW WILL HE FARE AGAINST DAN?!
RYU!

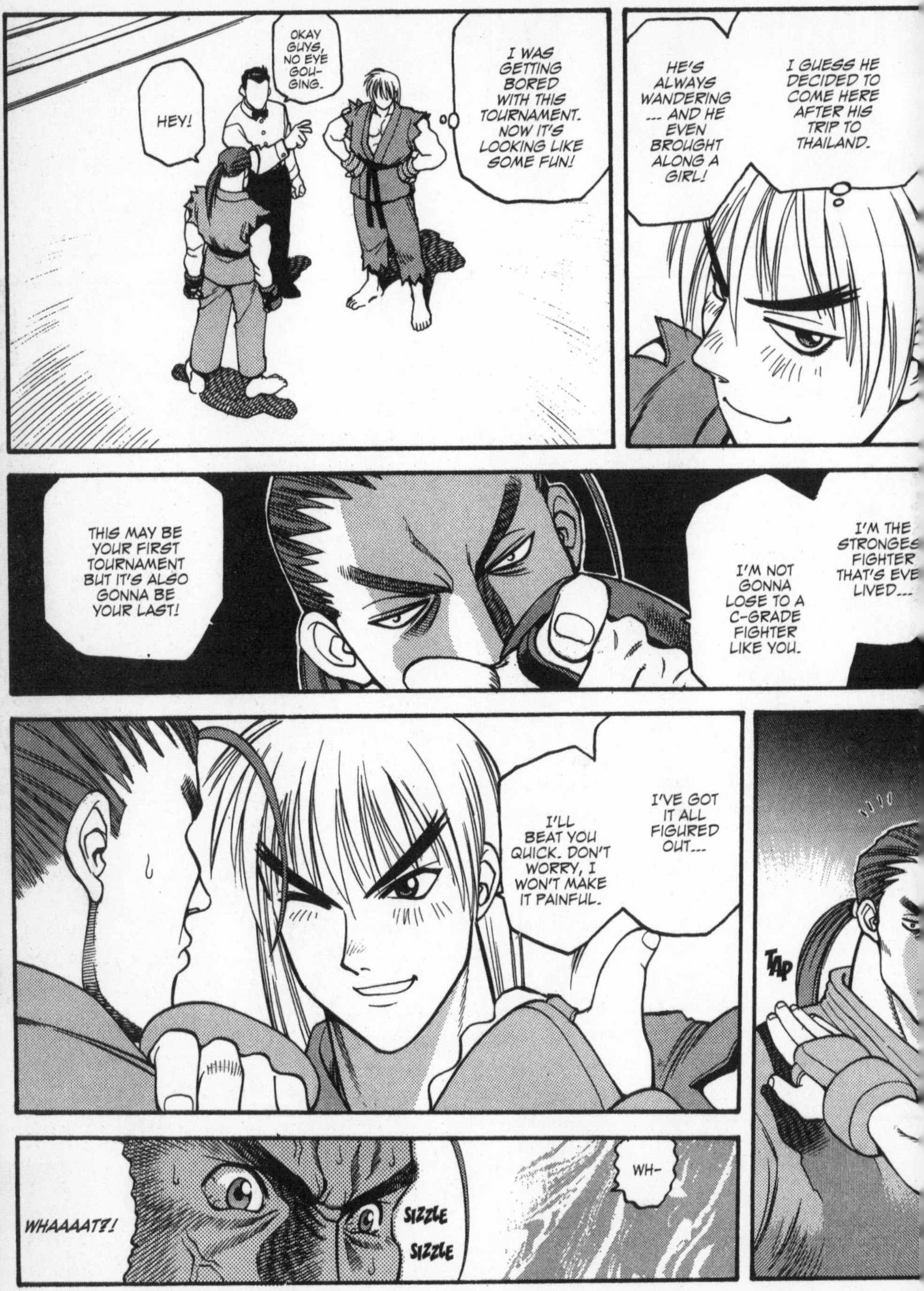
I GUESS HE DECIDED TO COME HERE AFTER HIS TRIP TO THAILAND.
HE'S ALWAYS WANDERING --- AND HE EVEN BROUGHT ALONG A GIRL!
I WAS GETTING BORED WITH THIS TOURNAMENT. NOW IT'S LOOKING LIKE SOME FUN!
OKAY GUYS, NO EYE GOU-GING.
HEY!
I'M THE STRONGES FIGHTER THAT'S EVE LIVED...
I'M NOT GONNA LOSE TO A C-GRADE FIGHTER LIKE YOU.
THIS MAY BE YOUR FIRST TOURNAMENT BUT IT'S ALSO GONNA BE YOUR LAST!
TAP
I'VE GOT IT ALL FIGURED OUT...
I'LL BEAT YOU QUICK. DON'T WORRY, I WON'T MAKE IT PAINFUL.
WH-
SIZZLE
SIZZLE
WHAAAAT?!

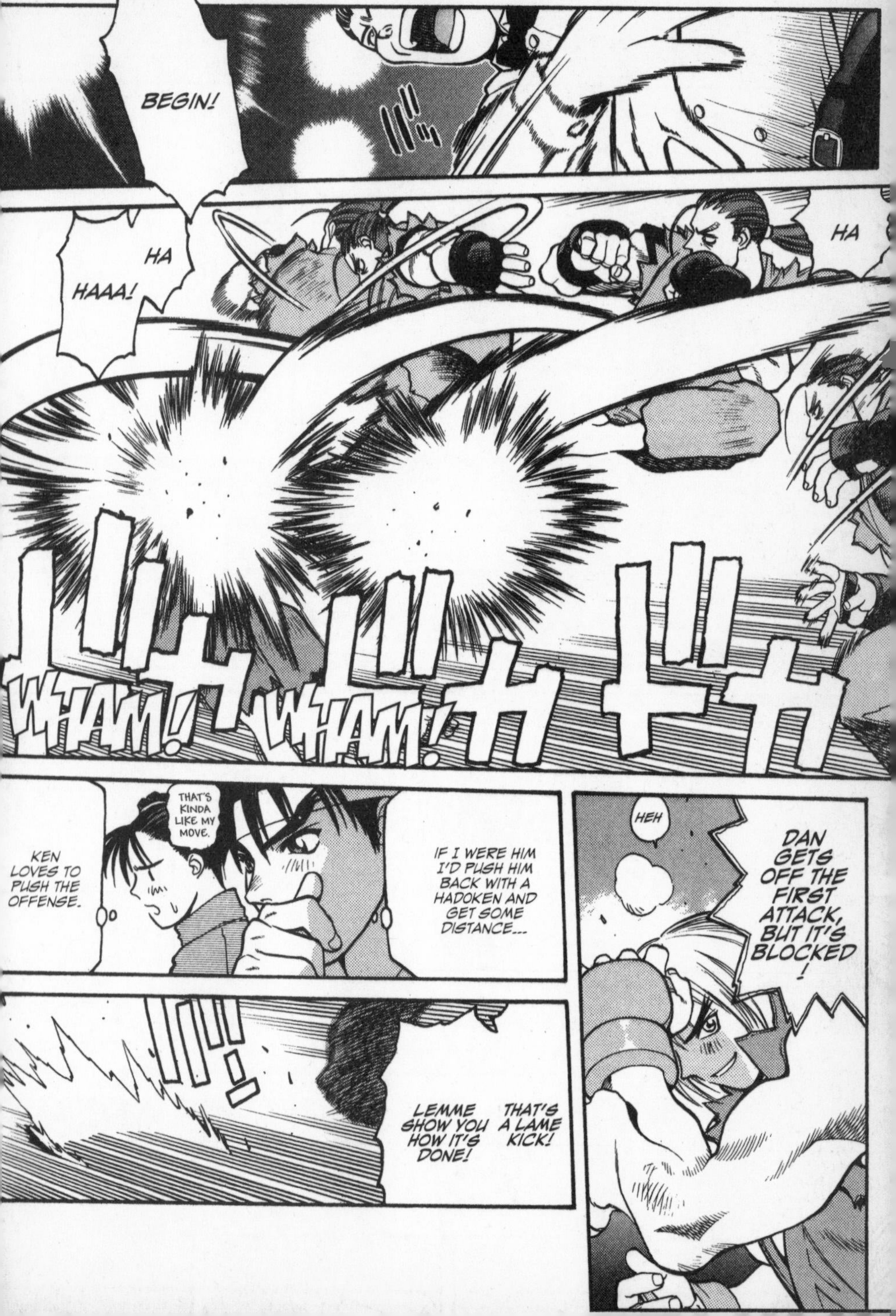
BEGIN!
HA
HA HAAA!
WHAM! WHAM!
HEH
DAN GETS OFF THE FIRST ATTACK, BUT IT'S BLOCKED!
IF I WERE HIM I'D PUSH HIM BACK WITH A HADOKEN AND GET SOME DISTANCE...
THAT'S KINDA LIKE MY MOVE.
KEN LOVES TO PUSH THE OFFENSE.
THAT'S A LAME KICK!
LEMME SHOW YOU HOW IT'S DONE!

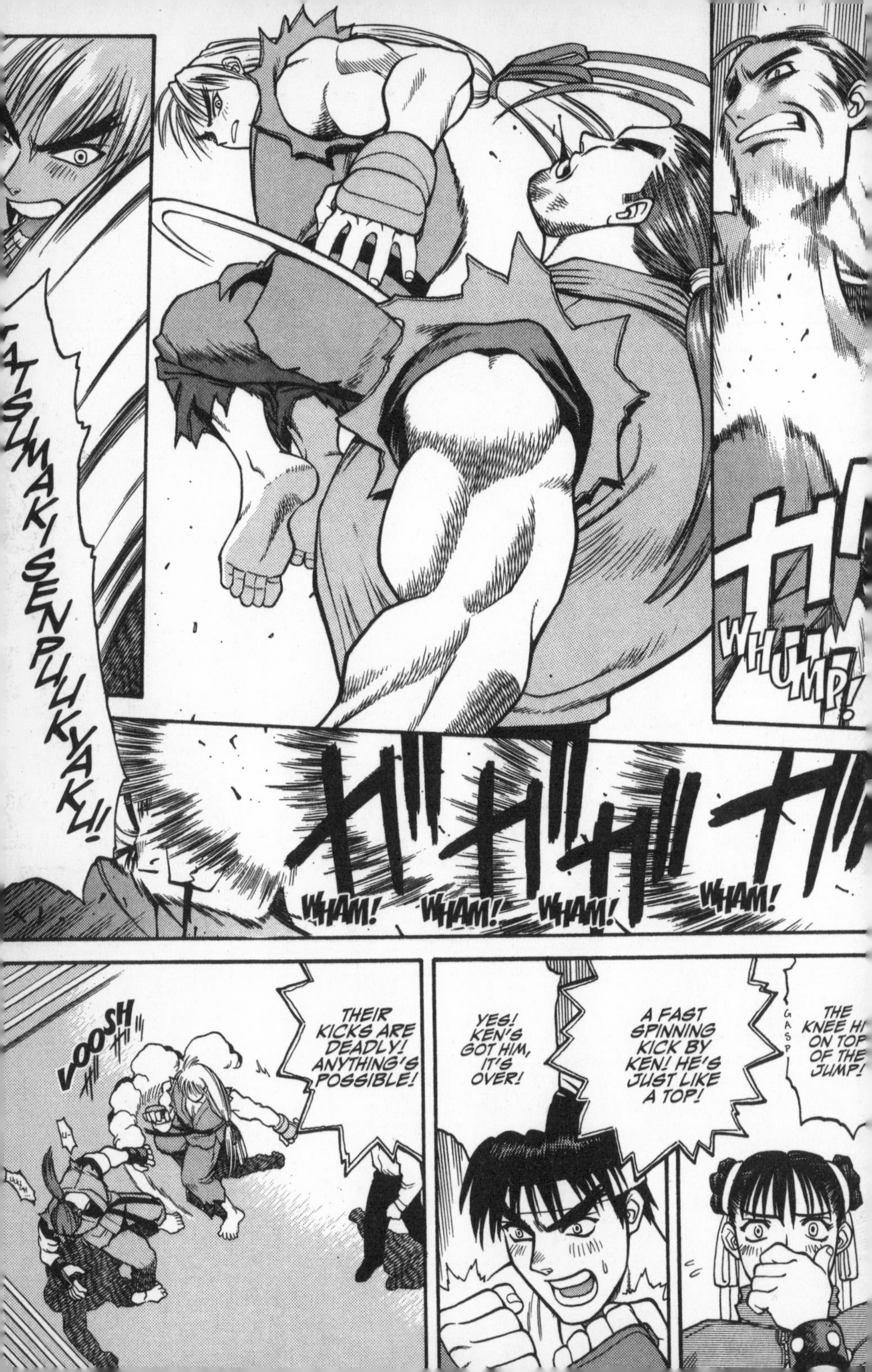
WHUMP!
TATSUMAKI SENPUUKYAKU!!
WHAM!
WHAM!
WHAM!
WHAM!
GASP
THE KNEE HI
ON TOP OF THE JUMP!
A FAST SPINNING KICK BY KEN! HE'S JUST LIKE A TOP!
YES! KEN'S GOT HIM, IT'S OVER!
THEIR KICKS ARE DEADLY! ANYTHING'S POSSIBLE!
VOOSH
U-

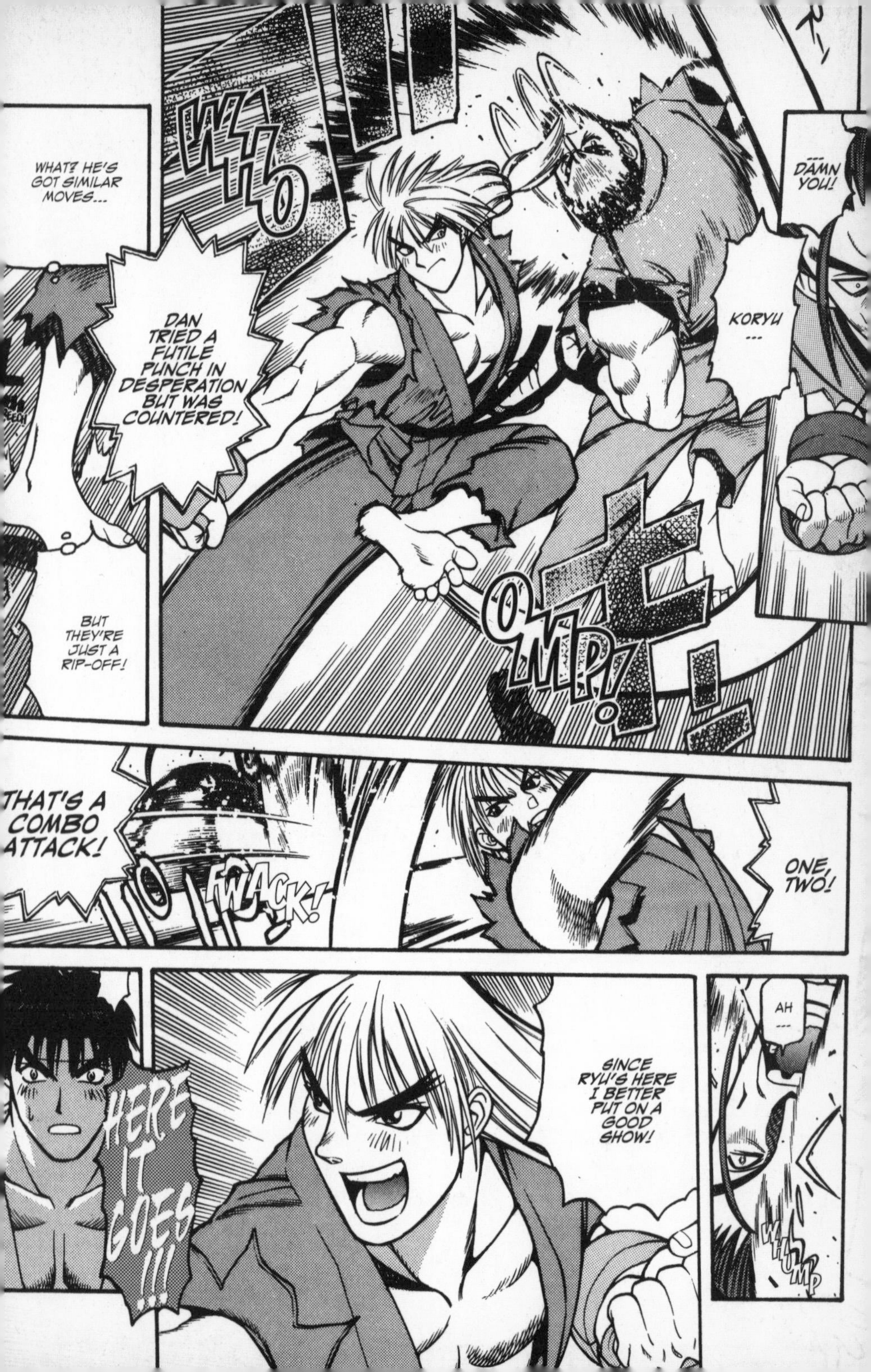
...DAMN YOU!
KORYU...
WHO
O-OMP!
WHAT? HE'S GOT SIMILAR MOVES...
DAN TRIED A FUTILE PUNCH IN DESPERATION BUT WAS COUNTERED!
BUT THEY'RE JUST A RIP-OFF!
ONE, TWO!
FWACK!
THAT'S A COMBO ATTACK!
AH...
WHUMP
SINCE RYU'S HERE I BETTER PUT ON A GOOD SHOW!
HERE IT GOES!!!

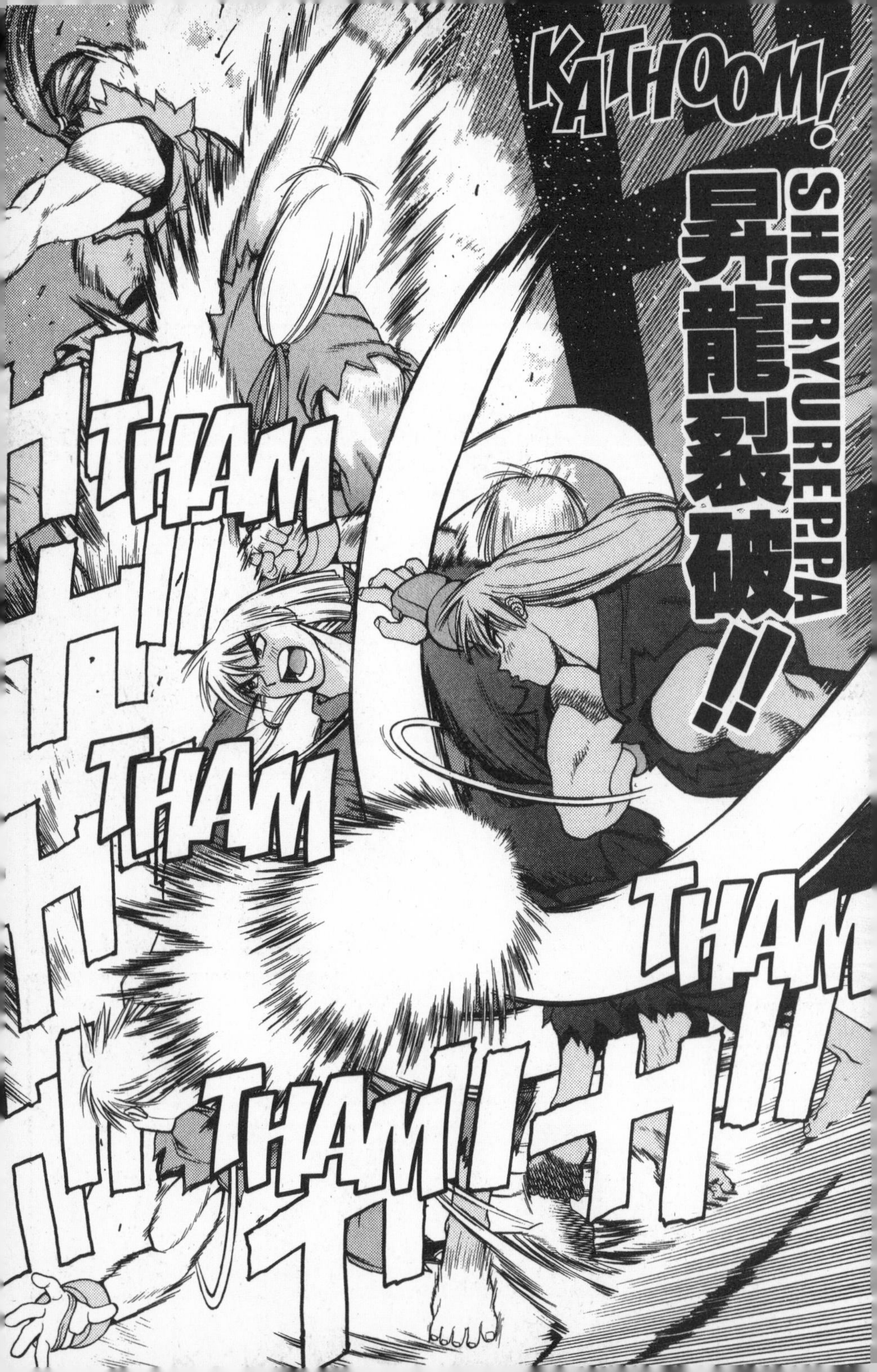

KATHOOM!
SHORYUREPPA
昇龍裂破!!
THAM
THAM
THAM
THAM

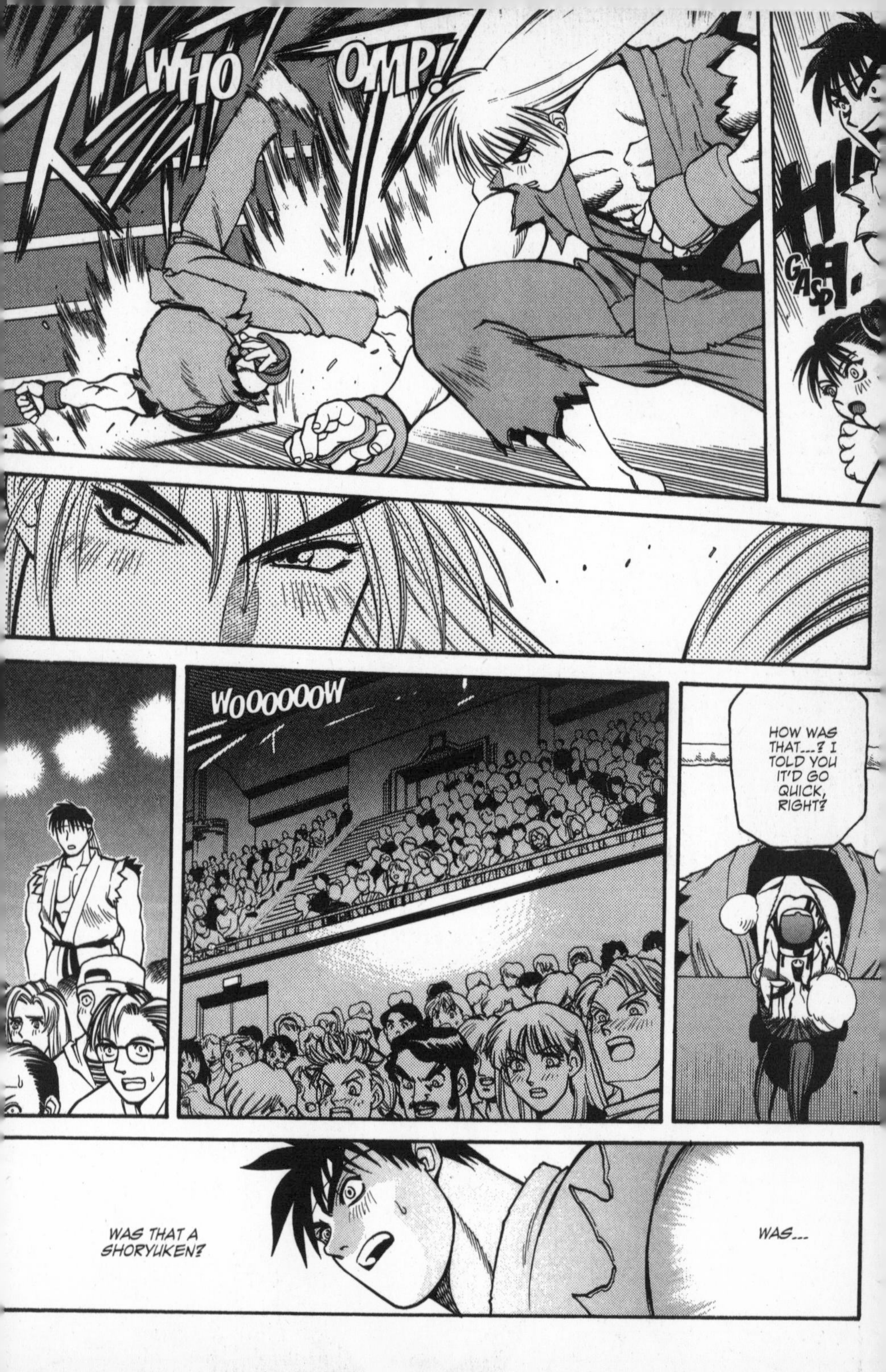
HA!!
GASP!
WHO OMP!
HOW WAS THAT...? I TOLD YOU IT'D GO QUICK, RIGHT?
WOOOOOOW
WAS...
WAS THAT A SHORYUKEN?

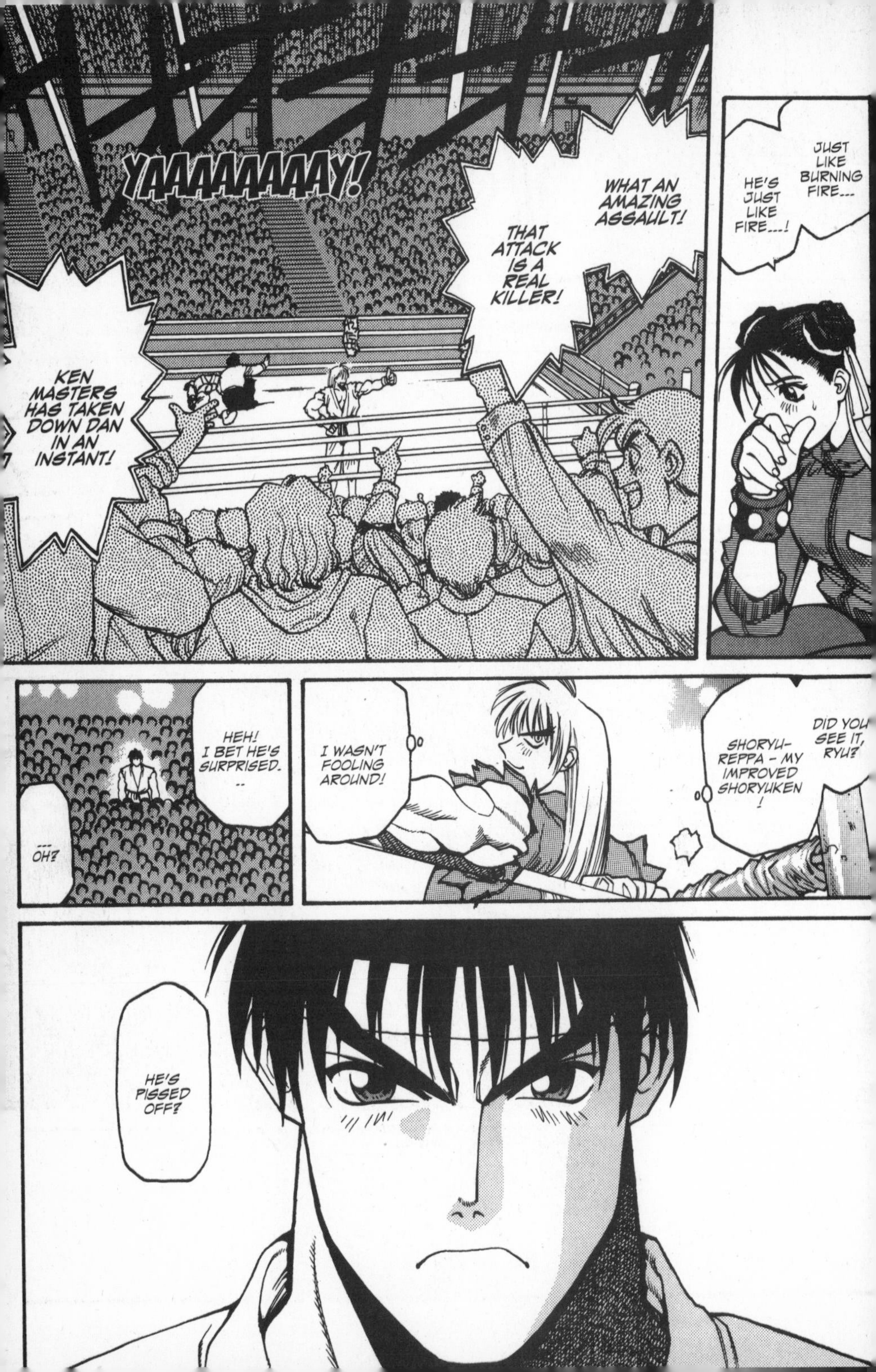
JUST LIKE BURNING FIRE...
HE'S JUST LIKE FIRE...!
WHAT AN AMAZING ASSAULT!
THAT ATTACK IS A REAL KILLER!
YAAAAAAAAY!
KEN MASTERS HAS TAKEN DOWN DAN IN AN INSTANT!
DID YOU SEE IT, RYU?
SHORYU-REPPA - MY IMPROVED SHORYUKEN!
I WASN'T FOOLING AROUND!
HEH! I BET HE'S SURPRISED...
...OH?
HE'S PISSED OFF?

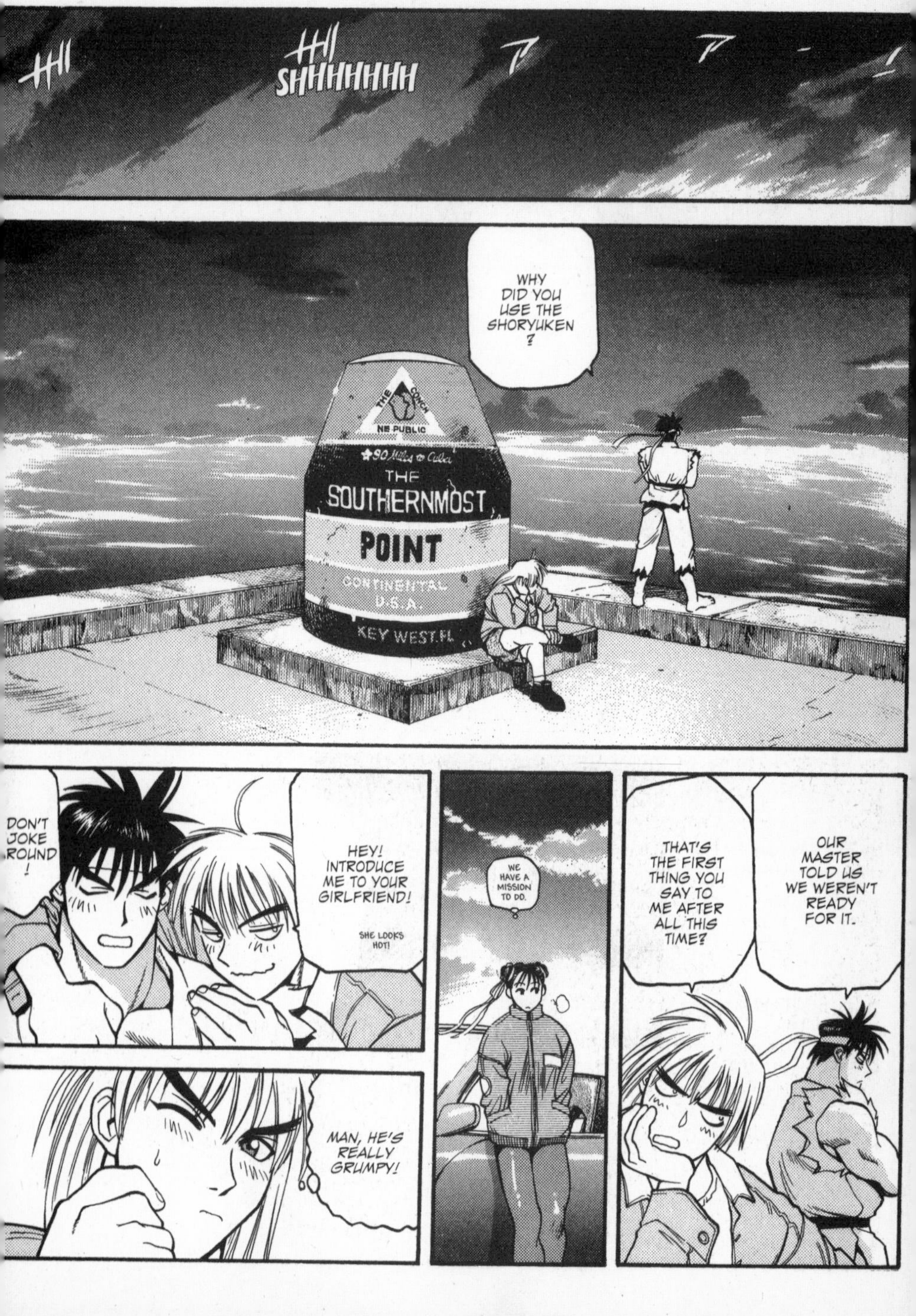
SHHHHHHH
WHY DID YOU USE THE SHORYUKEN?
90 Miles to Cuba
THE SOUTHERNMOST
POINT
CONTINENTAL U.S.A.
KEY WEST.FL
OUR MASTER TOLD US WE WEREN'T READY FOR IT.
THAT'S THE FIRST THING YOU SAY TO ME AFTER ALL THIS TIME?
WE HAVE A MISSION TO DO.
HEY! INTRODUCE ME TO YOUR GIRLFRIEND!
SHE LOOKS HOT!
DON'T JOKE ROUND!
MAN, HE'S REALLY GRUMPY!

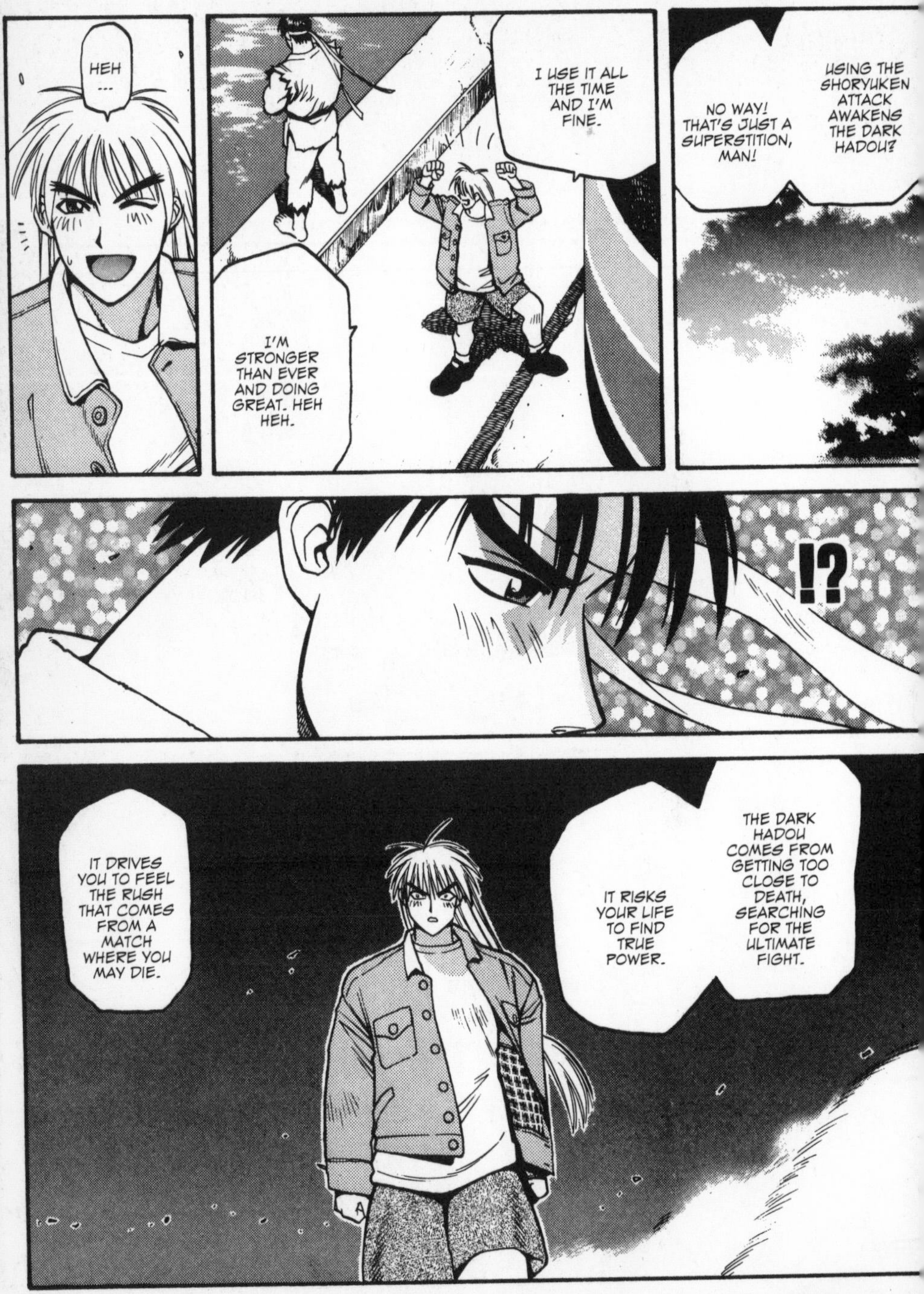
USING THE SHORYUKEN ATTACK AWAKENS THE DARK HADOU?
NO WAY! THAT'S JUST A SUPERSTITION, MAN!
I USE IT ALL THE TIME AND I'M FINE.
I'M STRONGER THAN EVER AND DOING GREAT. HEH HEH.
HEH ...
!?
THE DARK HADOU COMES FROM GETTING TOO CLOSE TO DEATH, SEARCHING FOR THE ULTIMATE FIGHT.
IT RISKS YOUR LIFE TO FIND TRUE POWER.
IT DRIVES YOU TO FEEL THE RUSH THAT COMES FROM A MATCH WHERE YOU MAY DIE.

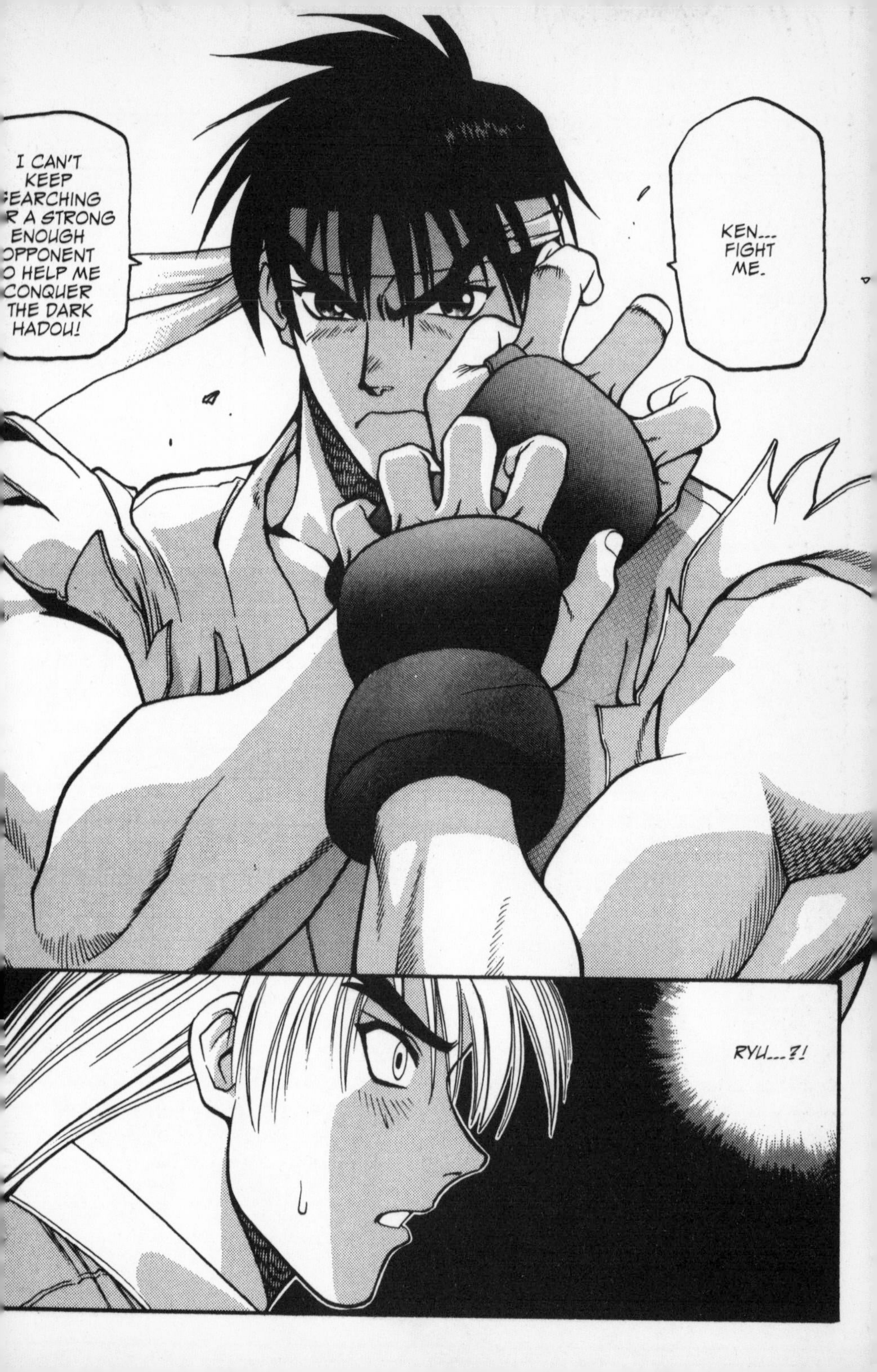
KEN... FIGHT ME.
I CAN'T KEEP EARCHING R A STRONG ENOUGH OPPONENT O HELP ME CONQUER THE DARK HADOU!
RYU...?!

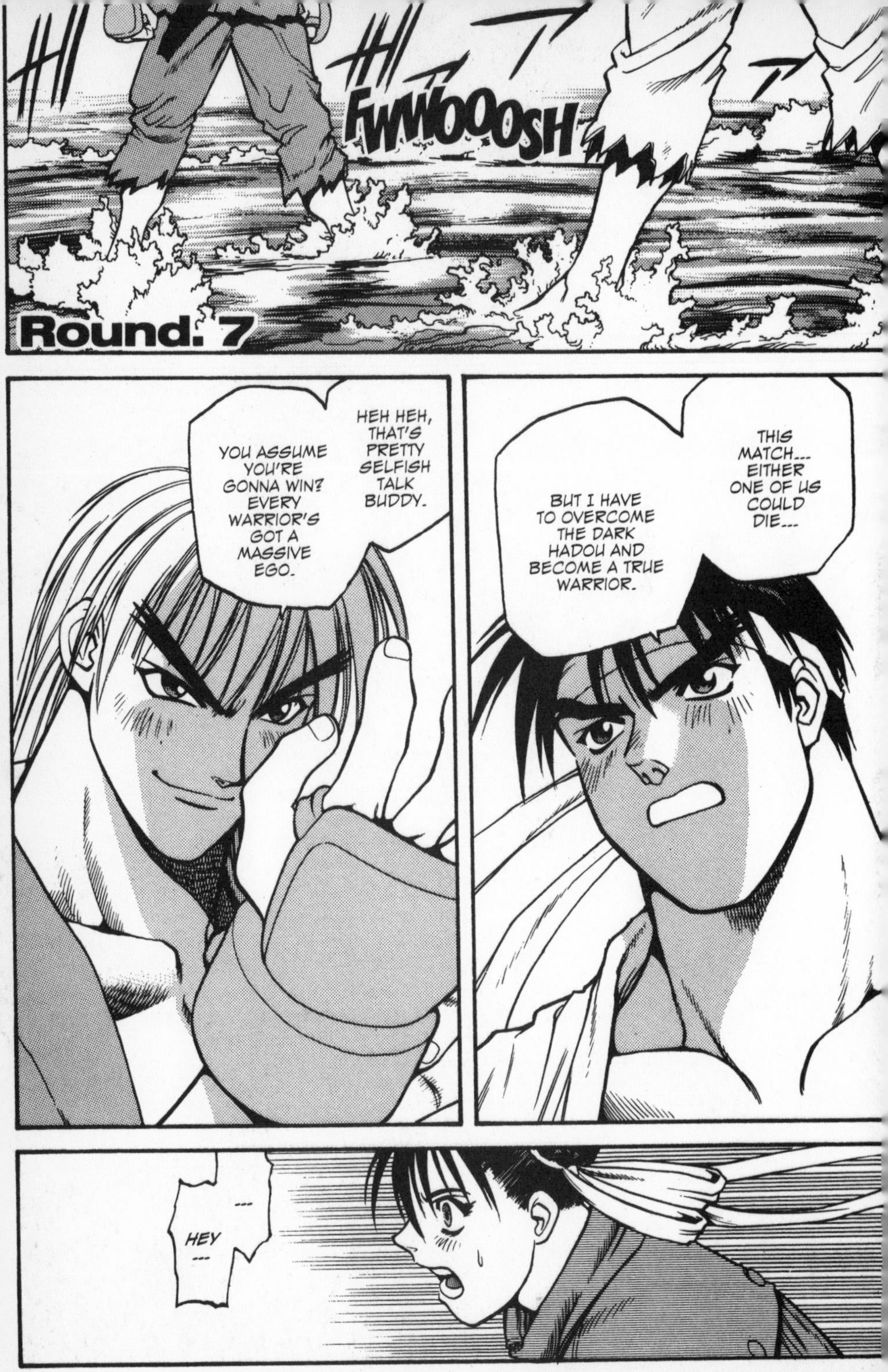
FWWOOOSH
Round. 7
THIS MATCH... EITHER ONE OF US COULD DIE...
BUT I HAVE TO OVERCOME THE DARK HADOU AND BECOME A TRUE WARRIOR.
HEH HEH, THAT'S PRETTY SELFISH TALK BUDDY.
YOU ASSUME YOU'RE GONNA WIN? EVERY WARRIOR'S GOT A MASSIVE EGO.
... HEY ...

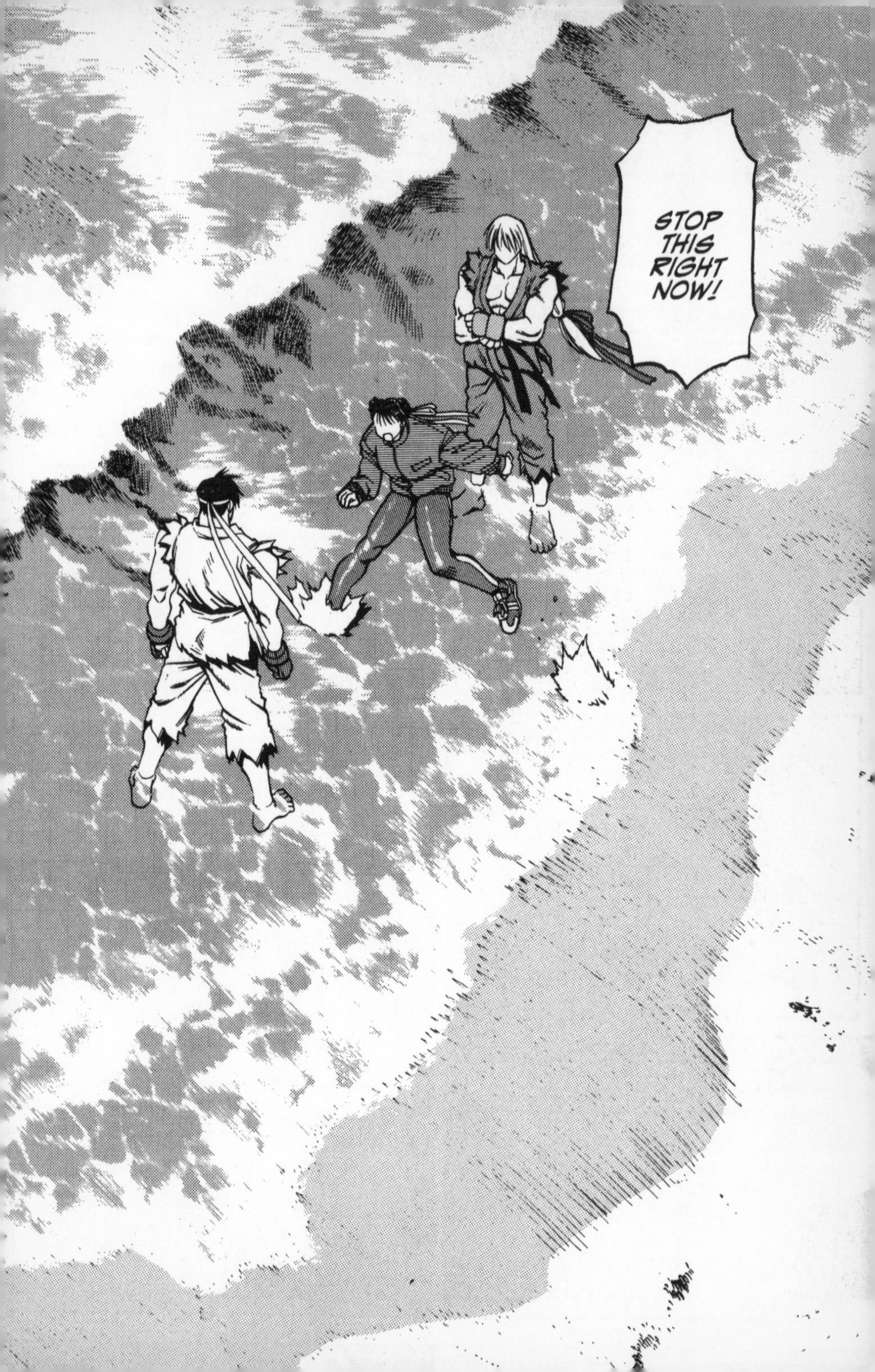
STOP THIS RIGHT NOW!

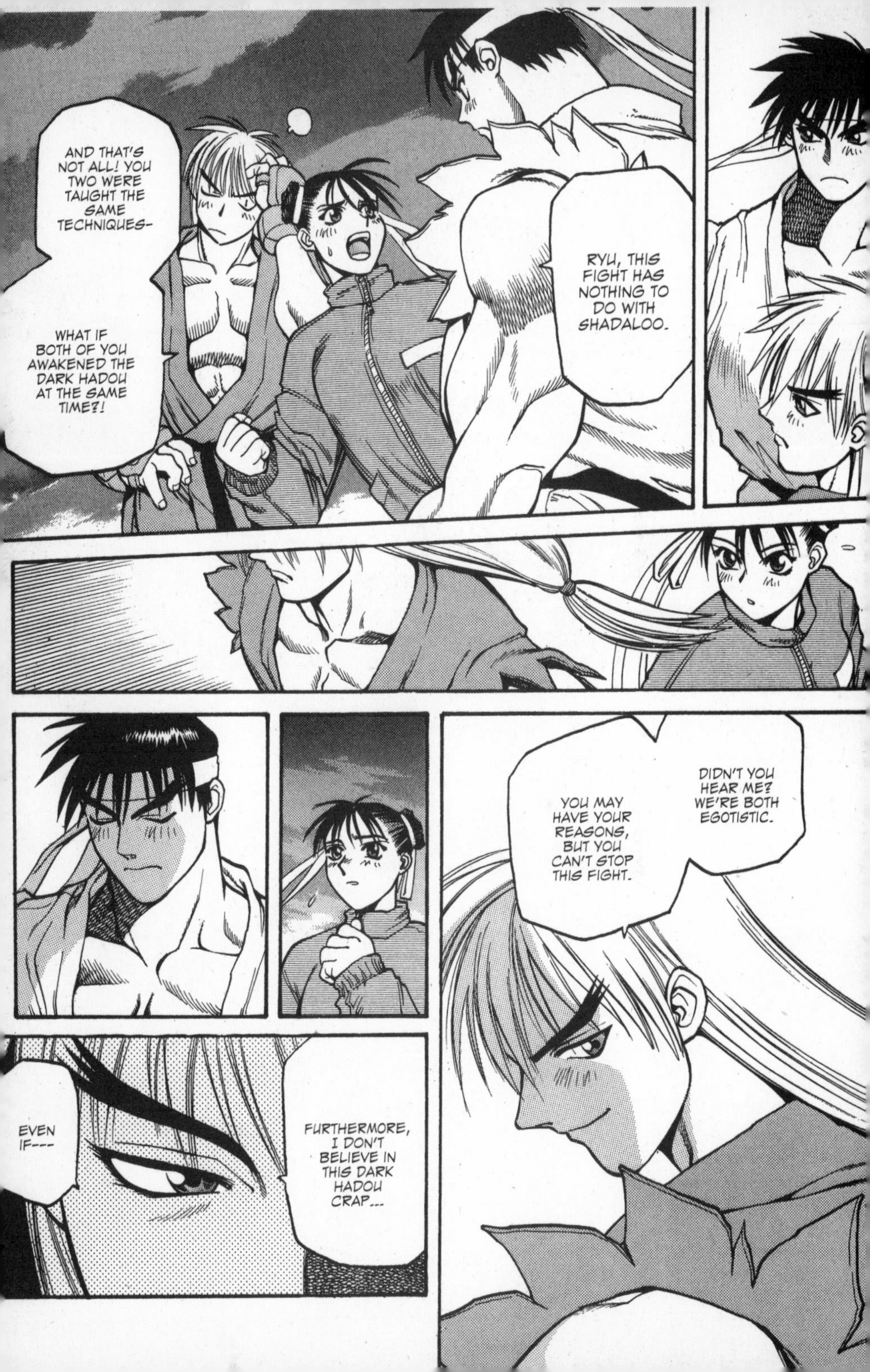
AND THAT'S NOT ALL! YOU TWO WERE TAUGHT THE SAME TECHNIQUES-
WHAT IF BOTH OF YOU AWAKENED THE DARK HADOU AT THE SAME TIME?!
RYU, THIS FIGHT HAS NOTHING TO DO WITH SHADALOO.
DIDN'T YOU HEAR ME? WE'RE BOTH EGOTISTIC.
YOU MAY HAVE YOUR REASONS, BUT YOU CAN'T STOP THIS FIGHT.
FURTHERMORE, I DON'T BELIEVE IN THIS DARK HADOU CRAP---
EVEN IF---

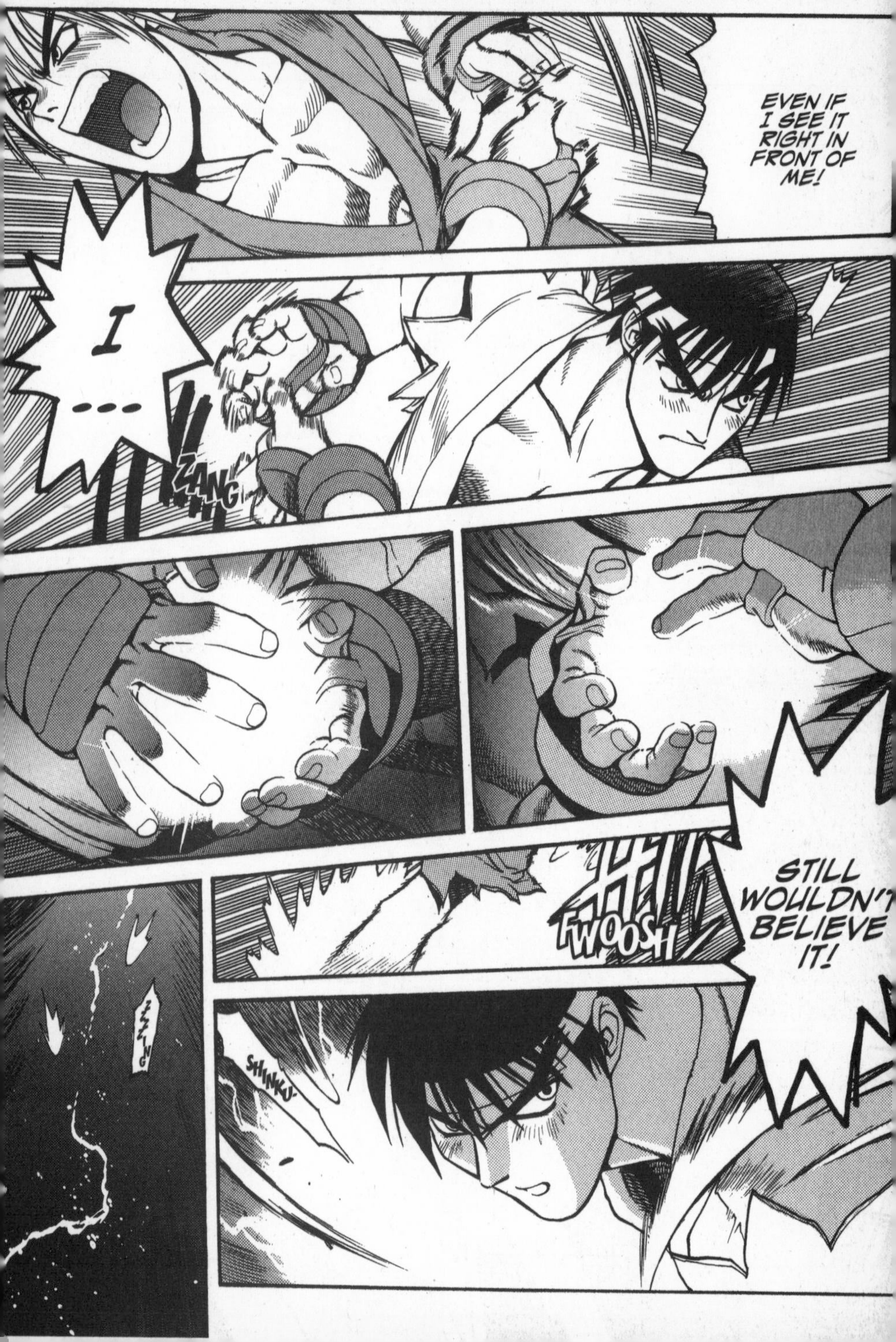
EVEN IF I SEE IT RIGHT IN FRONT OF ME!
I ...
ZANG
STILL WOULDN'T BELIEVE IT!
FWOOSH
SHINKU-
ZZZING

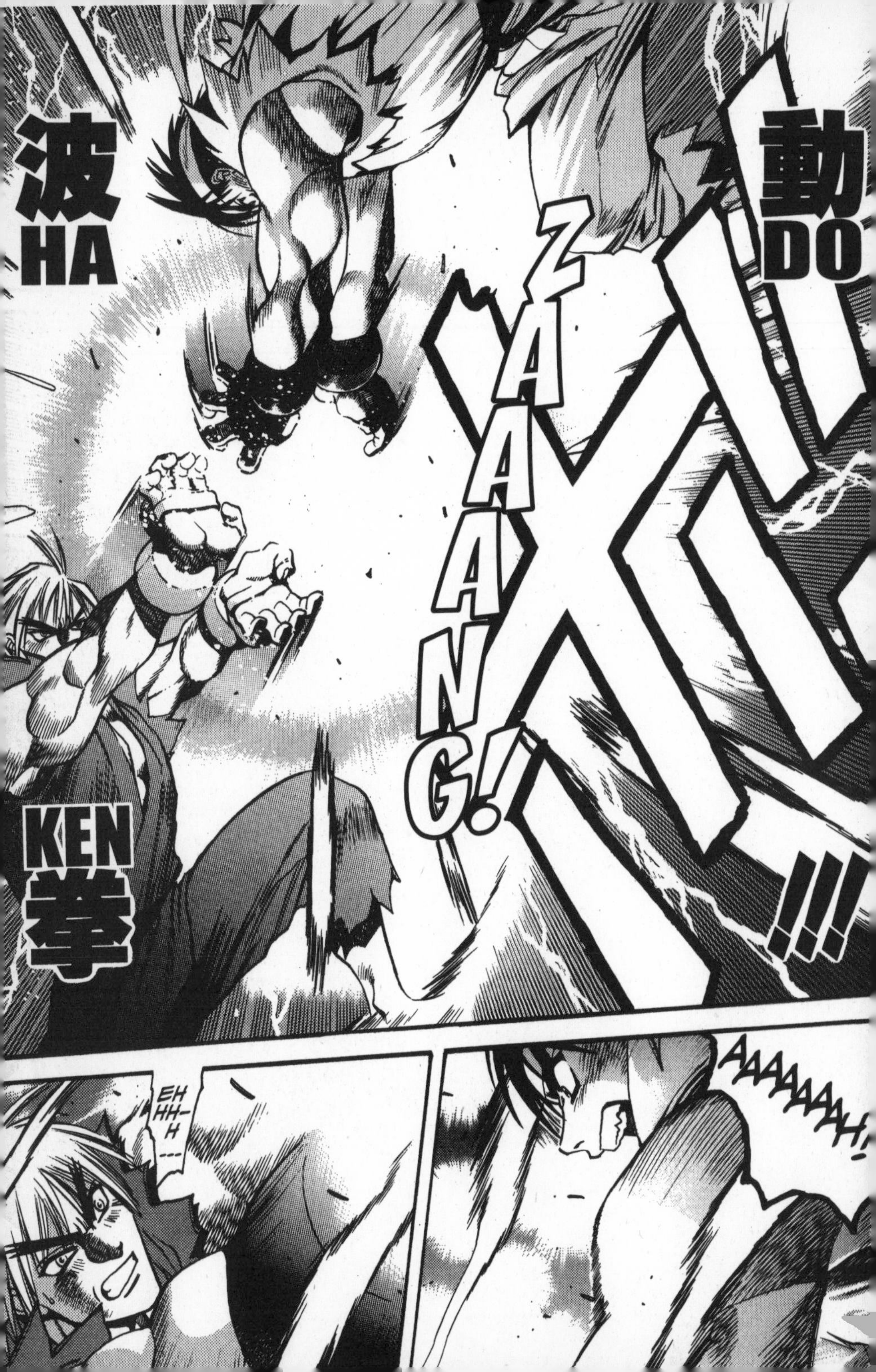

動 DO
ZAAAANG!
!!!
波 HA
KEN 拳
AAAAAAAH!
EHHH-H---

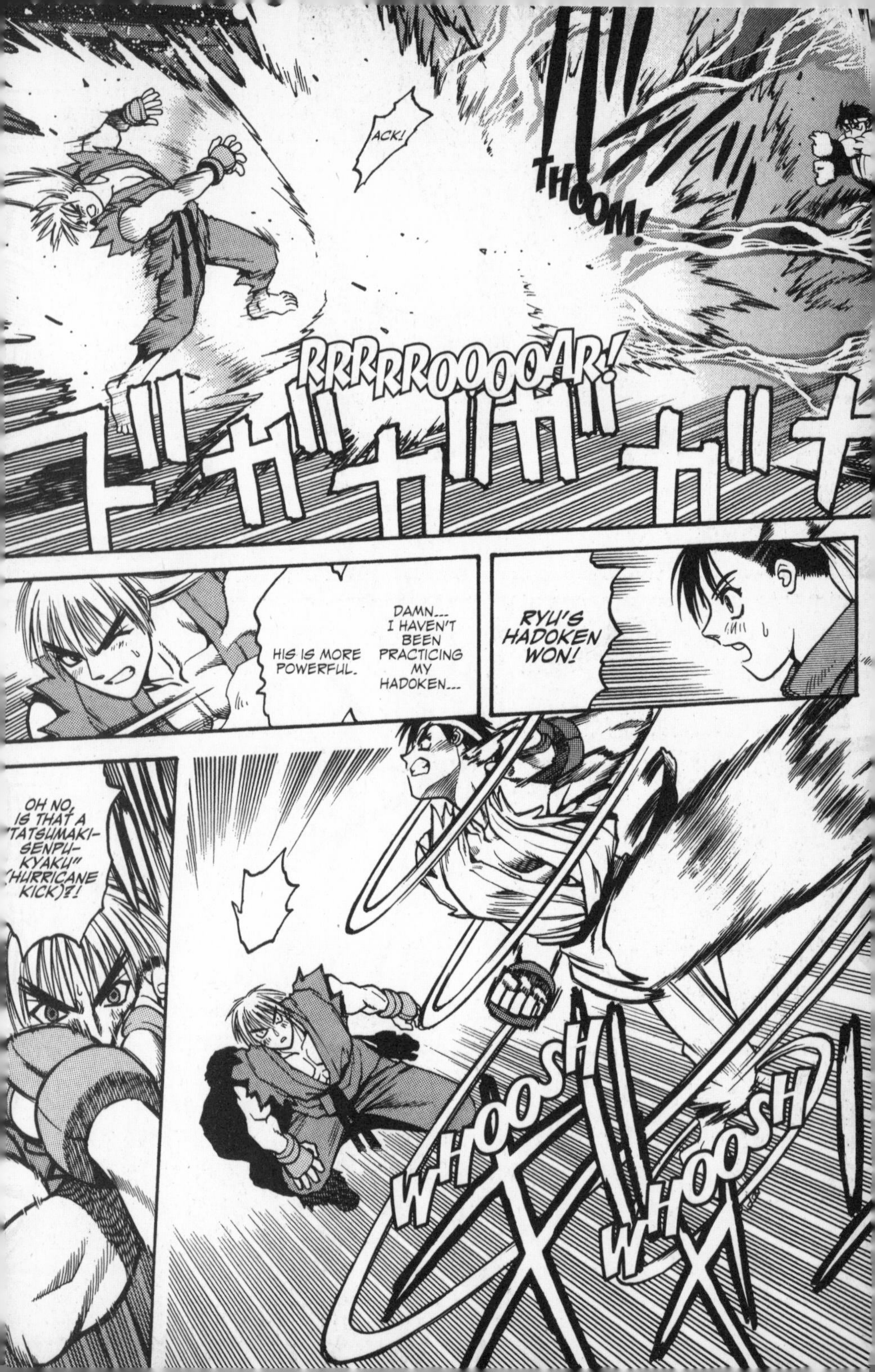
THOOM!
ACK!
RRRRROOOOOAR!
RYU'S HADOKEN WON!
DAMN... I HAVEN'T BEEN PRACTICING MY HADOKEN...
HIS IS MORE POWERFUL.
WHOOSH
WHOOSH
OH NO, IS THAT A "TATSUMAKI-SENPU-KYAKU" (HURRICANE KICK)?!

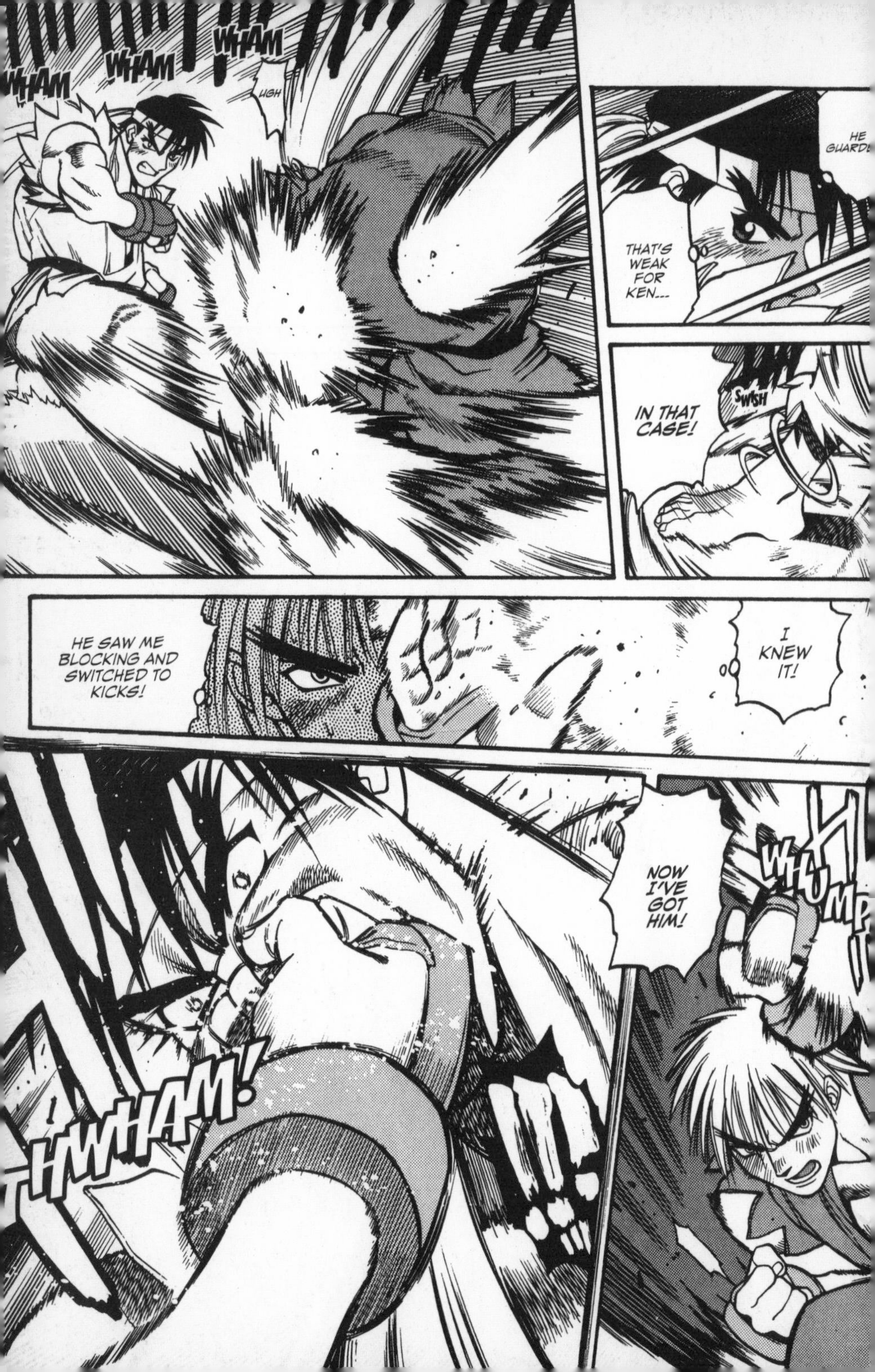
HE GUARDE
THAT'S WEAK FOR KEN...
SWISH
IN THAT CASE!
WHAM
WHAM
WHAM
UGH
I KNEW IT!
HE SAW ME BLOCKING AND SWITCHED TO KICKS!
WHUMP!
NOW I'VE GOT HIM!
THWHAM!

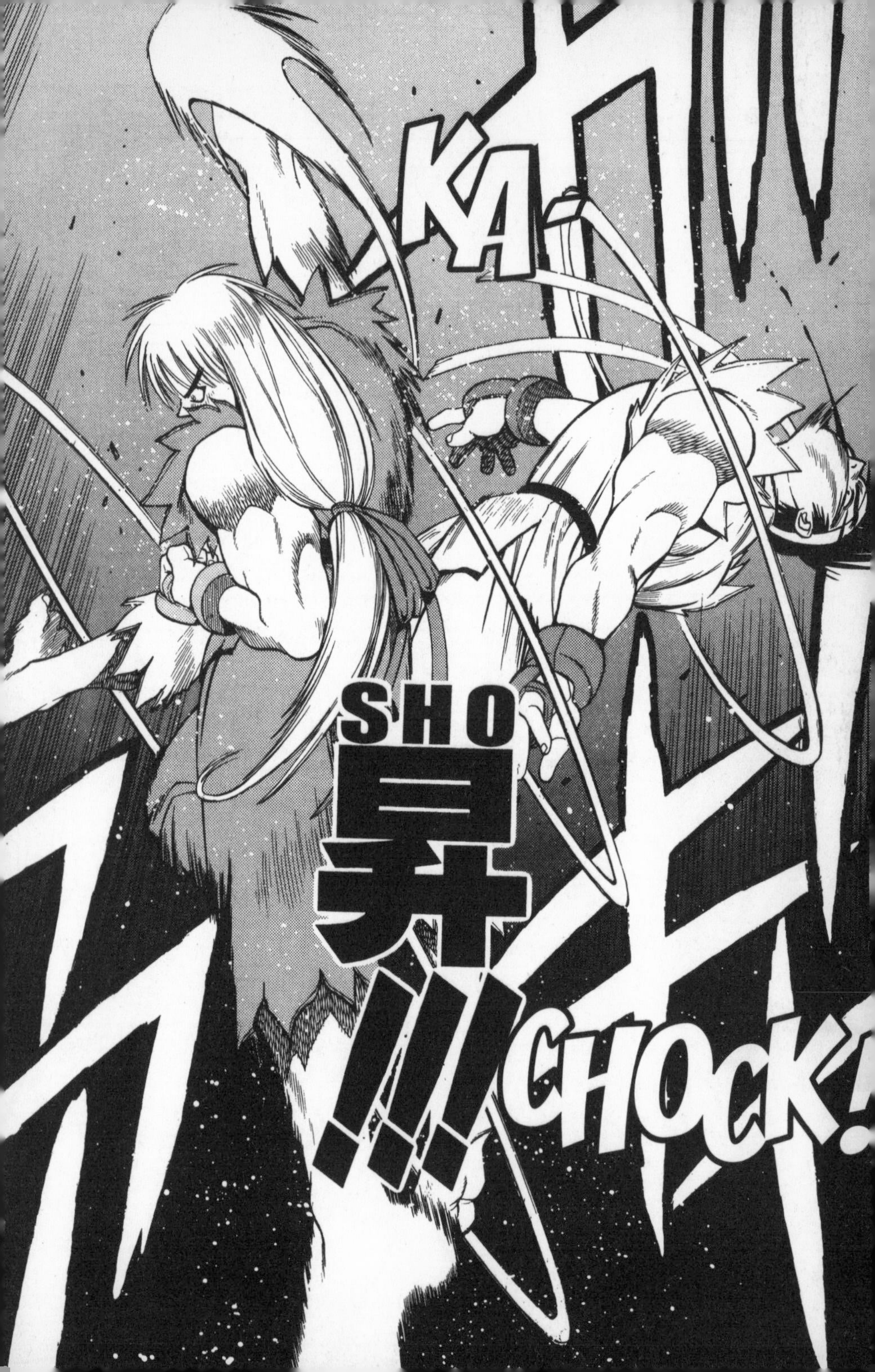
KA-
SHO
昇!!!
CHOCK!

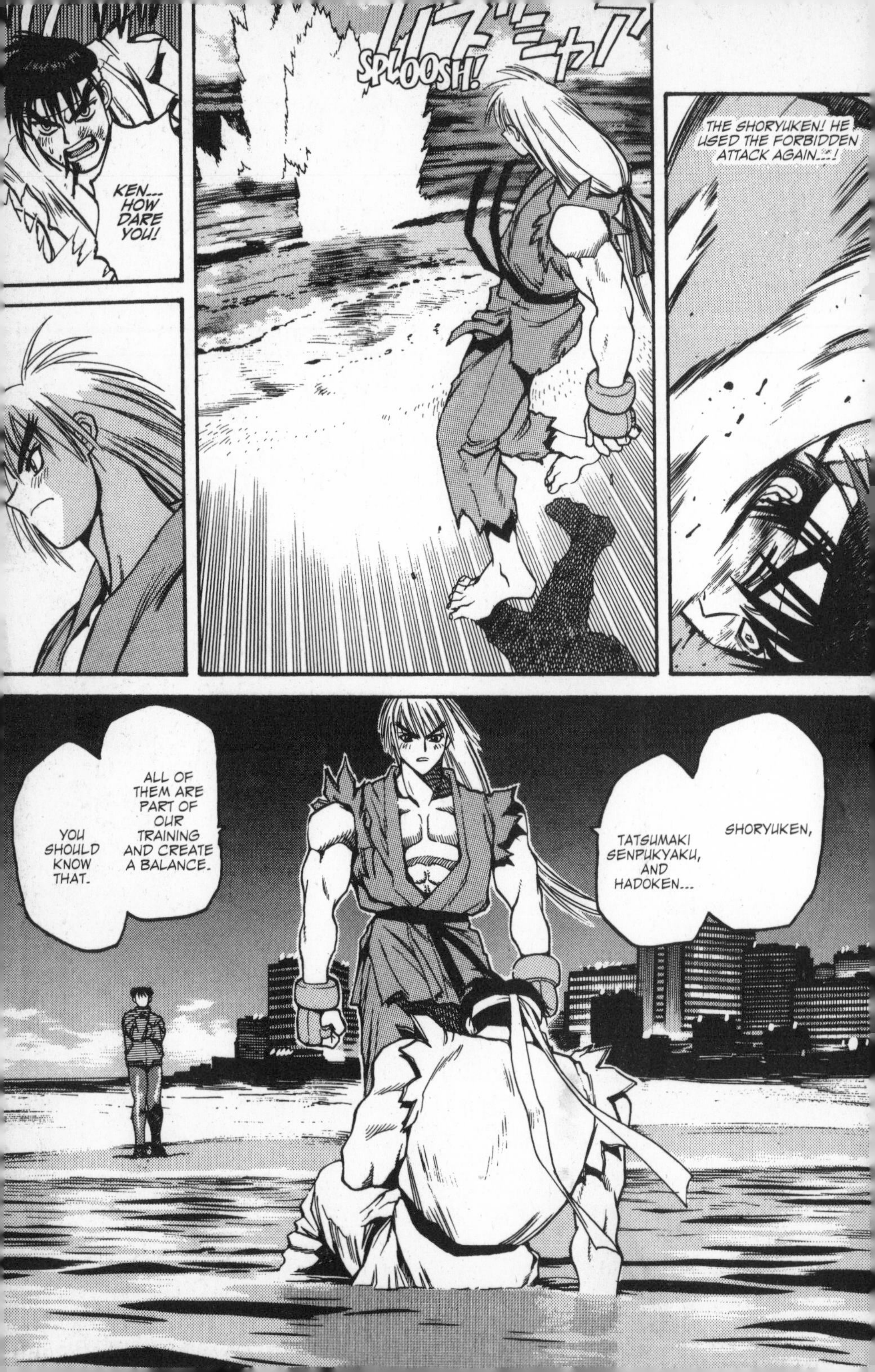
THE SHORYUKEN! HE USED THE FORBIDDEN ATTACK AGAIN...!
SPLOOSH!
KEN... HOW DARE YOU!
SHORYUKEN,
TATSUMAKI SENPUKYAKU, AND HADOKEN...
ALL OF THEM ARE PART OF OUR TRAINING AND CREATE A BALANCE.
YOU SHOULD KNOW THAT.

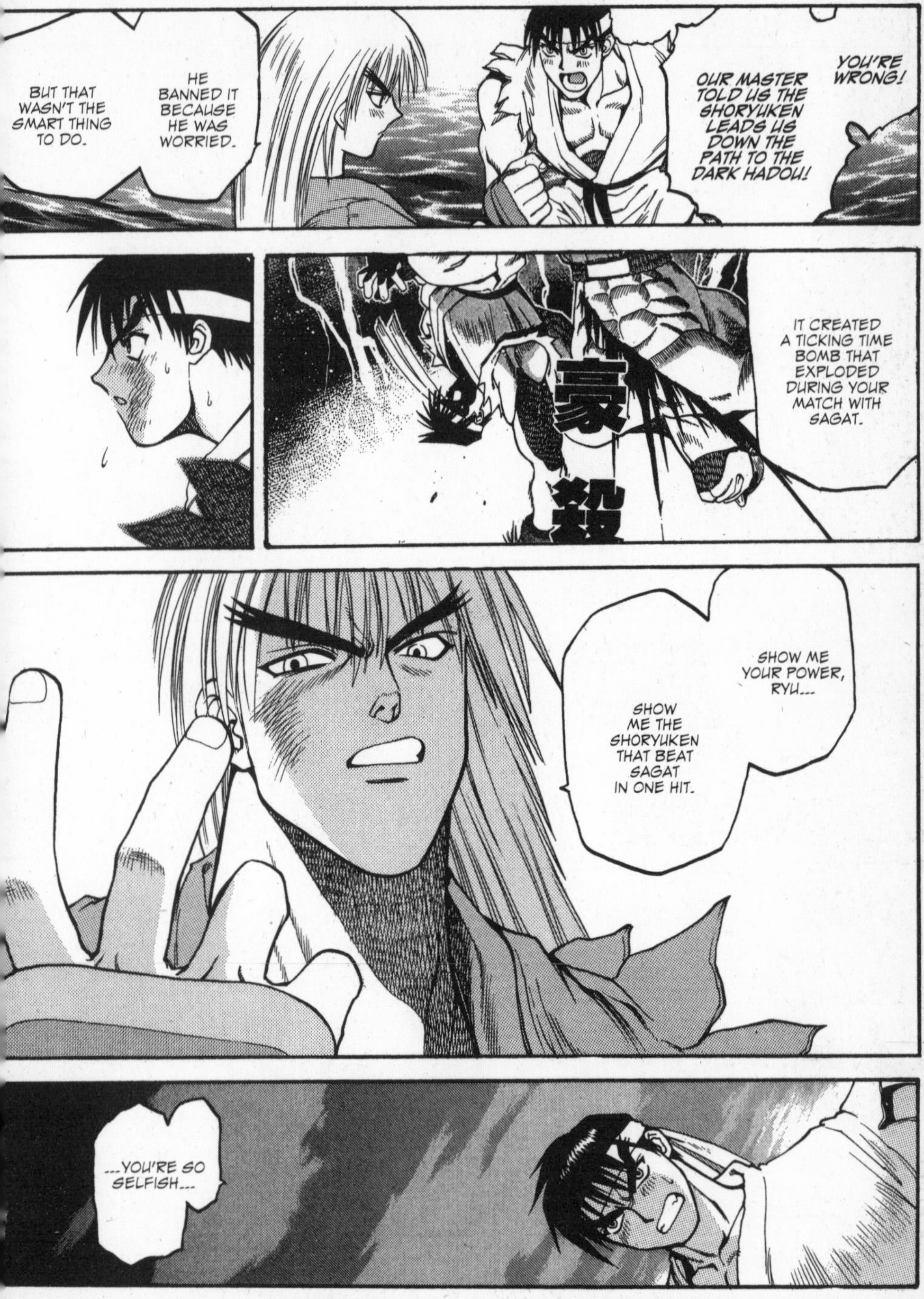
YOU'RE WRONG!
OUR MASTER TOLD US THE SHORYUKEN LEADS US DOWN THE PATH TO THE DARK HADOU!
HE BANNED IT BECAUSE HE WAS WORRIED.
BUT THAT WASN'T THE SMART THING TO DO.
IT CREATED A TICKING TIME BOMB THAT EXPLODED DURING YOUR MATCH WITH SAGAT.
豪殺
SHOW ME YOUR POWER, RYU...
SHOW ME THE SHORYUKEN THAT BEAT SAGAT IN ONE HIT.
...YOU'RE SO SELFISH...

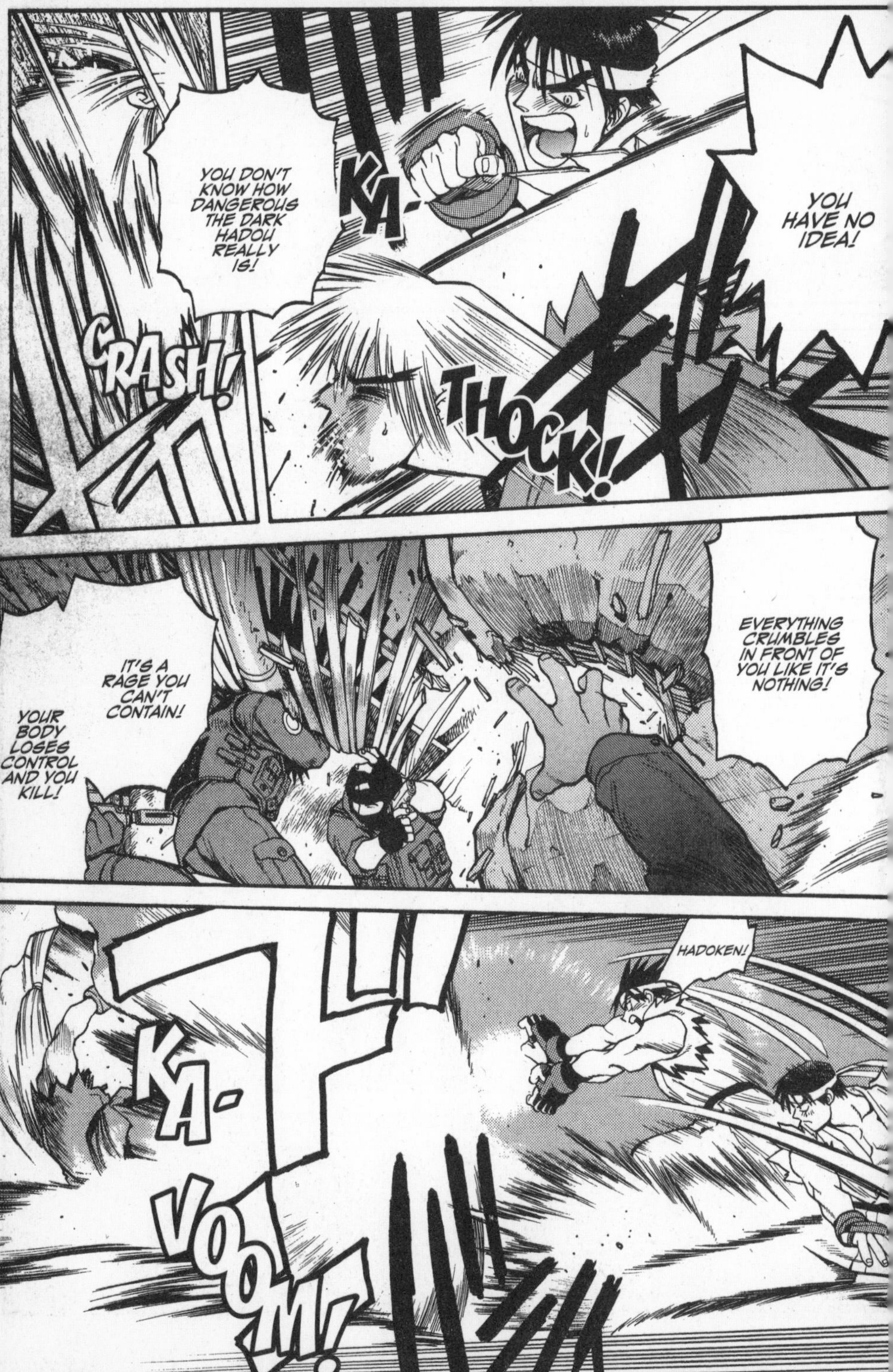
YOU HAVE NO IDEA!
KA-
YOU DON'T KNOW HOW DANGEROUS THE DARK HADOU REALLY IS!
THOCK!
CRASH!
EVERYTHING CRUMBLES IN FRONT OF YOU LIKE IT'S NOTHING!
IT'S A RAGE YOU CAN'T CONTAIN!
YOUR BODY LOSES CONTROL AND YOU KILL!
HADOKEN!
KA-
VOOM!

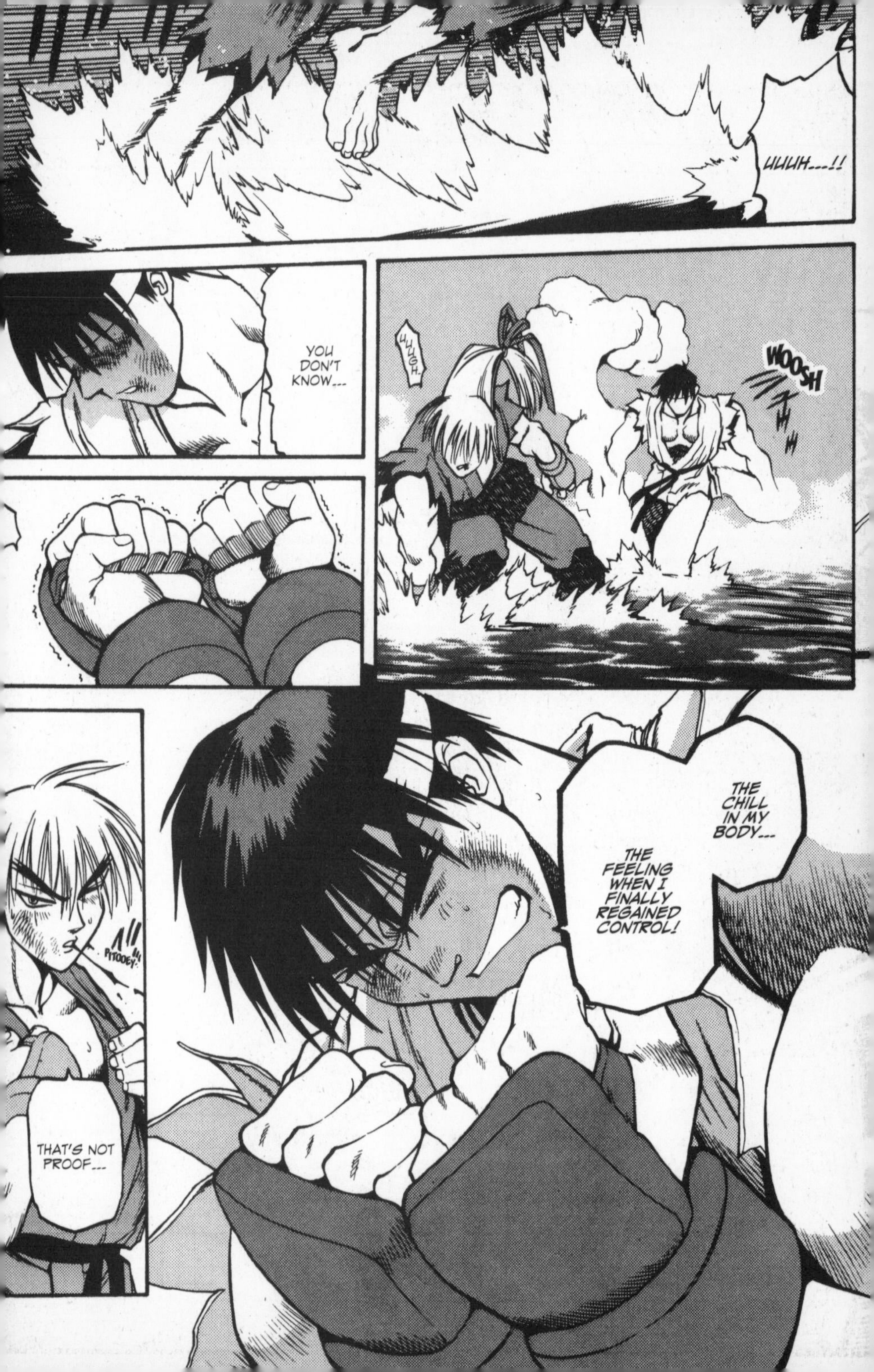
UUUH...!!
UUUGH...
WOOSH
YOU DON'T KNOW...
THE CHILL IN MY BODY...
THE FEELING WHEN I FINALLY REGAINED CONTROL!
PITOOEY
THAT'S NOT PROOF...

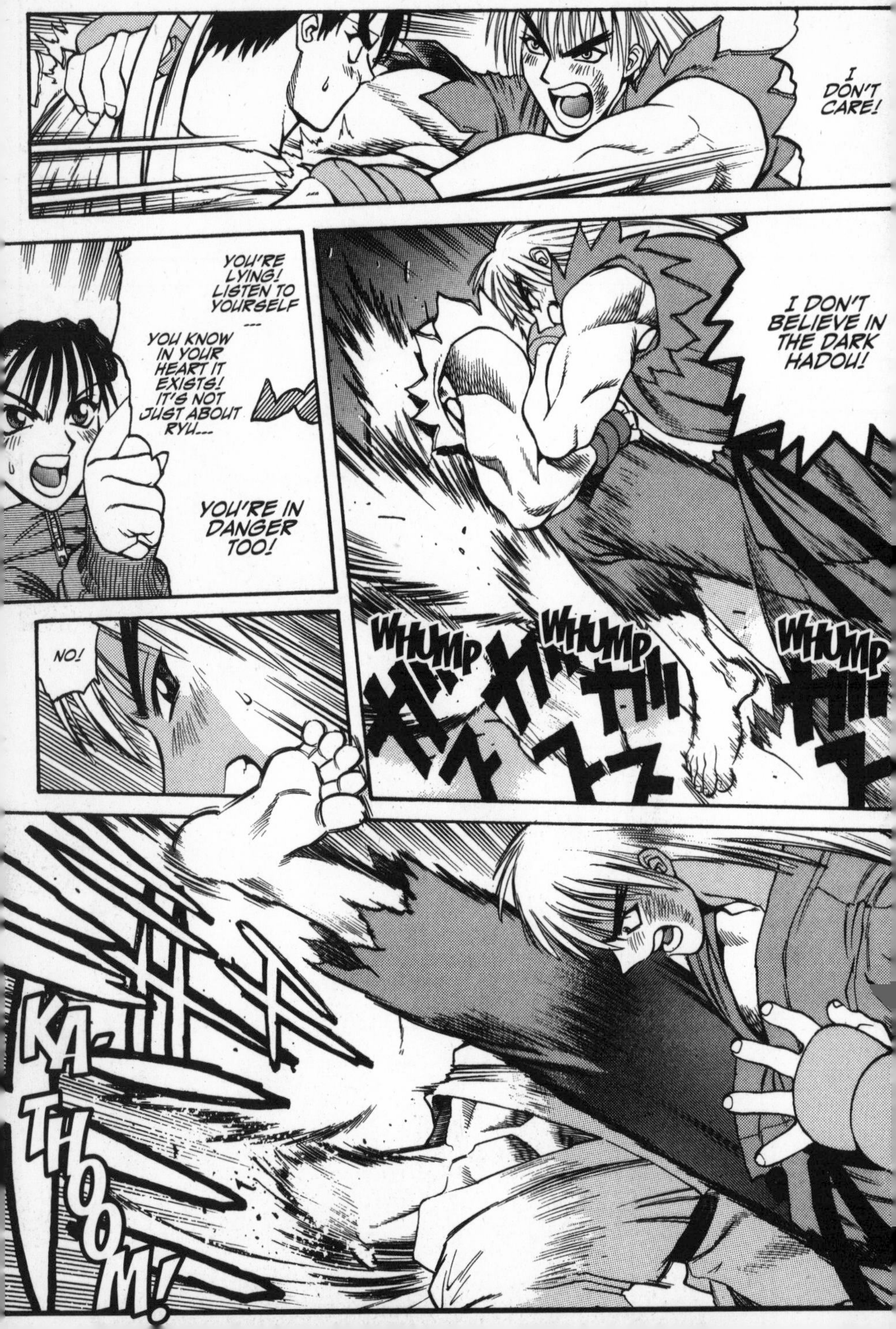
I DON'T CARE!
I DON'T BELIEVE IN THE DARK HADOU!
WHUMP
WHUMP
WHUMP
YOU'RE LYING! LISTEN TO YOURSELF ---
YOU KNOW IN YOUR HEART IT EXISTS! IT'S NOT JUST ABOUT RYU...
YOU'RE IN DANGER TOO!
NO!
KA-THOOM!

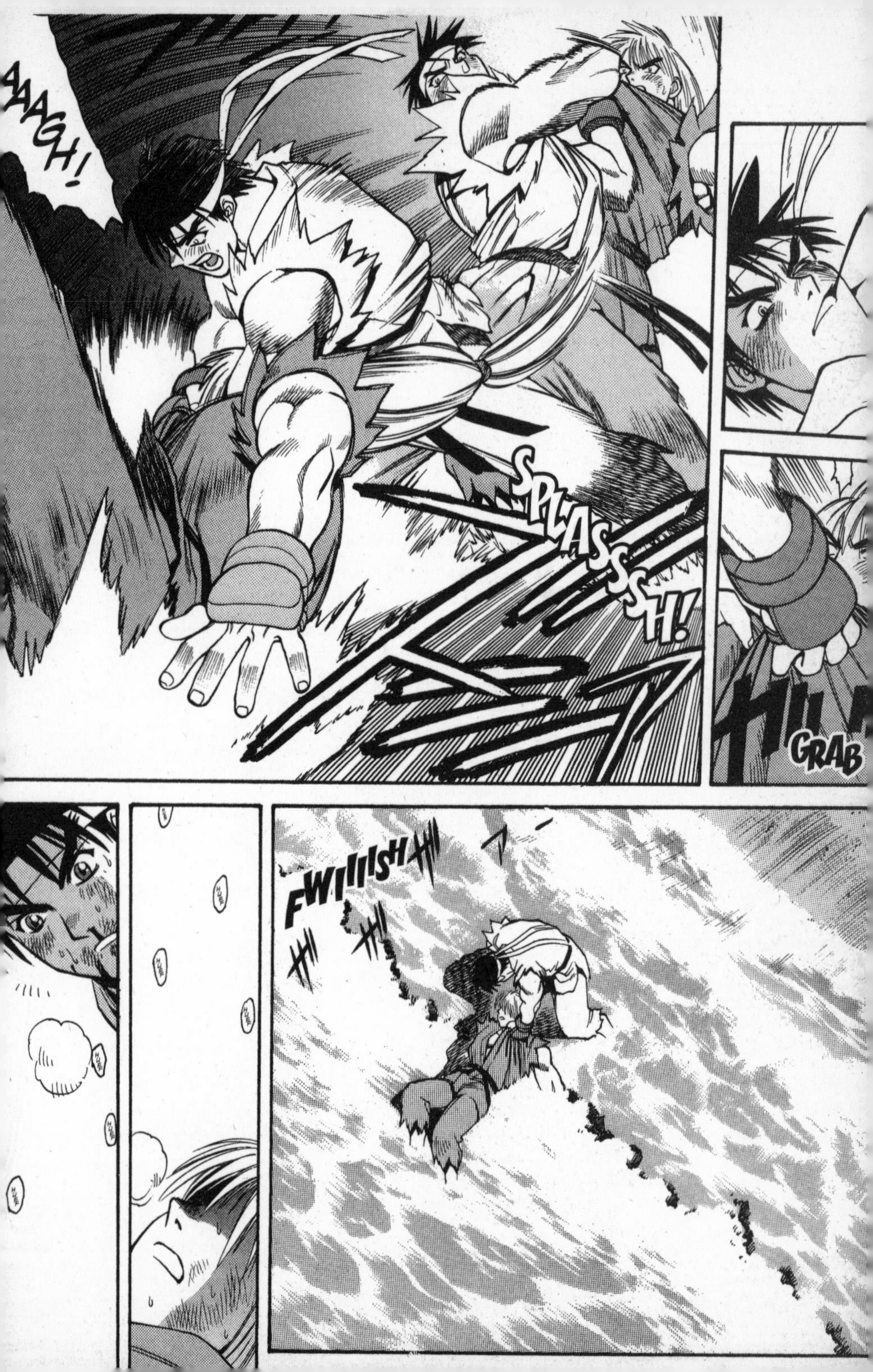
GRAB
AAAGH!
SPLASSSH!
FWIIIISH

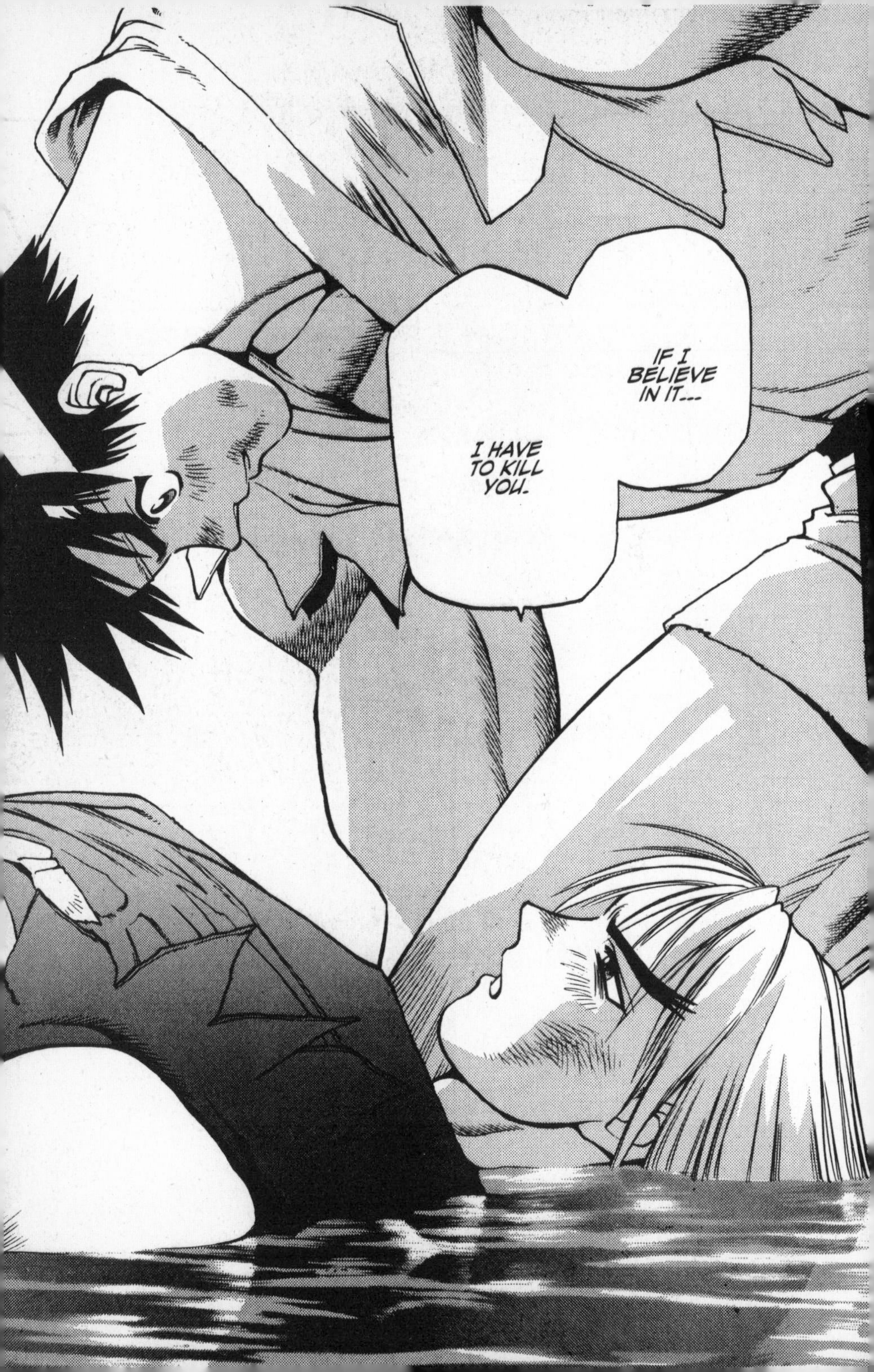
IF I BELIEVE IN IT...
I HAVE TO KILL YOU.

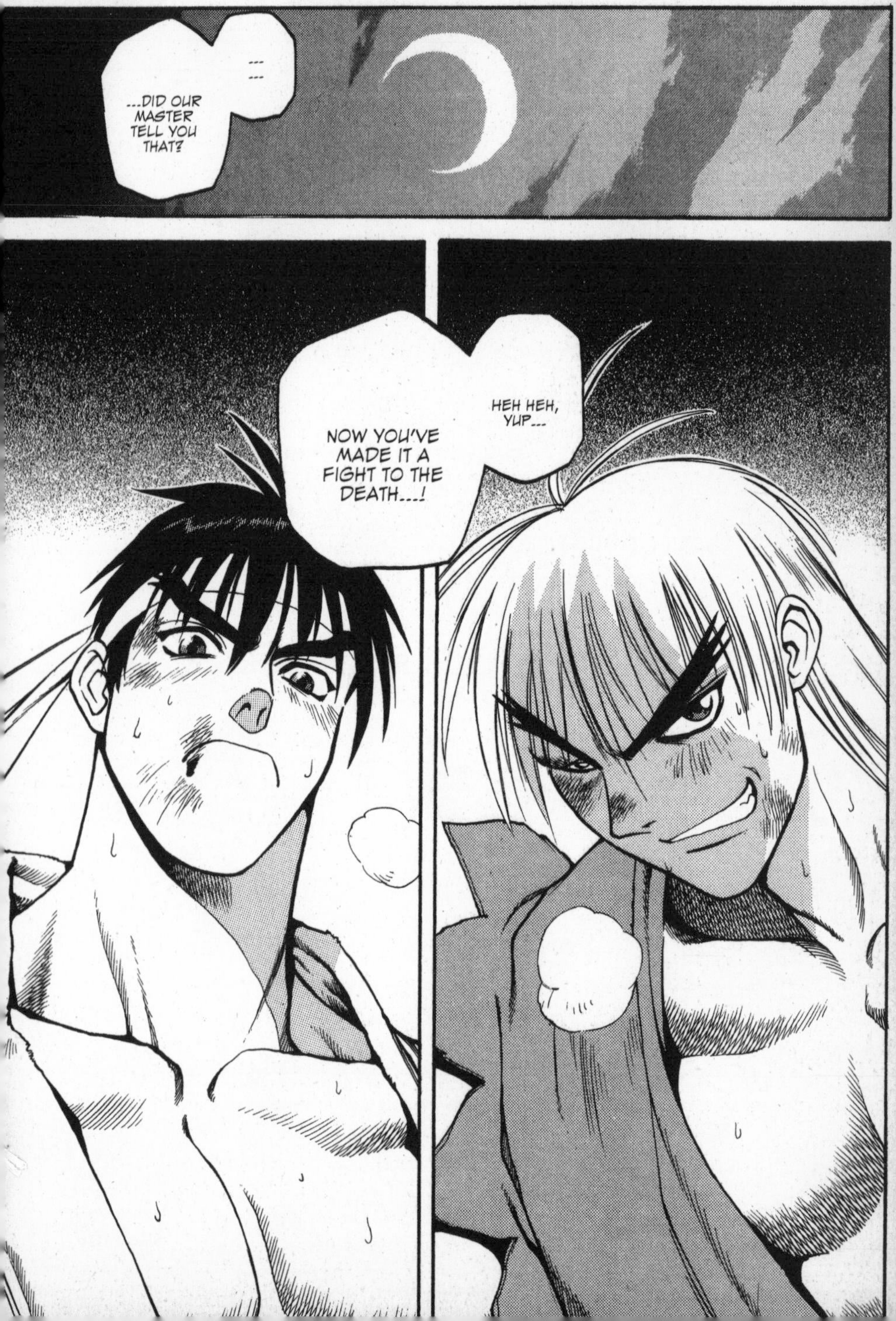
...
...
...DID OUR MASTER TELL YOU THAT?
HEH HEH, YUP...
NOW YOU'VE MADE IT A FIGHT TO THE DEATH...!

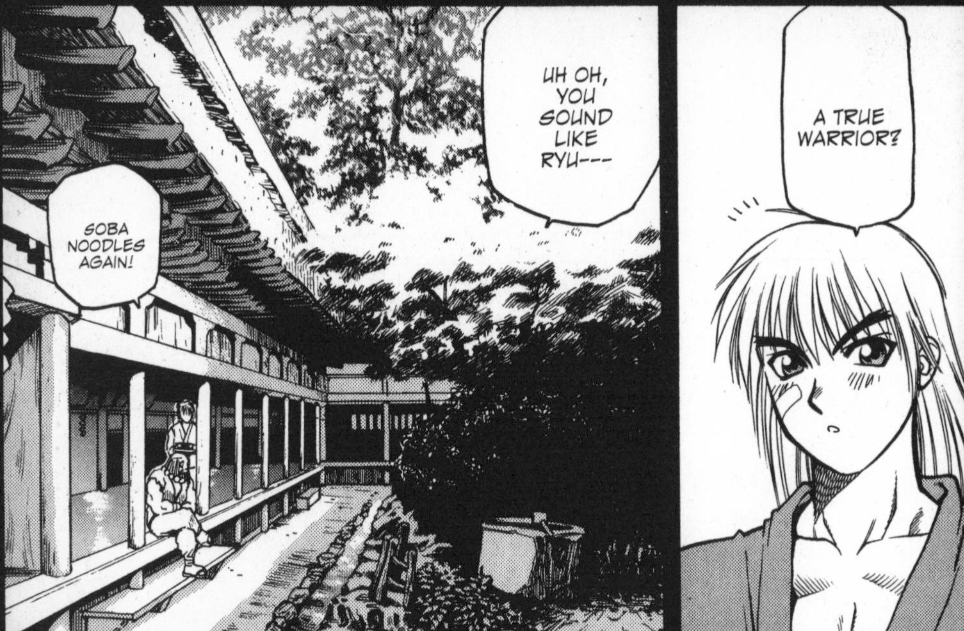
A TRUE WARRIOR?
UH OH, YOU SOUND LIKE RYU---
SOBA NOODLES AGAIN!
IT'S POMODORI SAUCE, ACTUALLY ---
SPAGHETTI, MASTER.

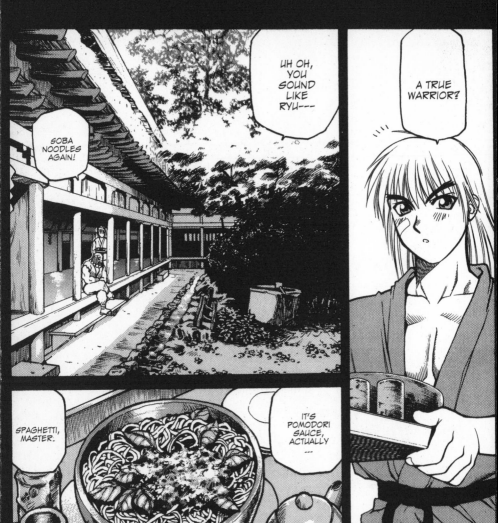

Round. 8

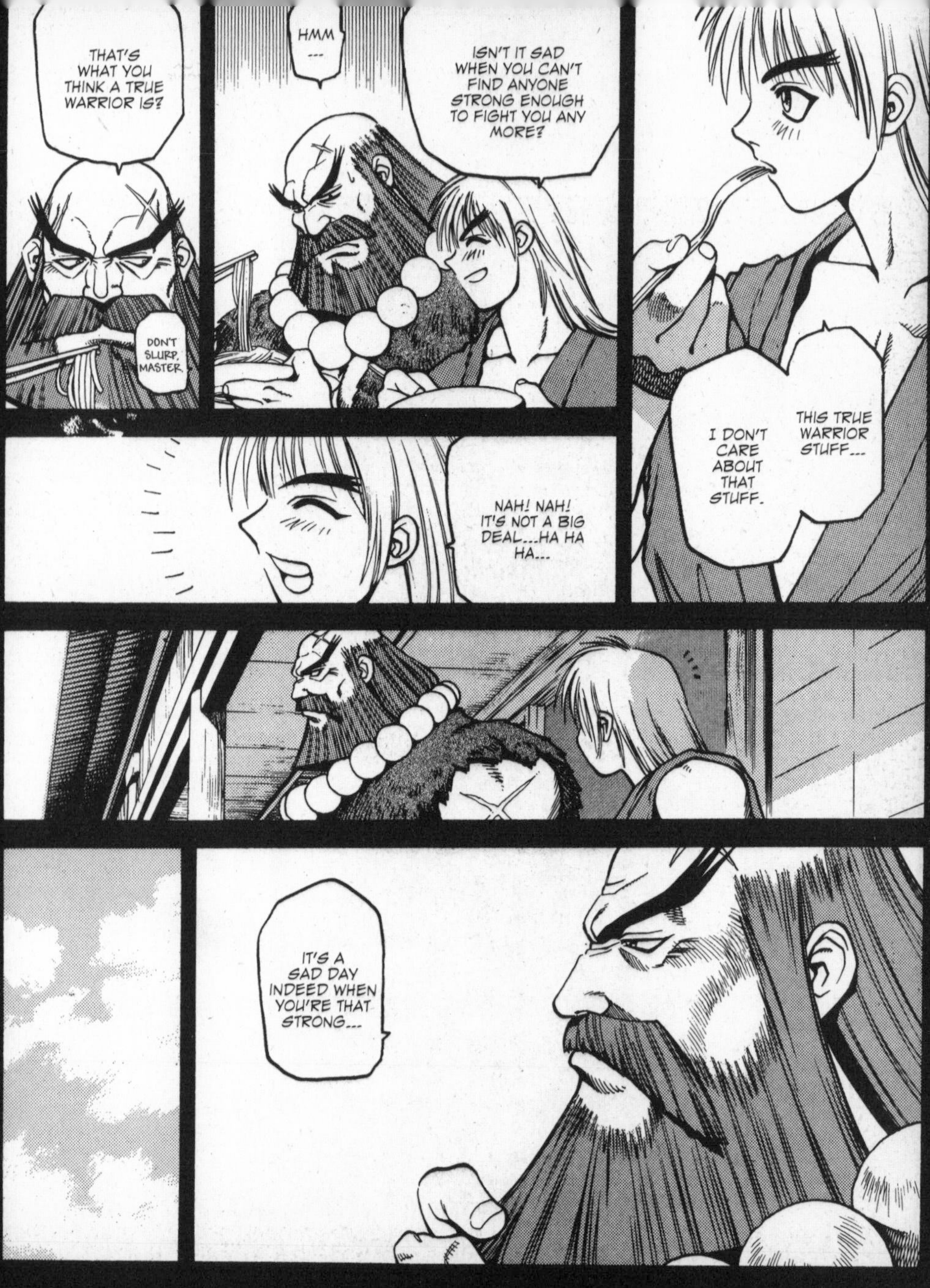
THIS TRUE WARRIOR STUFF...
I DON'T CARE ABOUT THAT STUFF.
ISN'T IT SAD WHEN YOU CAN'T FIND ANYONE STRONG ENOUGH TO FIGHT YOU ANY MORE?
HMM...
THAT'S WHAT YOU THINK A TRUE WARRIOR IS?
DON'T SLURP, MASTER.
NAH! NAH! IT'S NOT A BIG DEAL...HA HA HA...
IT'S A SAD DAY INDEED WHEN YOU'RE THAT STRONG...

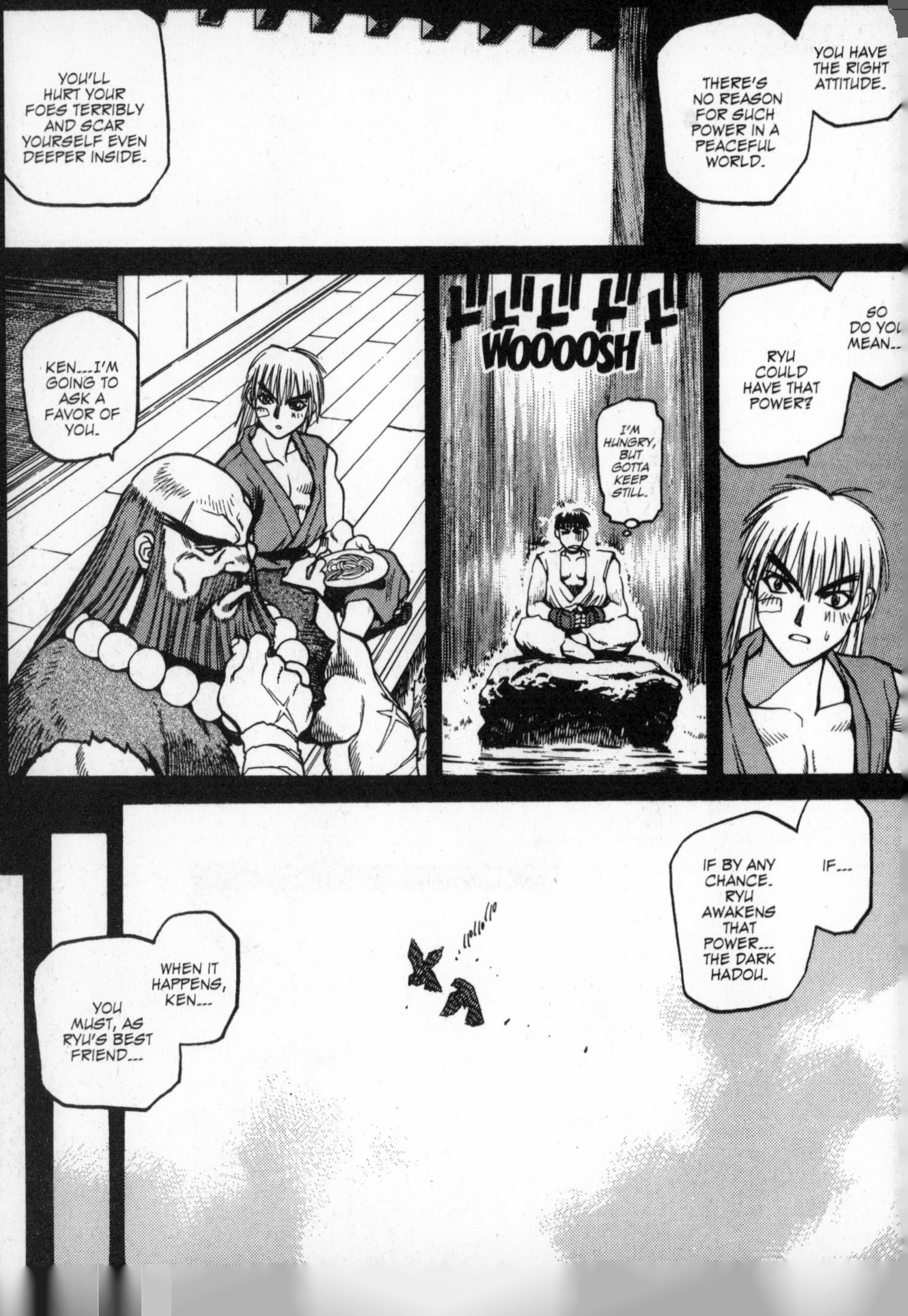
YOU HAVE THE RIGHT ATTITUDE.
THERE'S NO REASON FOR SUCH POWER IN A PEACEFUL WORLD.
YOU'LL HURT YOUR FOES TERRIBLY AND SCAR YOURSELF EVEN DEEPER INSIDE.
SO DO YOU MEAN...
RYU COULD HAVE THAT POWER?
WOOOOSH
I'M HUNGRY, BUT GOTTA KEEP STILL.
KEN...I'M GOING TO ASK A FAVOR OF YOU.
IF...
IF BY ANY CHANCE, RYU AWAKENS THAT POWER... THE DARK HADOU.
WHEN IT HAPPENS, KEN...
YOU MUST, AS RYU'S BEST FRIEND...

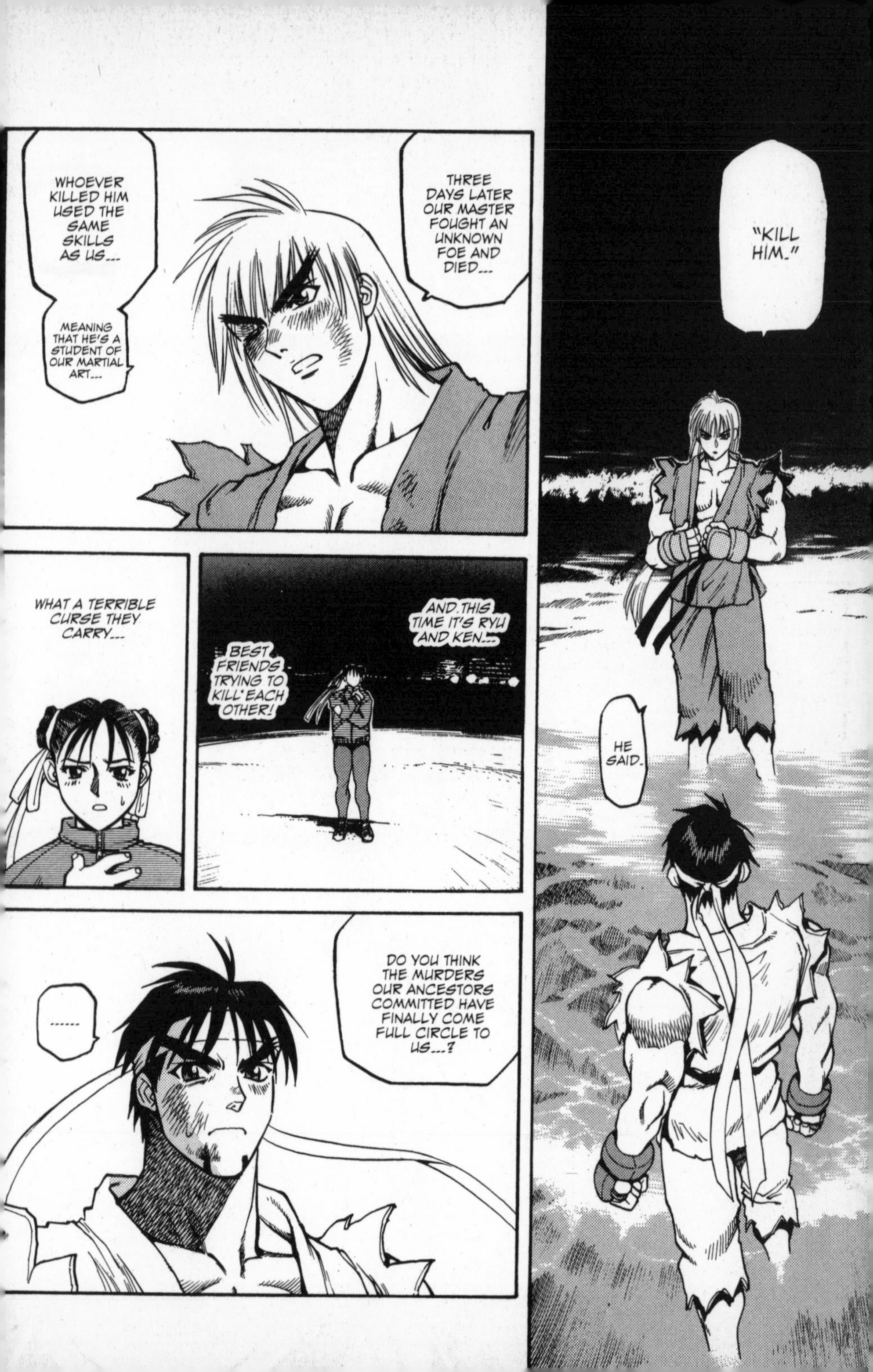
"KILL HIM."
HE SAID.
THREE DAYS LATER OUR MASTER FOUGHT AN UNKNOWN FOE AND DIED...
WHOEVER KILLED HIM USED THE SAME SKILLS AS US...
MEANING THAT HE'S A STUDENT OF OUR MARTIAL ART...
AND THIS TIME IT'S RYU AND KEN...
BEST FRIENDS TRYING TO KILL EACH OTHER!
WHAT A TERRIBLE CURSE THEY CARRY...
DO YOU THINK THE MURDERS OUR ANCESTORS COMMITTED HAVE FINALLY COME FULL CIRCLE TO US...?
......

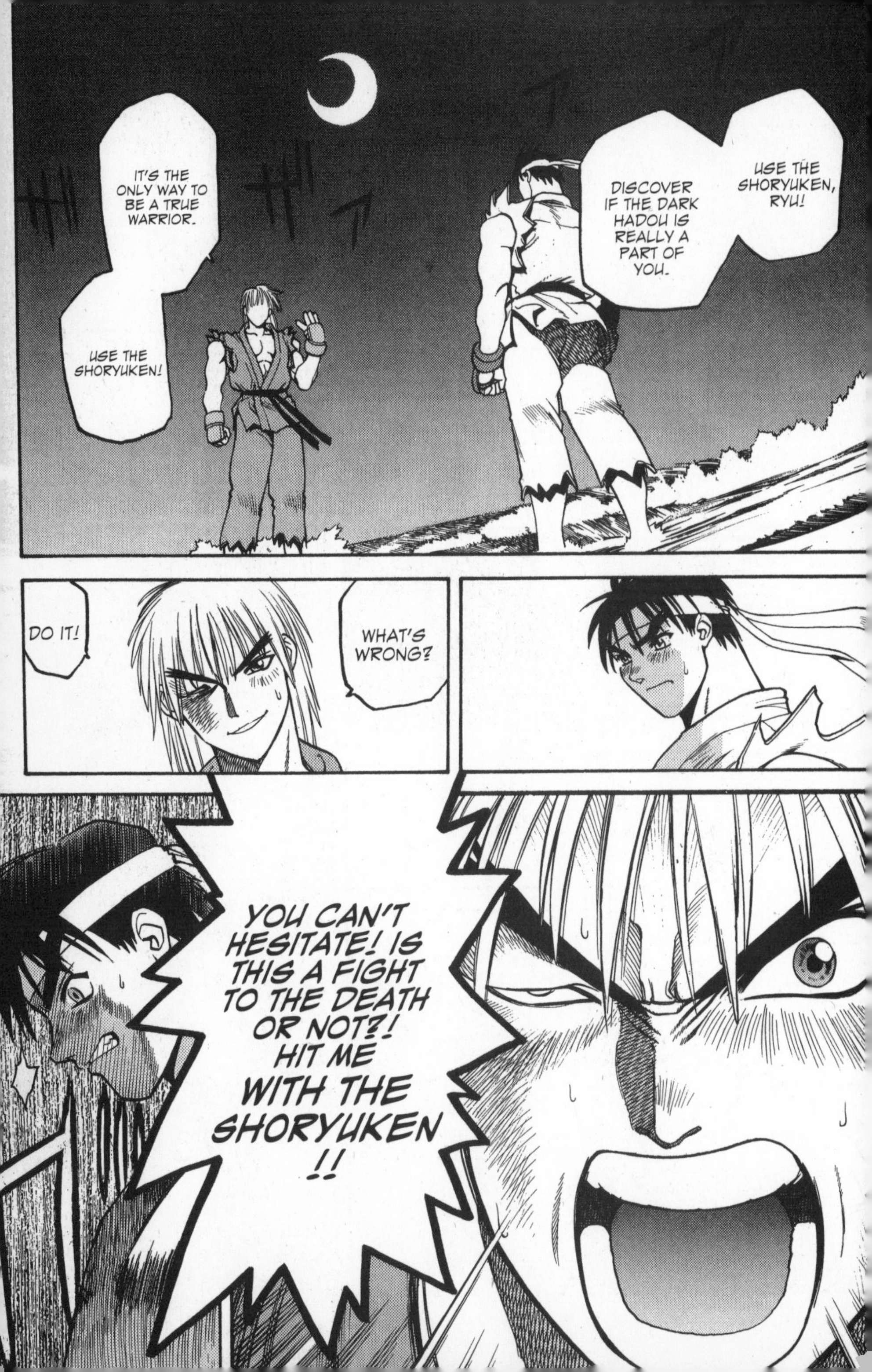
USE THE SHORYUKEN, RYU!
DISCOVER IF THE DARK HADOU IS REALLY A PART OF YOU.
IT'S THE ONLY WAY TO BE A TRUE WARRIOR.
USE THE SHORYUKEN!
WHAT'S WRONG?
DO IT!
YOU CAN'T HESITATE! IS THIS A FIGHT TO THE DEATH OR NOT?! HIT ME WITH THE SHORYUKEN!!

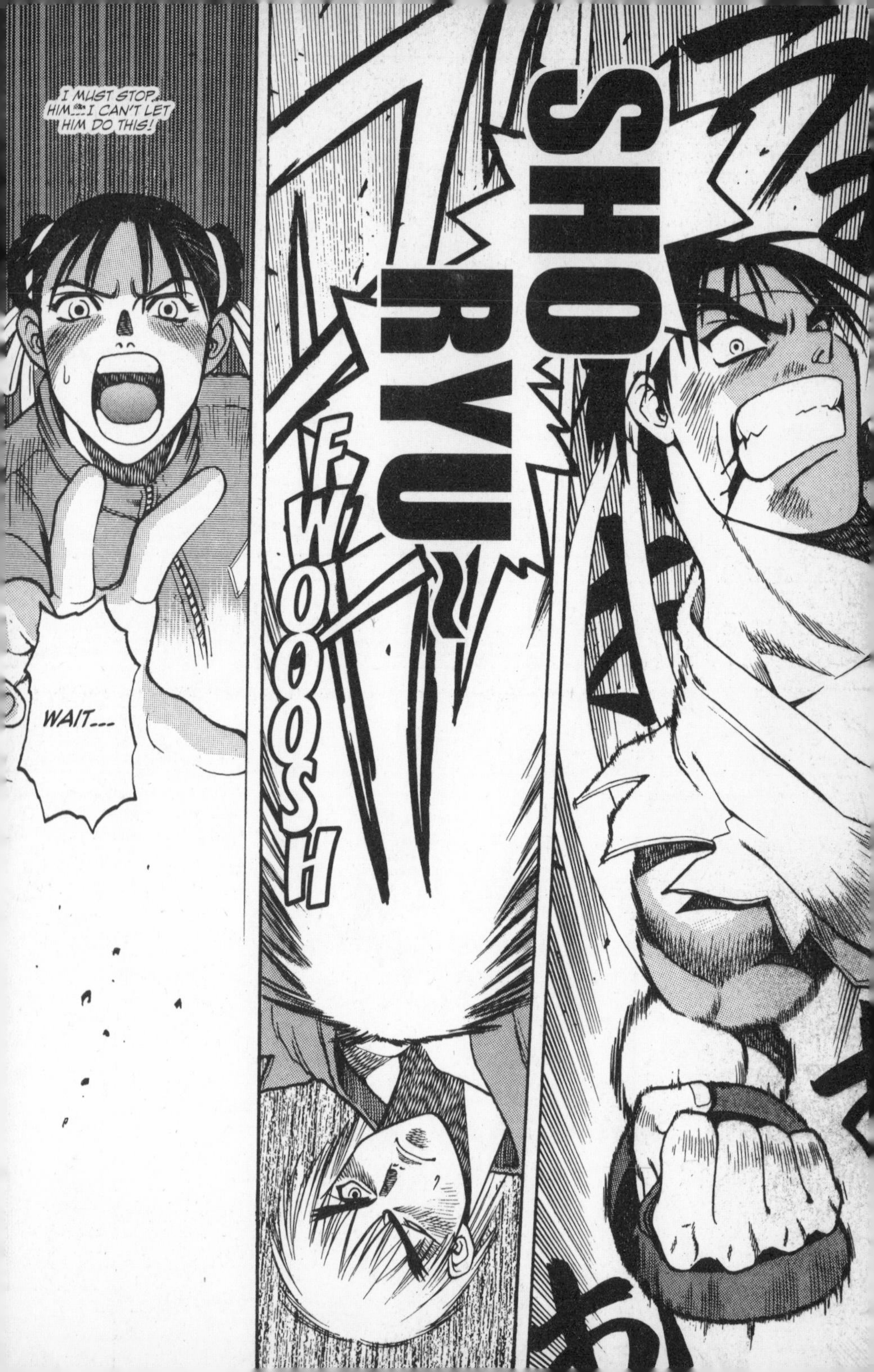
SHORYU~
FWOOOOSH
I MUST STOP HIM... I CAN'T LET HIM DO THIS!
WAIT...

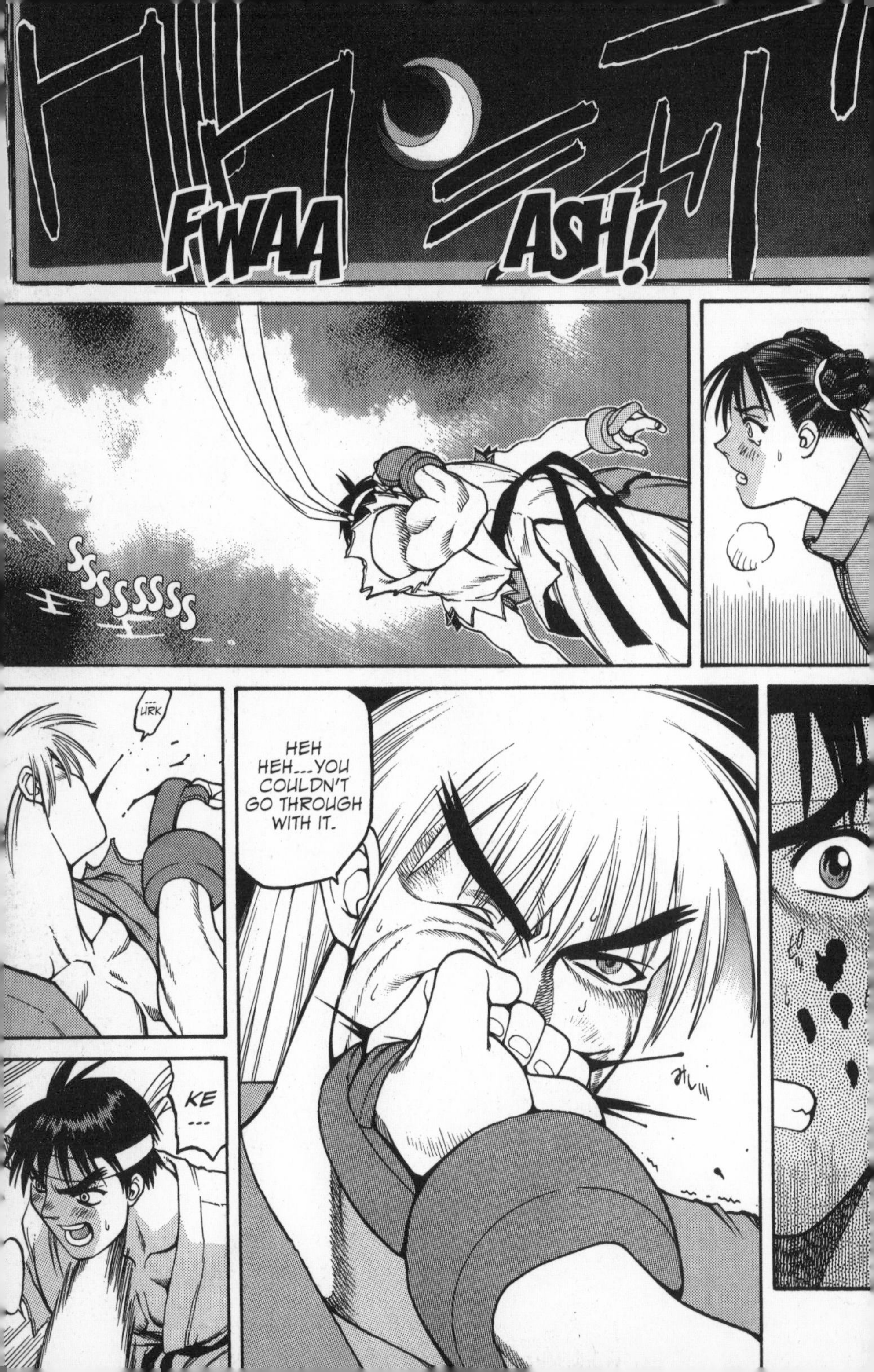
FWAA ASH!
SSSSSSSS
HEH HEH...YOU COULDN'T GO THROUGH WITH IT.
...URK
KE ---

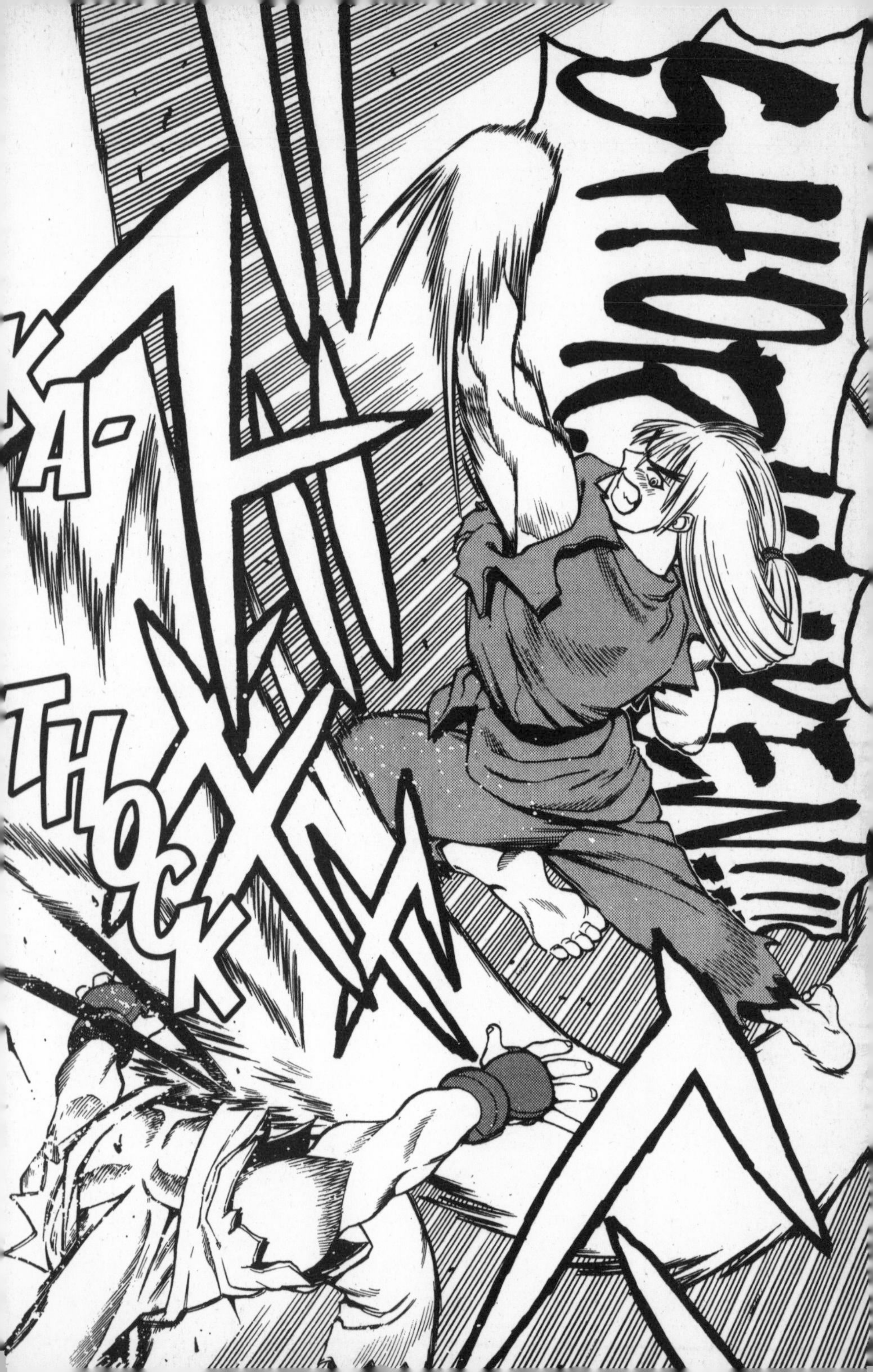
SHOR
KEN!!!
A-
THOCK

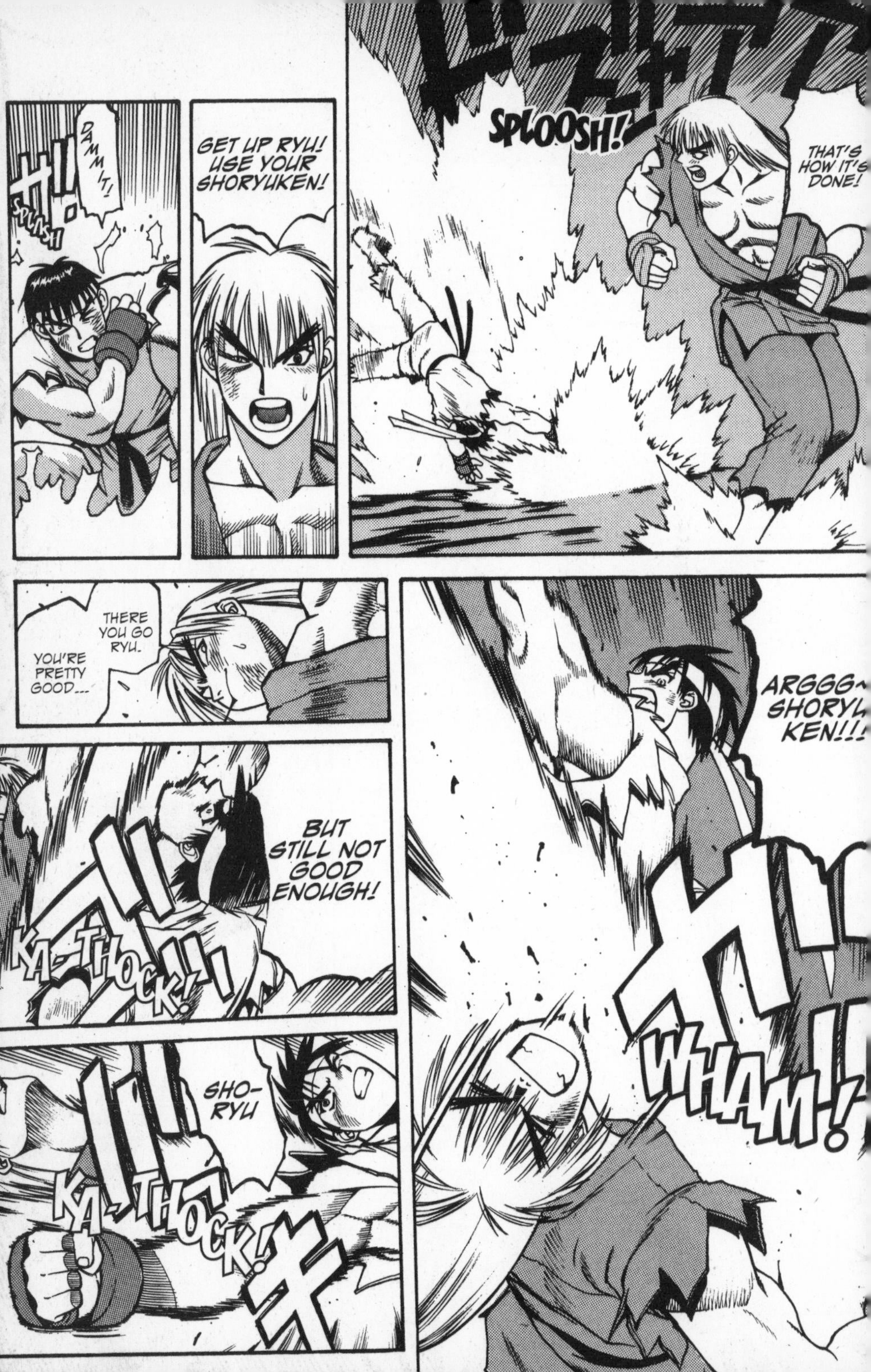
SPLOOSH!
THAT'S HOW IT'S DONE!
GET UP RYU! USE YOUR SHORYUKEN!
DAMMIT!
SPLASH
ARGGG- SHORYU- KEN!!!
WHAM!!
THERE YOU GO RYU.
YOU'RE PRETTY GOOD...
BUT STILL NOT GOOD ENOUGH!
KA-THOCK!!
SHO- RYU
KA-THOCK!

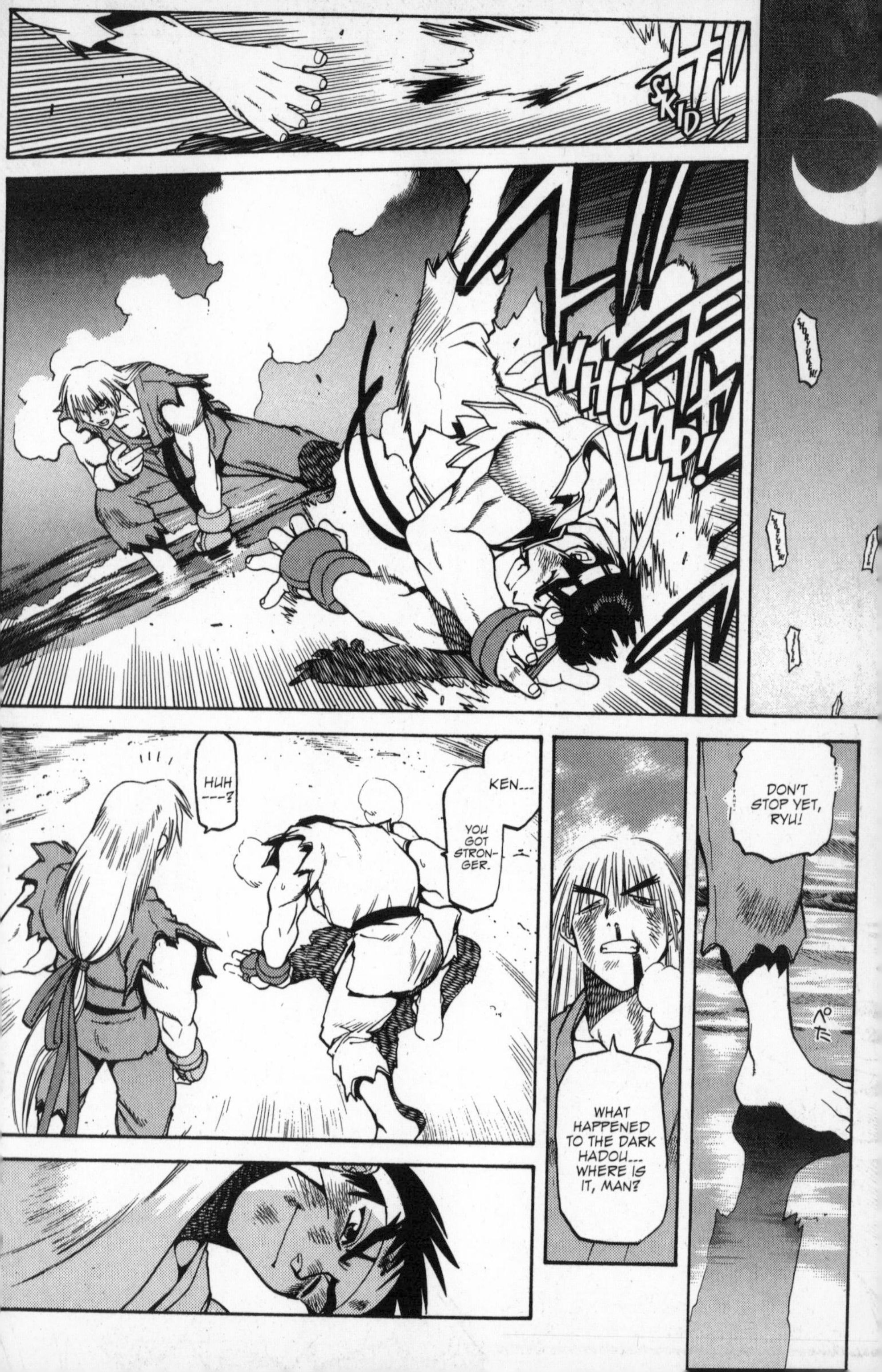
SHORYUKEN!
SHORYUKEN!
SKID
WHUMP!
PANT
DON'T STOP YET, RYU!
WHAT HAPPENED TO THE DARK HADOU... WHERE IS IT, MAN?
HUH---?
KEN...
YOU GOT STRONG-ER.

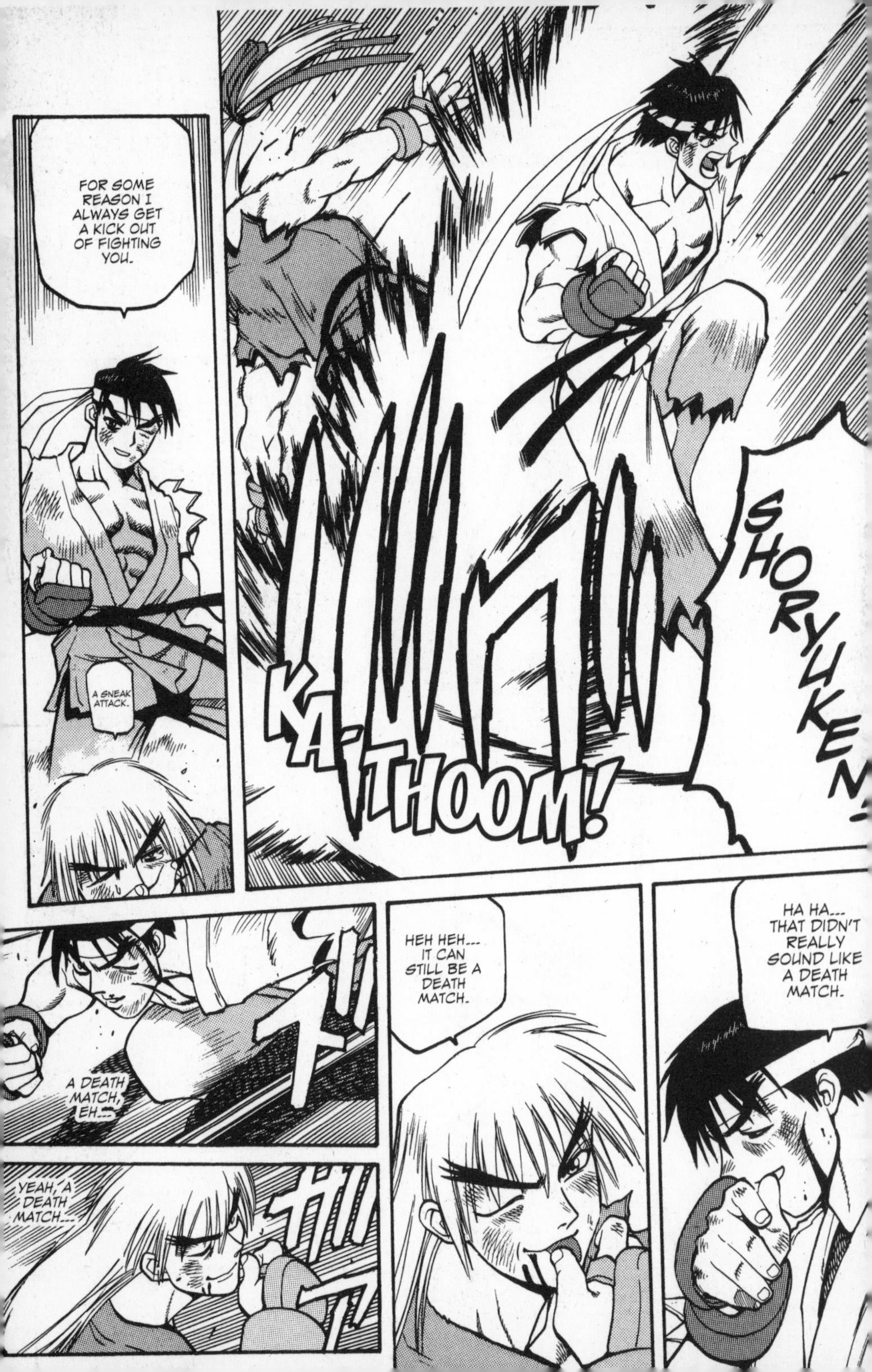
SHORYUKEN!
KA-THOOM!
FOR SOME REASON I ALWAYS GET A KICK OUT OF FIGHTING YOU.
A SNEAK ATTACK.
HA HA... THAT DIDN'T REALLY SOUND LIKE A DEATH MATCH.
HEH HEH... IT CAN STILL BE A DEATH MATCH.
A DEATH MATCH, EH...
YEAH, A DEATH MATCH...

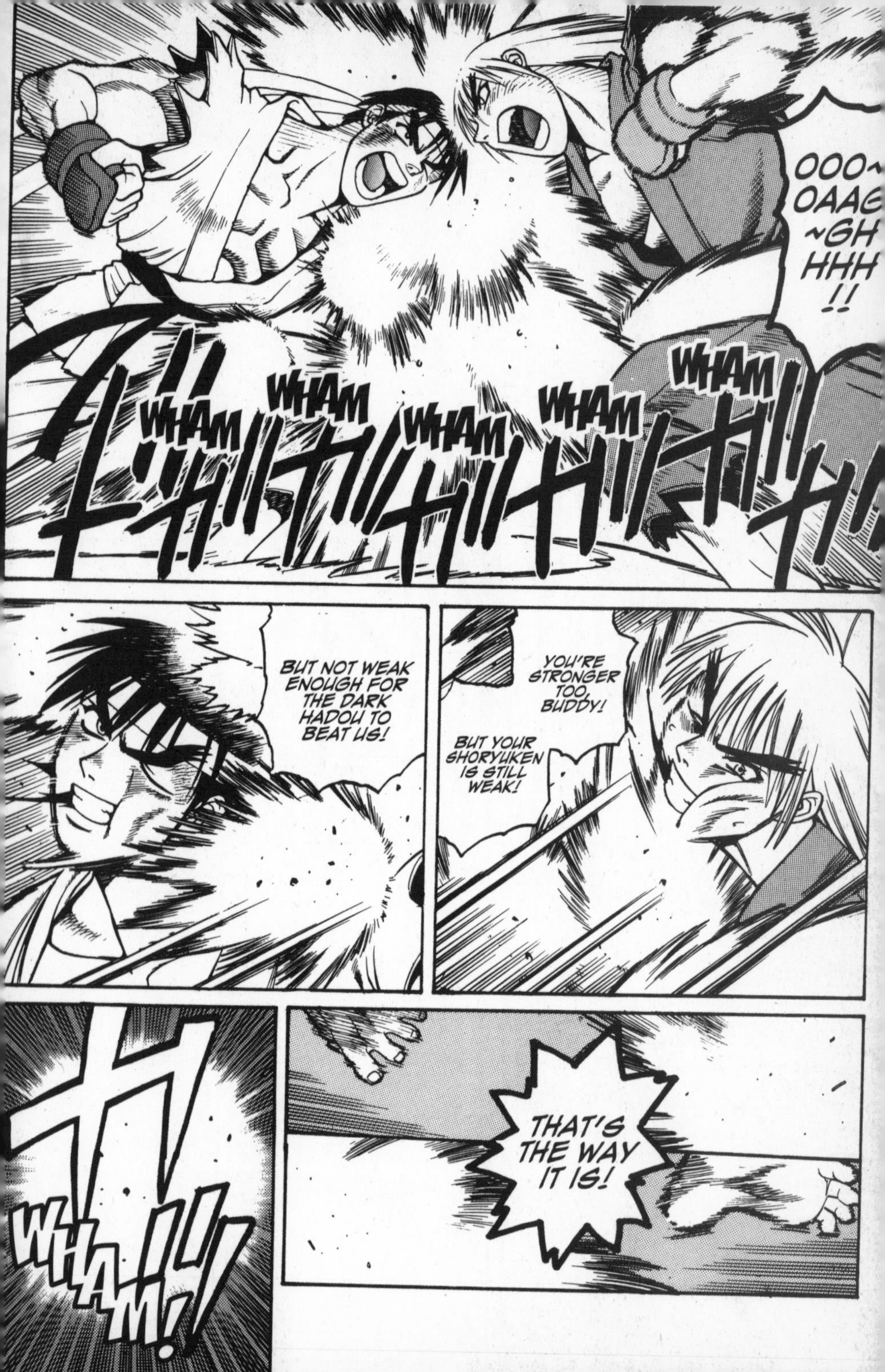
OOO~OAAG~GHHHH!!
WHAM
WHAM
WHAM
WHAM
WHAM
YOU'RE STRONGER TOO, BUDDY!
BUT YOUR SHORYUKEN IS STILL WEAK!
BUT NOT WEAK ENOUGH FOR THE DARK HADOU TO BEAT US!
THAT'S THE WAY IT IS!
WHAM!!

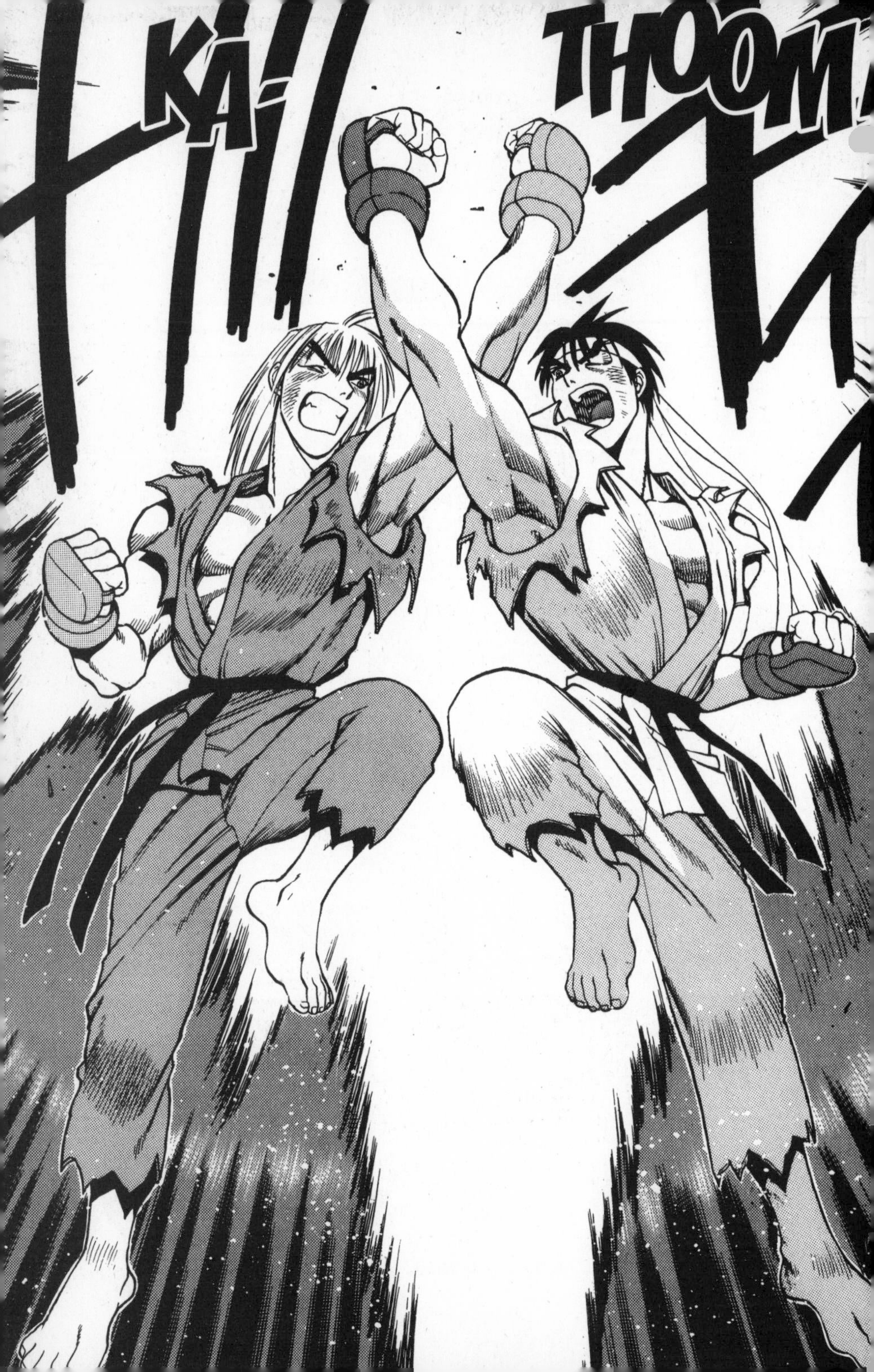
KA-
THOOM

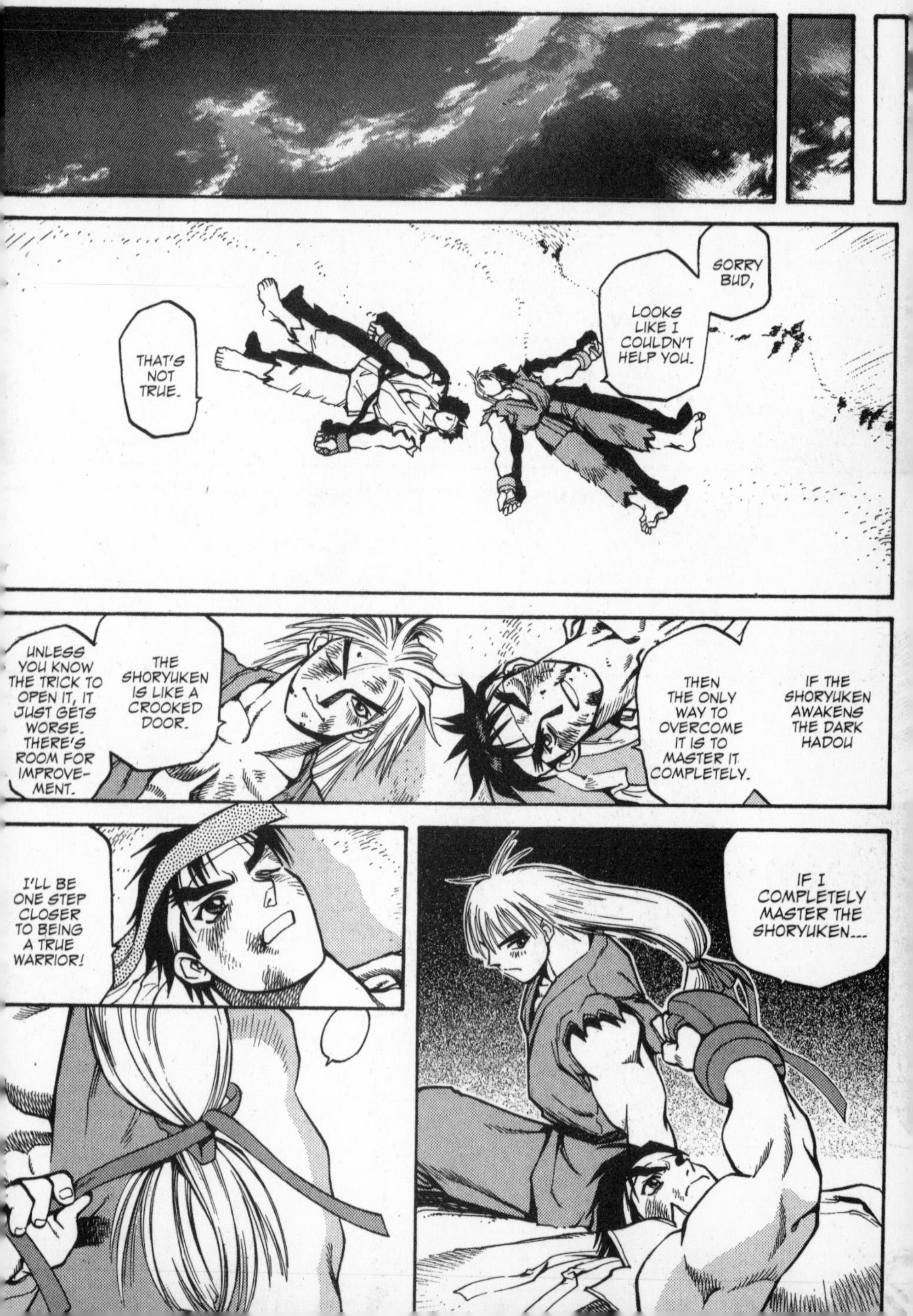
SORRY BUD,
LOOKS LIKE I COULDN'T HELP YOU.
THAT'S NOT TRUE.
IF THE SHORYUKEN AWAKENS THE DARK HADOU
THEN THE ONLY WAY TO OVERCOME IT IS TO MASTER IT COMPLETELY.
THE SHORYUKEN IS LIKE A CROOKED DOOR.
UNLESS YOU KNOW THE TRICK TO OPEN IT, IT JUST GETS WORSE. THERE'S ROOM FOR IMPROVE-MENT.
IF I COMPLETELY MASTER THE SHORYUKEN...
I'LL BE ONE STEP CLOSER TO BEING A TRUE WARRIOR!

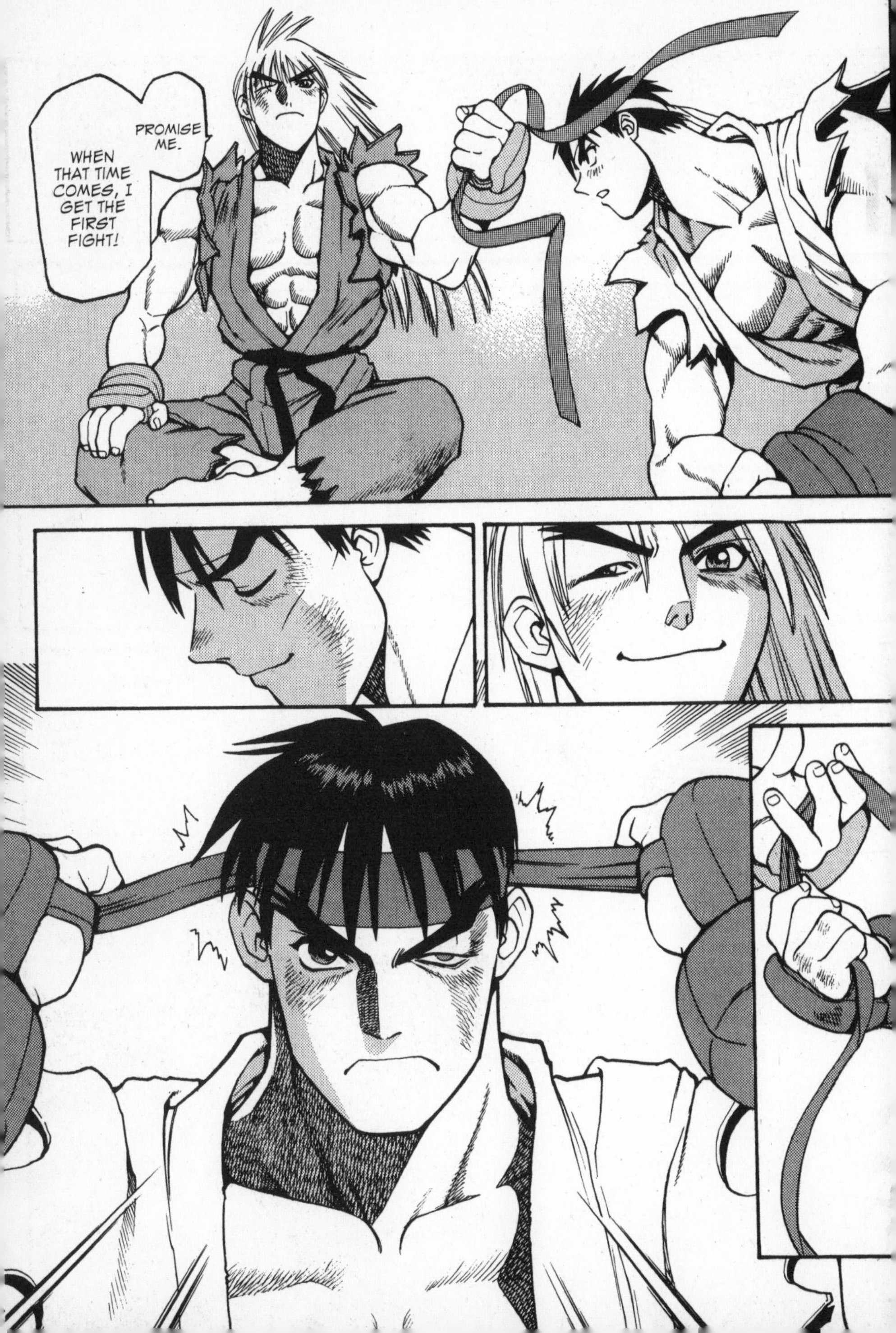
PROMISE ME.
WHEN THAT TIME COMES, I GET THE FIRST FIGHT!

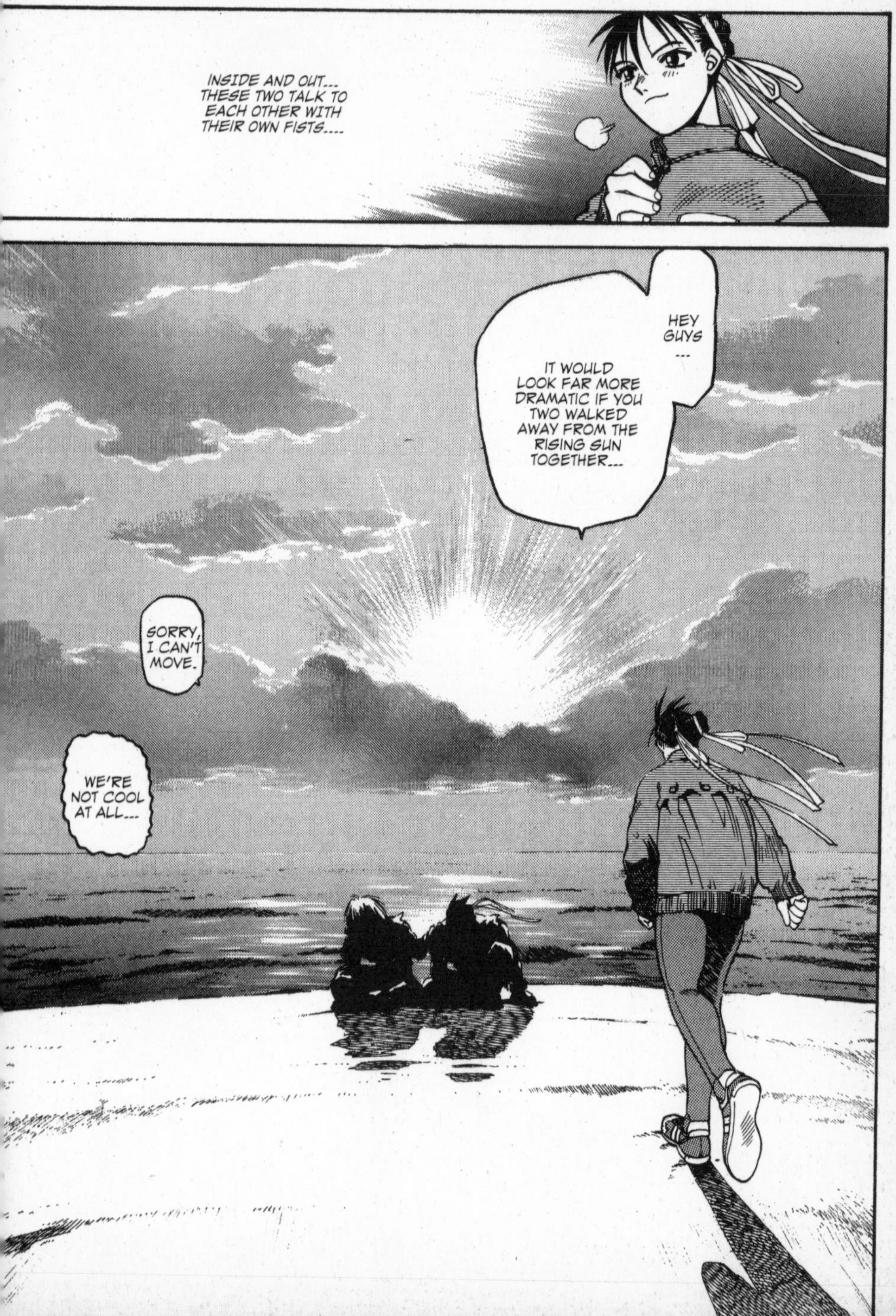
INSIDE AND OUT... THESE TWO TALK TO EACH OTHER WITH THEIR OWN FISTS....
HEY GUYS ---
IT WOULD LOOK FAR MORE DRAMATIC IF YOU TWO WALKED AWAY FROM THE RISING SUN TOGETHER...
SORRY, I CAN'T MOVE.
WE'RE NOT COOL AT ALL...

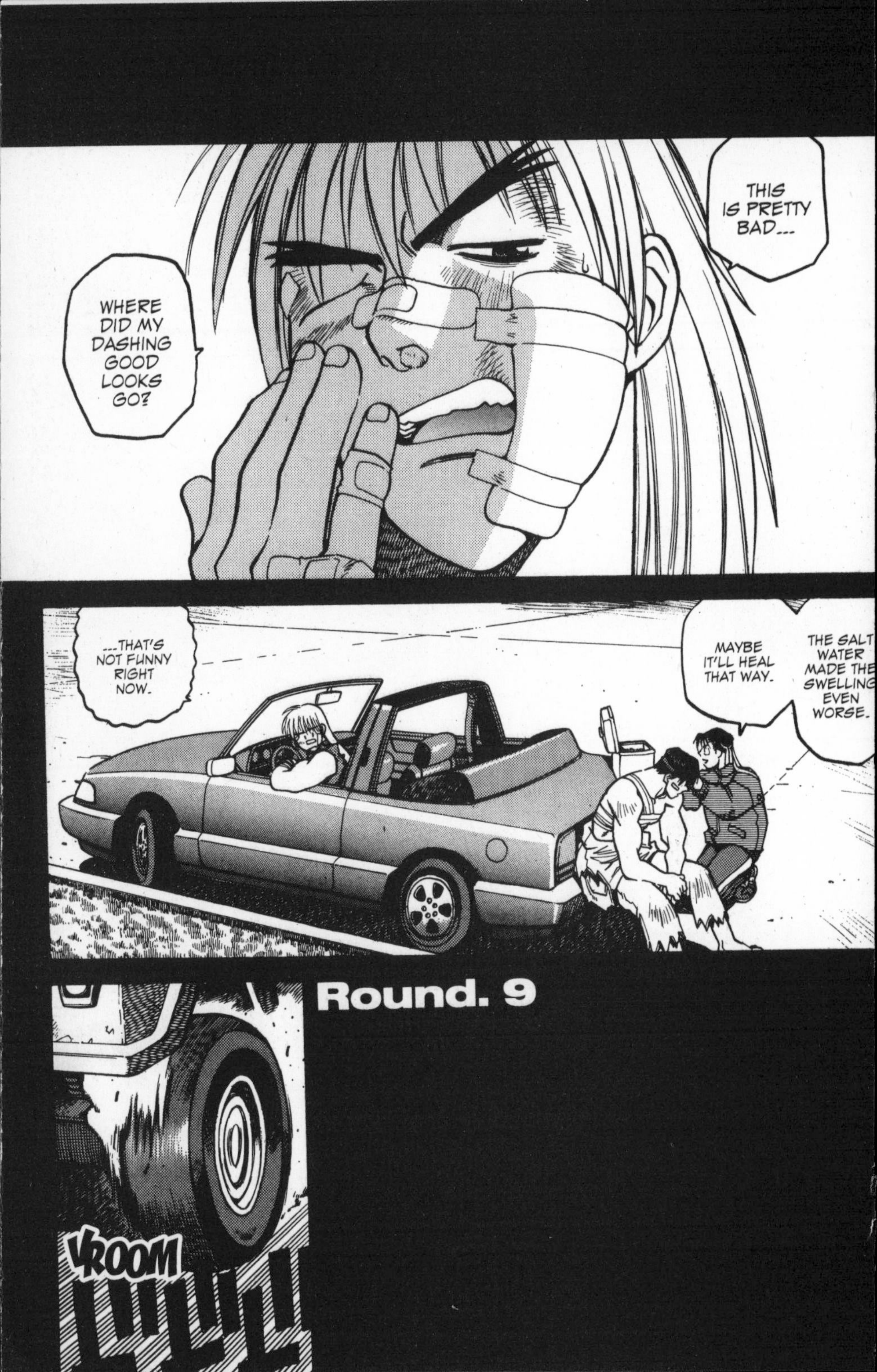
THIS IS PRETTY BAD...
WHERE DID MY DASHING GOOD LOOKS GO?
THE SALT WATER MADE THE SWELLING EVEN WORSE.
MAYBE IT'LL HEAL THAT WAY.
...THAT'S NOT FUNNY RIGHT NOW.
Round. 9
VROOM

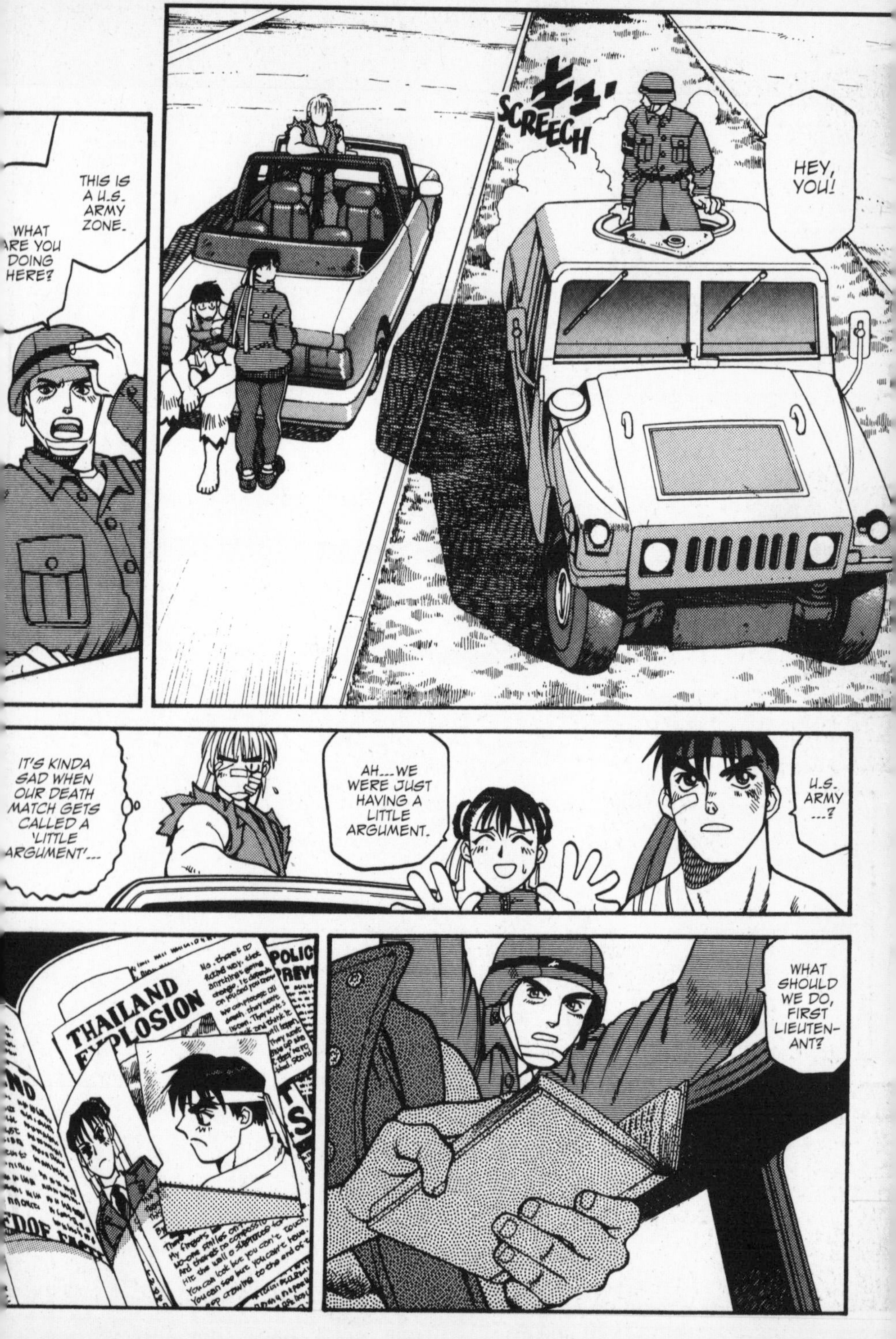
SCREECH
HEY, YOU!
THIS IS A U.S. ARMY ZONE.
WHAT ARE YOU DOING HERE?
U.S. ARMY...?
AH...WE WERE JUST HAVING A LITTLE ARGUMENT.
IT'S KINDA SAD WHEN OUR DEATH MATCH GETS CALLED A 'LITTLE ARGUMENT'...
WHAT SHOULD WE DO, FIRST LIEUTENANT?
THAILAND EXPLOSION

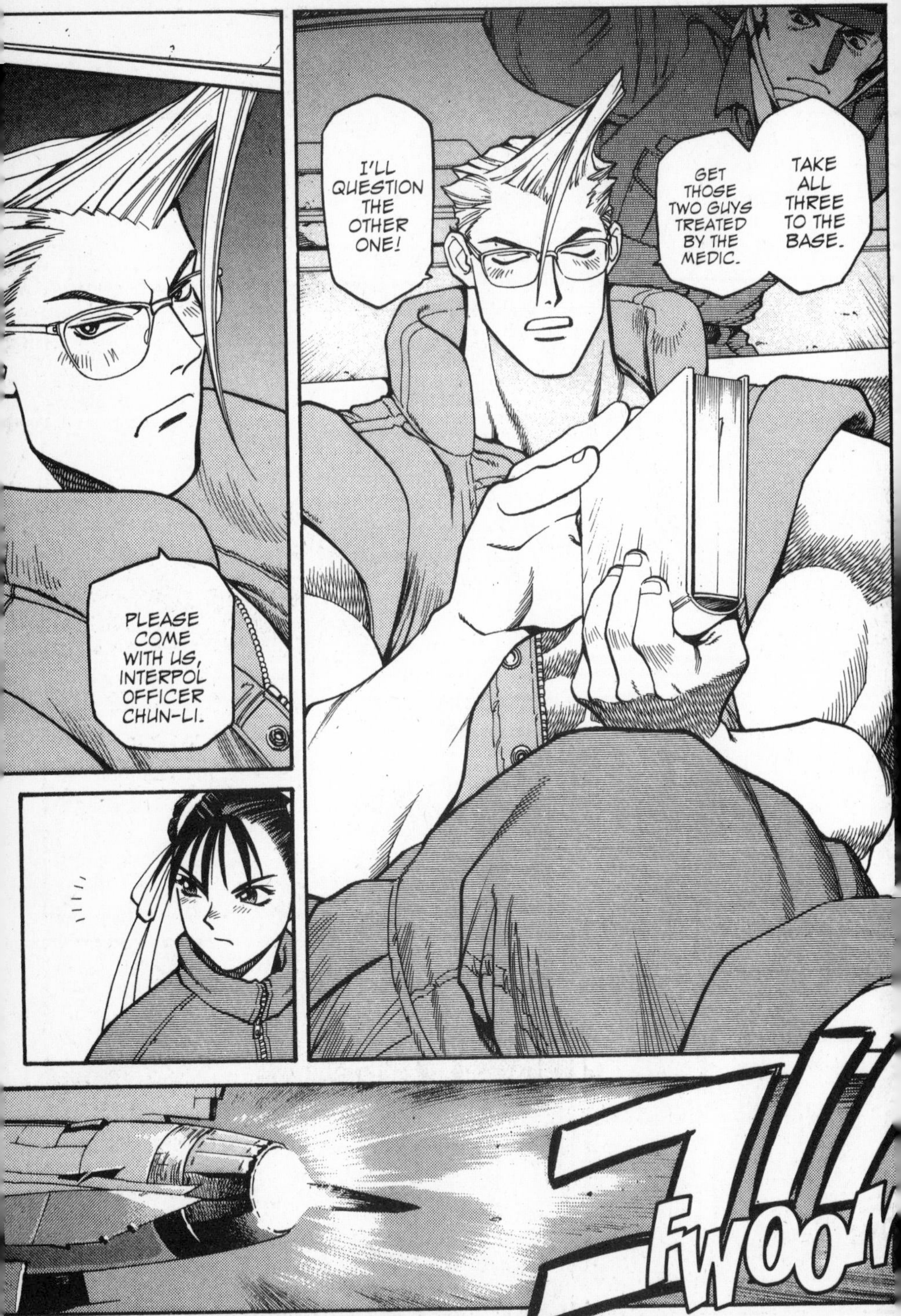
TAKE ALL THREE TO THE BASE.
GET THOSE TWO GUYS TREATED BY THE MEDIC.
I'LL QUESTION THE OTHER ONE!
PLEASE COME WITH US, INTERPOL OFFICER CHUN-LI.
FWOOM

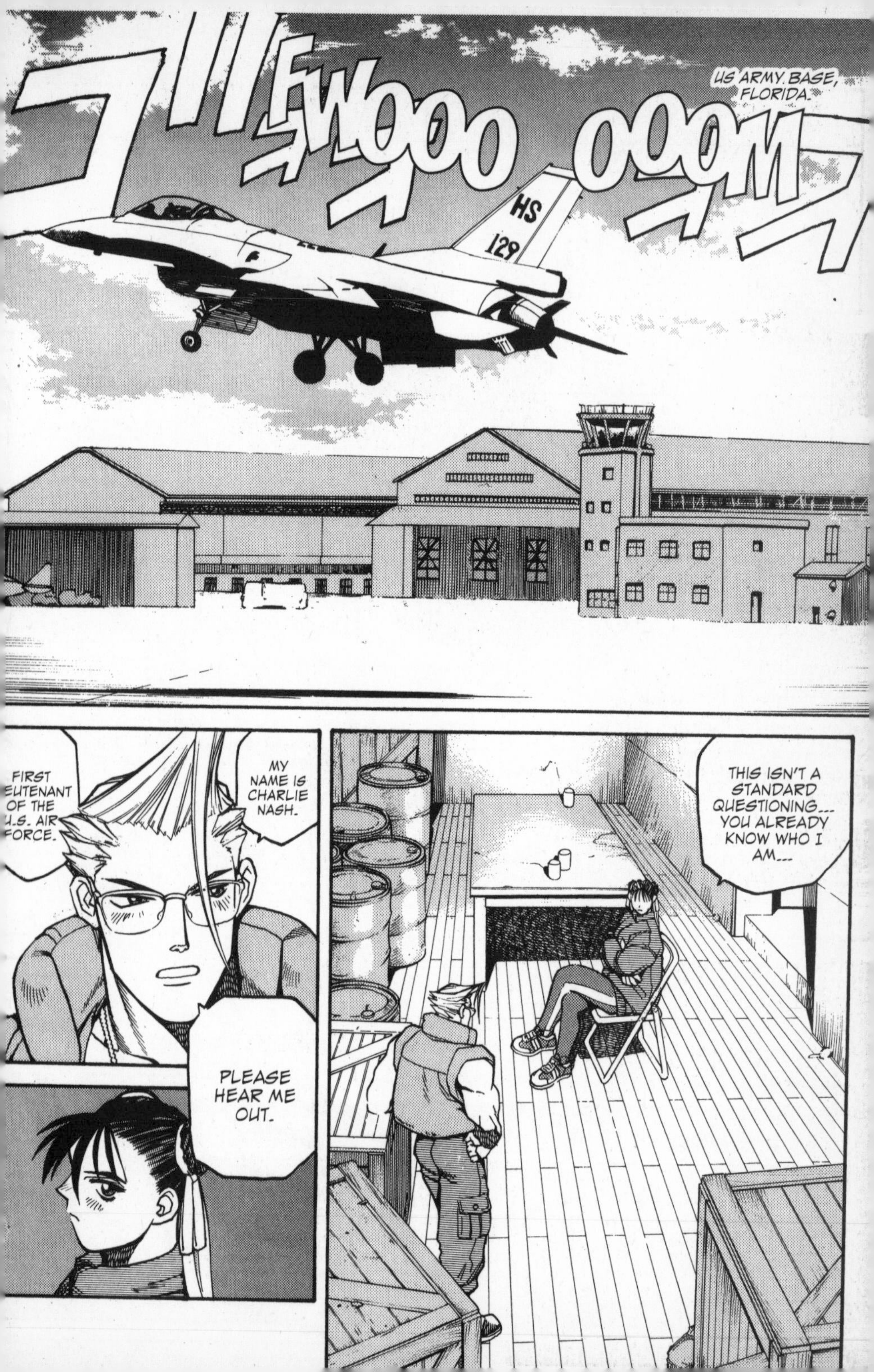
FWOOO OOOM
US ARMY BASE, FLORIDA.
THIS ISN'T A STANDARD QUESTIONING... YOU ALREADY KNOW WHO I AM...
MY NAME IS CHARLIE NASH.
FIRST EUTENANT OF THE .S. AIR FORCE.
PLEASE HEAR ME OUT.

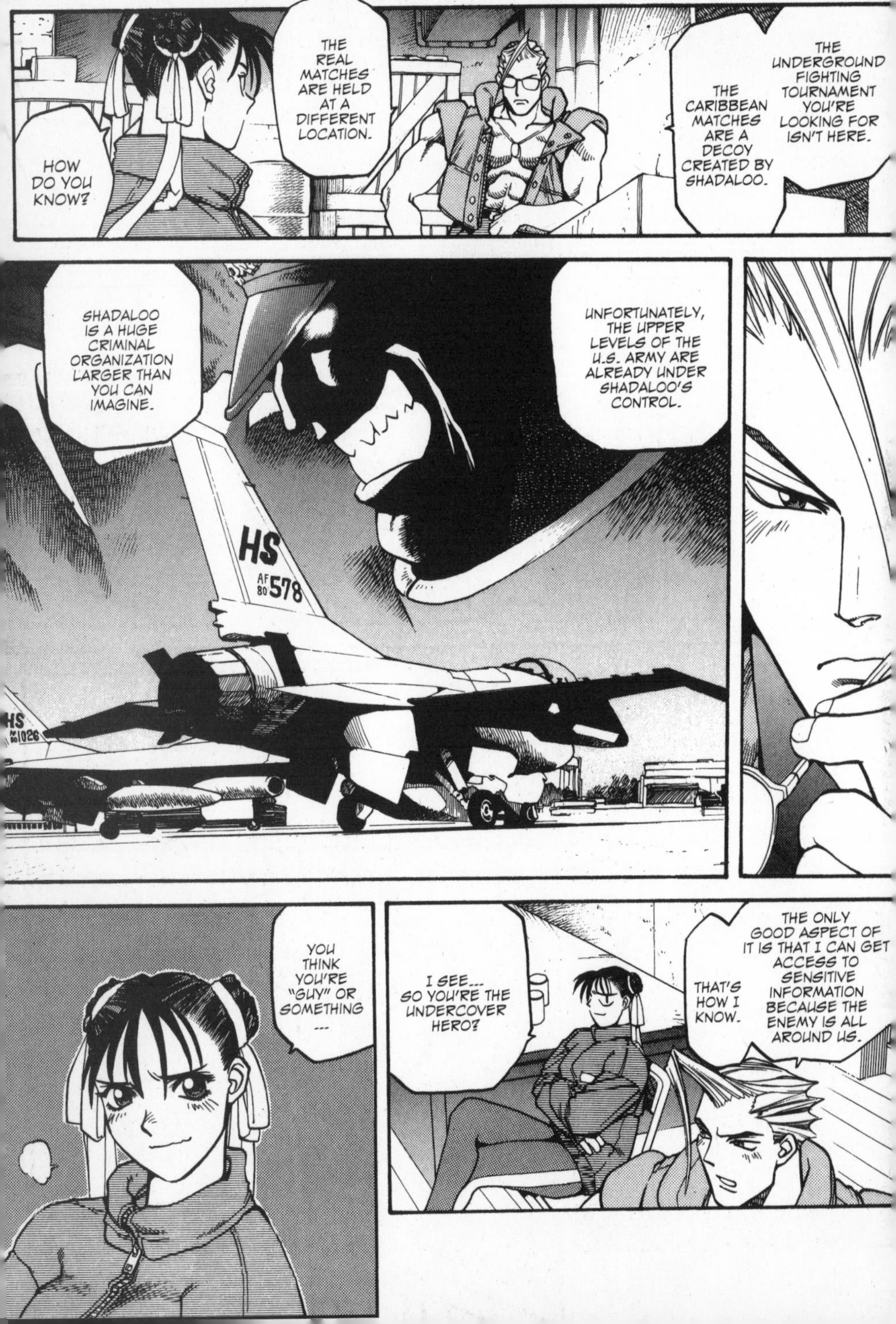
THE UNDERGROUND FIGHTING TOURNAMENT YOU'RE LOOKING FOR ISN'T HERE.
THE CARIBBEAN MATCHES ARE A DECOY CREATED BY SHADALOO.
THE REAL MATCHES ARE HELD AT A DIFFERENT LOCATION.
HOW DO YOU KNOW?
UNFORTUNATELY, THE UPPER LEVELS OF THE U.S. ARMY ARE ALREADY UNDER SHADALOO'S CONTROL.
SHADALOO IS A HUGE CRIMINAL ORGANIZATION LARGER THAN YOU CAN IMAGINE.
HS
AF 80 578
THE ONLY GOOD ASPECT OF IT IS THAT I CAN GET ACCESS TO SENSITIVE INFORMATION BECAUSE THE ENEMY IS ALL AROUND US.
THAT'S HOW I KNOW.
I SEE... SO YOU'RE THE UNDERCOVER HERO?
YOU THINK YOU'RE "GUY" OR SOMETHING ---

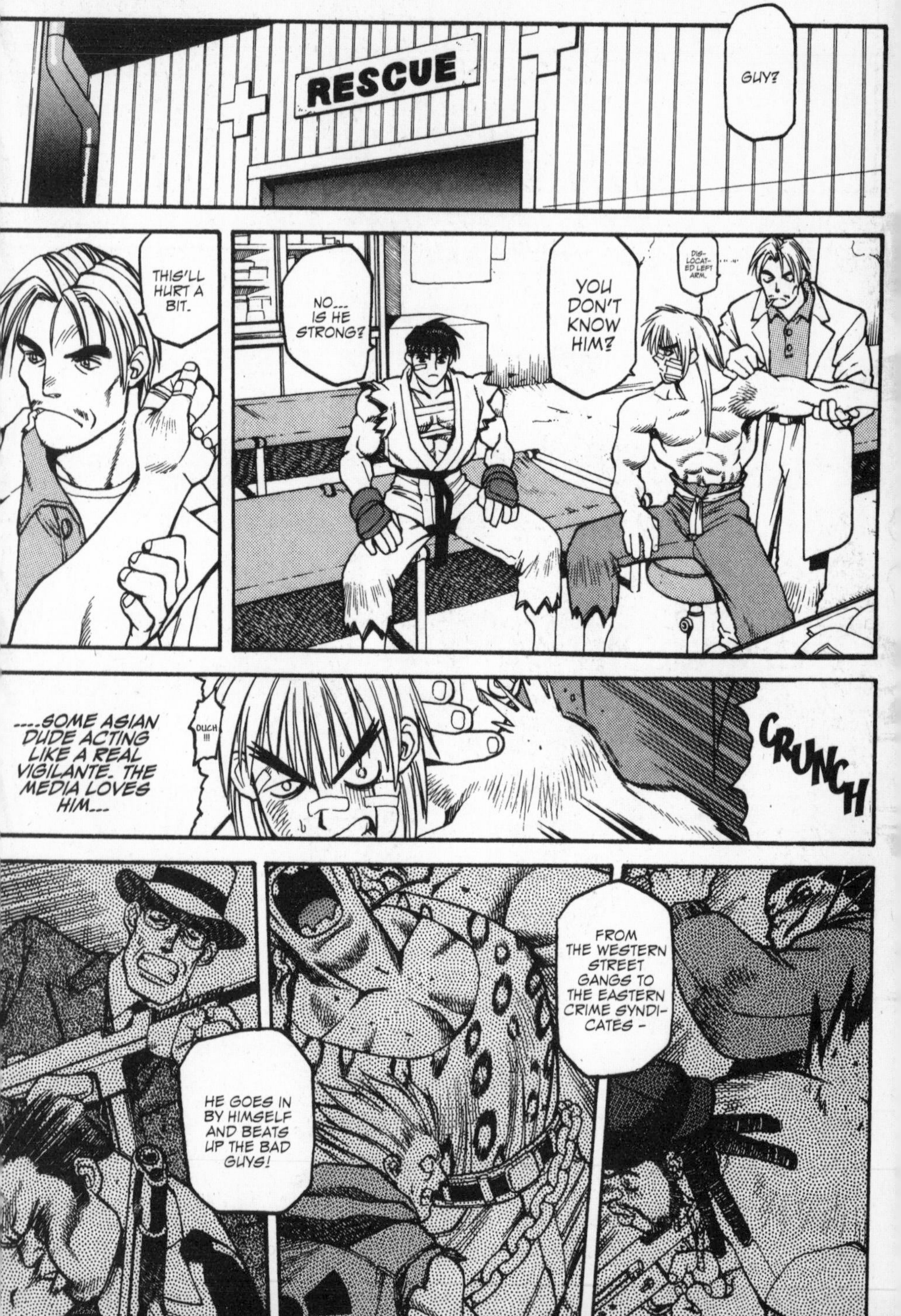

GUY?
DISLOCATED LEFT ARM.
...
YOU DON'T KNOW HIM?
NO... IS HE STRONG?
THIS'LL HURT A BIT.
CRUNCH
OUCH!!!
....SOME ASIAN DUDE ACTING LIKE A REAL VIGILANTE. THE MEDIA LOVES HIM...
FROM THE WESTERN STREET GANGS TO THE EASTERN CRIME SYNDICATES -
HE GOES IN BY HIMSELF AND BEATS UP THE BAD GUYS!
RESCUE

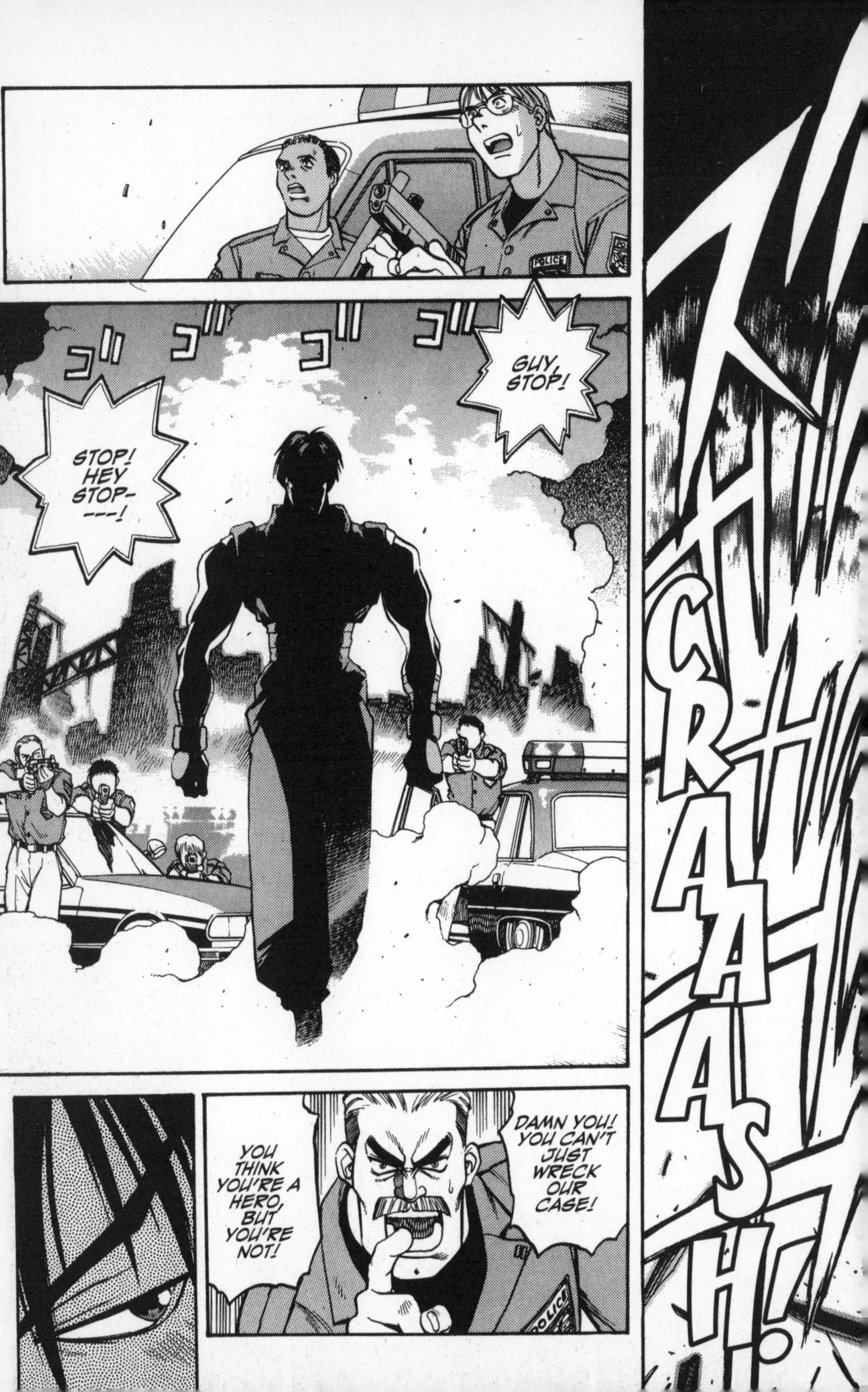
CRAAAASH!
ゴゴゴゴ
GUY, STOP!
STOP! HEY STOP----!
DAMN YOU! YOU CAN'T JUST WRECK OUR CASE!
YOU THINK YOU'RE A HERO, BUT YOU'RE NOT!

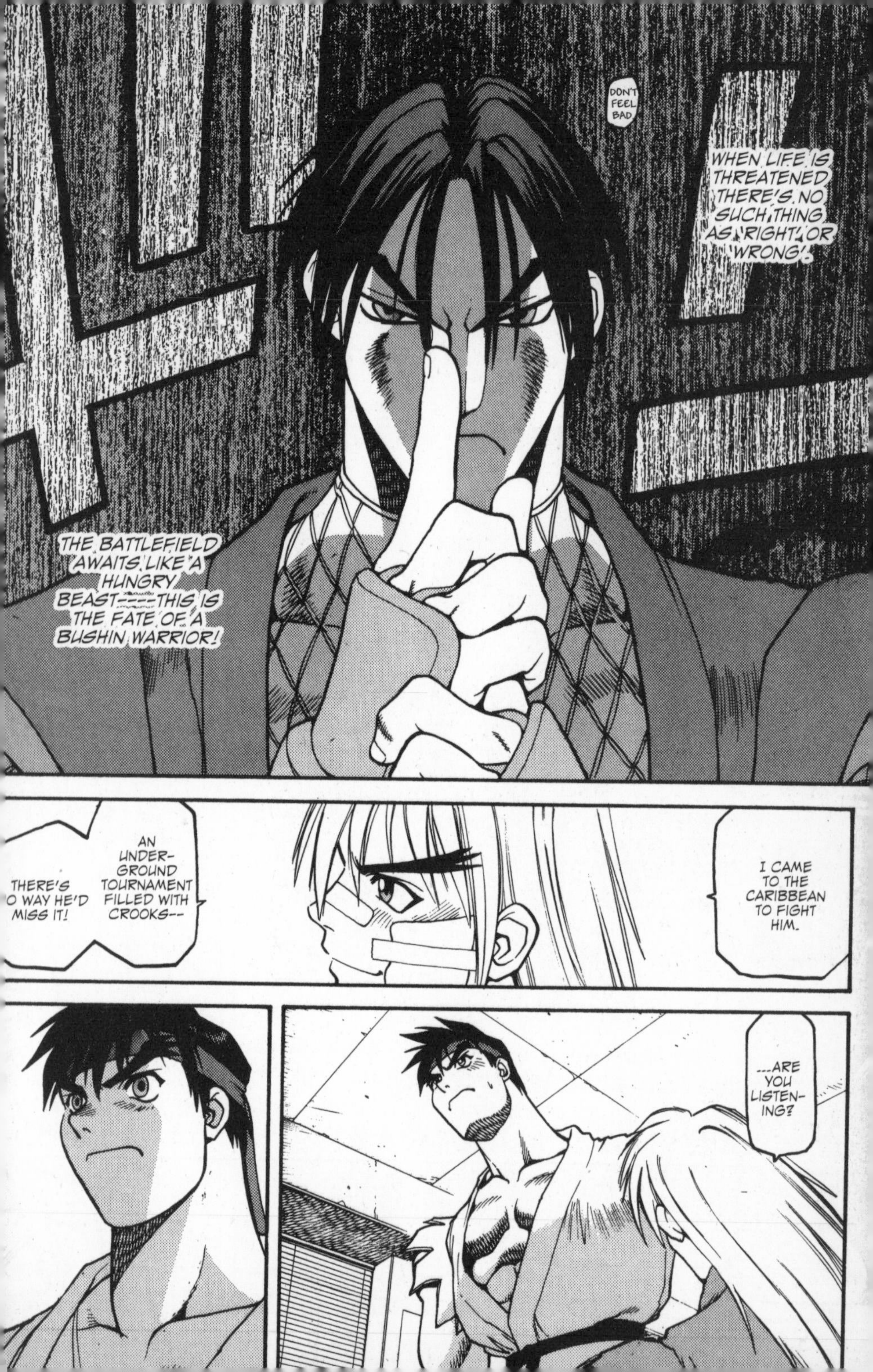
DON'T FEEL BAD
WHEN LIFE IS THREATENED THERE'S NO SUCH THING AS 'RIGHT' OR 'WRONG'.
THE BATTLEFIELD AWAITS LIKE A HUNGRY BEAST----THIS IS THE FATE OF A BUSHIN WARRIOR!
I CAME TO THE CARIBBEAN TO FIGHT HIM.
AN UNDER-GROUND TOURNAMENT FILLED WITH CROOKS--
THERE'S O WAY HE'D MISS IT!
---ARE YOU LISTEN-ING?

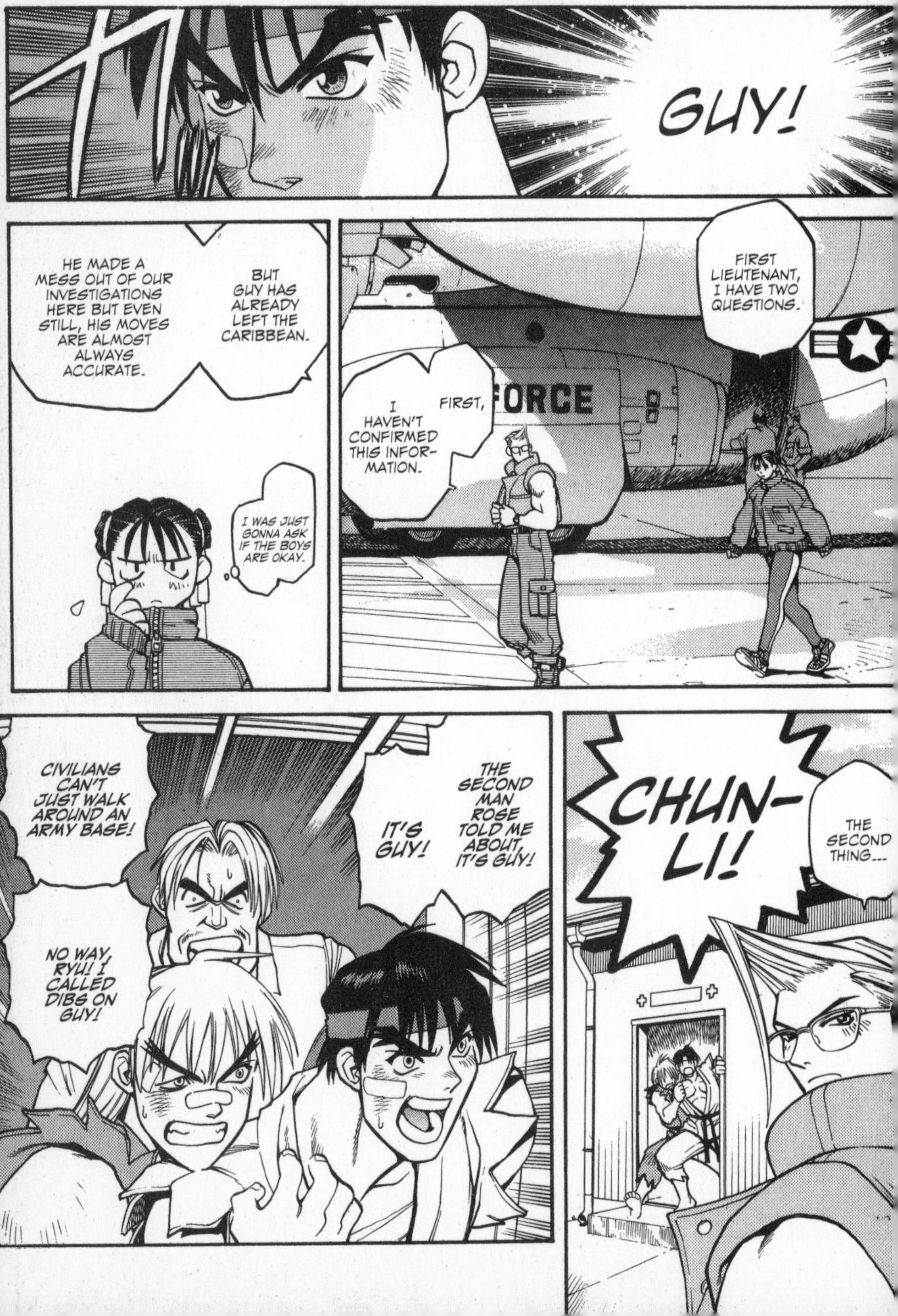
GUY!
FIRST LIEUTENANT, I HAVE TWO QUESTIONS.
FIRST,
I HAVEN'T CONFIRMED THIS INFORMATION.
FORCE
HE MADE A MESS OUT OF OUR INVESTIGATIONS HERE BUT EVEN STILL, HIS MOVES ARE ALMOST ALWAYS ACCURATE.
BUT GUY HAS ALREADY LEFT THE CARIBBEAN.
I WAS JUST GONNA ASK IF THE BOYS ARE OKAY.
THE SECOND THING...
CHUN-LI!
THE SECOND MAN ROSE TOLD ME ABOUT, IT'S GUY!
IT'S GUY!
CIVILIANS CAN'T JUST WALK AROUND AN ARMY BASE!
NO WAY, RYU! I CALLED DIBS ON GUY!

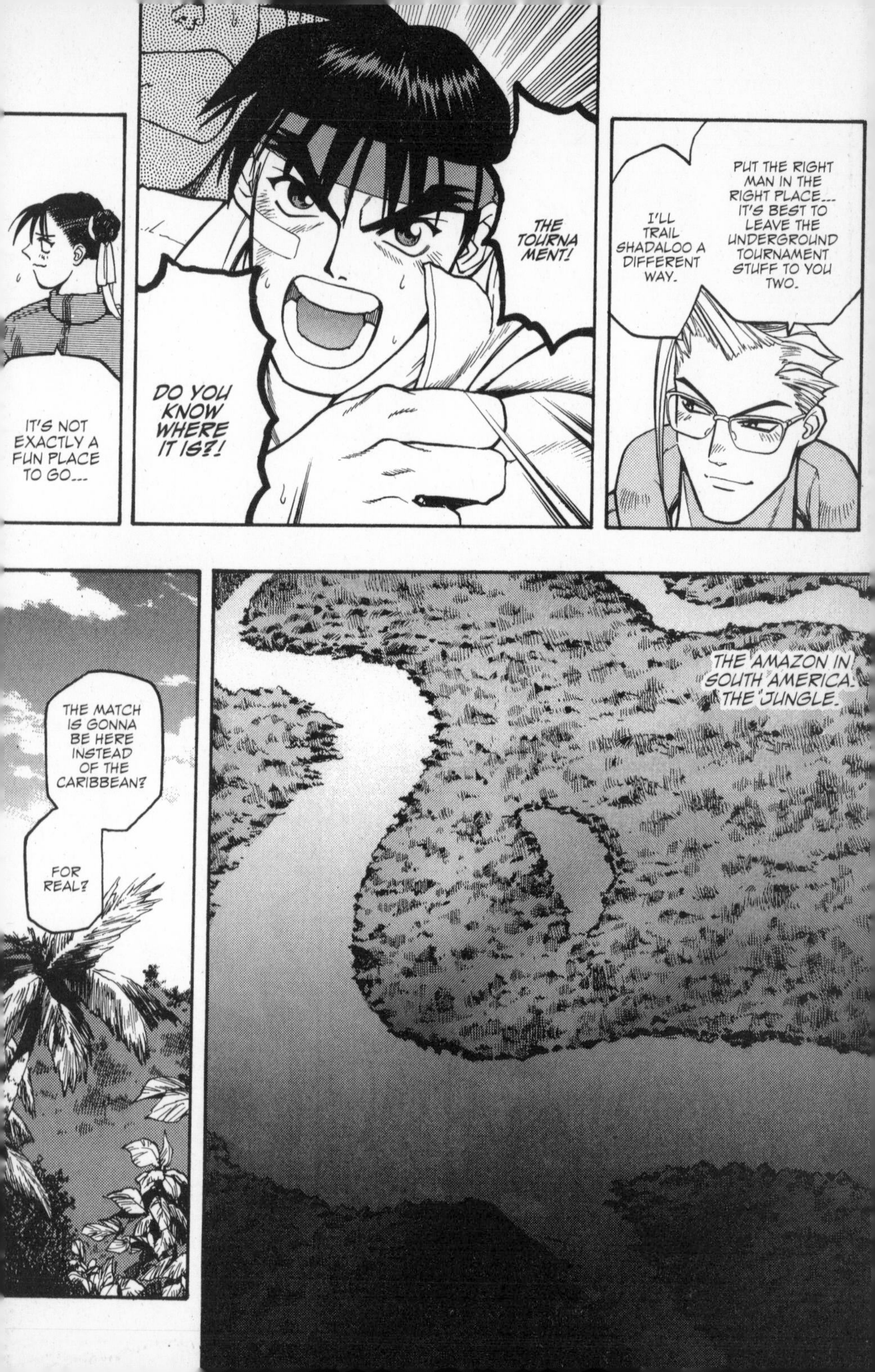
PUT THE RIGHT MAN IN THE RIGHT PLACE... IT'S BEST TO LEAVE THE UNDERGROUND TOURNAMENT STUFF TO YOU TWO.
I'LL TRAIL SHADALOO A DIFFERENT WAY.
THE TOURNAMENT!
DO YOU KNOW WHERE IT IS?!
IT'S NOT EXACTLY A FUN PLACE TO GO...
THE AMAZON IN SOUTH AMERICA. THE JUNGLE.
THE MATCH IS GONNA BE HERE INSTEAD OF THE CARIBBEAN?
FOR REAL?

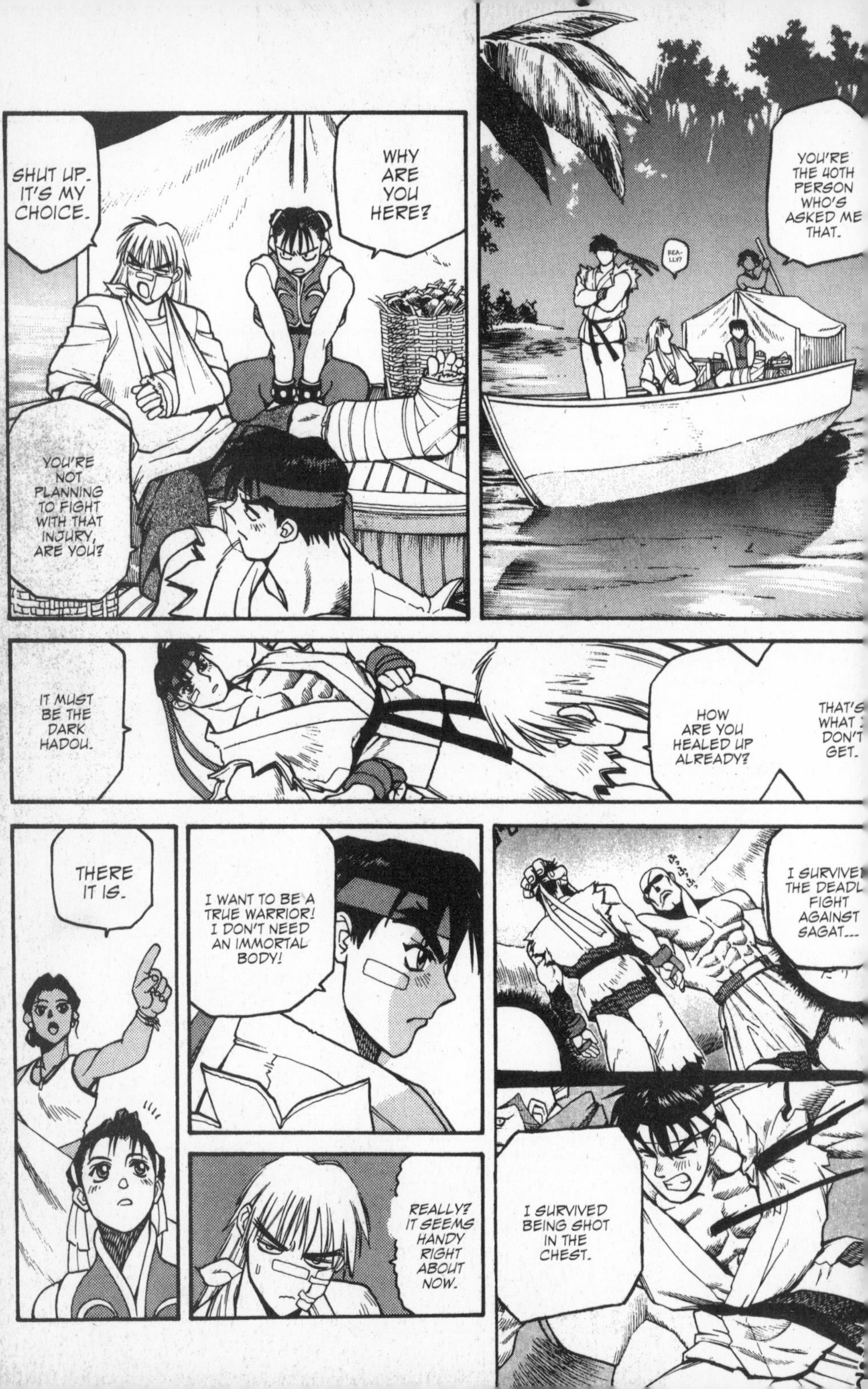
YOU'RE THE 40TH PERSON WHO'S ASKED ME THAT.
REALLY?
WHY ARE YOU HERE?
SHUT UP. IT'S MY CHOICE.
YOU'RE NOT PLANNING TO FIGHT WITH THAT INJURY, ARE YOU?
THAT'S WHAT I DON'T GET.
HOW ARE YOU HEALED UP ALREADY?
IT MUST BE THE DARK HADOU.
I SURVIVE THE DEADL FIGHT AGAINST SAGAT...
I SURVIVED BEING SHOT IN THE CHEST.
I WANT TO BE A TRUE WARRIOR! I DON'T NEED AN IMMORTAL BODY!
REALLY? IT SEEMS HANDY RIGHT ABOUT NOW.
THERE IT IS.

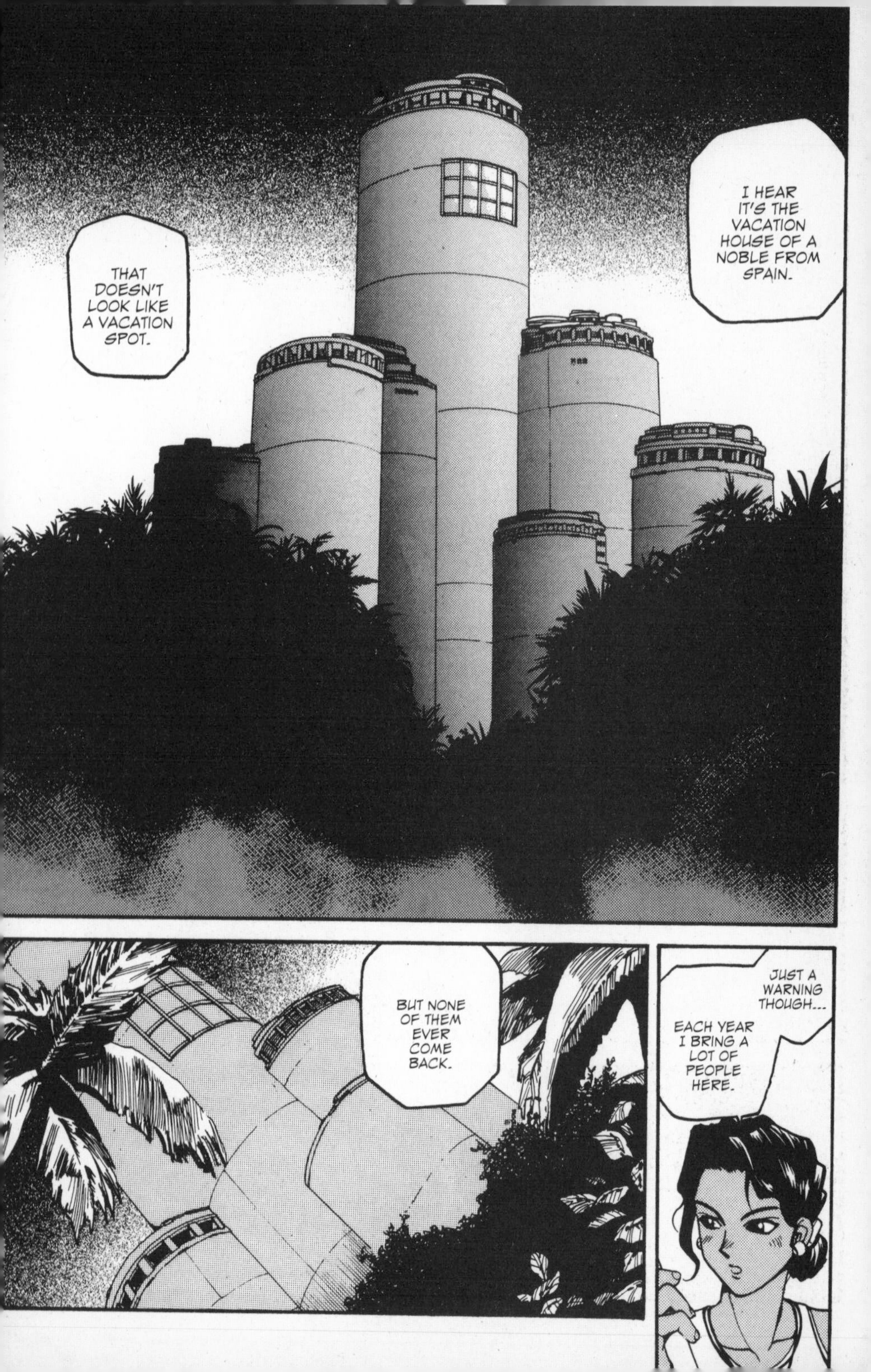
I HEAR IT'S THE VACATION HOUSE OF A NOBLE FROM SPAIN.
THAT DOESN'T LOOK LIKE A VACATION SPOT.
JUST A WARNING THOUGH...
EACH YEAR I BRING A LOT OF PEOPLE HERE.
BUT NONE OF THEM EVER COME BACK.

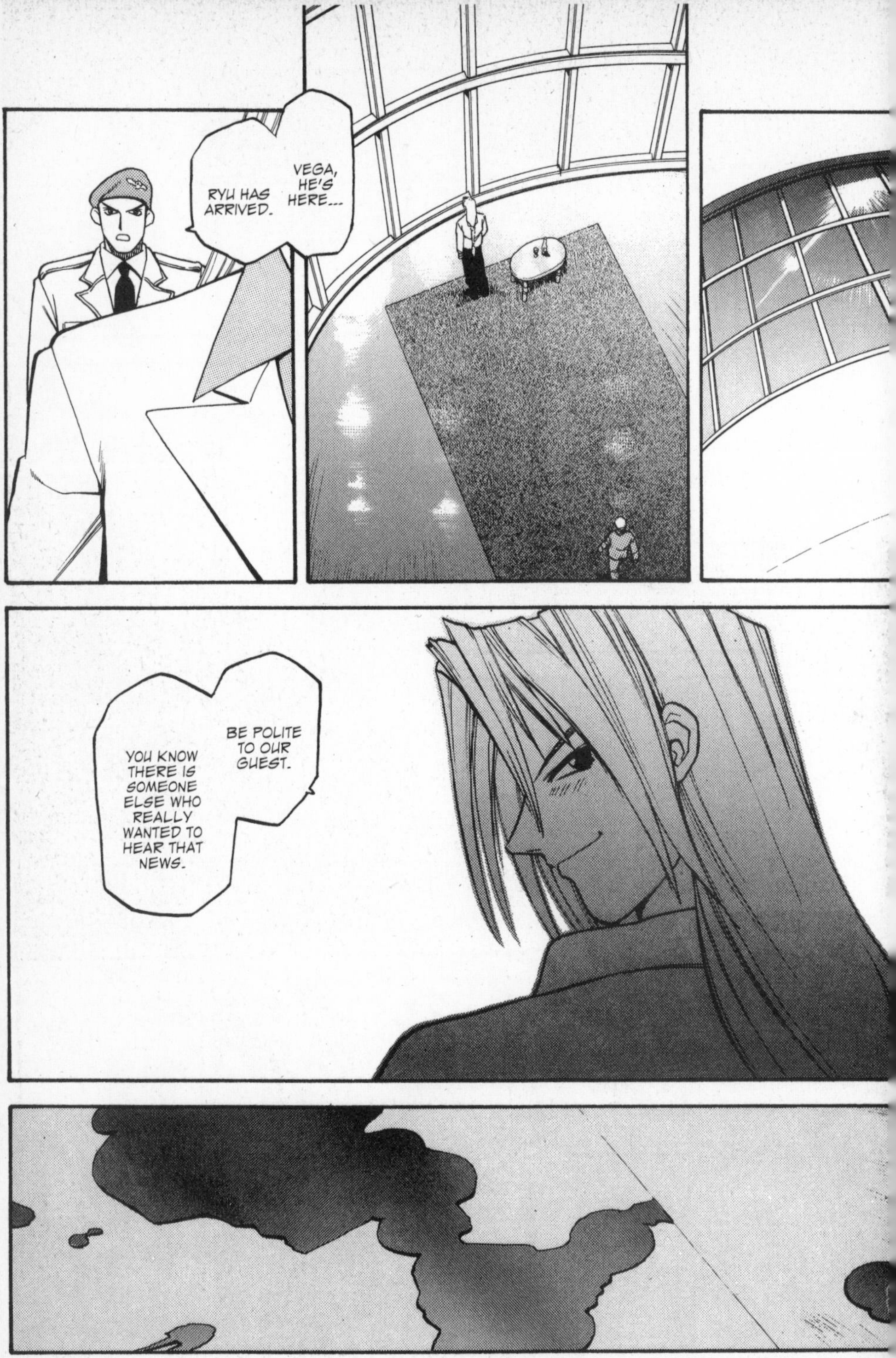
VEGA, HE'S HERE...
RYU HAS ARRIVED.
BE POLITE TO OUR GUEST.
YOU KNOW THERE IS SOMEONE ELSE WHO REALLY WANTED TO HEAR THAT NEWS.

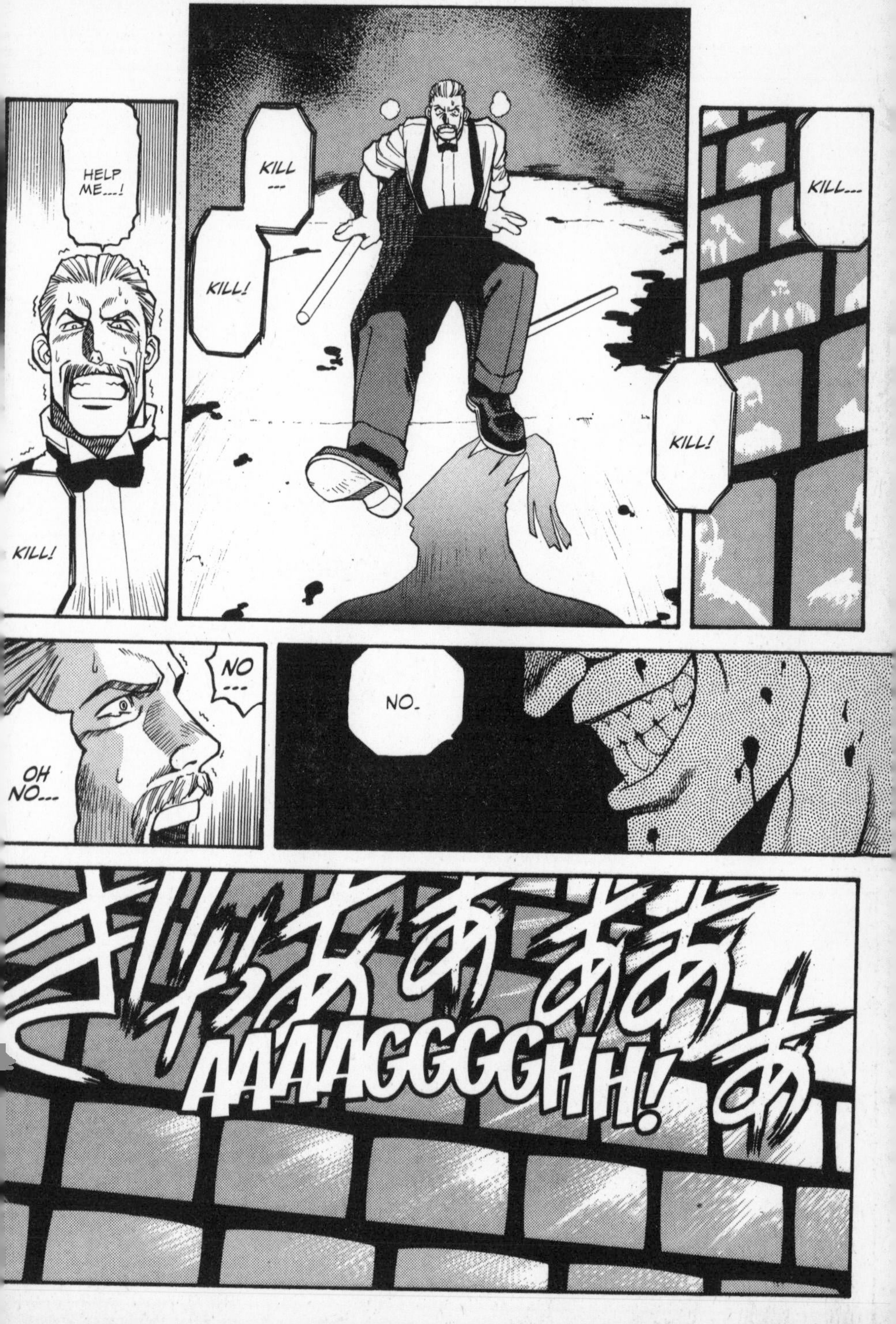
KILL...
KILL!
KILL ---
KILL!
HELP ME...!
KILL!
NO.
NO ---
OH NO...
AAAAGGGGHH!

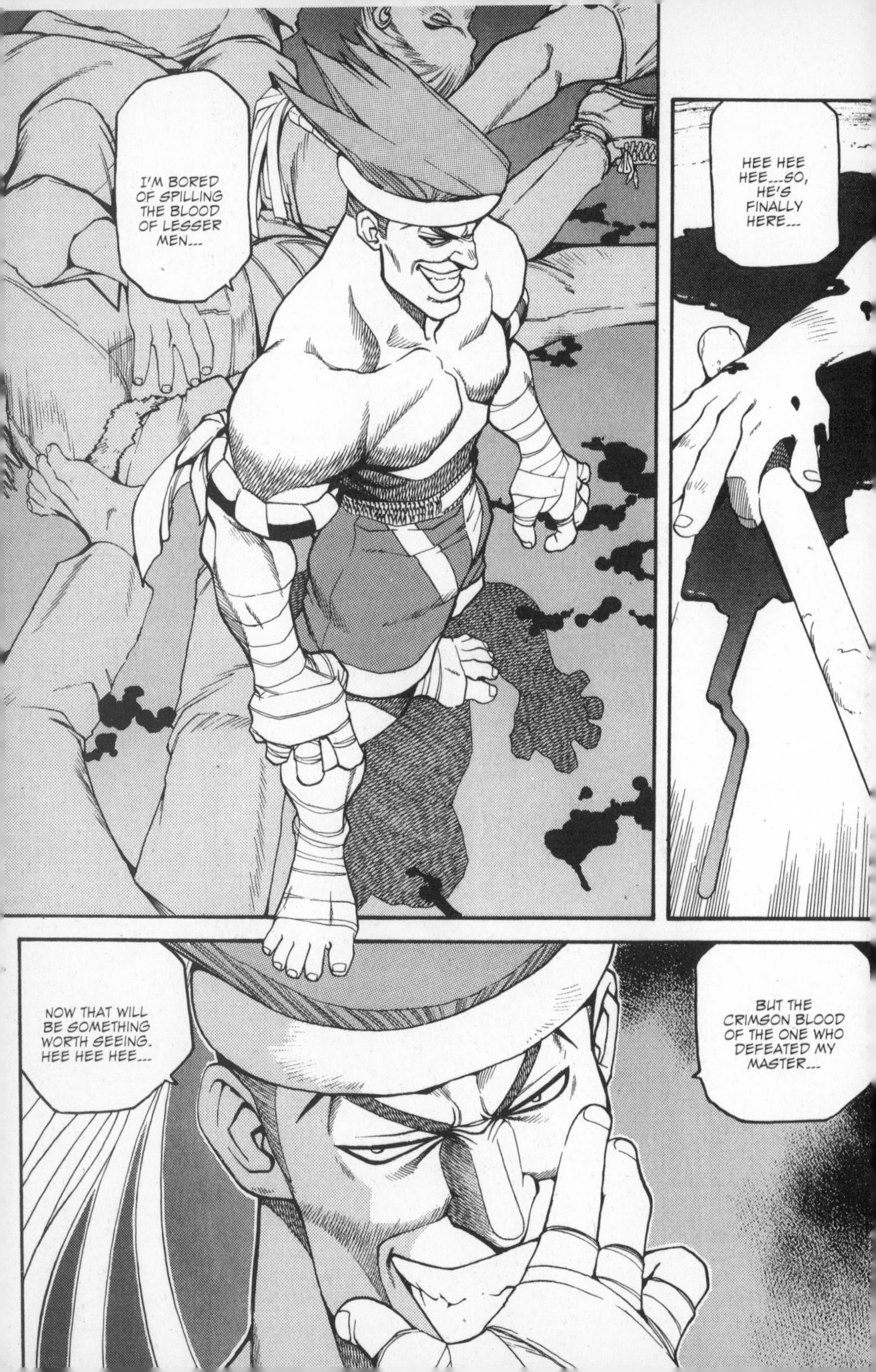
HEE HEE HEE...SO, HE'S FINALLY HERE...
I'M BORED OF SPILLING THE BLOOD OF LESSER MEN...
BUT THE CRIMSON BLOOD OF THE ONE WHO DEFEATED MY MASTER...
NOW THAT WILL BE SOMETHING WORTH SEEING. HEE HEE HEE...

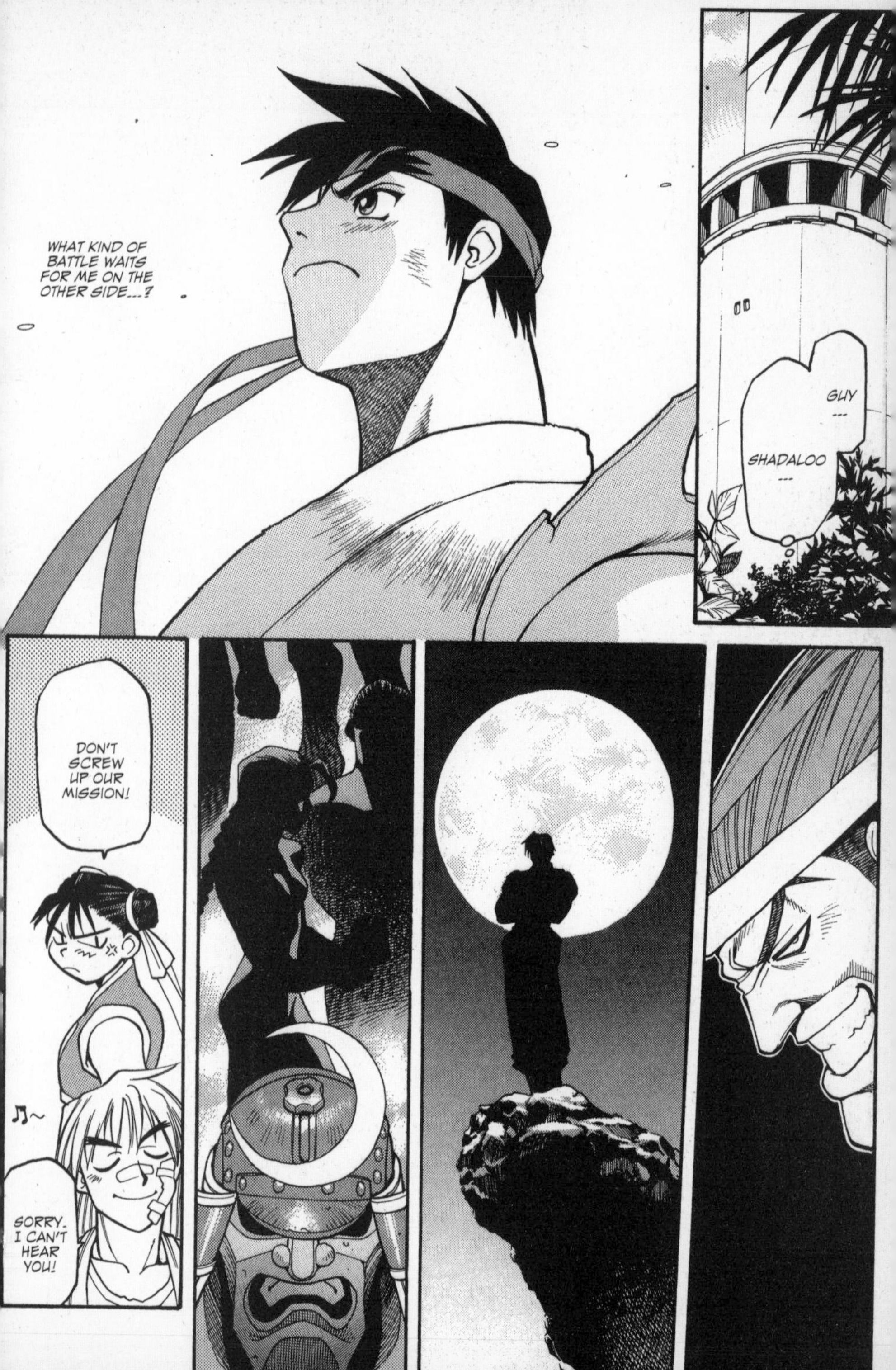
GUY --- SHADALOO ---
WHAT KIND OF BATTLE WAITS FOR ME ON THE OTHER SIDE...?
DON'T SCREW UP OUR MISSION!
♫~
SORRY. I CAN'T HEAR YOU!

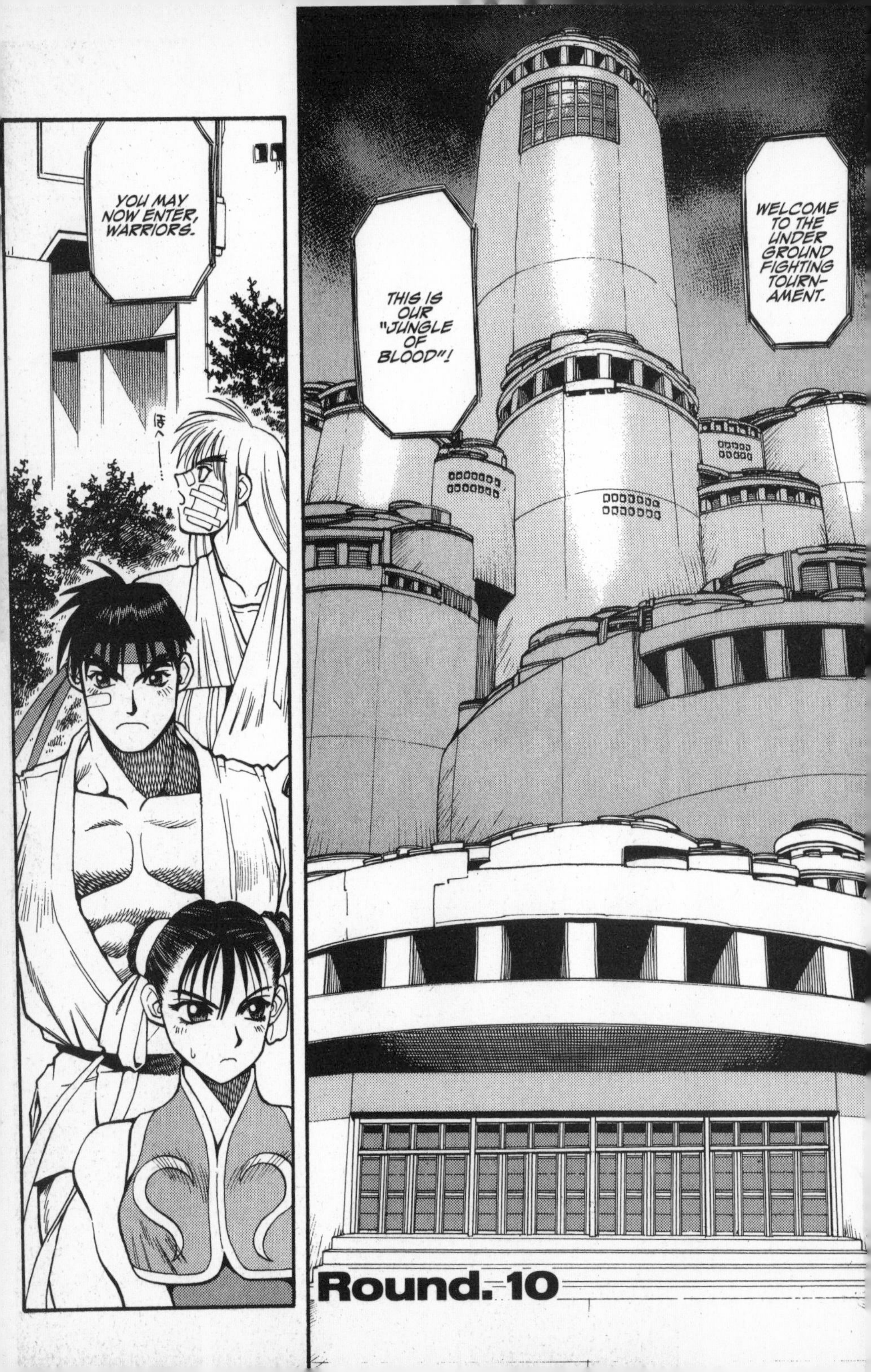
WELCOME TO THE UNDER GROUND FIGHTING TOURN-AMENT.
THIS IS OUR "JUNGLE OF BLOOD"!
Round. 10
YOU MAY NOW ENTER, WARRIORS.
ほへ―…

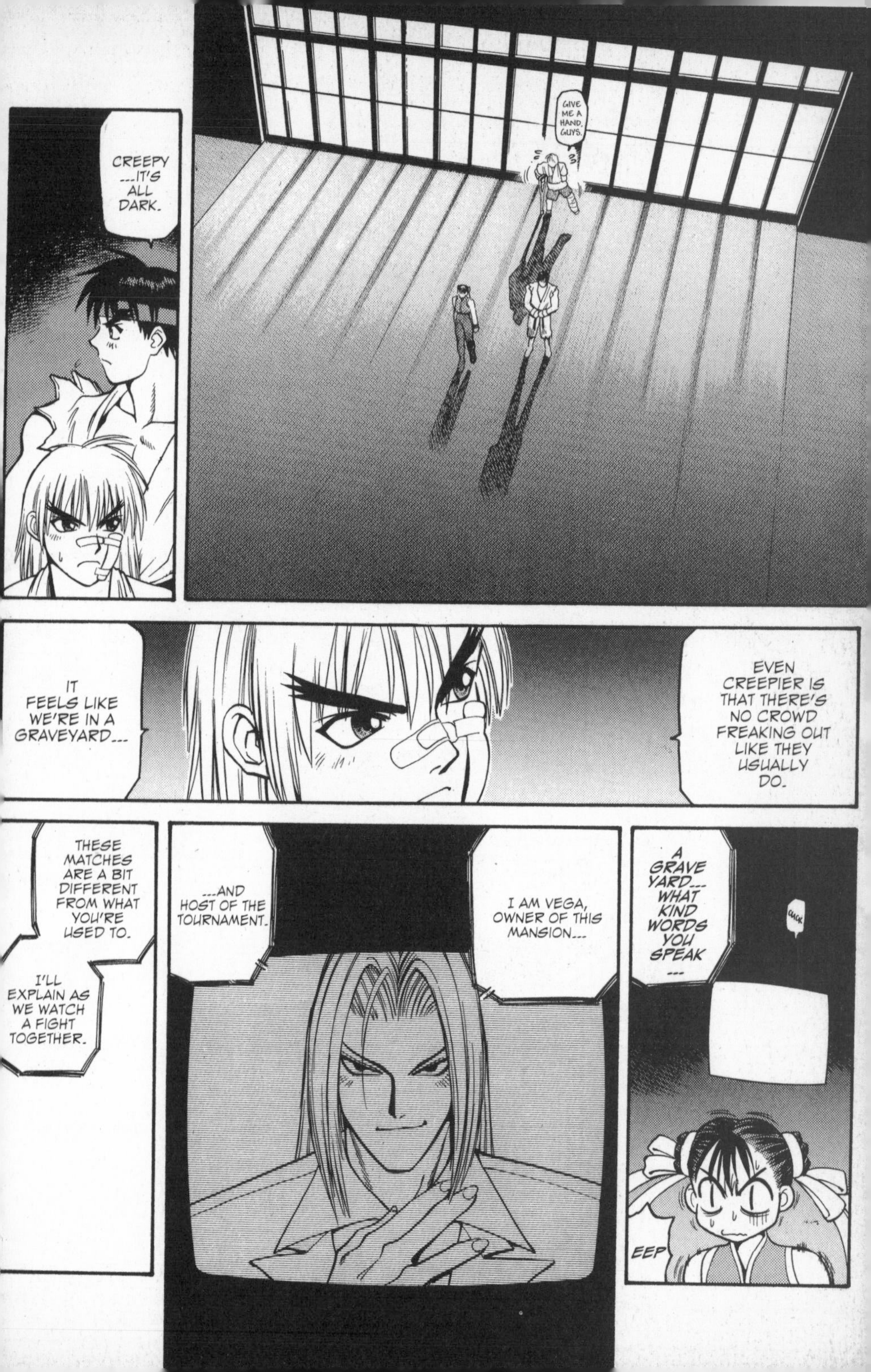
GIVE ME A HAND, GUYS.
CREEPY ---IT'S ALL DARK.
EVEN CREEPIER IS THAT THERE'S NO CROWD FREAKING OUT LIKE THEY USUALLY DO.
IT FEELS LIKE WE'RE IN A GRAVEYARD---
A GRAVE YARD--- WHAT KIND WORDS YOU SPEAK ---
CLICK
EEP
I AM VEGA, OWNER OF THIS MANSION---
---AND HOST OF THE TOURNAMENT.
THESE MATCHES ARE A BIT DIFFERENT FROM WHAT YOU'RE USED TO.
I'LL EXPLAIN AS WE WATCH A FIGHT TOGETHER.

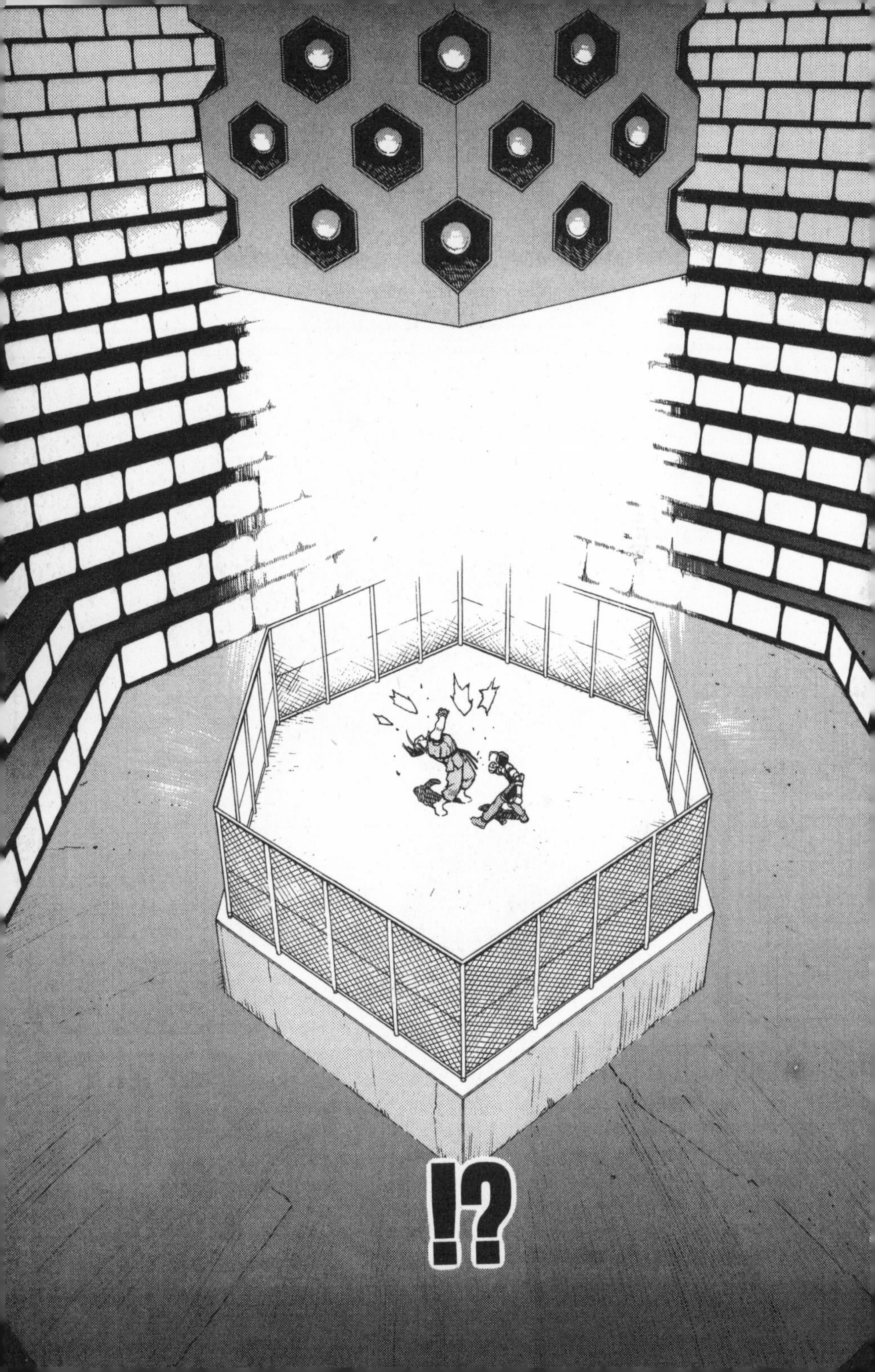
!?

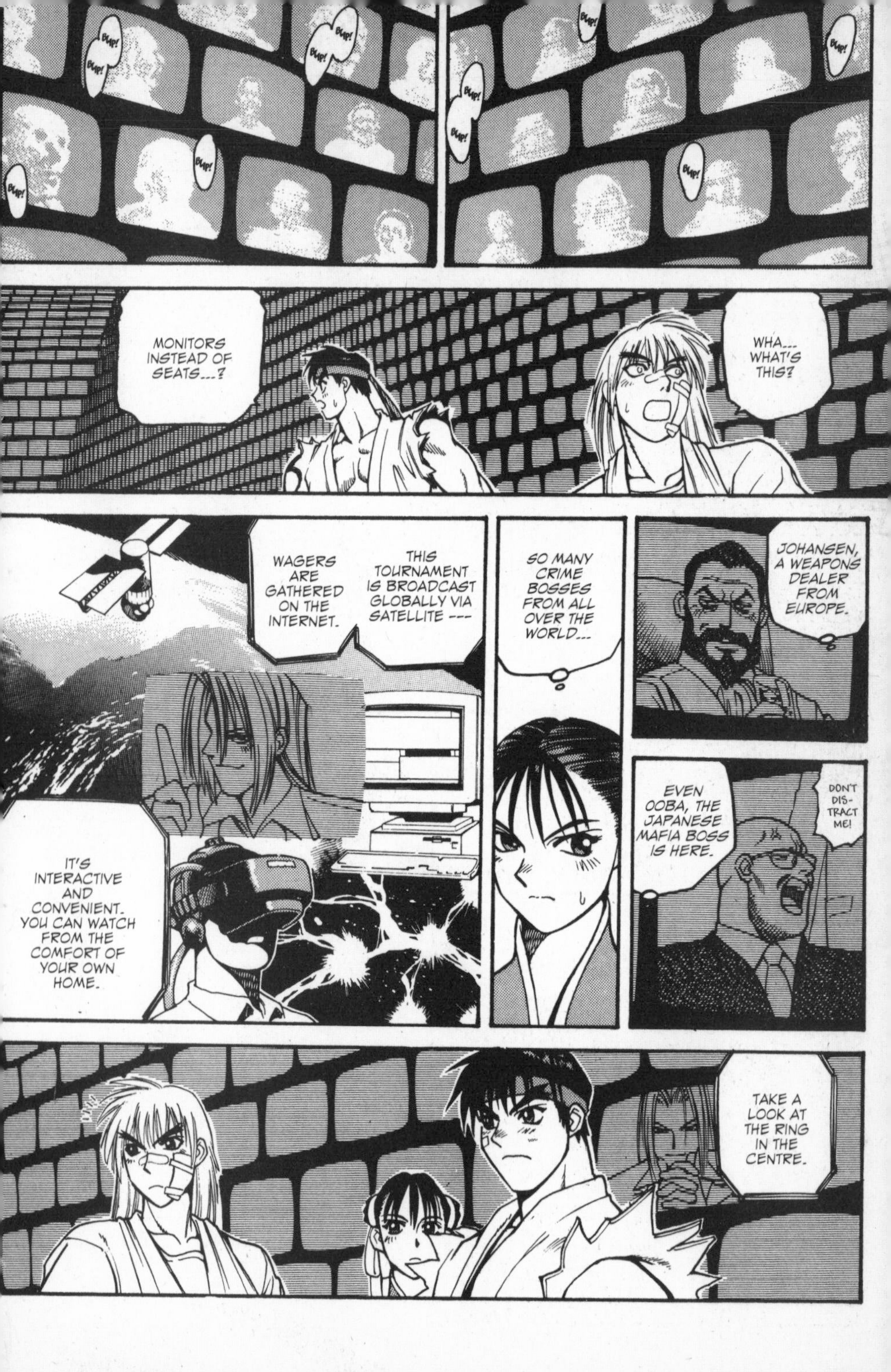
BLIP!
BLIP!
BLIP!
BLIP!
BLIP!
BLIP!
BLIP!
BLIP!
BLIP!
BLIP!
WHA... WHAT'S THIS?
MONITORS INSTEAD OF SEATS...?
JOHANSEN, A WEAPONS DEALER FROM EUROPE.
DON'T DIS-TRACT ME!
EVEN OOBA, THE JAPANESE MAFIA BOSS IS HERE.
SO MANY CRIME BOSSES FROM ALL OVER THE WORLD...
THIS TOURNAMENT IS BROADCAST GLOBALLY VIA SATELLITE ---
WAGERS ARE GATHERED ON THE INTERNET.
IT'S INTERACTIVE AND CONVENIENT. YOU CAN WATCH FROM THE COMFORT OF YOUR OWN HOME.
TAKE A LOOK AT THE RING IN THE CENTRE.

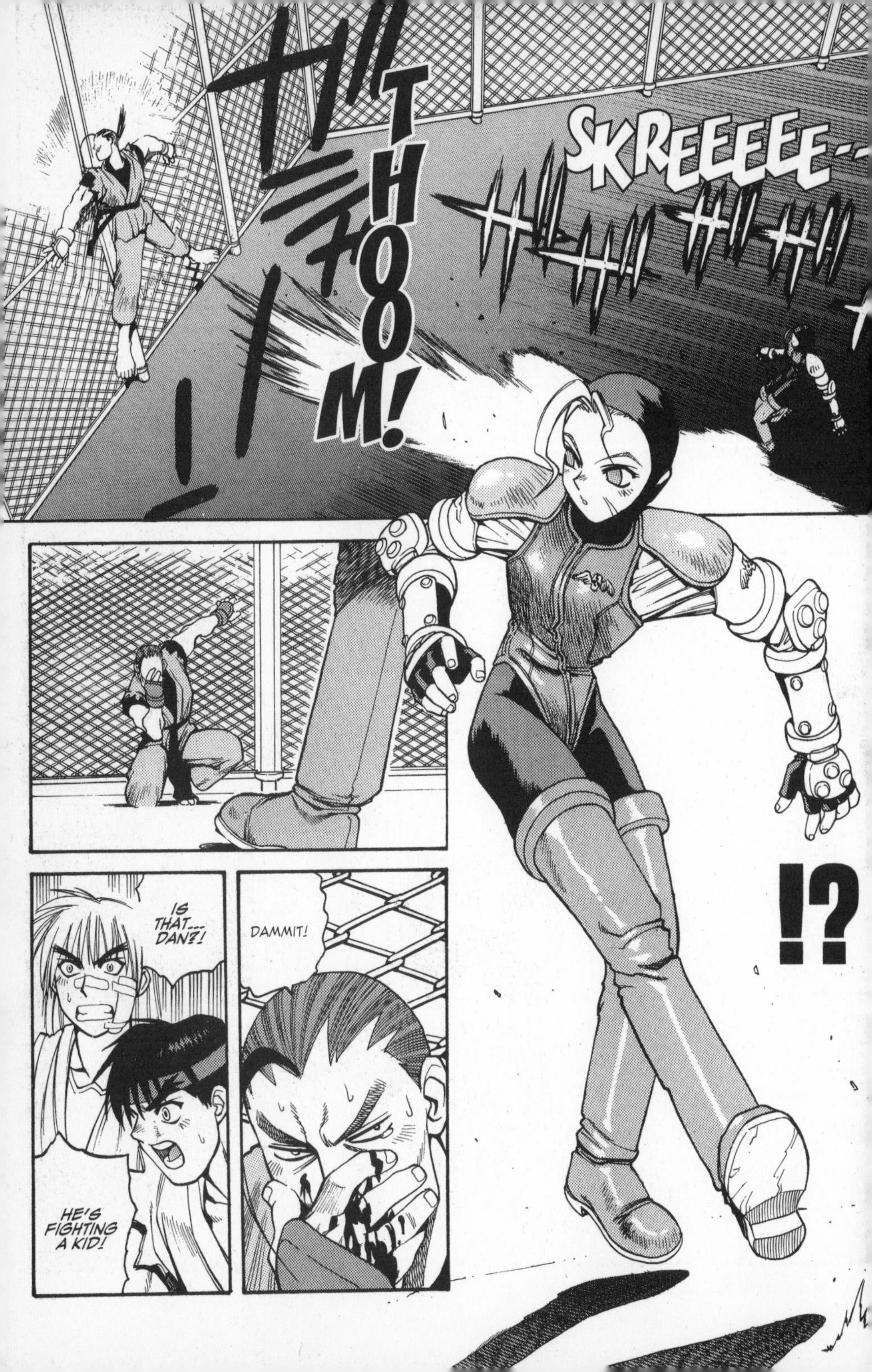
SKREEEEE...
THOOM!
!?
DAMMIT!
IS THAT... DAN?!
HE'S FIGHTING A KID!

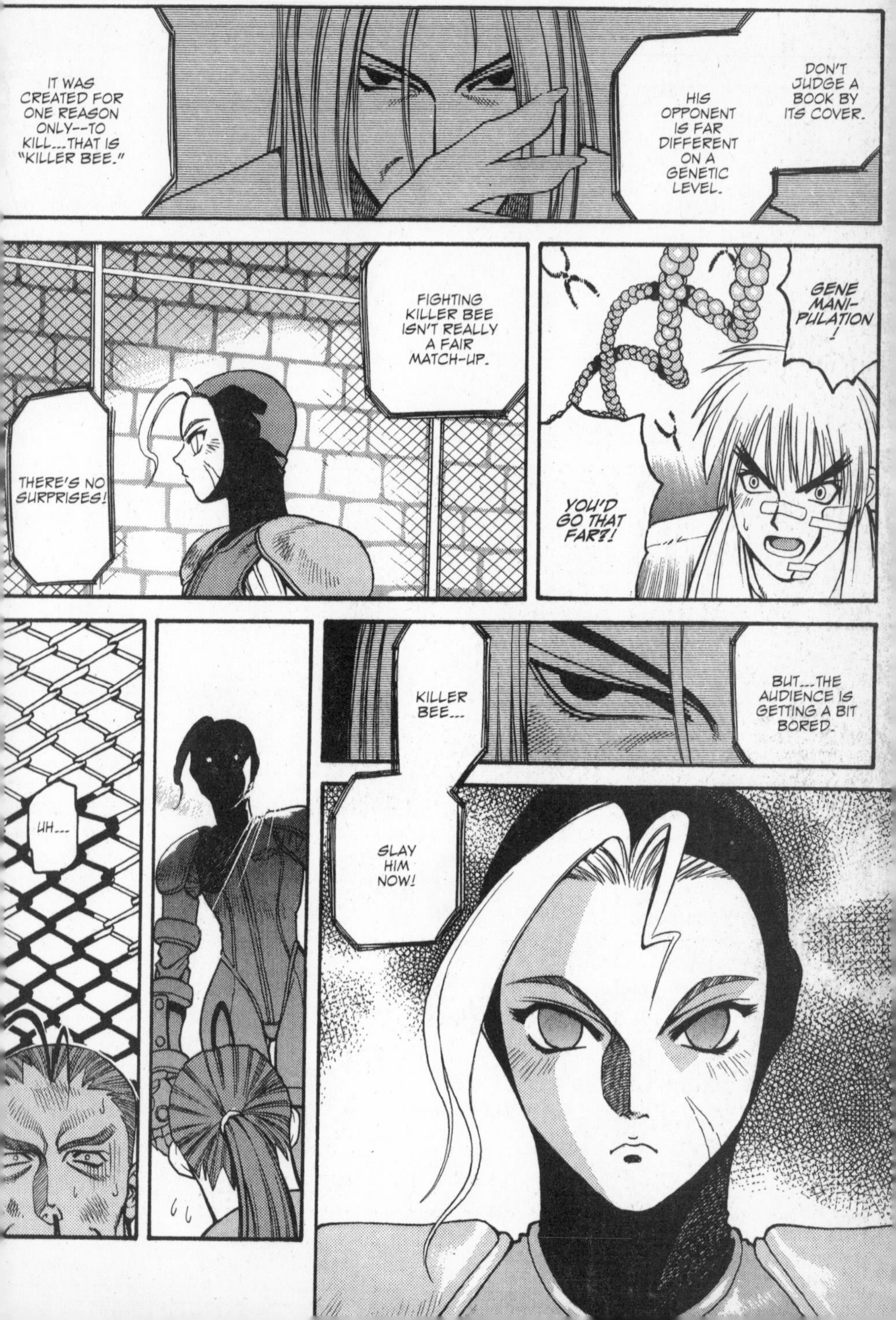
DON'T JUDGE A BOOK BY ITS COVER.
HIS OPPONENT IS FAR DIFFERENT ON A GENETIC LEVEL.
IT WAS CREATED FOR ONE REASON ONLY--TO KILL...THAT IS "KILLER BEE."
GENE MANI-PULATION!
YOU'D GO THAT FAR?!
FIGHTING KILLER BEE ISN'T REALLY A FAIR MATCH-UP.
THERE'S NO SURPRISES!
BUT...THE AUDIENCE IS GETTING A BIT BORED.
KILLER BEE...
SLAY HIM NOW!
UH...

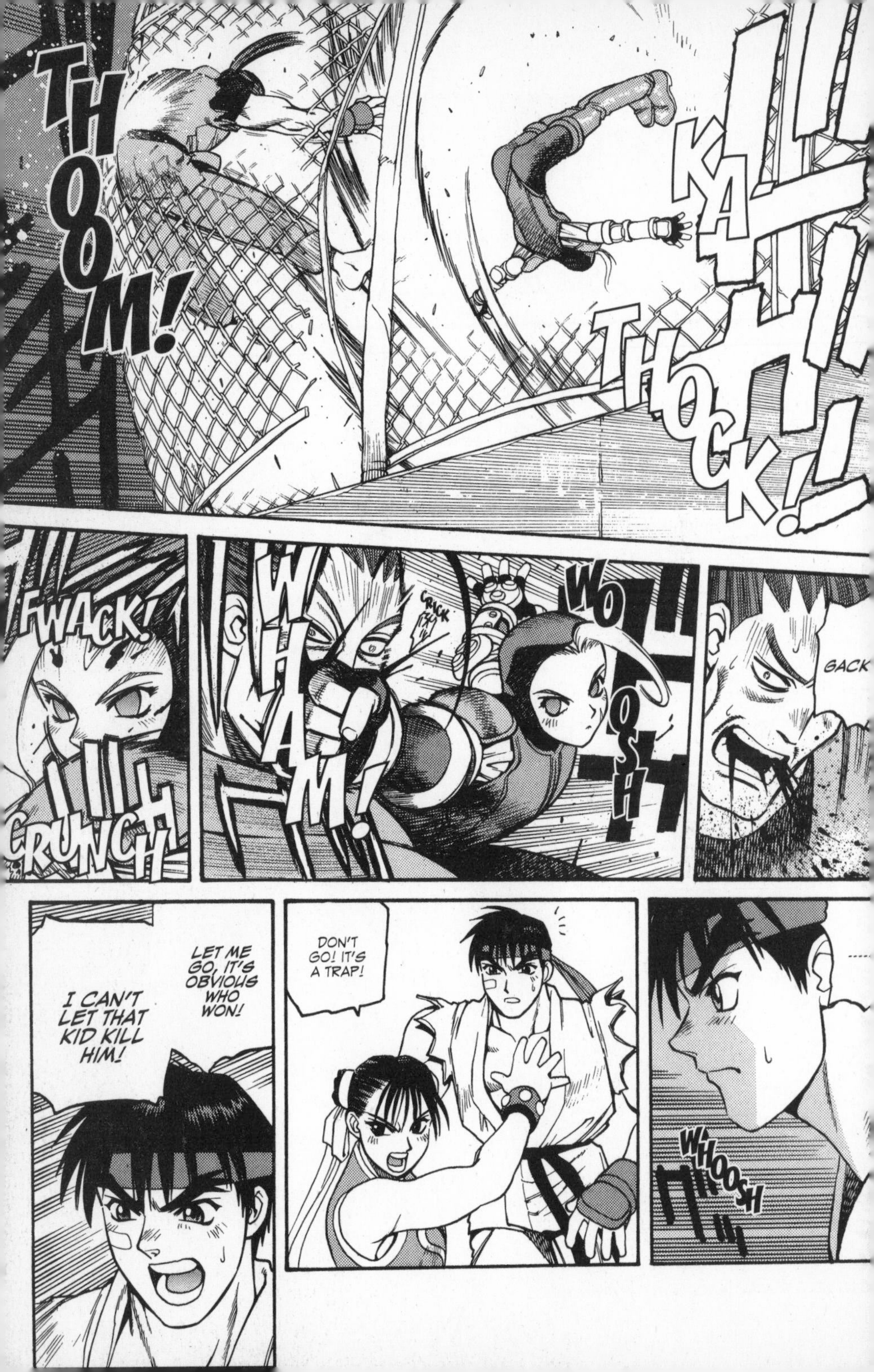
KA
THOCK!!
THOOM!
GACK
WOOSH
CRICK
WHAM!
FWACK!
CRUNCH
......
WHOOSH
DON'T GO! IT'S A TRAP!
LET ME GO, IT'S OBVIOUS WHO WON!
I CAN'T LET THAT KID KILL HIM!

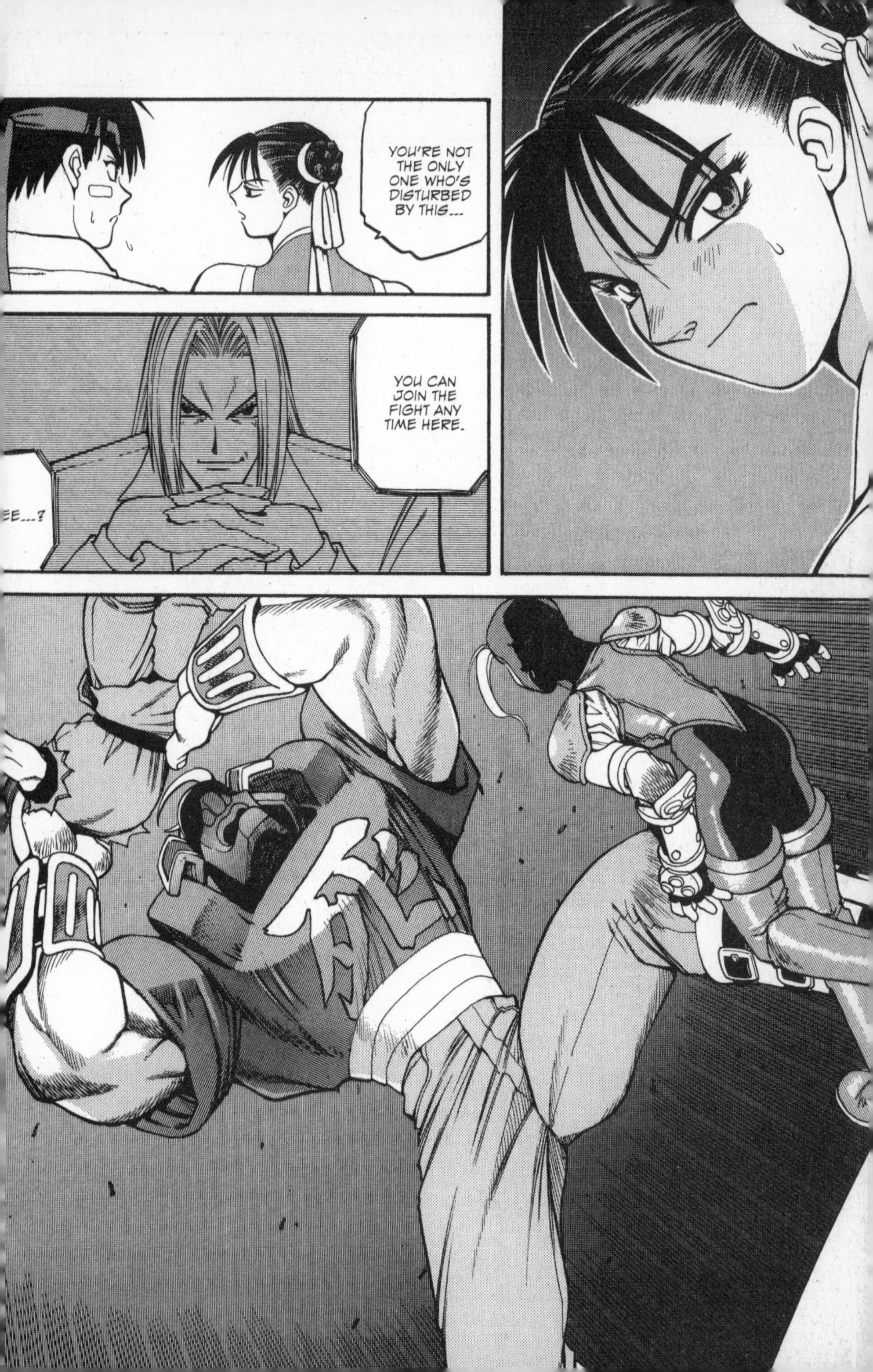
YOU'RE NOT THE ONLY ONE WHO'S DISTURBED BY THIS...
YOU CAN JOIN THE FIGHT ANY TIME HERE.
EE...?

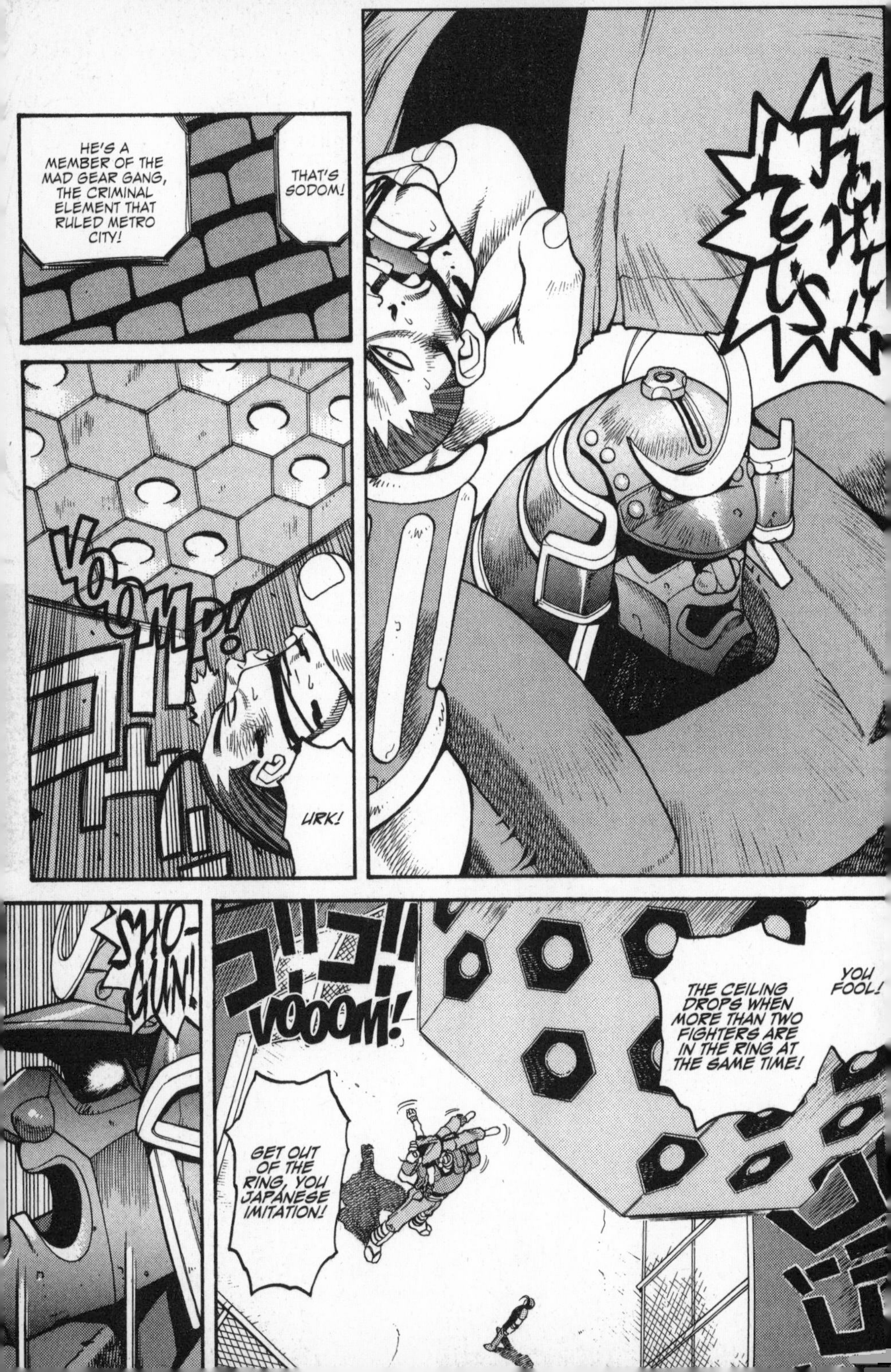
THAT'S SODOM!
HE'S A MEMBER OF THE MAD GEAR GANG, THE CRIMINAL ELEMENT THAT RULED METRO CITY!
VOOOMP!
URK!
YOU FOOL!
THE CEILING DROPS WHEN MORE THAN TWO FIGHTERS ARE IN THE RING AT THE SAME TIME!
VOOOM!
GET OUT OF THE RING, YOU JAPANESE IMITATION!
SHO-GUN!

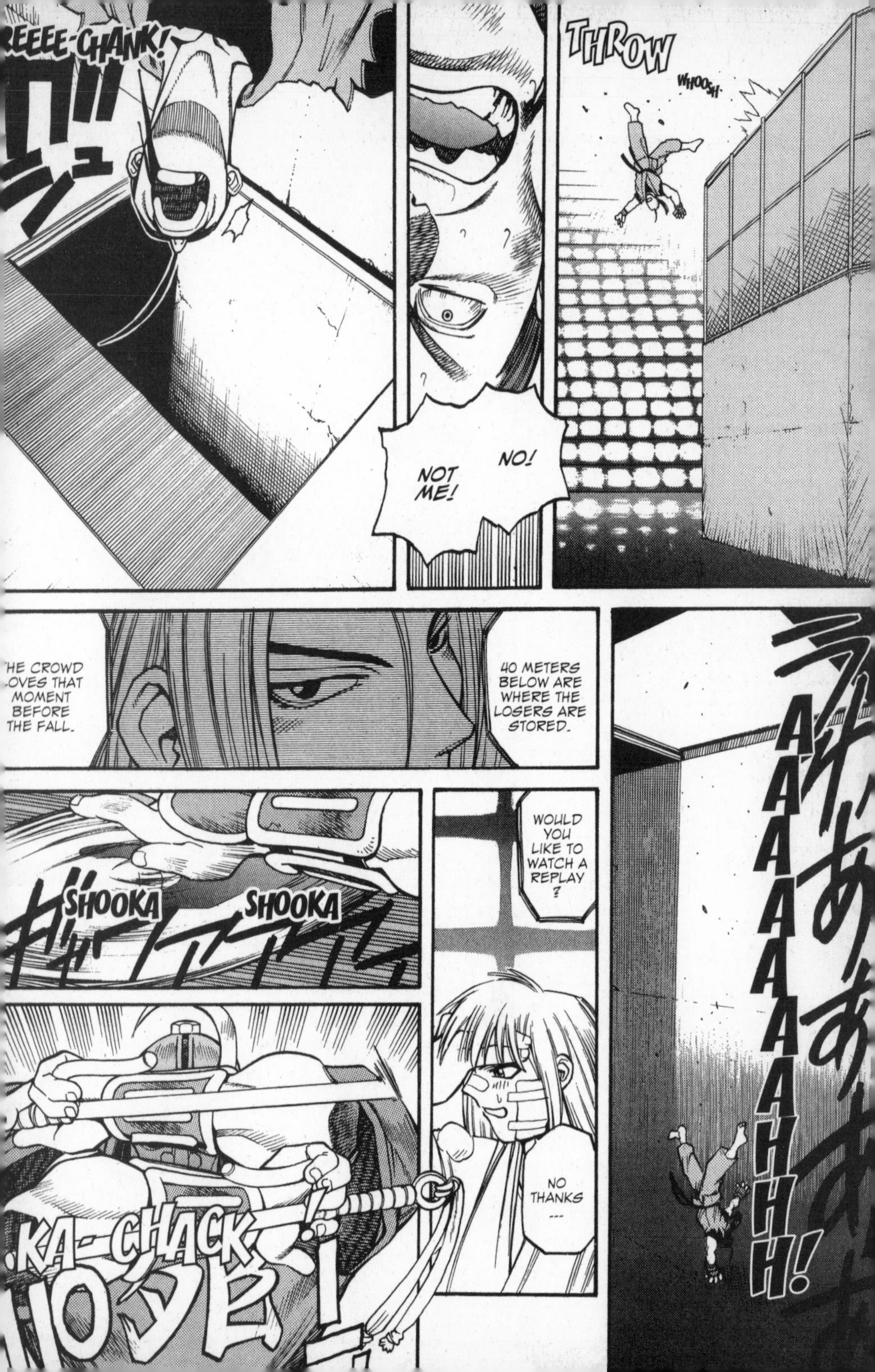
THROW
WHOOSH
NO! NOT ME!
REEEE-CHANK!
AAAAAAAAHHHH!
40 METERS BELOW ARE WHERE THE LOSERS ARE STORED.
HE CROWD OVES THAT MOMENT BEFORE THE FALL.
WOULD YOU LIKE TO WATCH A REPLAY?
SHOOKA
SHOOKA
NO THANKS ...
KA-CHACK!

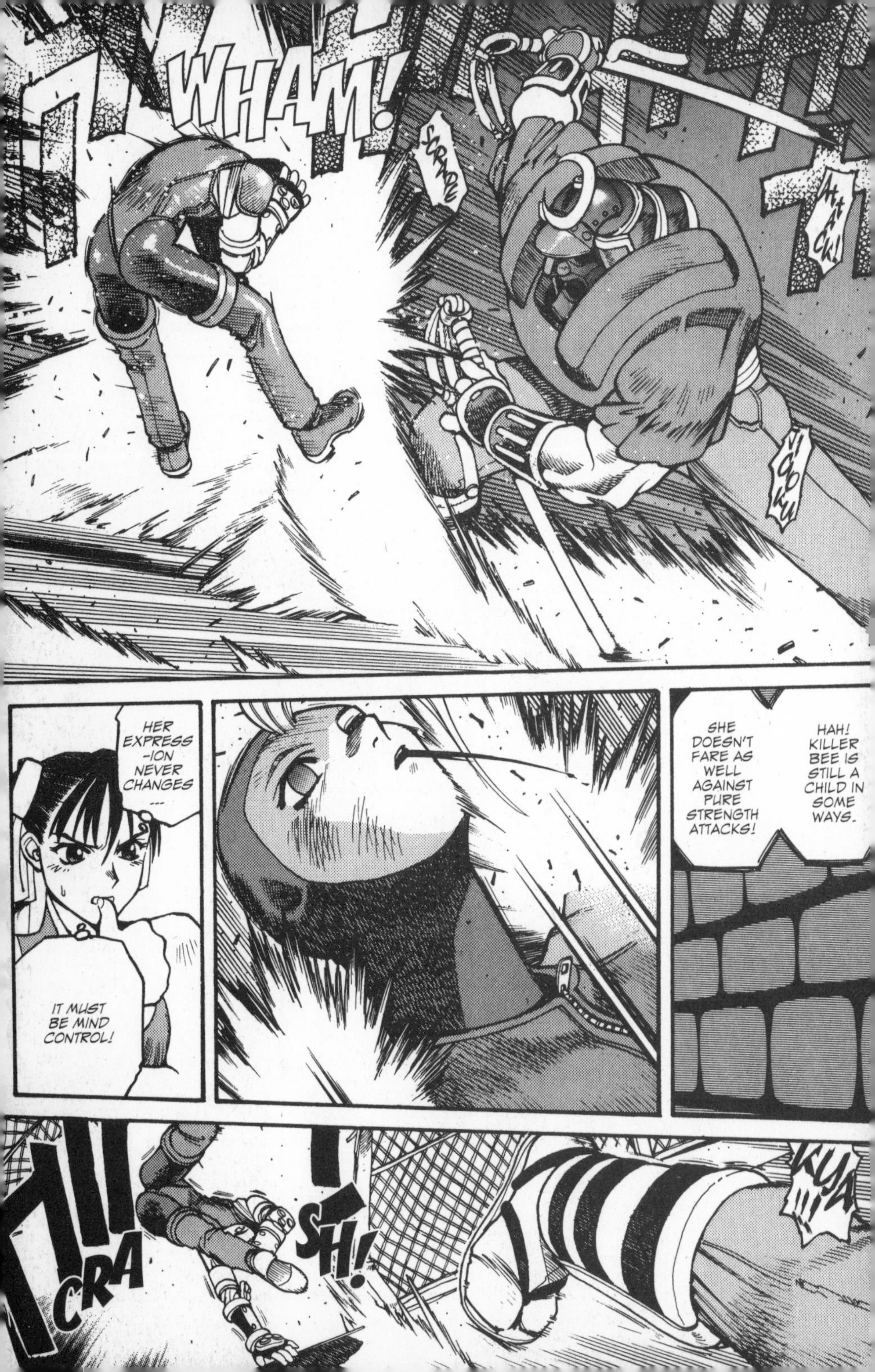
ATTACK!
JIGOKU
SCRAPE
WHAM!
HAH! KILLER BEE IS STILL A CHILD IN SOME WAYS.
SHE DOESN'T FARE AS WELL AGAINST PURE STRENGTH ATTACKS!
HER EXPRESS-ION NEVER CHANGES...
IT MUST BE MIND CONTROL!
KYA!!!
CRASH!!

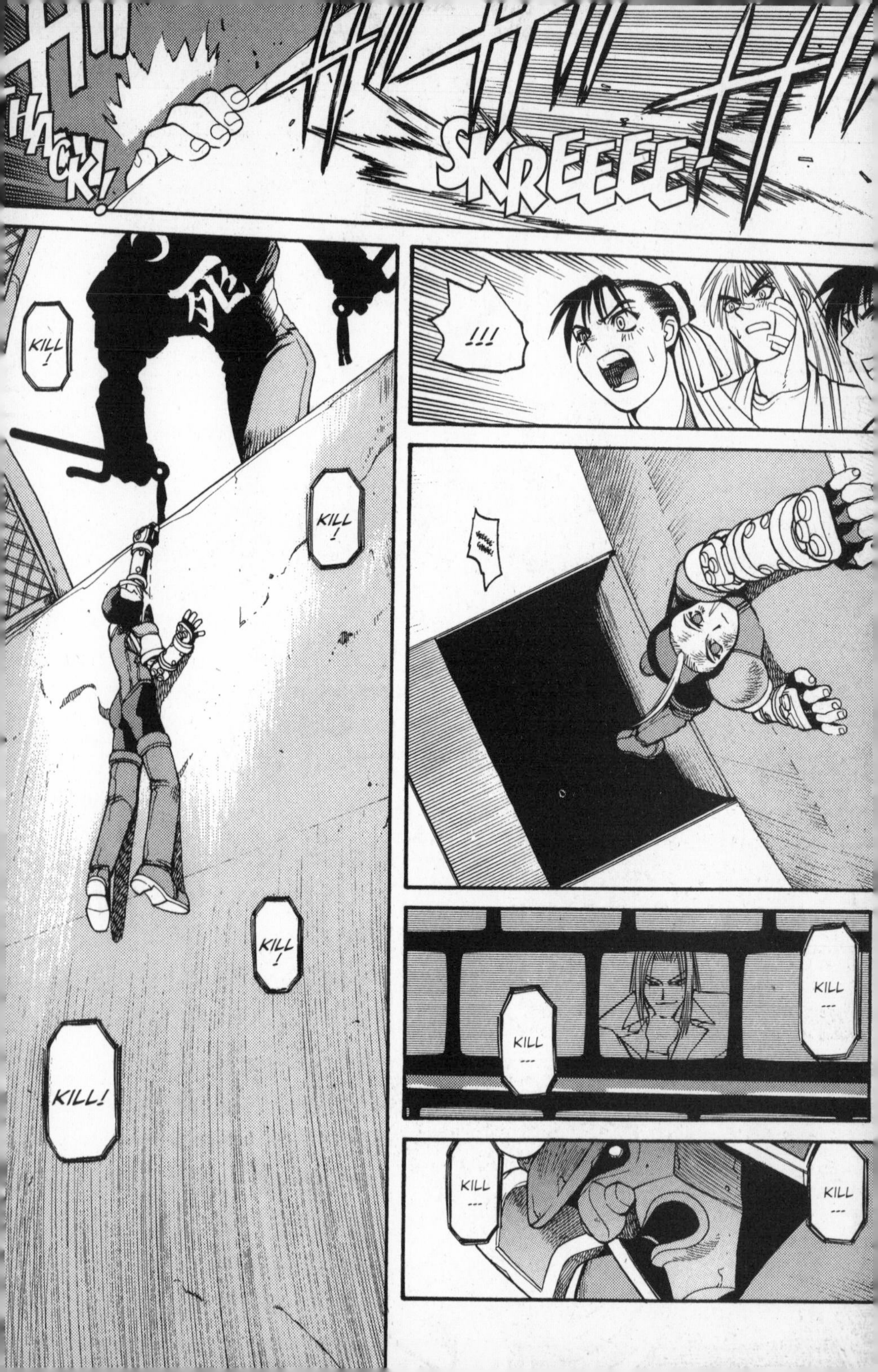
SKREEEE-
HACK!
!!!
KILL ---
KILL ---
KILL ---
KILL ---
KILL !
KILL !
KILL !
KILL!

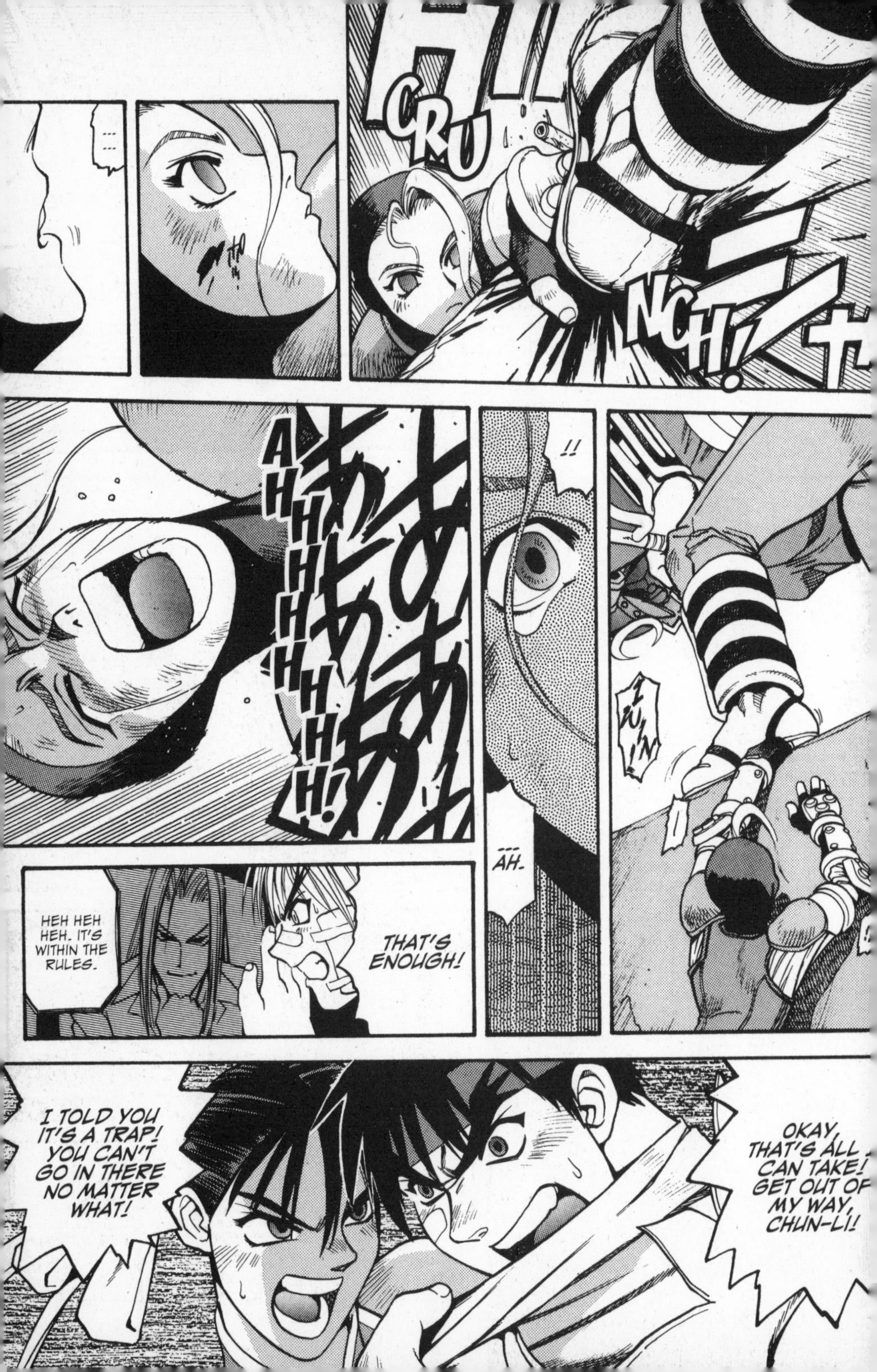
CRU
NCH!
ZUIN!
!!
...AH-
AHHHHHHHHHH!
THAT'S ENOUGH!
HEH HEH HEH. IT'S WITHIN THE RULES.
OKAY, THAT'S ALL I CAN TAKE! GET OUT OF MY WAY, CHUN-LI!
I TOLD YOU IT'S A TRAP! YOU CAN'T GO IN THERE NO MATTER WHAT!

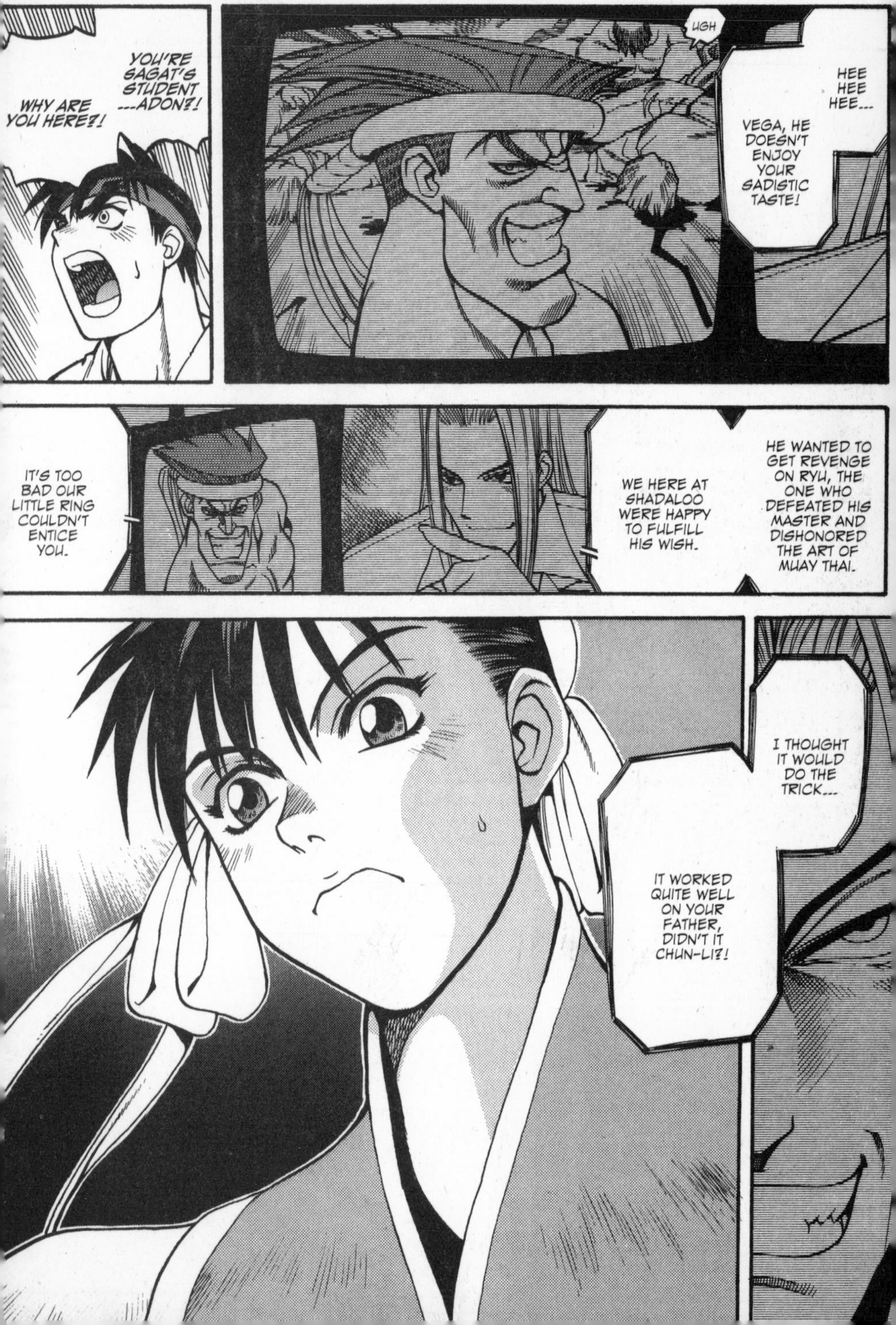
UGH
HEE HEE HEE...
VEGA, HE DOESN'T ENJOY YOUR SADISTIC TASTE!
YOU'RE SAGAT'S STUDENT ---ADON?!
WHY ARE YOU HERE?!
HE WANTED TO GET REVENGE ON RYU, THE ONE WHO DEFEATED HIS MASTER AND DISHONORED THE ART OF MUAY THAI.
WE HERE AT SHADALOO WERE HAPPY TO FULFILL HIS WISH.
IT'S TOO BAD OUR LITTLE RING COULDN'T ENTICE YOU.
I THOUGHT IT WOULD DO THE TRICK...
IT WORKED QUITE WELL ON YOUR FATHER, DIDN'T IT CHUN-LI?!

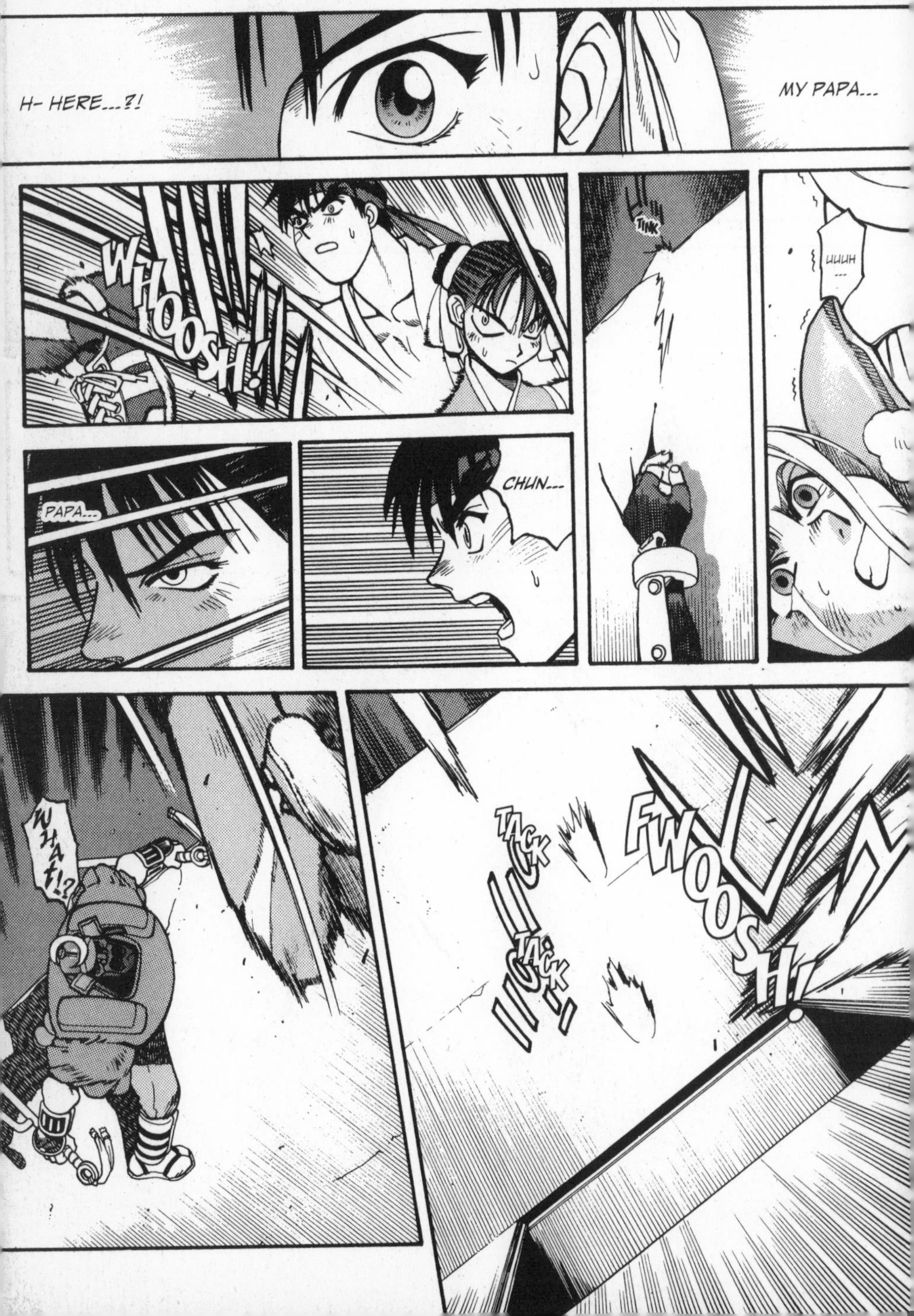
MY PAPA...
H- HERE...?!
UUUH...
TINK
WHOOSH!
CHUN...
PAPA...
FWOOSH!
TACK
TACK!
WHAT!?

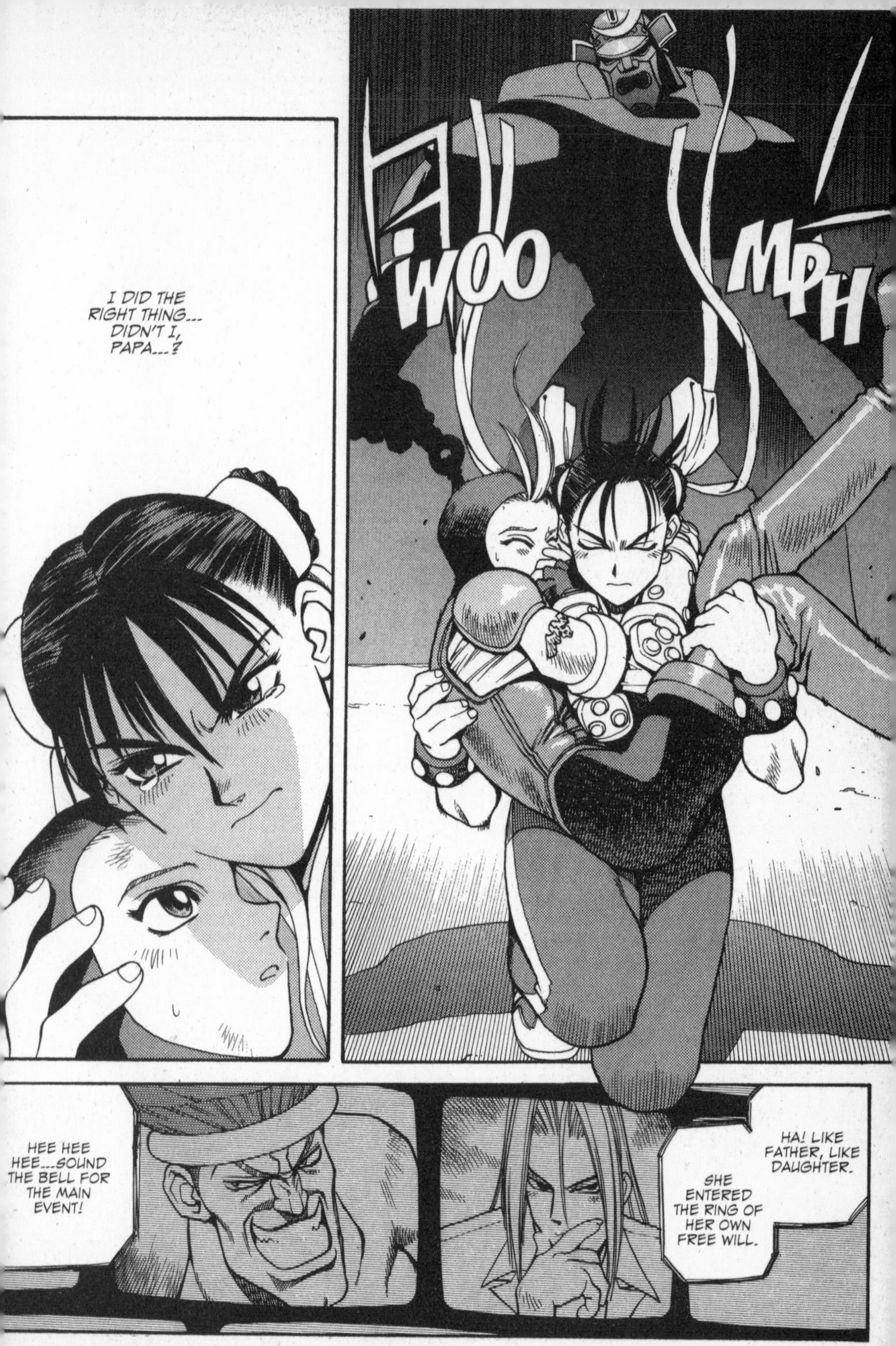
WOOMPH!
I DID THE RIGHT THING... DIDN'T I, PAPA...?
HA! LIKE FATHER, LIKE DAUGHTER.
SHE ENTERED THE RING OF HER OWN FREE WILL.
HEE HEE HEE...SOUND THE BELL FOR THE MAIN EVENT!

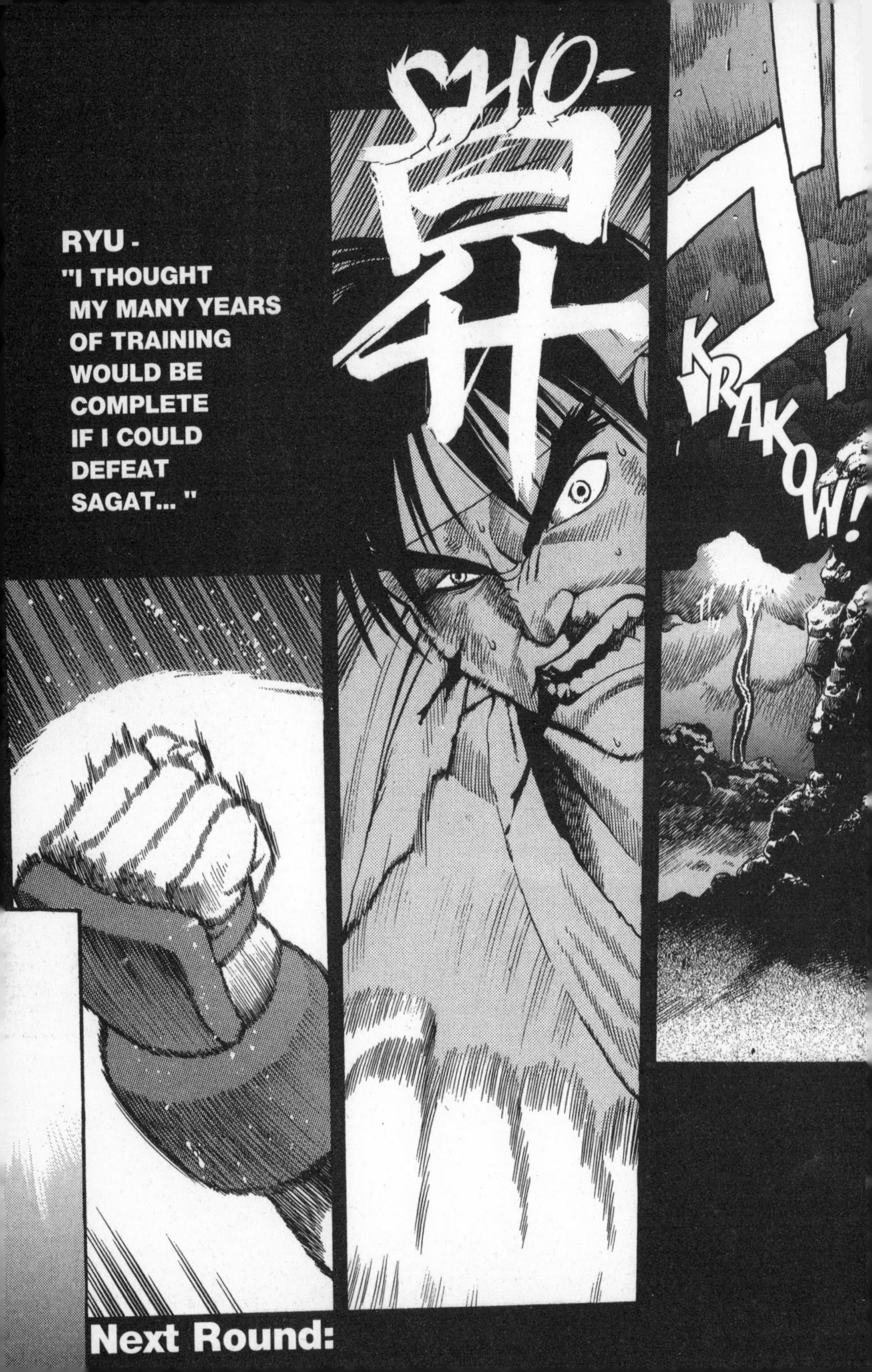
KRAKOW!
SHO-
昇
RYU -
"I THOUGHT MY MANY YEARS OF TRAINING WOULD BE COMPLETE IF I COULD DEFEAT SAGAT... "
Next Round:

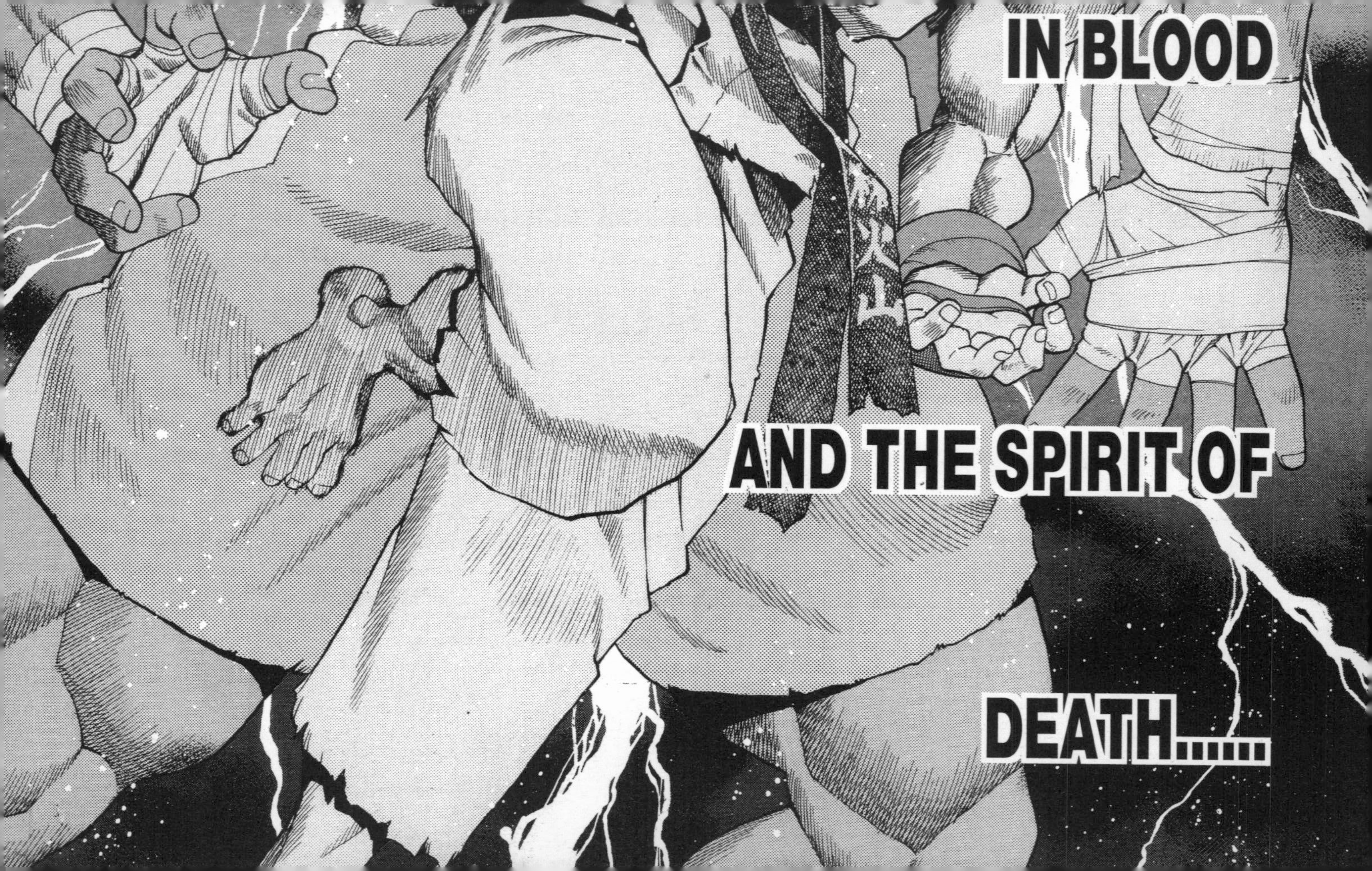
IN BLOOD
AND THE SPIRIT OF
DEATH......

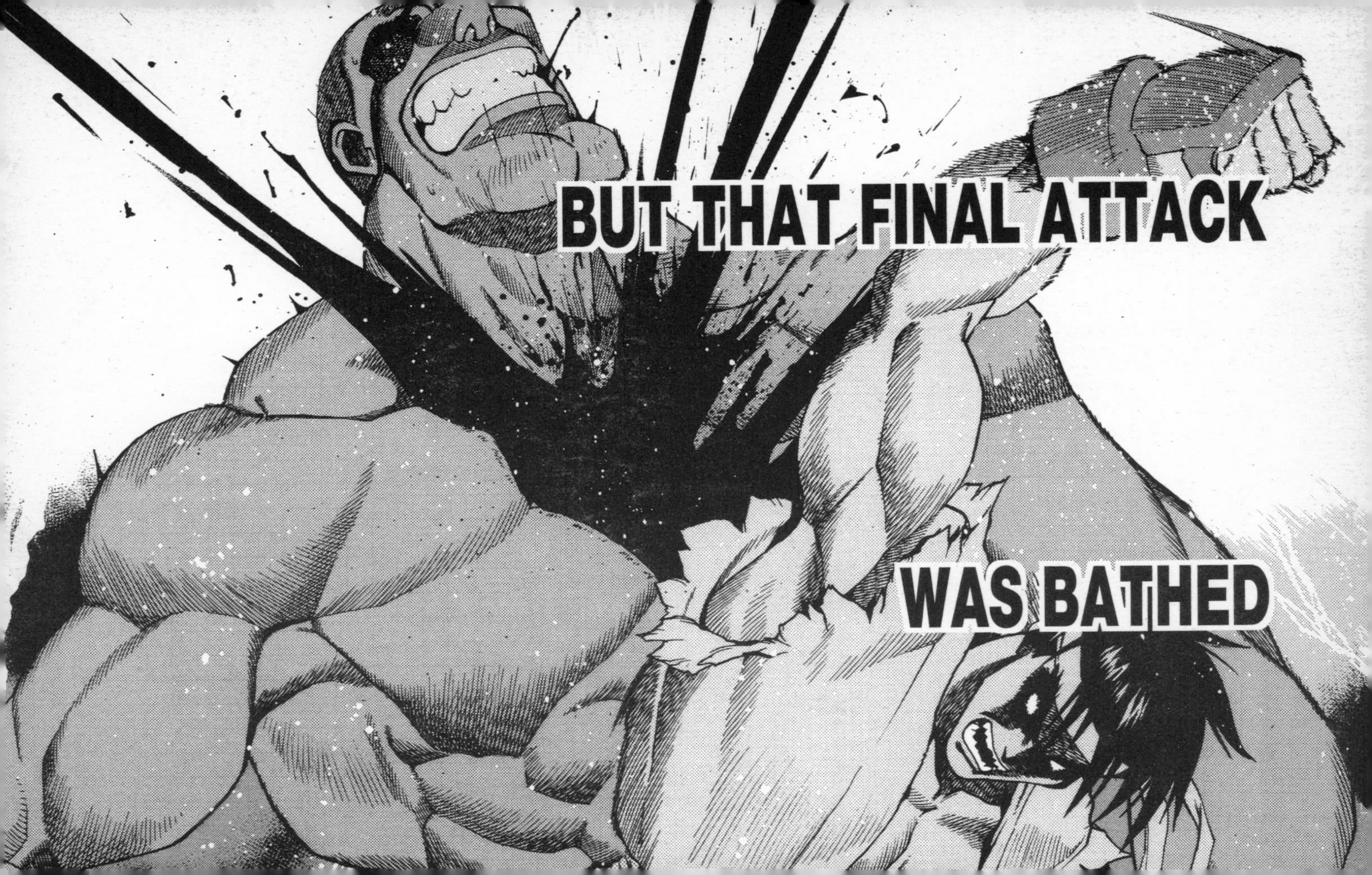
BUT THAT FINAL ATTACK
WAS BATHED

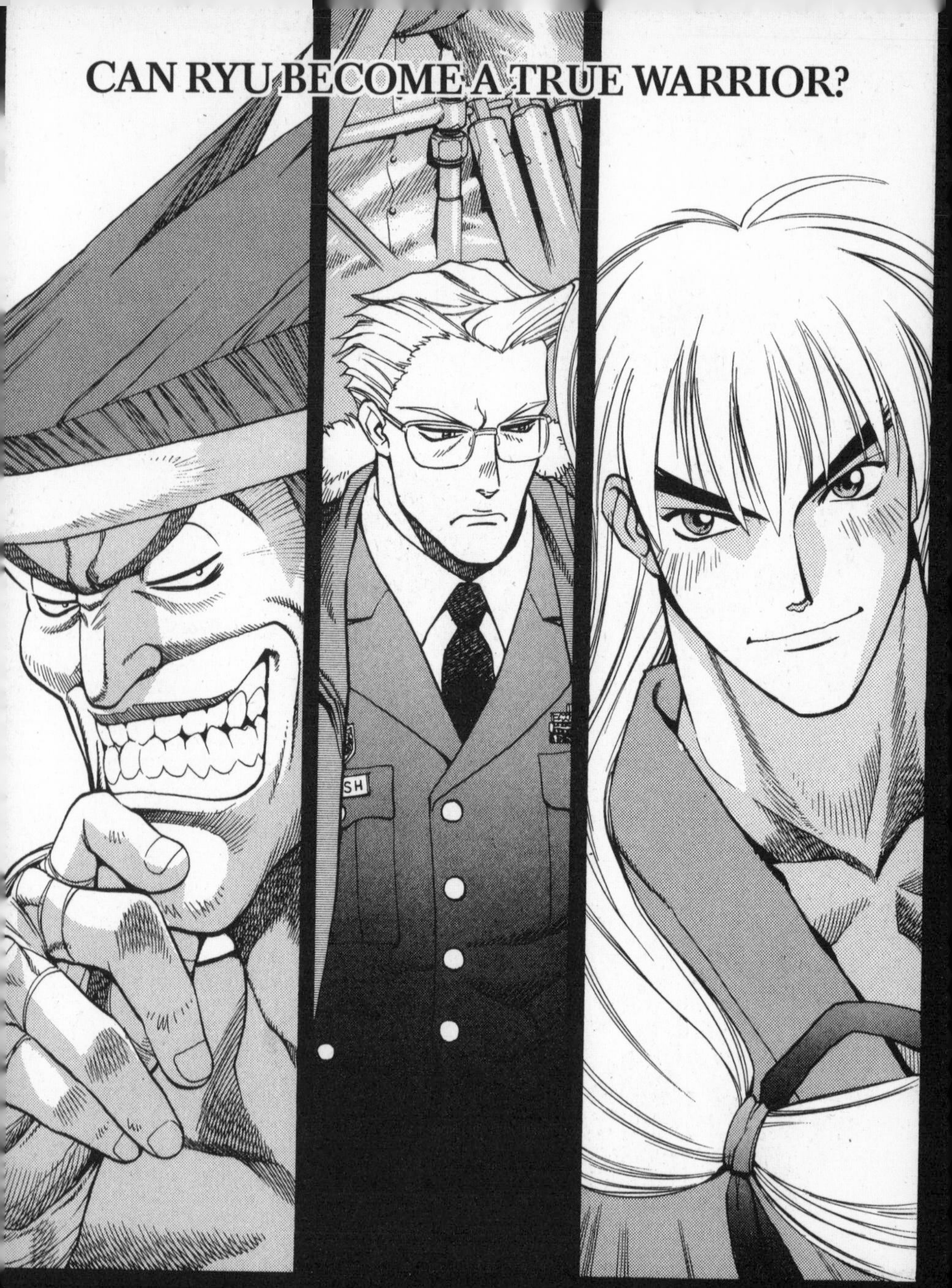
CAN RYU BECOME A TRUE WARRIOR?

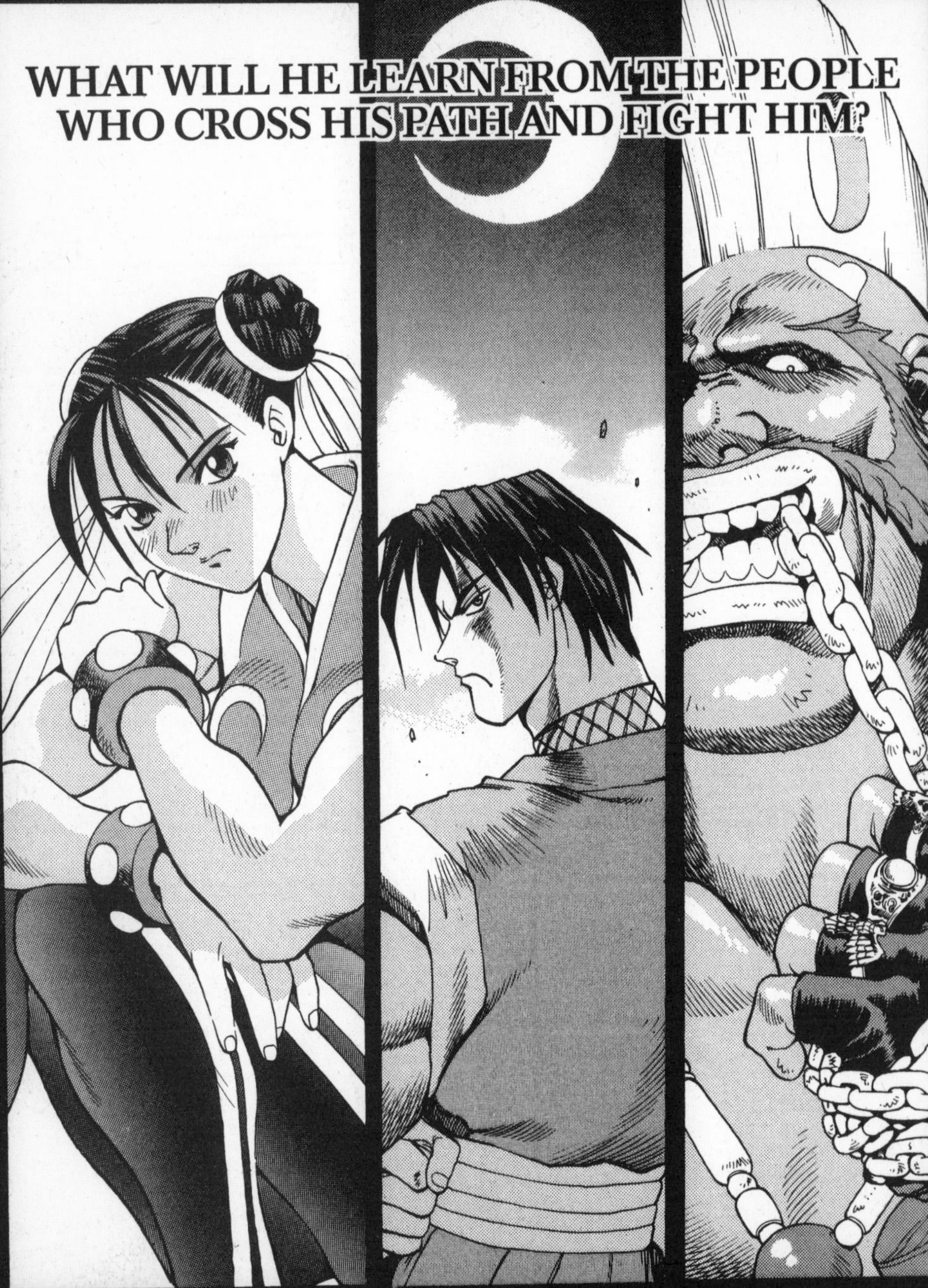
WHAT WILL HE LEARN FROM THE PEOPLE
WHO CROSS HIS PATH AND FIGHT HIM?

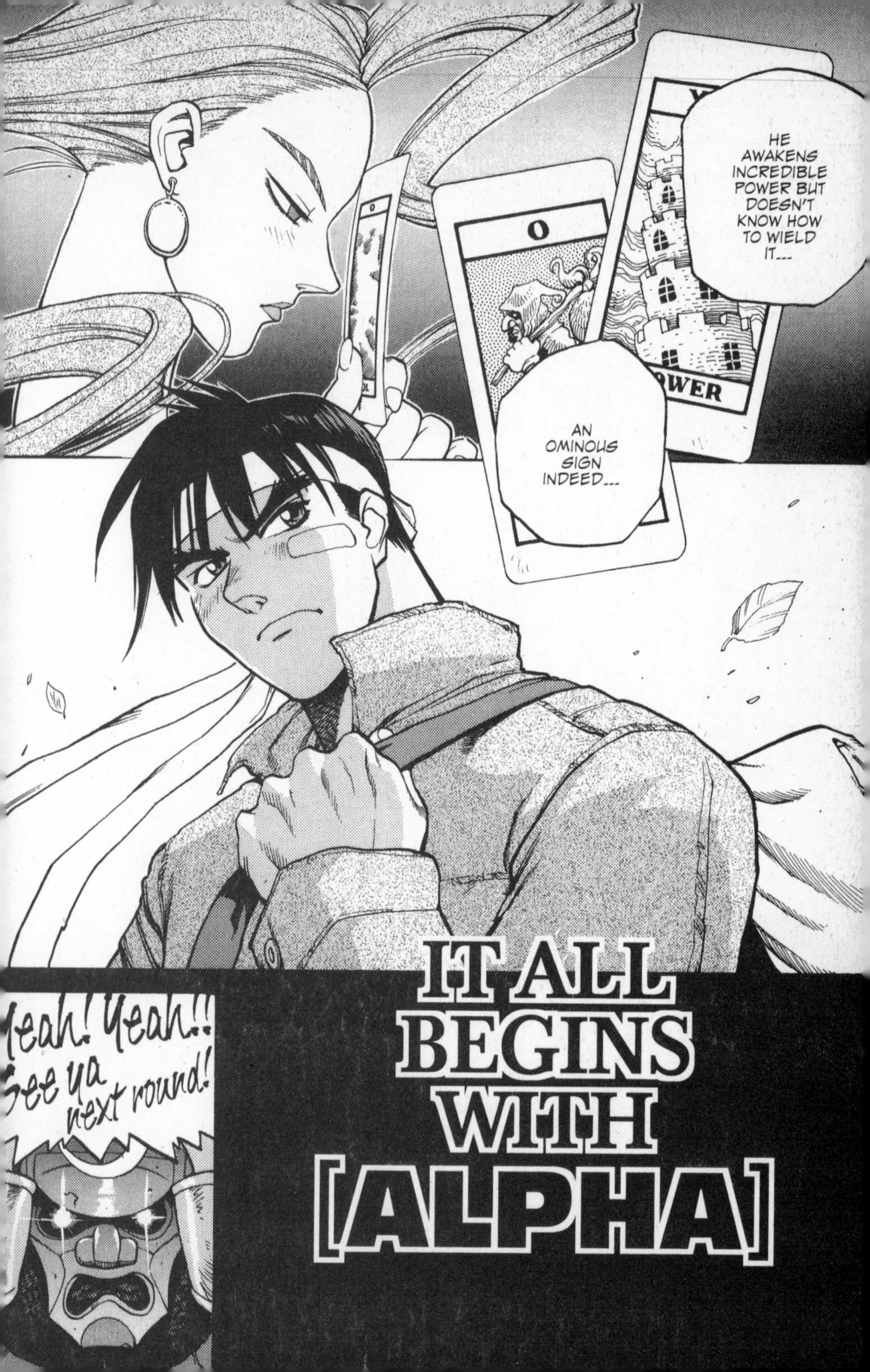
HE AWAKENS INCREDIBLE POWER BUT DOESN'T KNOW HOW TO WIELD IT...
AN OMINOUS SIGN INDEED...
IT ALL BEGINS WITH [ALPHA]
Yeah! Yeah!! See ya next round!

To be continued in Volume 2

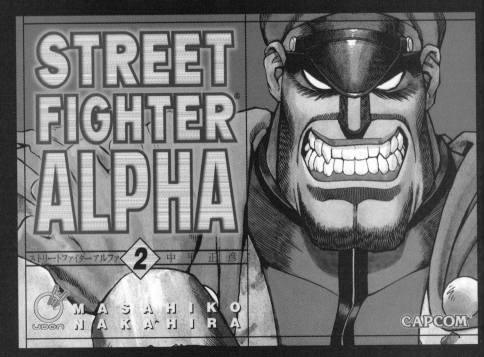

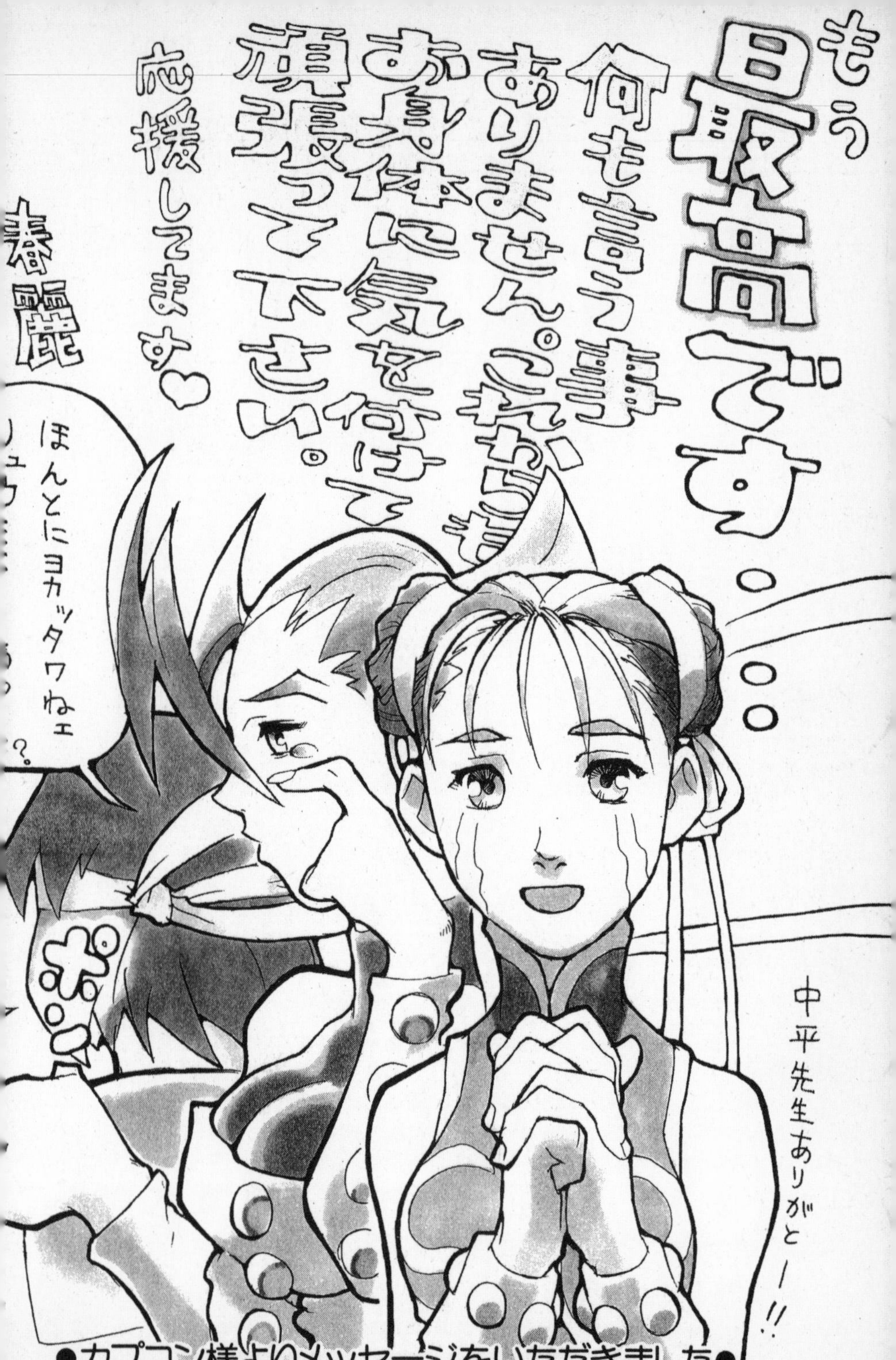
もう
最高です。。。
何も言う事
ありません。それからも
お身体に気を付けて
頑張って下さい。
応援してます♥
春麗
ほんとにヨカッタワねェ
ポッ
中平先生ありがとー!!

●カプコン様よりメッセージをいただきました●

<Translations of the opposite page>

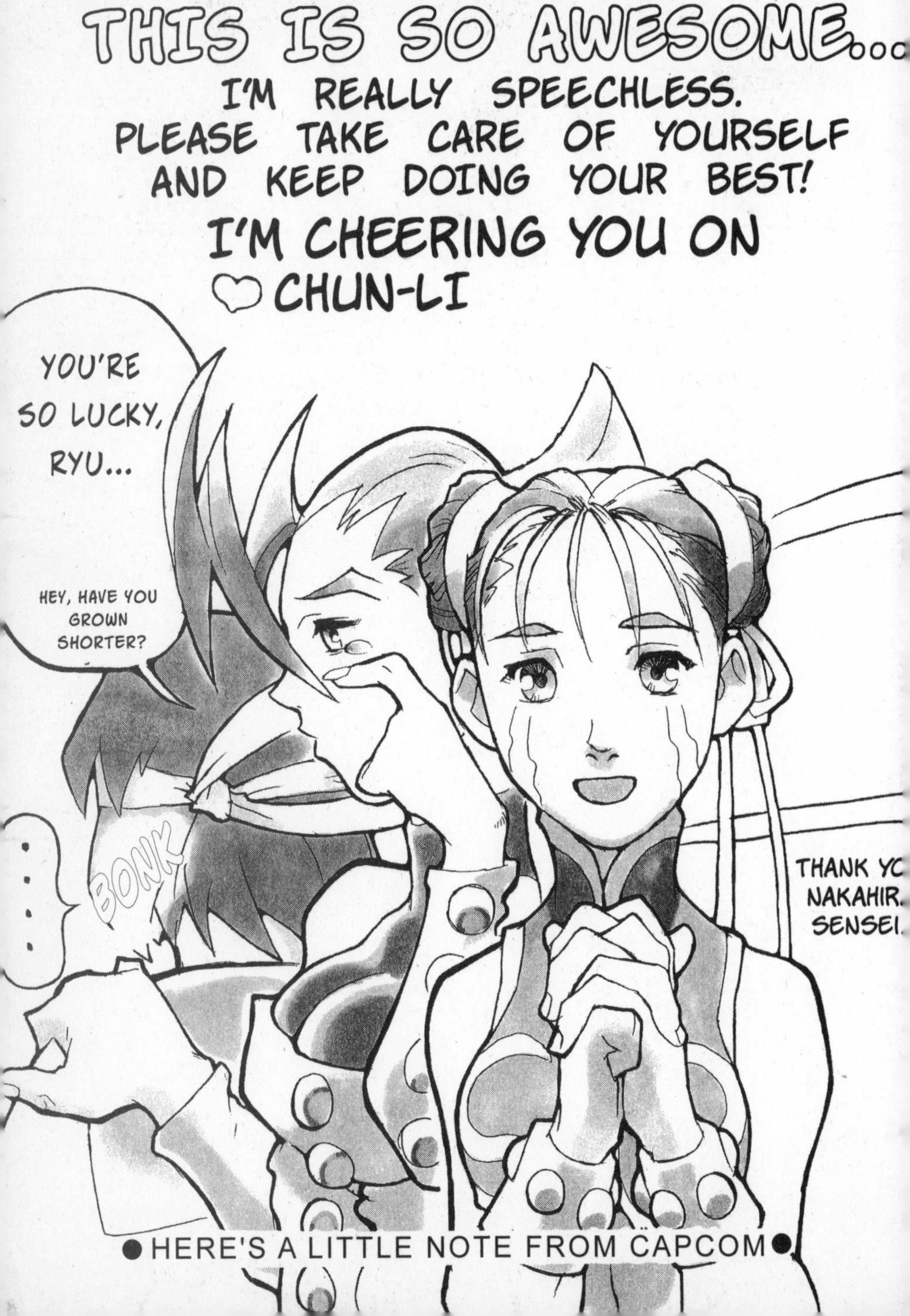
THIS IS SO AWESOME...
I'M REALLY SPEECHLESS.
PLEASE TAKE CARE OF YOURSELF AND KEEP DOING YOUR BEST!
I'M CHEERING YOU ON
CHUN-LI
THANK Y NAKAHIR SENSEI.
YOU'RE SO LUCKY, RYU...
HEY, HAVE YOU GROWN SHORTER?
BONK
....

● HERE'S A LITTLE NOTE FROM CAPCOM ●

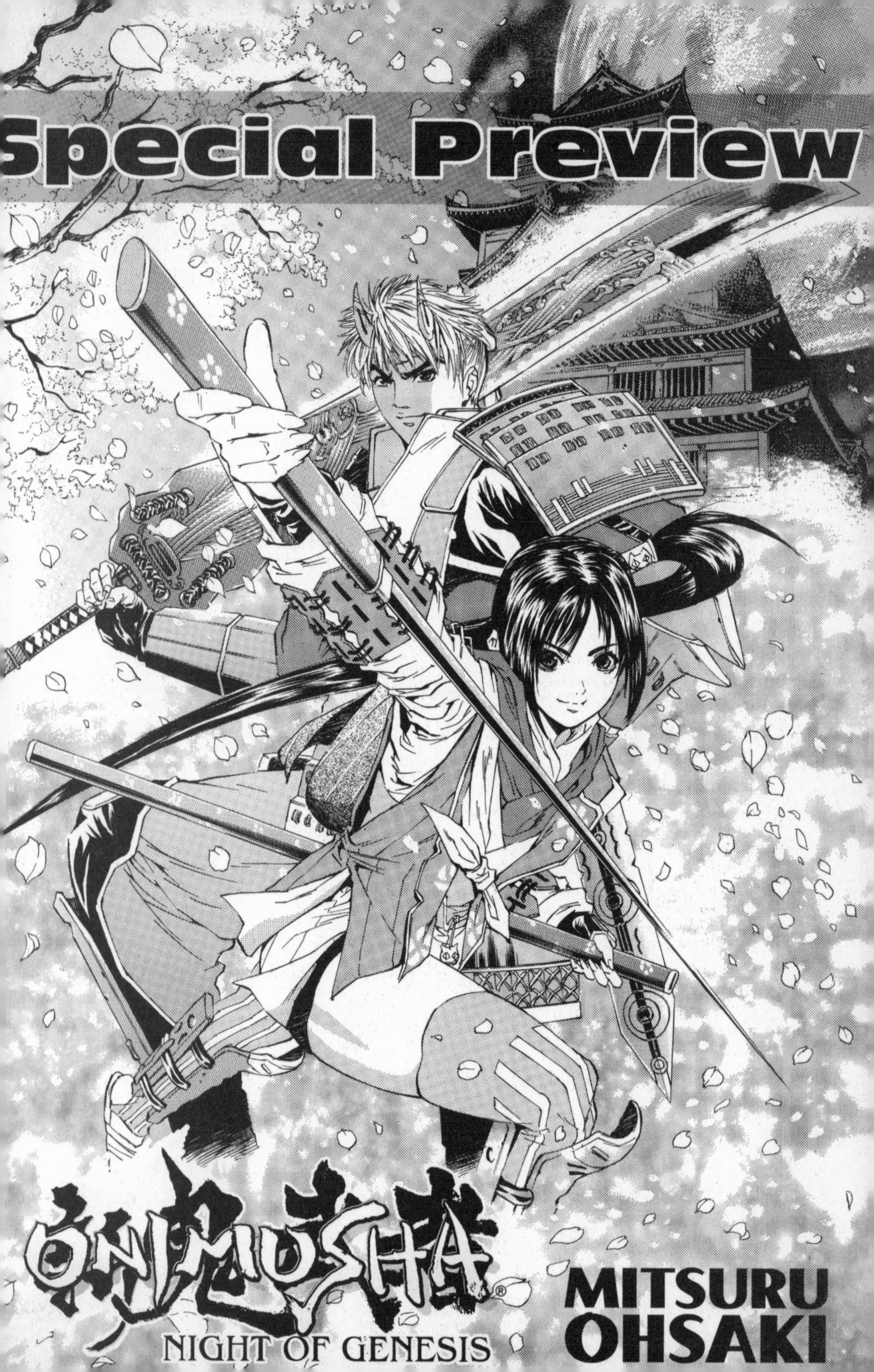
Special Preview
ONIMUSHA®
NIGHT OF GENESIS
MITSURU
OHSAKI

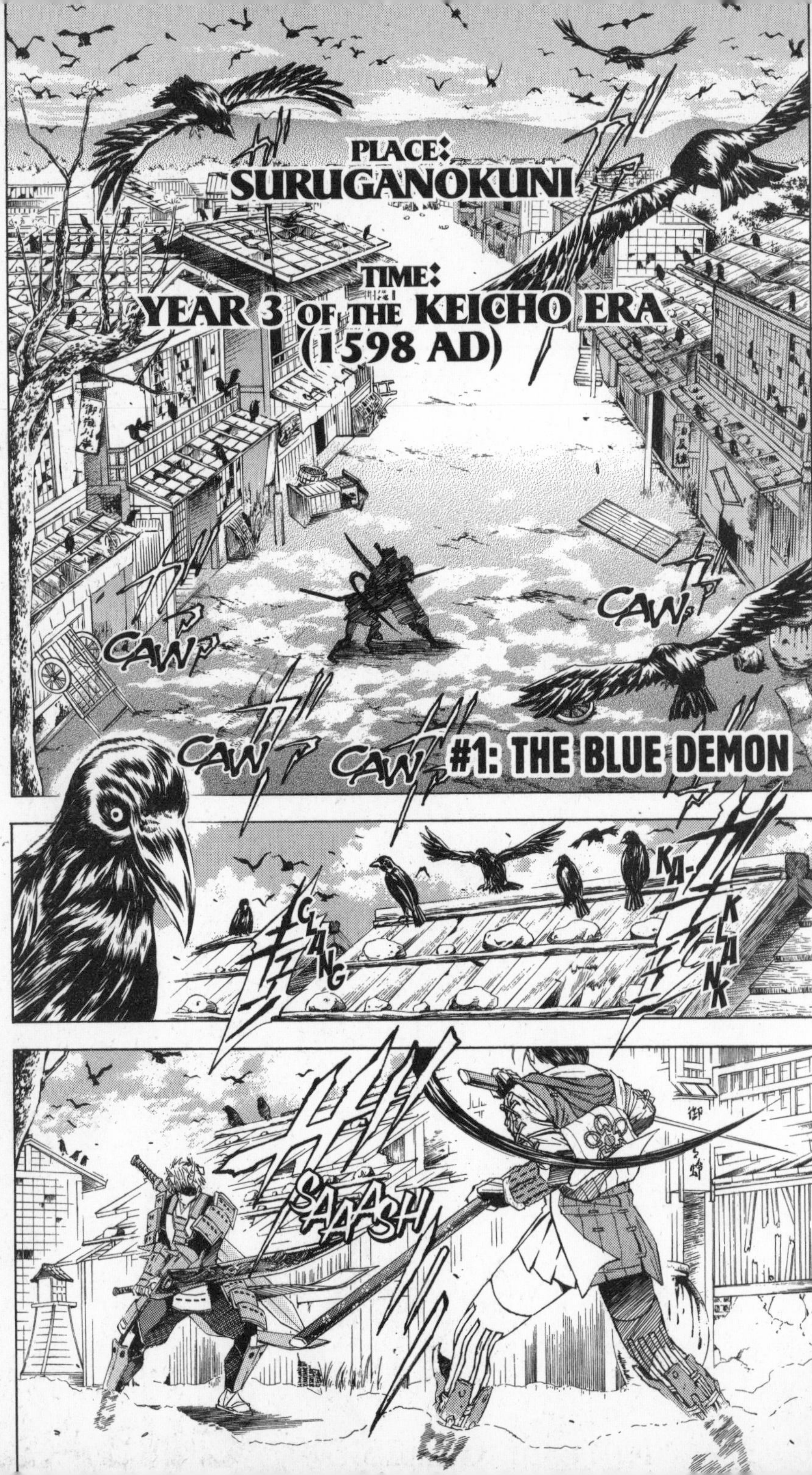
PLACE:
SURUGANOKUNI
TIME:
YEAR 3 OF THE KEICHO ERA
(1598 AD)
CAW
CAW
CAW
CAW
#1: THE BLUE DEMON
KA-KLANK
CLANG
SAAASH

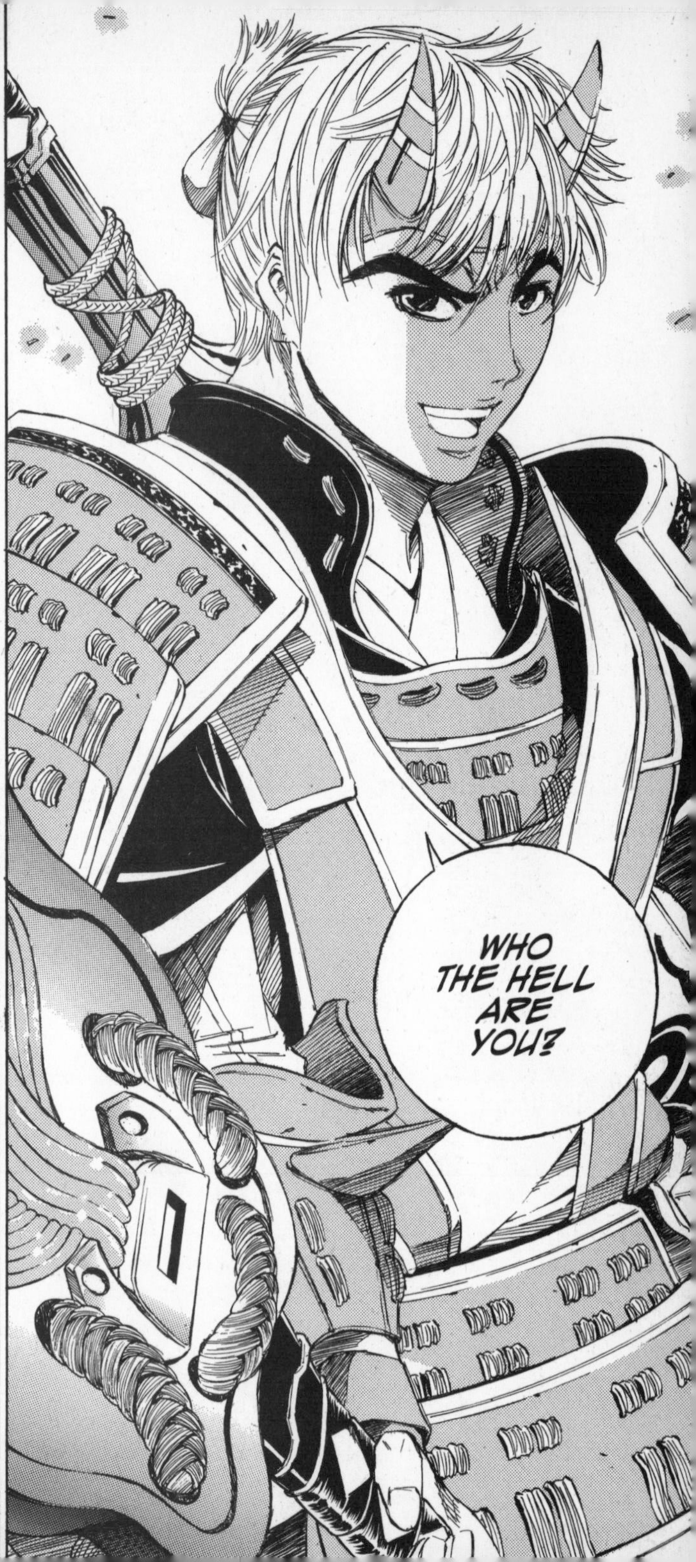
WHO THE HELL ARE YOU?
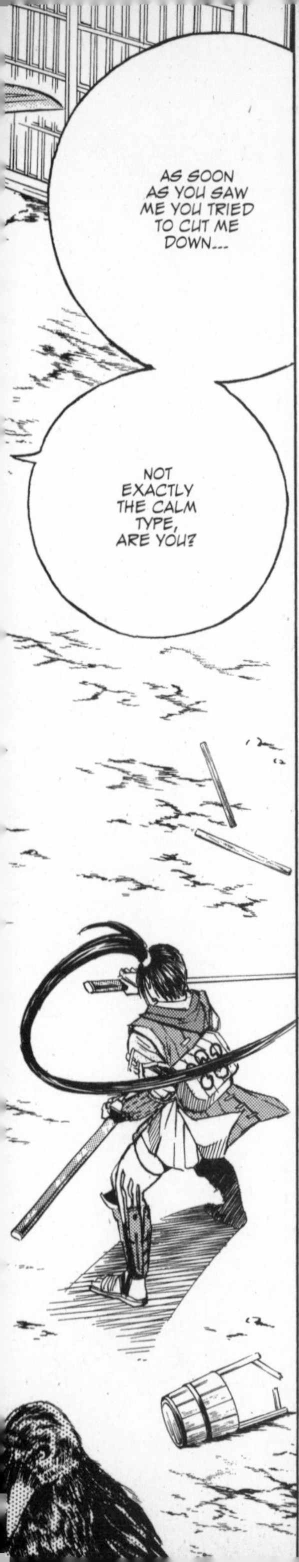
AS SOON AS YOU SAW ME YOU TRIED TO CUT ME DOWN...
NOT EXACTLY THE CALM TYPE, ARE YOU?

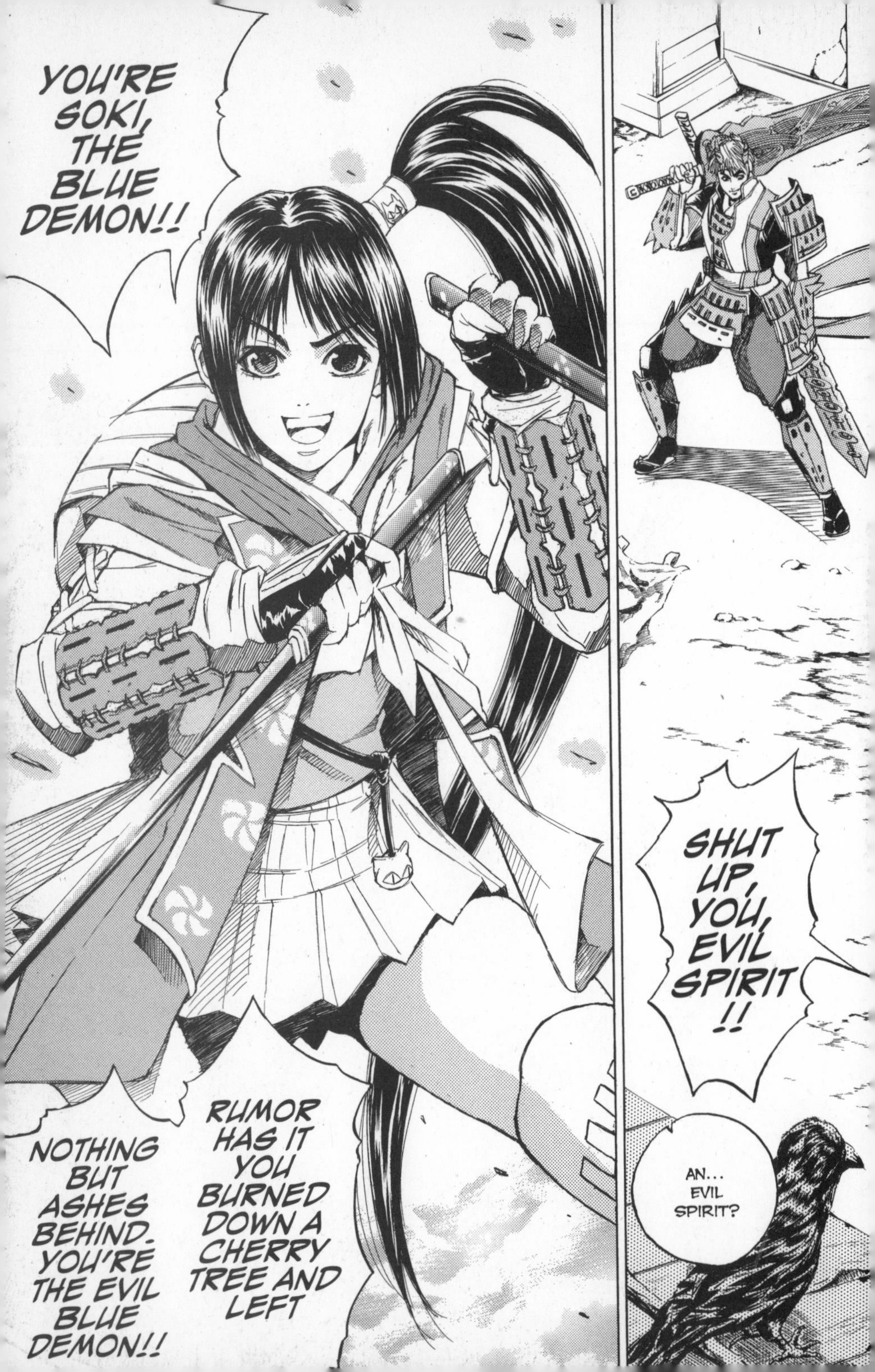
SHUT UP, YOU, EVIL SPIRIT!!
AN... EVIL SPIRIT?
YOU'RE SOKI, THE BLUE DEMON!!
RUMOR HAS IT YOU BURNED DOWN A CHERRY TREE AND LEFT
NOTHING BUT ASHES BEHIND. YOU'RE THE EVIL BLUE DEMON!!

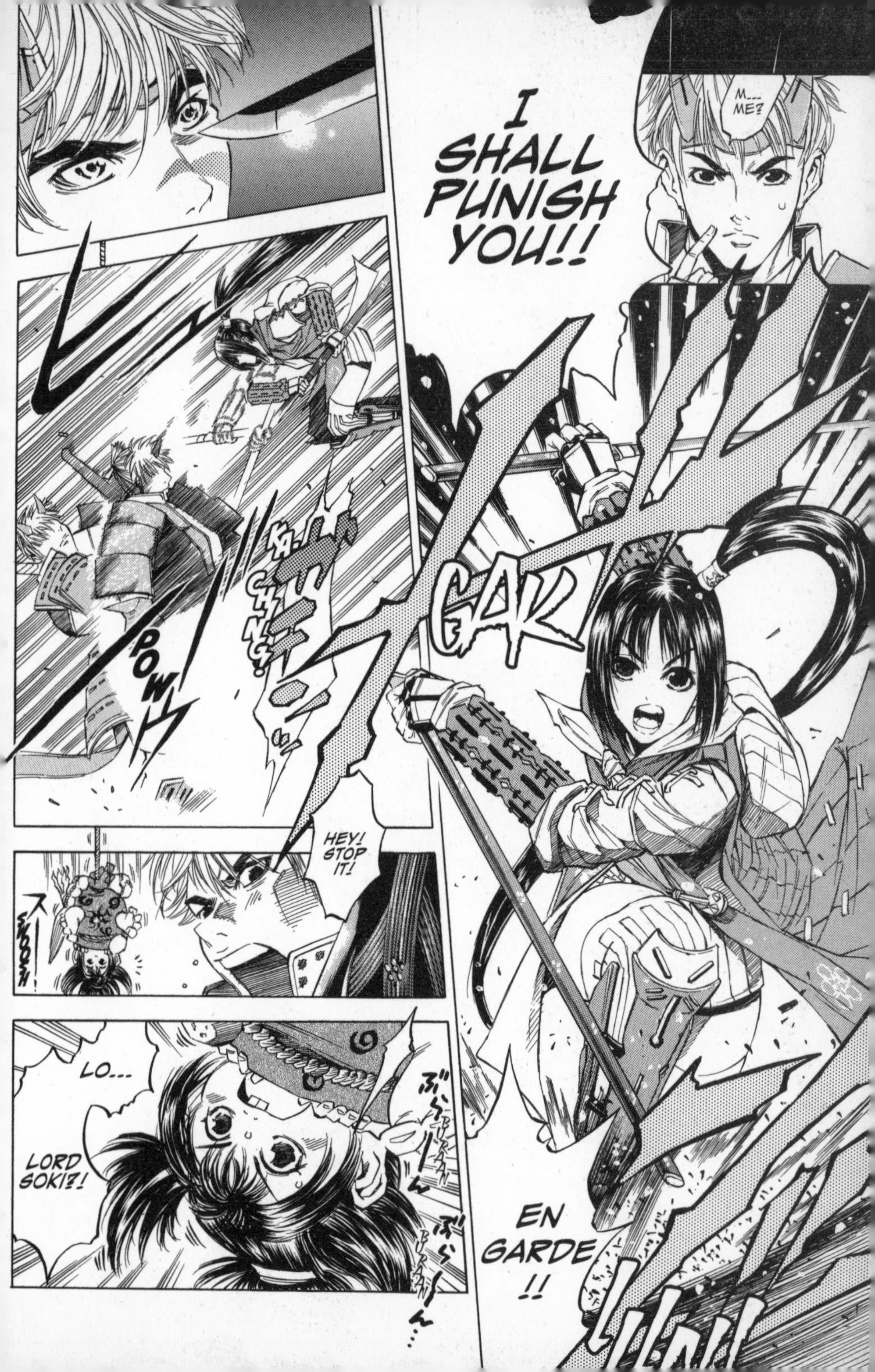
M... ME?
I SHALL PUNISH YOU!!
GAK
EN GARDE!!
KA-CHING!
POW
HEY! STOP IT!
SWOOSH!
LO...
LORD SOKI!?!
ぶらーん
BURAAN
ぶらーん…
BURAAN

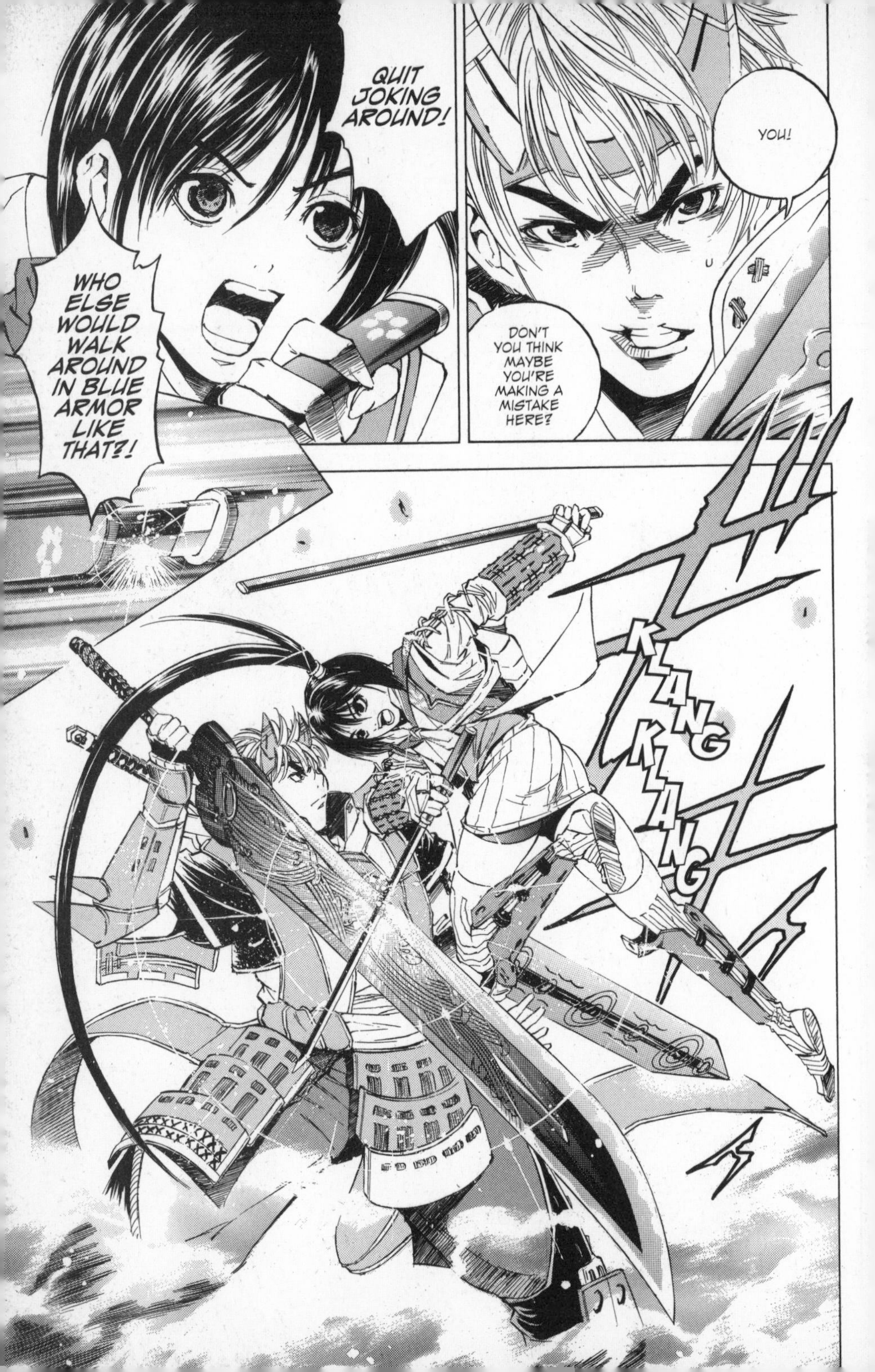
YOU!
DON'T YOU THINK MAYBE YOU'RE MAKING A MISTAKE HERE?
QUIT JOKING AROUND!
WHO ELSE WOULD WALK AROUND IN BLUE ARMOR LIKE THAT?!
KLANG
KLANG
KLANG

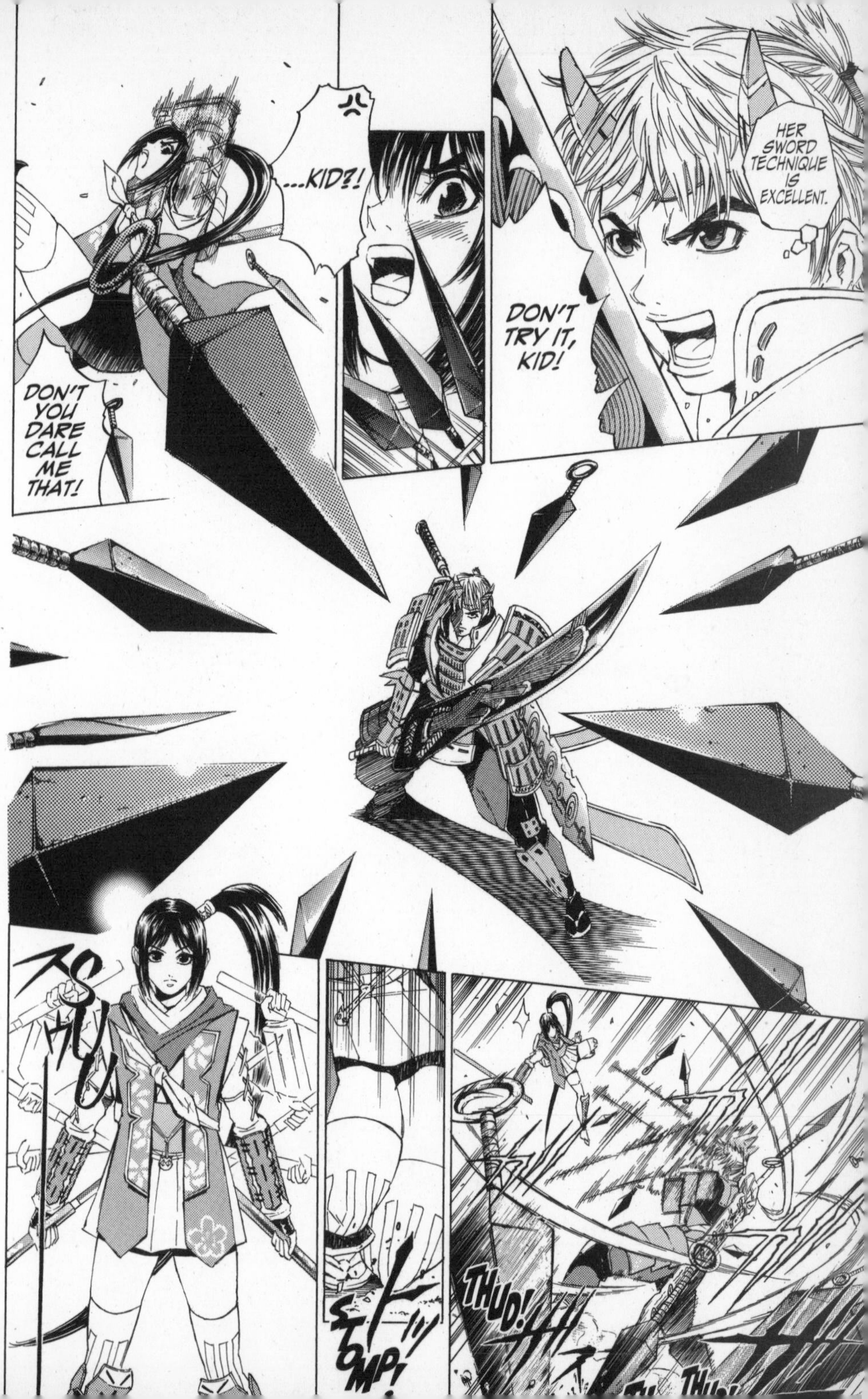
HER SWORD TECHNIQUE IS EXCELLENT.
DON'T TRY IT, KID!
...KID?!
DON'T YOU DARE CALL ME THAT!
THUD!
STOMP!

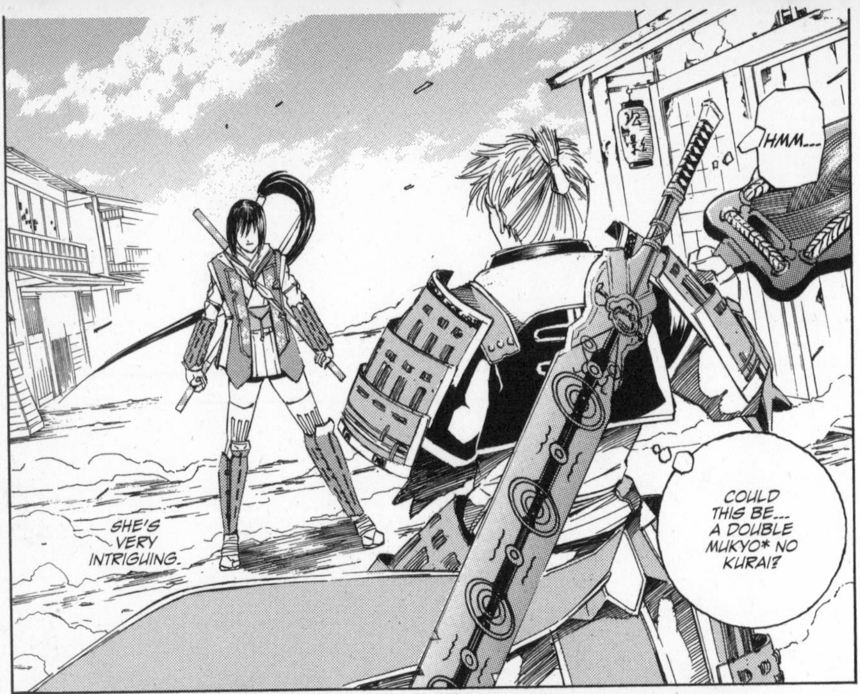
HMM...
COULD THIS BE... A DOUBLE MUKYO* NO KURAI?
SHE'S VERY INTRIGUING.

*MUKYU NO KURAI = ROUGHLY TRANSLATES AS THE INVISIBLE POSITION.

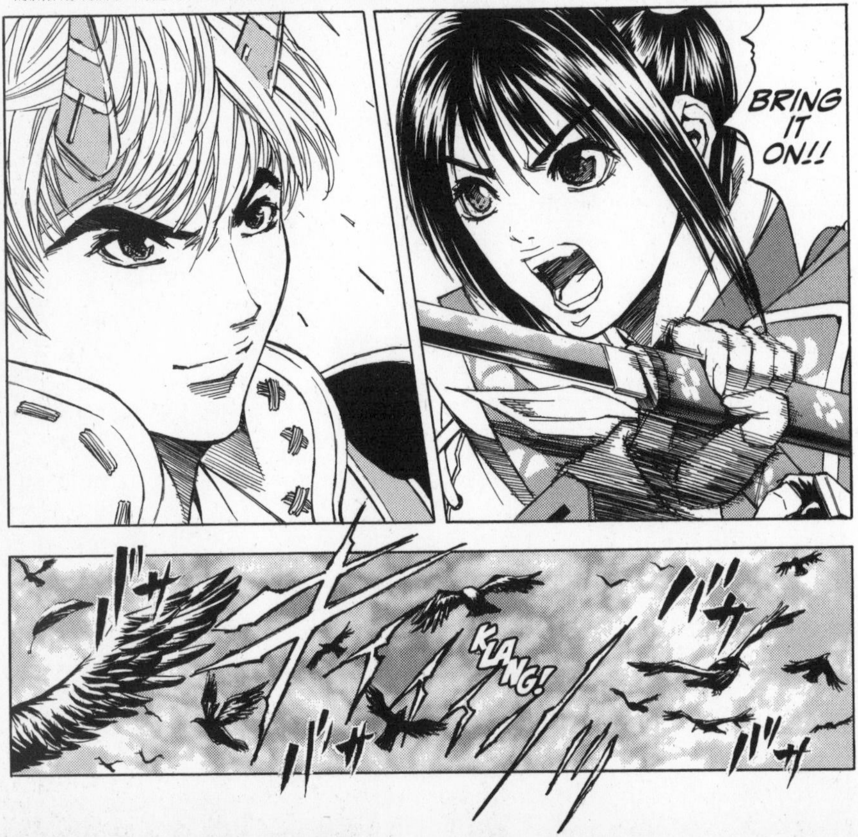
BRING IT ON!!
KLANG!

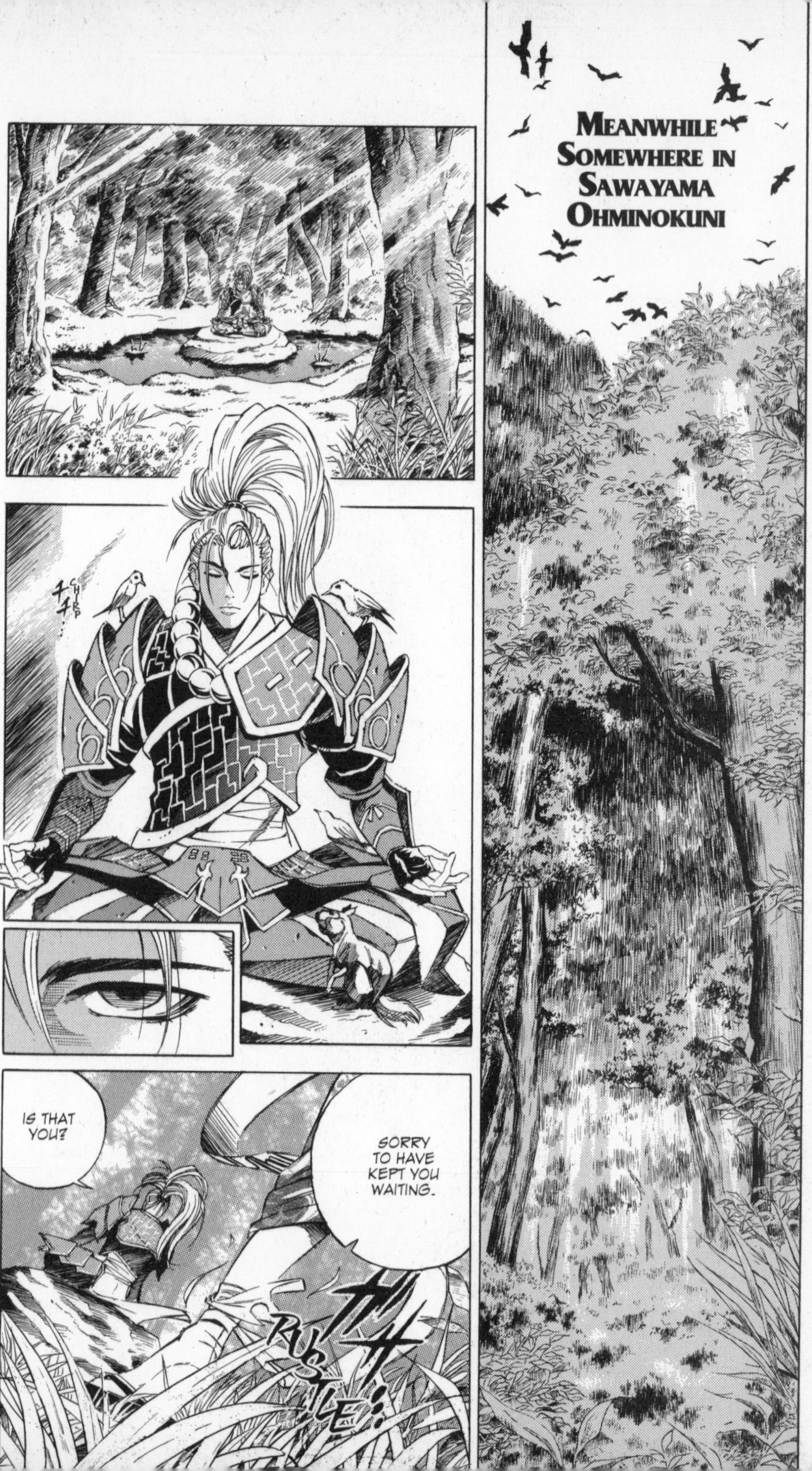
MEANWHILE SOMEWHERE IN SAWAYAMA OHMINOKUNI
CHIRP
IS THAT YOU?
SORRY TO HAVE KEPT YOU WAITING.
RUSTLE...

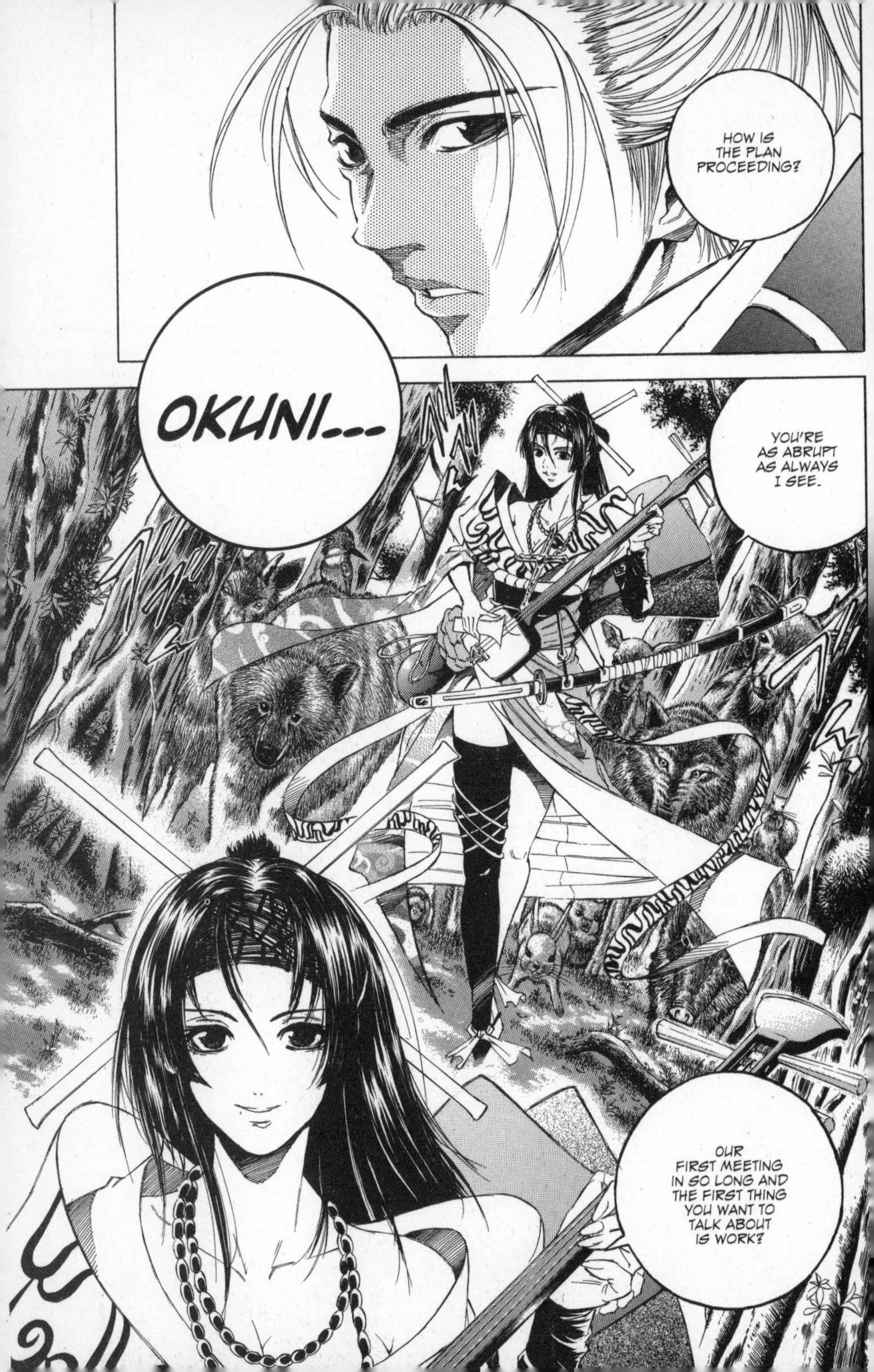
HOW IS THE PLAN PROCEEDING?
OKUNI...
YOU'RE AS ABRUPT AS ALWAYS I SEE.
OUR FIRST MEETING IN SO LONG AND THE FIRST THING YOU WANT TO TALK ABOUT IS WORK?

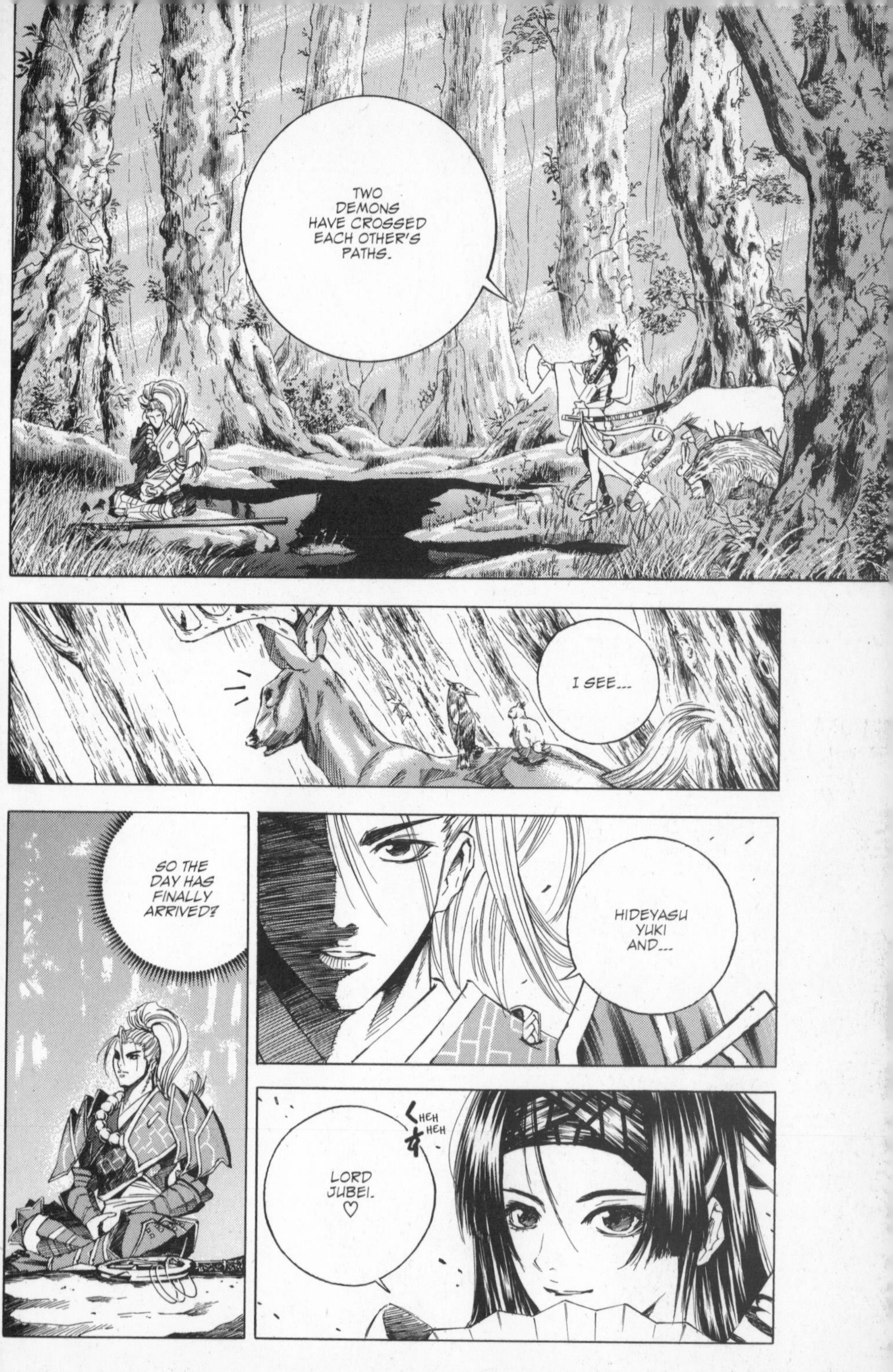
TWO DEMONS HAVE CROSSED EACH OTHER'S PATHS.
I SEE...
HIDEYASU YUKI AND...
HEH HEH
LORD JUBEI. ♡
SO THE DAY HAS FINALLY ARRIVED?

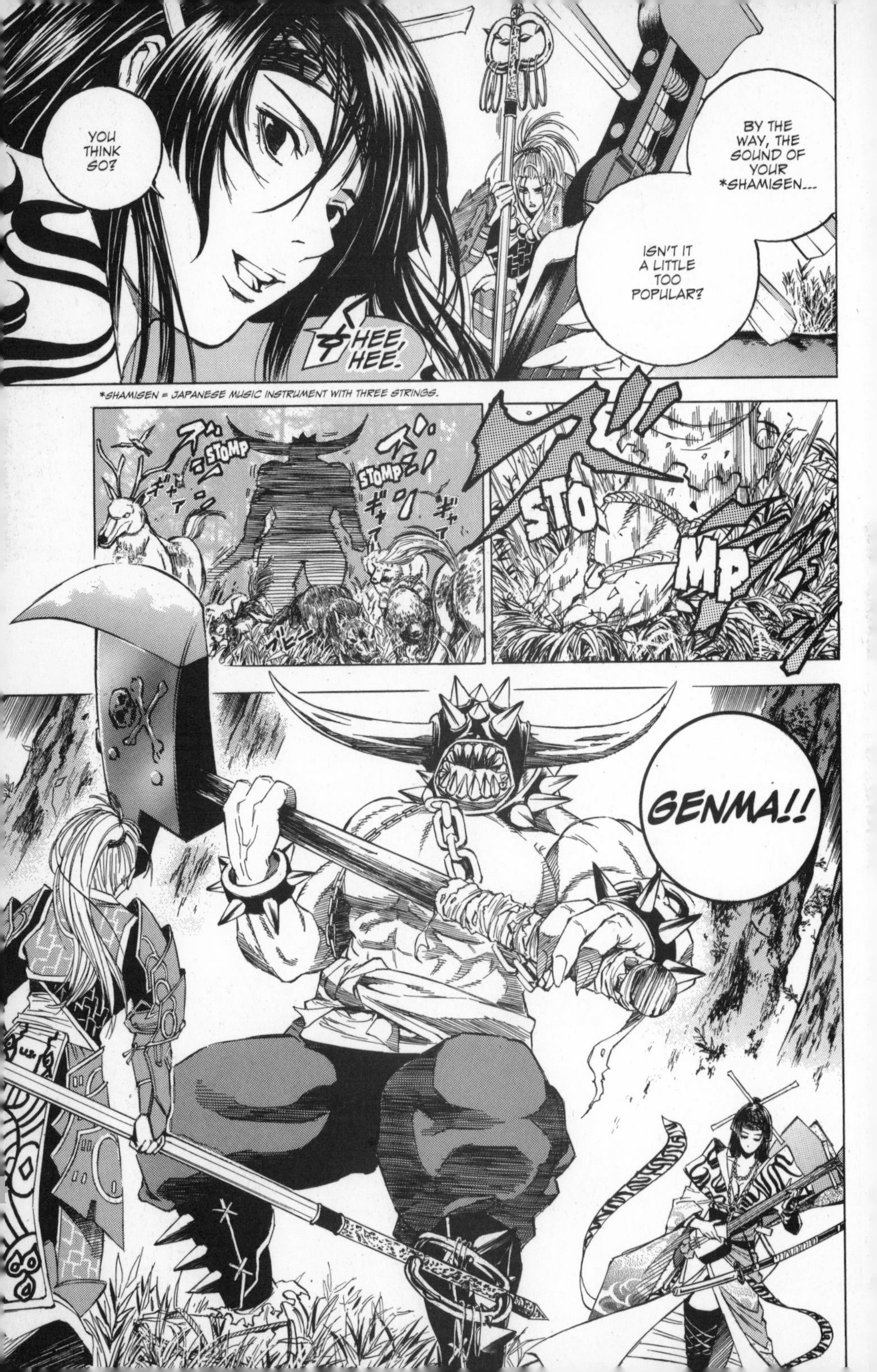
BY THE WAY, THE SOUND OF YOUR *SHAMISEN...
ISN'T IT A LITTLE TOO POPULAR?
YOU THINK SO?
HEE, HEE.
*SHAMISEN = JAPANESE MUSIC INSTRUMENT WITH THREE STRINGS.
STO MP
STOMP
STOMP
GENMA!!

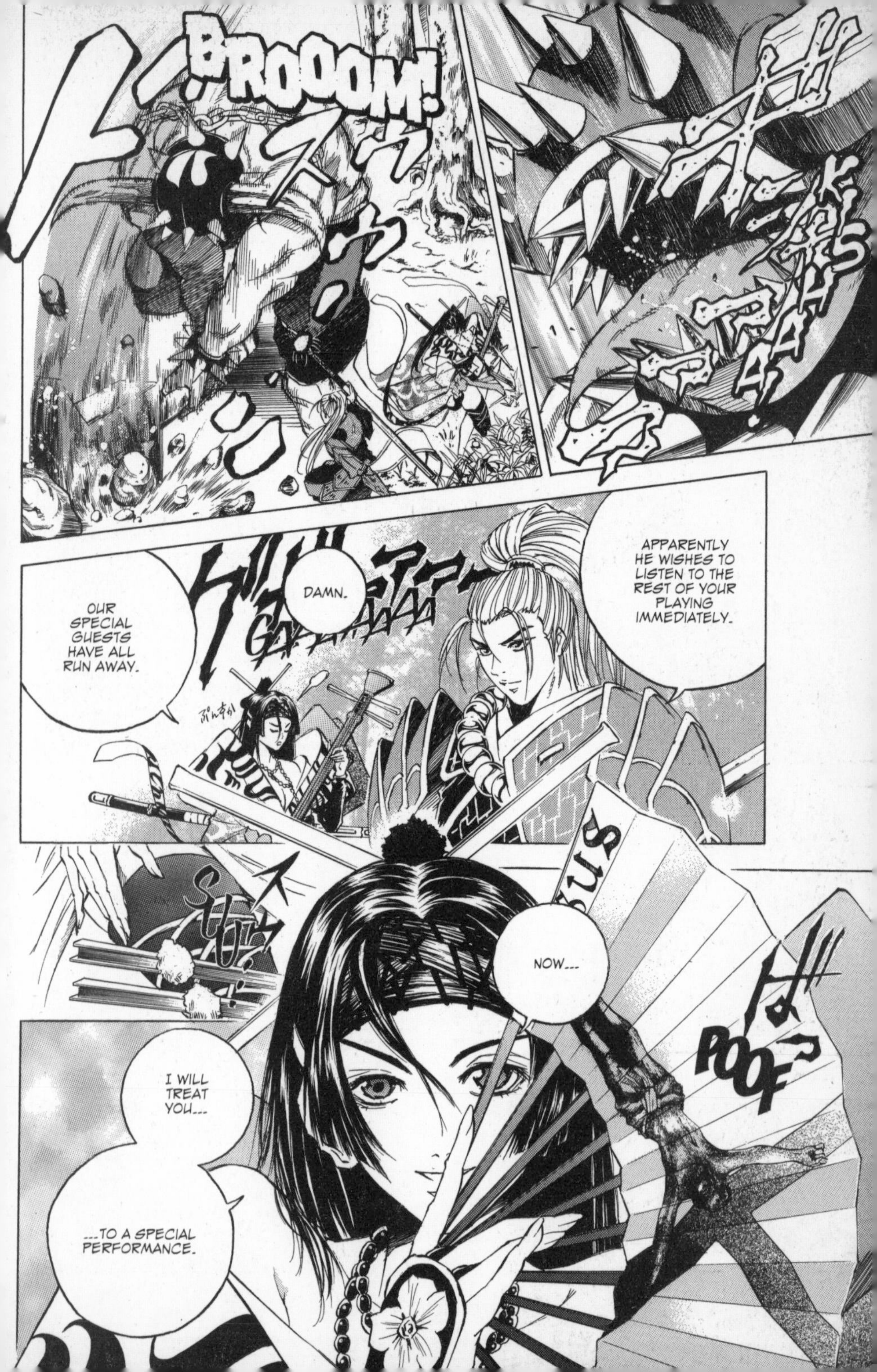
KSHAA
BROOOM!
APPARENTLY HE WISHES TO LISTEN TO THE REST OF YOUR PLAYING IMMEDIATELY.
DAMN.
GAWAWA
OUR SPECIAL GUESTS HAVE ALL RUN AWAY.
SUS
NOW...
SUU
POOF
I WILL TREAT YOU...
...TO A SPECIAL PERFORMANCE.

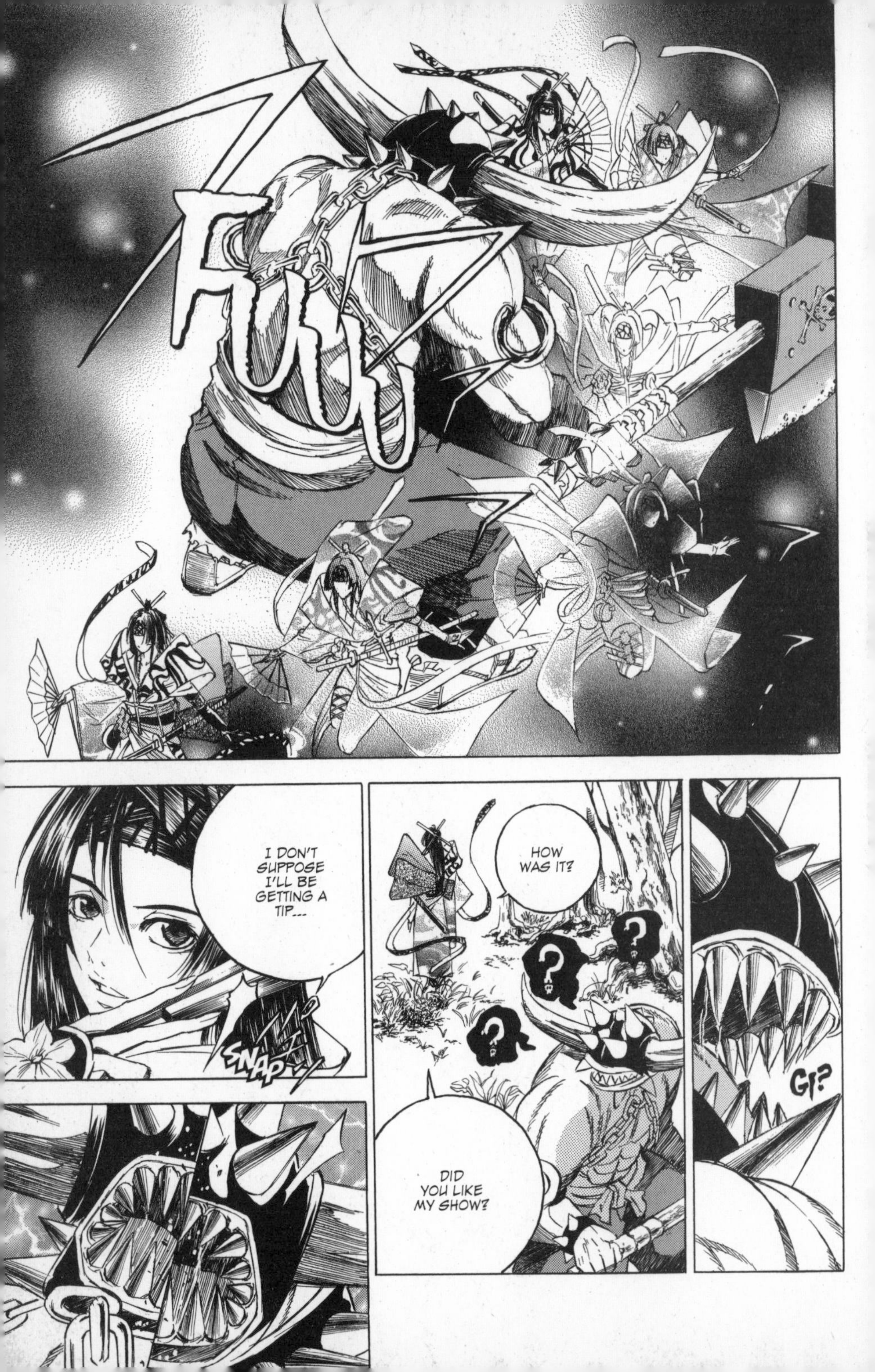
FUUU
GI?
HOW WAS IT?
DID YOU LIKE MY SHOW?
I DON'T SUPPOSE I'LL BE GETTING A TIP...
SNAP

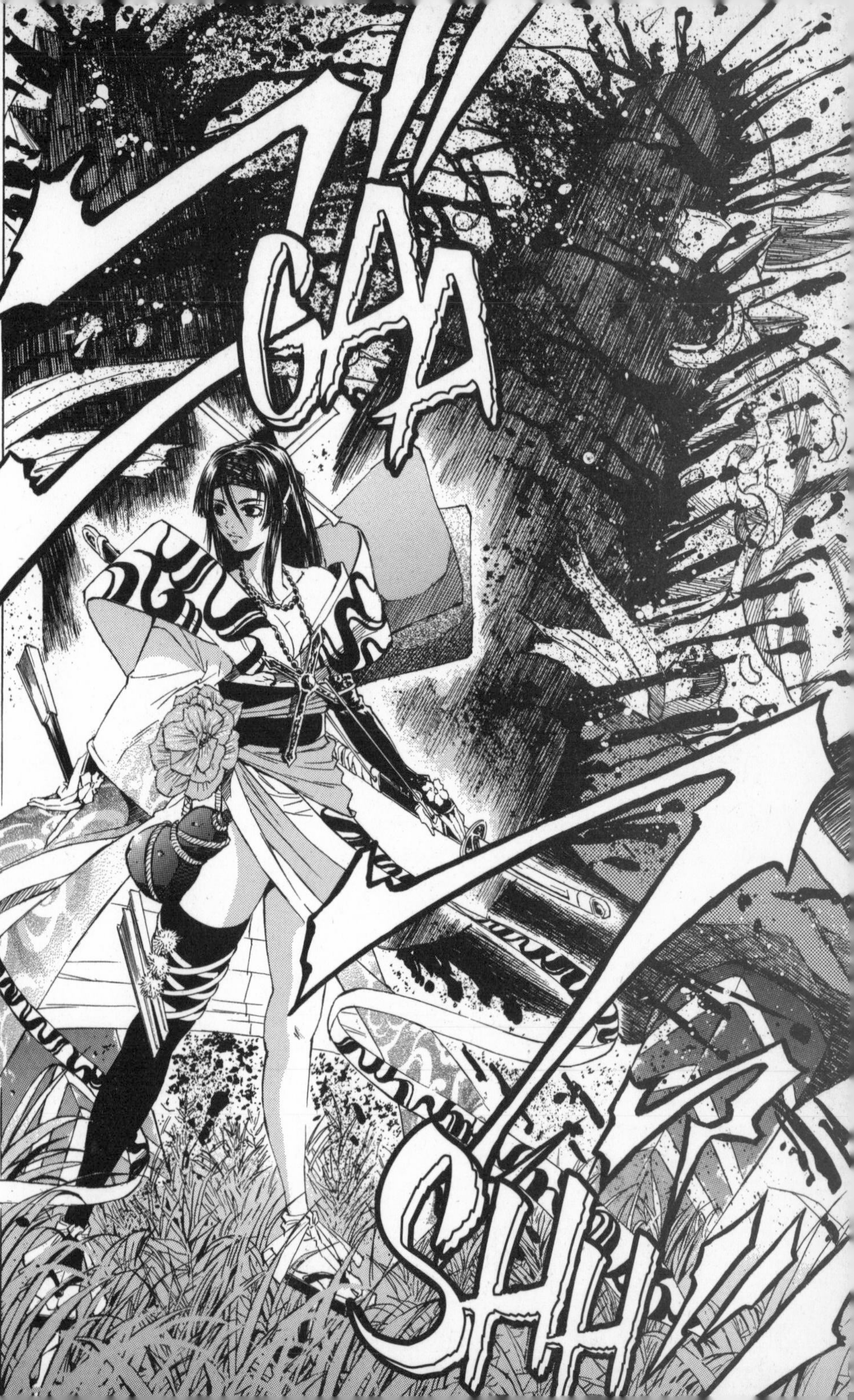
GAA
SHH

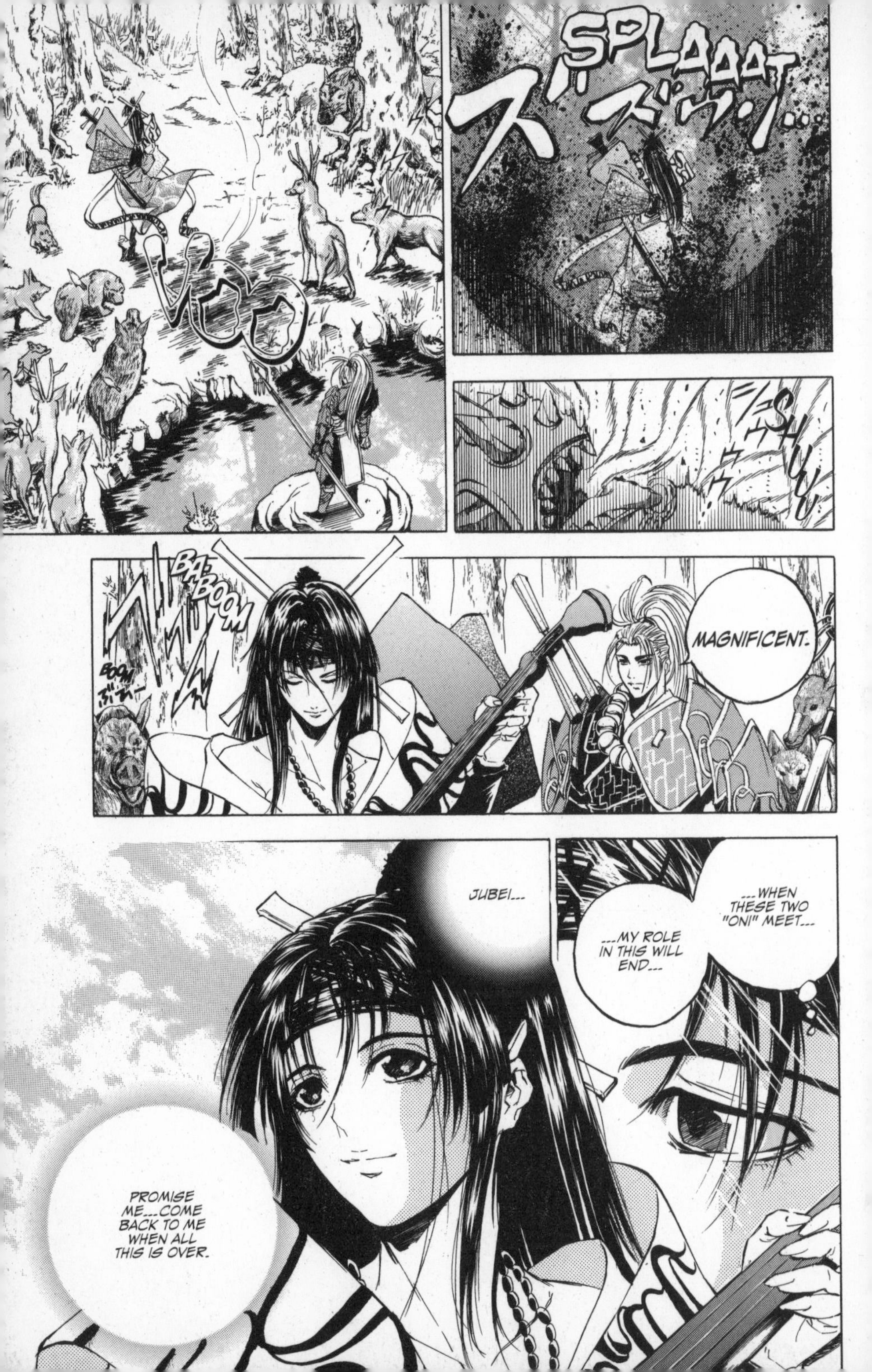
SPLAAAT
SHUUU
VOOO
MAGNIFICENT.
BA-BOOM
BOOM
...WHEN THESE TWO "ONI" MEET...
...MY ROLE IN THIS WILL END...
JUBEI...
PROMISE ME...COME BACK TO ME WHEN ALL THIS IS OVER.

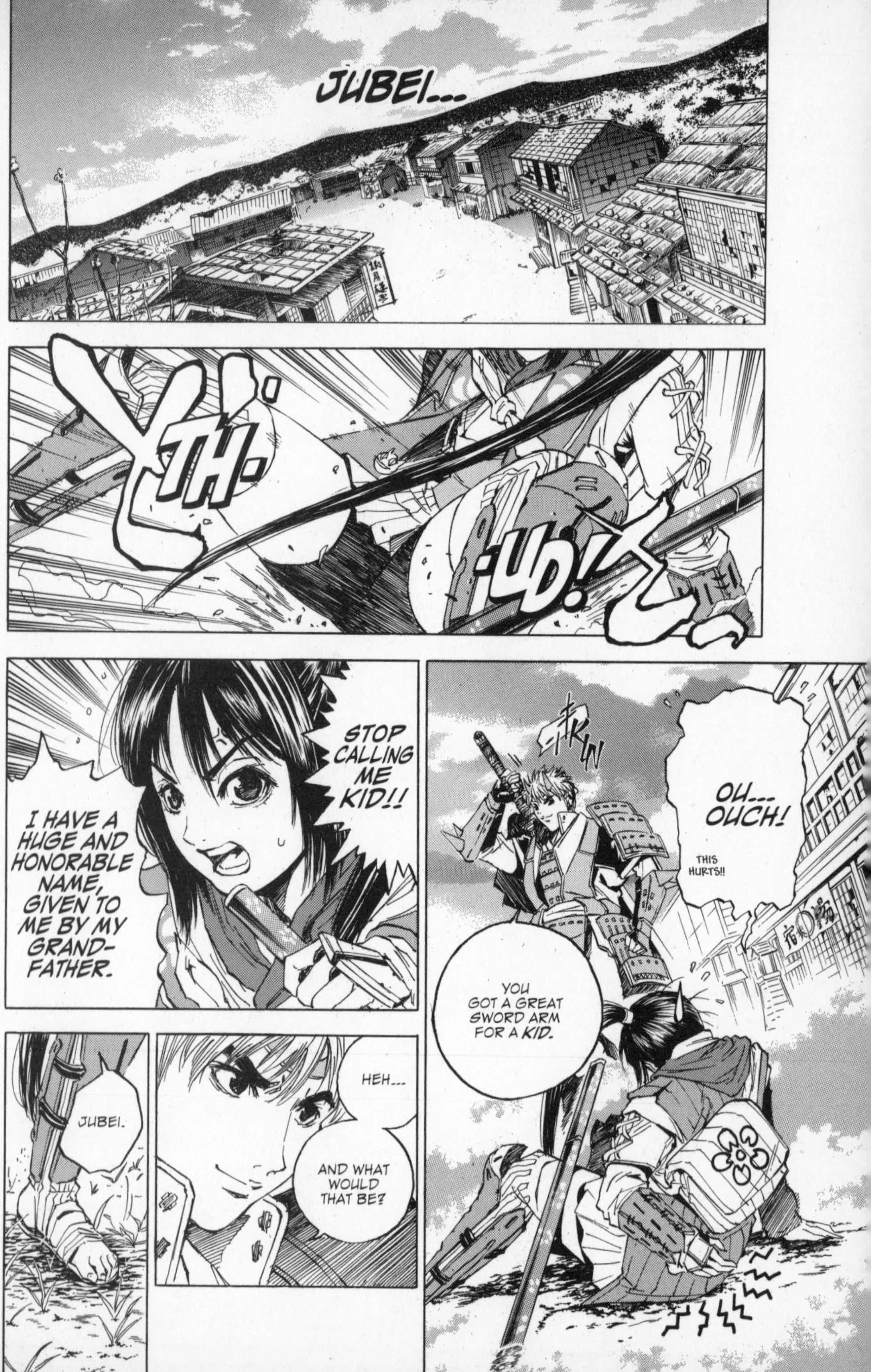
JUBEI...
TH-
-UD!
OU... OUCH!
THIS HURTS!!
YOU GOT A GREAT SWORD ARM FOR A KID.
STOP CALLING ME KID!!
I HAVE A HUGE AND HONORABLE NAME, GIVEN TO ME BY MY GRANDFATHER.
HEH...
AND WHAT WOULD THAT BE?
JUBEI.

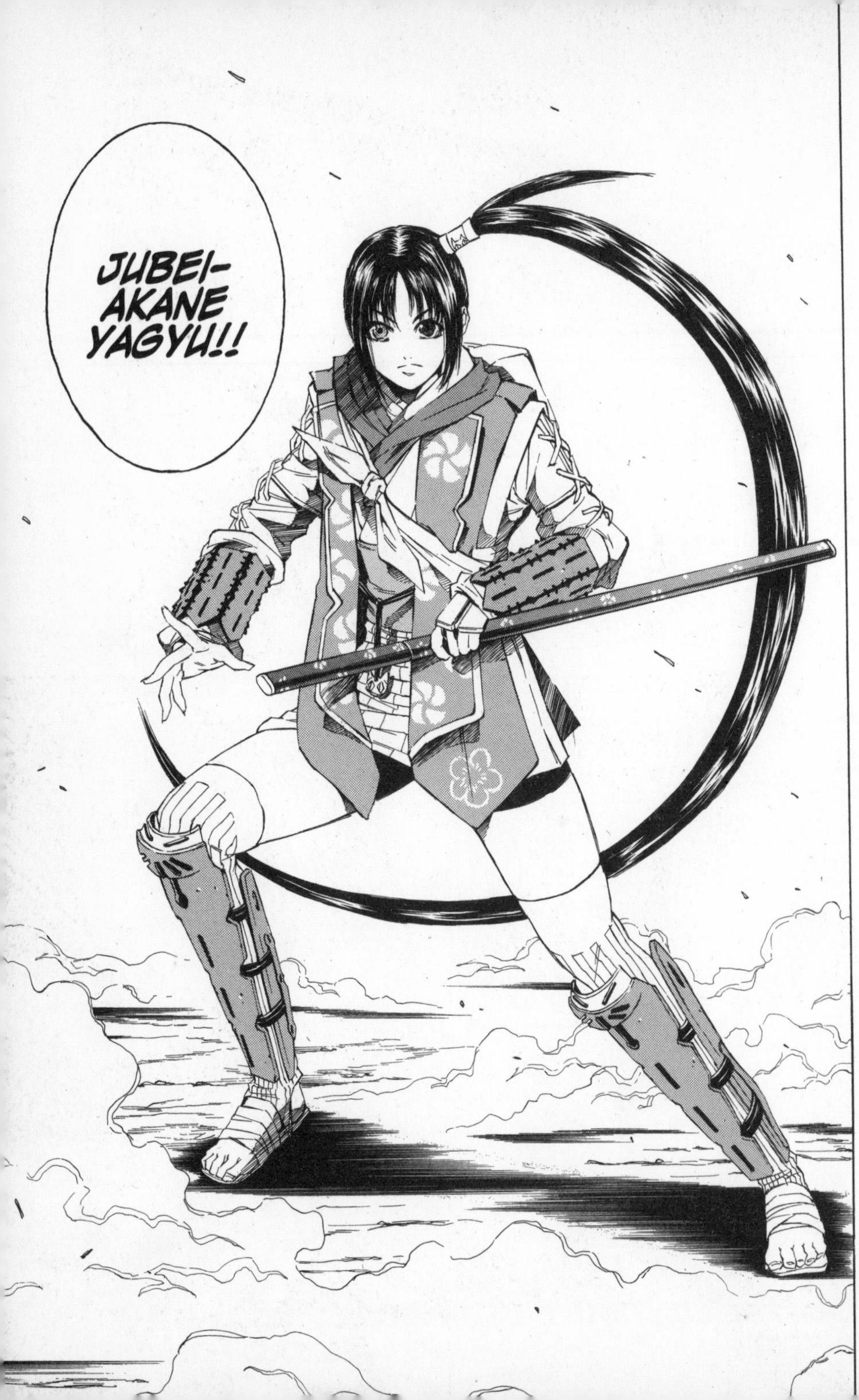
JUBEI-AKANE YAGYU!!

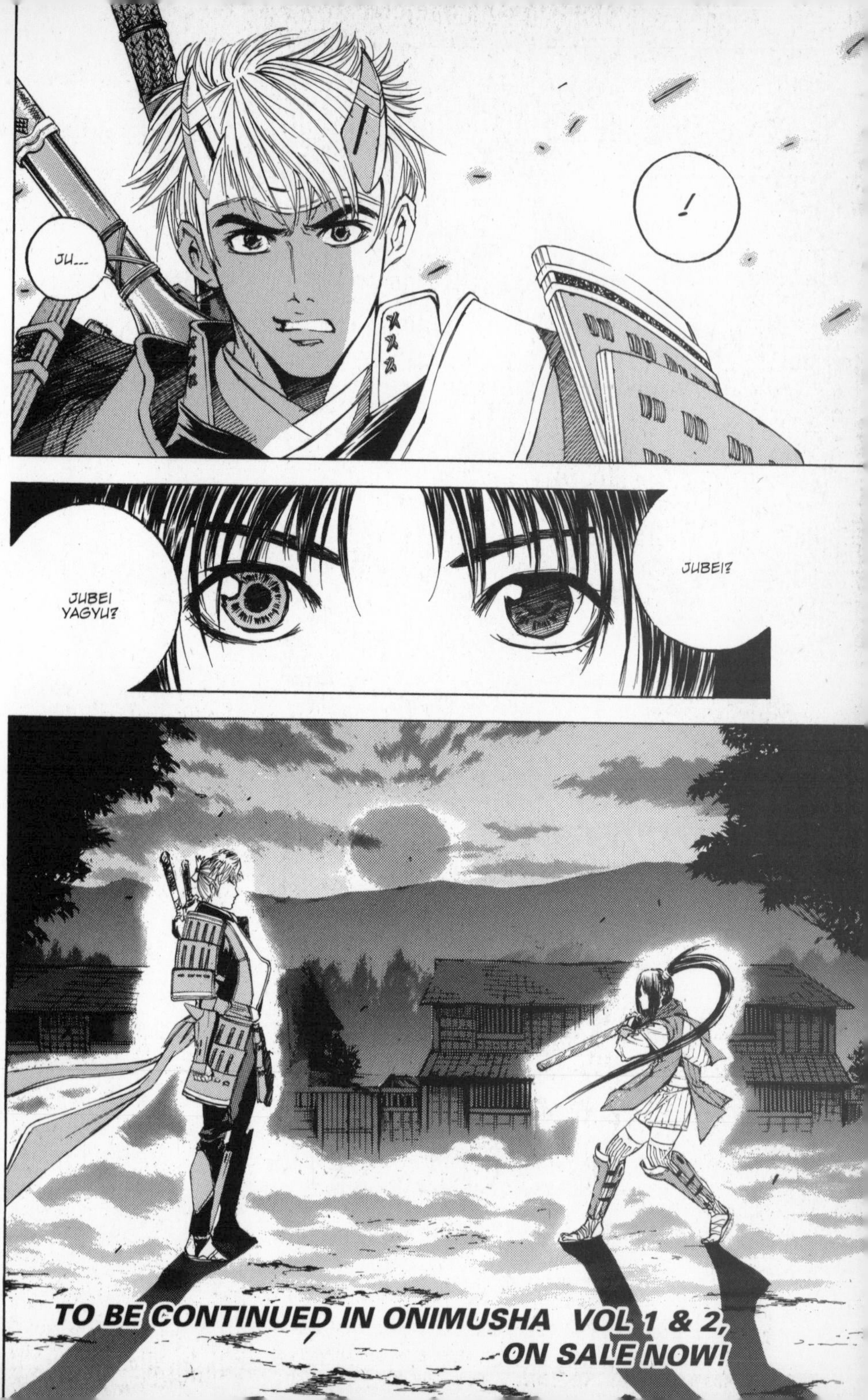
!
JU...
JUBEI?
JUBEI YAGYU?
TO BE CONTINUED IN ONIMUSHA VOL 1 & 2,
ON SALE NOW!

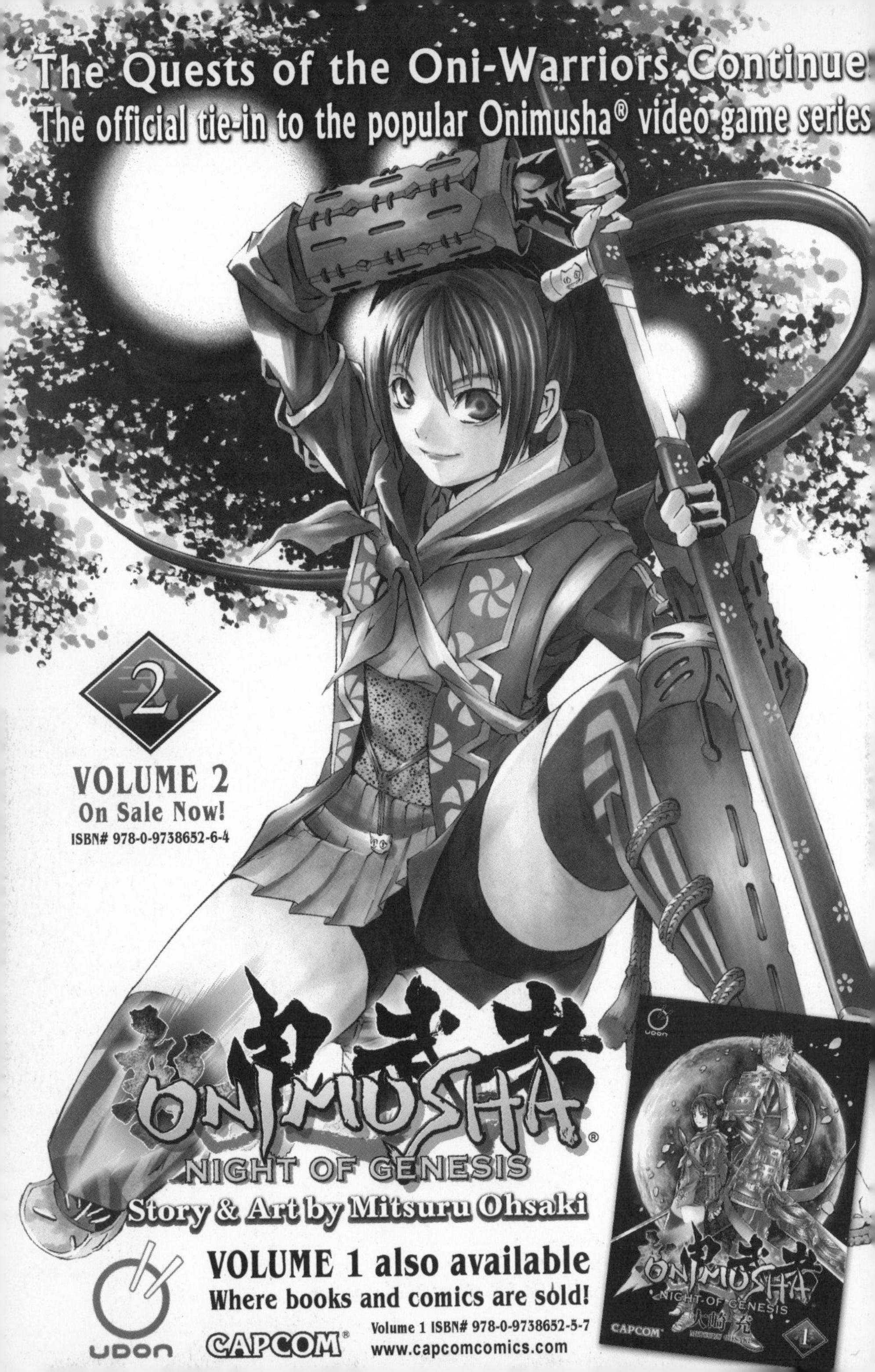
The Quests of the Oni-Warriors Continue!
The official tie-in to the popular Onimusha® video game series
2
VOLUME 2
On Sale Now!
ISBN# 978-0-9738652-6-4
ONIMUSHA®
NIGHT OF GENESIS
Story & Art by Mitsuru Ohsaki
VOLUME 1 also available
Where books and comics are sold!
Volume 1 ISBN# 978-0-9738652-5-7
www.capcomcomics.com
UDON
CAPCOM®
UDON
ONIMUSHA
NIGHT OF GENESIS
CAPCOM
1

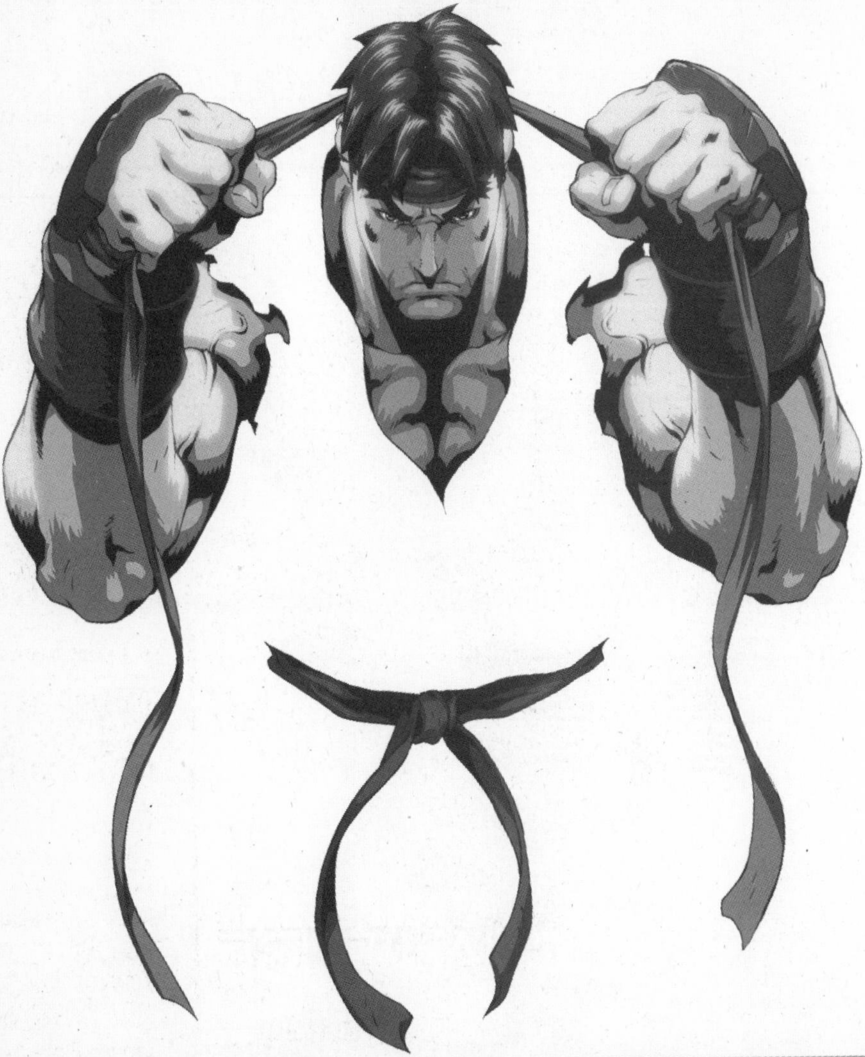

these CAPCOM® posters.

Above: Street Fighter: World Warriors (24 X 30 inches)
Right: Darkstalkers: Sisters (24 X 36 inches)

Licensed by:
CAPCOM®

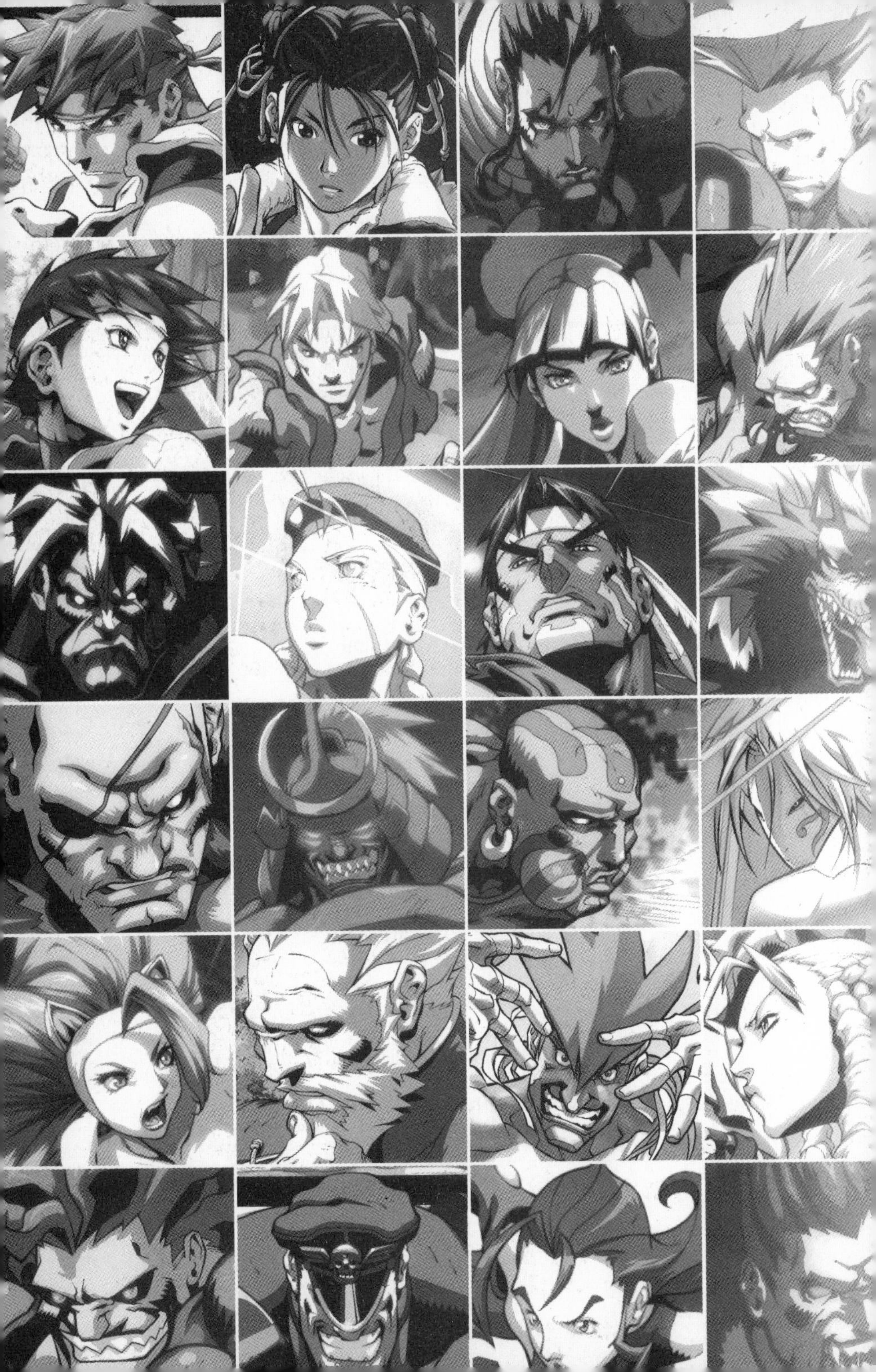

STREET FIGHTER® ALPHA
Volume 1

Story and Art : Masahiko Nakahira

English Translations: Mai Kusuyama
English Adaptations: Jim Zubkavich and Erik Ko

Lettering: Marshall Dillon with Terri Delgado

File Preparations: Clarence Lim
Color Pages Touch Up: Robert Ruffolo
Logo: Alex Chung

Cover Design: Erik Ko

For Capcom Licensing:
Toshi Tokumaru, Taki Enomoto, Toru Kusano of Capcom Co. Ltd.
Tommy Yoshida, Jean-Ralph Parillon, Rob Pereyda of Capcom Entertainment, Inc.
Marc Mostman of Most Management.

Originally published in Japanese language by Shinseisha.

English language version produced by UDON Entertainment Corp.

www.capcomcomics.com
www.udoncomics.com

Published by UDON Entertainment Corp.
P.O. Box 32662, P.O. Village Gate, Richmond Hill, Ontario, L4X 0A2, Canada

First Printing: May 2007
ISBN-13:978-1-897376-50-8
ISBN-10:1-897376-50-2

Printed in Canada

WHOOPS

This is the back of the book!

You're looking at the last page, not the first one.

STREET FIGHTER®ALPHA is a comic originally published in Japan (known as manga). Traditional manga is read in a 'reversed' format, starting on the right and heading towards the left. The story begins where english readers expect to find the last page because the spine of the book is on the opposite side.

Preserving the original artwork, we've decided to leave the Japanese format intact. Check the examples below to see how to read the word balloons in proper order.

Now head to the real front of the book and enjoy the pulse-pounding action the way it was meant to be read. **ENJOY!**